THE ORIGINS OF ORGANIZED CHARITY IN RABBINIC JUDAISM

This book examines the origins of communal and institutional almsgiving in rabbinic Judaism. It undertakes a close reading of foundational rabbinic texts (Mishnah, Tosefta, and Tannaitic Midrashim) and places their discourses on organized giving in their second to third century C.E. contexts. Gregg E. Gardner finds that the Tannaim promoted giving through the soup kitchen (*tamhui*) and charity fund (*quppa*), which enabled anonymous and collective support for the poor. This protected the dignity of the poor and provided an alternative to begging, which benefited the community as a whole – poor and non-poor alike. By contrast, later Jewish and Christian writers would see organized charity as a means to promote their own religious authority. This book contributes to the study of Jews and Judaism, history of religions, biblical studies, and ethics.

Gregg E. Gardner is Assistant Professor and the Diamond Chair in Jewish Law and Ethics at the University of British Columbia. He earned his PhD from Princeton University and MA degrees from Princeton University and the Hebrew University of Jerusalem. He held a Doctoral Dissertation Completion Fellowship from the Charlotte W. Newcombe Foundation (2008–09), a Starr Fellowship in Judaica at the Center for Jewish Studies at Harvard University (2009–10), and a Mellon/American Council of Learned Societies Fellowship at the Cogut Center for the Humanities at Brown University (2010–11). Gardner is the coeditor of *Antiquity in Antiquity: Jewish and Christian Pasts in the Greco-Roman World* (2008). His work has been published in such journals as *Jewish Quarterly Review*, *Journal for the Study of Judaism*, and *Journal of Biblical Literature*.

The Origins of Organized Charity in Rabbinic Judaism

GREGG E. GARDNER
University of British Columbia

CAMBRIDGE
UNIVERSITY PRESS

CAMBRIDGE
UNIVERSITY PRESS

32 Avenue of the Americas, New York, NY 10013-2473, USA

Cambridge University Press is part of the University of Cambridge.

It furthers the University's mission by disseminating knowledge in the pursuit of education, learning, and research at the highest international levels of excellence.

www.cambridge.org
Information on this title: www.cambridge.org/9781107095434

© Gregg E. Gardner 2015

This publication is in copyright. Subject to statutory exception and to the provisions of relevant collective licensing agreements, no reproduction of any part may take place without the written permission of Cambridge University Press.

First published 2015

Printed in the United States of America

A catalog record for this publication is available from the British Library.

ISBN 978-1-107-09543-4 Hardback

Cambridge University Press has no responsibility for the persistence or accuracy of URLs for external or third-party Internet Web sites referred to in this publication and does not guarantee that any content on such Web sites is, or will remain, accurate or appropriate.

For my parents,
Francine Iris Gardner and Dr. Marshall Keith Gardner
"And the glory of children is their parents"
Proverbs 17:6

Contents

Acknowledgments		*page* xi
Abbreviations and Conventions		xv
1	**Introduction**	1
	The Problem of Charity	1
	Begging in Late Antiquity	5
	The Problems: Beginnings and Ends	7
	The Ends of Organized Charity	8
	The Beginnings of Organized Charity	10
	The Reality of Organized Charity	22
	Tsedaqah and "Charity": Some Definitions	26
	Charity and Other Forms of Support	32
	Organized Charity as an End to Begging	33
	Organizing Charity: The Structure of This Book	35
	Appendix: A Brief Introduction to Tannaitic Literature	39
2	**The Poor and Poverty in Roman Palestine**	42
	Economy and Poverty in Roman Palestine	43
	The Third-Century Crisis	47
	The Poor and Poverty: Realia	48
	Food	49
	Clothing	52
	Shelter	53
	Two Poverties	56
	Urbanization and Urban Life	59
	Conclusion	62
3	**From Vessels to Institutions**	63
	Introduction	63
	Vessels and Institutions	64

	Tamhui: From Dish to Soup Kitchen	67
	Quppa: From Basket to Charity Fund	69
	Institutions	75
	From Vessels to Institutions	79
	Conclusion	82
4	**_Tamhui_, The Soup Kitchen**	84
	Introduction	84
	Daily Alms	85
	Bread	86
	Legumes	87
	Olive Oil	89
	Biological Poverty	91
	Provisions for the Sabbath and Passover	91
	Three Meals	92
	Fish	93
	Vegetables	94
	Wine at the Passover Seder	95
	Conclusion	97
	Lodging for the Poor	98
	Hospitality	99
	Communal Hospitality and the Synagogue	104
	Hospitality and the Origins of the *Tamhui*	105
	Conclusion	109
5	**_Quppa_, The Charity Fund**	111
	Introduction	111
	Clothing, Money, and Food	112
	Clothing	112
	Money	114
	Bread	116
	Wives, Slaves, and Horses	118
	Wife	118
	Slave and a Horse	121
	The Poor's Needs	125
	Unlimited Giving	128
	Prodigious Giving	129
	The "Usha Ordinance"	134
	Conclusion	137
6	**Charity with Dignity**	139
	The Conjunctural Poor	139
	The *Quppa* as a Civic Institution	142
	Anonymous Giving	151

	Empathy for the Conjunctural Poor's Dignity	153
	Conclusion	155
7	**The Charity Supervisor**	157
	Introduction	157
	Charity Supervisor	158
	Collection	163
	Distribution	167
	The Poor Who Refuse Alms	167
	Imposters	169
	Supervisors as Judges	172
	Supervisors as Communal Officials	175
	Instructions for Handling Funds	176
	Conclusion	179
8	**Conclusion: After the Tannaim**	180
	Organized Charity in Palestinian Amoraic Texts	180
	The *Tamhui* and *Quppa* in Palestinian Amoraic Texts	181
	The Urgency of Poverty	183
	Organized Charity and Authority	185
	Conclusion	192

Bibliography	193
Ancient Sources Index	219
Subject Index	229

Acknowledgments

I would like to thank the many friends, colleagues, and institutions who helped make this book a reality. This book began its life as my doctoral dissertation written in the Department of Religion at Princeton University. My dissertation advisor, Peter Schäfer, provided expert guidance, mentorship, and erudite feedback as this project evolved from a paper for his graduate seminar, to a thesis proposal, through many drafts, and finally to the completed dissertation. He always encouraged me to follow my own interests and explore new ideas, while ensuring that I remained true to the sources and focused on what they can – and cannot – tell us. Likewise, my debt to my two tireless and generous readers, Martha Himmelfarb and AnneMarie Luijendijk, is beyond measure. They provided exhaustive and insightful comments on numerous drafts, which were followed up with long and enjoyable discussions. The elaborate feedback and supportive mentorship that I received from John Gager and Simeon Chavel was likewise invaluable. Altogether, I could not have asked for a better team to guide me through my doctoral work, as these scholars and friends brought to life the words of Mishnah *Avot* 1:6: "Appoint for yourself a *rav*; acquire for yourself a *haver*." Together with my cohort of graduate students and the Department of Religion's amazing staff, I could not have hoped for a more supportive and nurturing environment.

I received generous financial support for my doctoral studies from Princeton University, particularly the Department of Religion, Graduate School, Program in Judaic Studies, Princeton Institute for International and Regional Studies, and Program in the Ancient World. I was fortunate to receive a Doctoral Dissertation Fellowship from the Charlotte W. Newcombe Foundation for my final year of writing (2008–09).

Upon completion of my doctorate, I had the opportunity to research the topic further and revise my work as Harry Starr Fellow in Judaica and Alan M. Stroock Postdoctoral Fellow at Harvard University (2009–10), and as an

Andrew W. Mellon Foundation/American Council of Learned Societies Recent Doctoral Recipients Fellow at Brown University in 2010–11. I thank Shaye Cohen, Eric Nelson, Bernard Septimus, and the Center for Jewish Studies at Harvard. At Brown, I thank Katharina Galor, Michael Satlow, Michael Steinberg, and the Cogut Center for the Humanities. My fellow Fellows in these programs provided lively and stimulating intellectual environments. This book was completed at the University of British Columbia, and I express my deep gratitude to my wonderful colleagues and the excellent staff in the Department of Classical, Near Eastern, and Religious Studies, who have supported my work in too many ways to possibly list.

I am very grateful to Ra'anan Boustan, Franco De Angelis, David Downs, Ari Finkelstein, Adam Gregerman, Jonathan Kaplan, Tzvi Novick, Jonathan Schofer, and Moulie Vidas for providing feedback on chapters of the manuscript as it took shape. Jordan Rosenblum has always been ready to exchange ideas, and his work has had an important impact on my own. Tracy Ames, Jamie Carrick, Justin Glessner, Courtney Innes, and Lisa Tweten provided valuable research assistance. The manuscript as a whole was greatly improved by comments from the two anonymous reviewers for the Press; I thank them for their time, effort, and investment in my work.

In addition to those already mentioned, this project benefited from conversations with and support from Elizabeth Shanks Alexander, Aryeh Amihay, Antje Ellermann, Laura Fisher, Eric Gregory, Cam Grey, Alan Jacobs, Joel Kaminsky, Joshua Karlip, Eitan Kensky, Lee Levine, Eric Meyers, Yoni Miller, Vered Noam, Annette Reed, Seth Schwartz, Aharon Shemesh, Benjamin Soskis, Jeffrey Stout, Nathan Sussman, my colleagues in the 2012–13 Early Career Faculty Fellowship of the American Academy for Jewish Research, and the participants in the Religious Competition in Late Antiquity program unit of the Society of Biblical Literature. My writing group in Cambridge – Rachel Greenblatt, Jane Kanarek, Yehuda Kurtzer, and Claire Sufrin – provided not only valuable feedback on my work, but also essential structure to my writing process. Various portions of this project were presented and workshopped at the annual meetings of the Association for Jewish Studies and the Society of Biblical Literature, the Judaism in Antiquity workshop at Harvard, and the Philadelphia Seminar on Christian Origins at the University of Pennsylvania. I thank the organizers for the opportunity to present my work and the participants for their feedback. Perhaps needless to say, all remaining errors are my responsibility alone.

Special thanks to the Diamond Foundation of Vancouver for supporting Jewish studies at the University of British Columbia and my work as the UBC Diamond Chair in Jewish Law and Ethics. I am very grateful to Lewis

Bateman, Elda Granata, Paul Smolenski, Shaun Vigil, and others at Cambridge University Press, as well as my copy editor Hillary Ford and Anamika Singh for their hard work and enthusiasm in turning this manuscript into a book.

I also extend my gratitude to the staff at Princeton's Firestone Library, Brown's Rockefeller Library, Harvard's Widener Library and the Andover-Harvard Theological Library, and the Koerner Library at the University of British Columbia for providing the resources that I needed for this project.

Last, but certainly not least, I owe a special debt to my family. I thank my parents, Fran and Keith, to whom this book is dedicated, and Kevin, Scott, Joy, Brandon, and Brooke Gardner, and Cindy, Don, Sam, Lacey, and Rhodes Brown for their support and love. Yael Deborah was born as I was finishing the dissertation and Jonah Edward was born just before we moved from Boston to Vancouver. Curious to know what Daddy was working on, they would hop onto my lap, take over my keyboard, and helpfully type the first letters of their names again and again. Yael and Jonah, I owe every *y* and *j* in this book to you. I love you and thank you for making sure that I do not lose sight of what is truly important. I never could have undertaken or completed this project without my wife, Rabbi Carey A. Brown. She read and commented upon multiple drafts of the entire manuscript, was my constant sounding board for ideas, and provided me with the support and strength that I needed to finish. Carey, you mean more to me than I can possibly put into words. I consider myself unbelievably lucky to have you as my partner on this journey.

Gregg E. Gardner

Abbreviations and Conventions

All translations of rabbinic texts, unless otherwise noted, are my own and based on the following Hebrew and Aramaic editions of the primary texts: the Kaufmann manuscript of the Mishnah; Lieberman's Tosefta – where incomplete, I have used Zuckermandel's edition; Horovitz-Rabin's *Mekhilta*; Weiss's *Sifra*; Kahana's *Sifre on Numbers*, Finkelstein's *Sifre on Deuteronomy*; Schäfer's Jerusalem Talmud; and the Vilna edition of the Babylonian Talmud.[1] Unless otherwise indicated, translations of the Hebrew Bible are according to the New Jewish Publication Society Translation, with my modifications.[2] Translations of the Apocrypha and New Testament are according to the New Revised Standard Version. References to Greek and Latin sources, unless

---

[1] Georg Beer, ed. *Faksimile-Ausgabe des Mischnacodex Kaufmann A 50* (The Hague, 1929 [repr. Jerusalem, 1968]); Louis Finkelstein and Saul Horovitz, eds., *Sifre on Deuteronomy [Hebrew]* (2nd ed.; New York: Jewish Theological Seminary of America, 1969; repr. 2001); H. S. Horovitz and I. A. Rabin, eds., *Mechilta d'Rabbi Ismael [Hebrew]* (2nd ed., 1931; repr. Jerusalem: Shalem Books, 1997); Menahem I. Kahana, *Sifre on Numbers: An Annotated Edition [Hebrew]* (3 vols.; Jerusalem: Hebrew University Magnes Press, 2011); Saul Lieberman, *The Tosefta: According to Codex Vienna, with Variants from Codex Erfurt, Genizah Mss. and Editio Princeps [Venice 1521] [Hebrew]* (4 vols.; New York: Jewish Theological Seminary of America, 1955–1988); Isaac Hirsch Weiss, *Sifra de-ve Rav hu sefer Torat kohanim [Hebrew]* (New York: Om Publishing, 1862; repr. 1946); M. S. Zuckermandel, *Tosephta: Based on the Erfurt and Vienna Codices, with Parallels and Variants, with Supplement to the Tosefta by Saul Lieberman* (Jerusalem: Wahrman, 1970; repr. 2003); and for the Yerushalmi, the Leiden manuscript as published in Peter Schäfer and Hans-Jürgen Becker, eds., *Synopse zum Talmud Yerushalmi* (TSAJ 31, 33, 35, 47, 67, 82–83; Tübingen: J.C.B. Mohr, 1991). I have also made use of the following electronic editions of these texts: Martin G. Abegg Jr. and Casey A. Toews, *Mishna: Based Upon the Kaufmann Manuscript* (Altamonte Springs, Fla.: Accordance 9.1 Bible Software, Oak Tree Software, Inc., 2010); *Ma'agarim: Historical Dictionary of the Academy of the Hebrew Language* (Jerusalem: Academy of the Hebrew Language, 1998); Bar Ilan University, *The Responsa Project: Version 20* (Ramat Gan, Israel: Bar-Ilan University, 1972–2012).

[2] Jewish Publication Society, *Tanakh: The Holy Scriptures: The New JPS Translation According to the Traditional Hebrew Text* (Philadelphia: The Jewish Publication Society, 1985).

otherwise noted, refer to their respective editions in the Loeb Classical Library series.

I have employed a general-purpose style of transliterating Hebrew and Aramaic words when the fully reversible style (with diacritics, etc.) is unnecessary. For common names (e.g., Judah, Shimon) and terms that appear in standard English dictionaries (e.g., midrash), I have used conventional spellings and roman type. References to rabbinic texts are abbreviated as follows: *m.* – Mishnah; *t.* – Tosefta; *y.* – Jerusalem Talmud or Yerushalmi; *b.* – Babylonian Talmud or Bavli (all followed by the name of the tractate); *Mekilta* – *Mekilta of Rabbi Ishmael*; *SifreNum* – *Sifre on Numbers*; and *SifreDeut* – *Sifre on Deuteronomy*. All other abbreviations are according to Alexander et al., *SBL Handbook of Style*, which I have also endeavored to follow for citations, spellings, and other conventions.[3]

In this book, *rabbis* and *Tannaim* refer to the editors and redactors of early rabbinic or Tannaitic compilations, as methodological difficulties limit what can be known about any particular individual or individuals depicted within the texts.[4] *Mishnah* indicates the entire corpus of six orders; each order contains about ten tractates, each tractate is divided into chapters; and each chapter consists of numerous mishnayoth (singular: mishnah) or pericopae. A pericope is divided into multiple lemmata; a lemma is defined as the smallest group of words that convey a coherent thought.[5] I have enumerated lemmata only as necessary.

---

[3] Patrick H. Alexander et al., eds., *The SBL Handbook of Style: For Ancient Near Eastern, Biblical, and Early Christian Studies* (Peabody, Mass.: Hendrickson, 1999).

[4] See H. L. Strack and Günter Stemberger, *Introduction to the Talmud and Midrash* (trans. M. N. A. Bockmuehl; Minneapolis, Minn.: Fortress Press, 1996), 59–62, and my discussion in Chapter 1.

[5] Martin S. Jaffee, "Rabbinic Authorship as a Collective Enterprise," in *The Cambridge Companion to the Talmud and Rabbinic Literature* (ed. C. E. Fonrobert and M. S. Jaffee; New York: Cambridge University Press, 2007), 17–37.

1

Introduction

In the late second and early third centuries C.E., the rabbis who authored and redacted the foundational texts of rabbinic Judaism outlined a system for giving to the poor through communal institutions. They saw organized charity as a way to bring an end to begging; their goal, however, was to solve not the problem of poverty – but rather the problem of charity.[1]

THE PROBLEM OF CHARITY

Charity, or *tsedaqah* in Hebrew, is a prominent concept in classical rabbinic literature, texts that took shape between the second and seventh centuries C.E. Living in Palestine under Roman rule and Babylonia under the Sasanians, the rabbis instruct that charity is a way to imitate God. Charity replaces sacrifices, brings one closer to the divine, and averts the evil decree on the day of judgment. Charity can redeem the world, the sages claim, and even save one from imminent death. The Babylonian Talmud instructs that giving charity adds twenty-two years to the benefactor's life. Indeed, charity is considered to be *the* commandment in some rabbinic texts. An examination of charity, therefore, will illuminate a central concept of rabbinic Judaism, the preeminent form of Judaism from the middle ages to today.[2]

---

[1] That charity could be a problem was not unique to the ancient world; see, e.g., Benjamin Soskis, "The Problem of Charity in Industrial America, 1873–1915" (Ph.D. diss., Columbia University, 2010).

[2] The most important discussions of charity in classical rabbinic literature are found in *m. Pe'ah* 8:7; *t. Pe'ah* 4:8–21; *y. Pe'ah* 1:1, 15b–c; *y. Pe'ah* 8:7–9, 21a–b (as noted earlier, citations from the Yerushalmi are according to the Leiden manuscript, as published in Schäfer and Becker, eds. *Synopse zum Talmud Yerushalmi*); *b. Bava Batra* 8a–11a; *b. Ketubbot* 66b–68a; and *Lev. Rab.* 5:4, 34:1–16. See also *t. Demai* 3:16–17; *y. Demai* 3:1, 23b; *b. Shabbat* 156a–b; *b. Sotah* 14a; *b. Sukkah* 49b; *Deut. Rab.* 5:3; *Exod. Rab.* 31:4. For collections of rabbinic sources on charity, see Alan J. Avery-Peck, "Charity in Judaism," in *The Encyclopaedia of Judaism* (ed. J. Neusner

Rabbinic texts instruct that charity is best performed in a collective and organized way. "Just as in a coat of mail every small scale joins with the others to form one piece of armor," we read in the Babylonian Talmud, "so every little sum given to charity combines with the rest to form a large sum."[3] The rabbis envision that everyone in a community would contribute to their local *tamhui* or soup kitchen and *quppa* or charity fund. In turn, these institutions would distribute provisions to the poor. Organized charity would become a hallmark of Jewish approaches to charity and, more broadly, Jewish life and thought. "Never have we seen or heard of a Jewish community," Maimonides wrote, "that does not have a *quppa*."[4]

What are the origins of organized charity in rabbinic Judaism and why was it formulated in the way that it was? This book seeks to answer these questions, which will help us better understand the foundations of Jewish ethics and law, as well as the rabbinic movement's gradual consolidation of socioreligious authority over Jewish society. Because care for the poor through organized charity played an important role in the development of Judaism and Christianity, this topic has important implications for the broader study of the history of religions and late antiquity. I find that early rabbinic or Tannaitic texts prescribe a system of institutionalized almsgiving that provides an alternative to giving to beggars. The early rabbis or Tannaim sought to end begging in order to transform the way that people gave charity, which was deeply problematic.

The simplest form of charity, when one individual hands over food, money, or some other asset to a beggar, was the most prevalent form of support for the poor in ancient world. This straightforward transfer, however, created moral, ethical, and social dilemmas. The problems caused by giving charity directly to beggars are timeless and have been brought to light by a number of prominent thinkers. Immanuel Kant writes, "Almsgiving is a form of kindliness associated with pride and costing no trouble.... Men are demeaned by it."[5]

---

et al.; Leiden and Boston: Brill, 2005), 1:335–47; Robert B. Becknell, "Almsgiving, the Jewish Legacy of Justice and Mercy" (Ph.D. diss., Miami University, 2000), 472–585; C. G. Montefiore and H. M. J. Loewe, eds., *A Rabbinic Anthology* (Cleveland, Ohio, and Philadelphia: Meridian Books and Jewish Publication Society of America, 1963), 412–39.

[3] *b. Bava Batra* 9b. Likewise, later in the same text: "Just as in a garment every thread unites with the rest to form a whole garment, so every farthing given to charity unites with the rest to form a large sum."

[4] Maimonides, *Mishneh Torah, Hilkhot mattenot ʿaniyyim* (Laws on Gifts to the Poor) 9.3; translation based on Joseph B. Meszler and Marc Lee Raphael, *Gifts for the Poor: Moses Maimonides' Treatise on Tzedakah* (Williamsburg, Va.: Department of Religion: The College of William and Mary, 2003), 64, with my emendations.

[5] Immanuel Kant, "Lectures on Ethics," in *The Cambridge Edition of the Works of Immanuel Kant* (ed. P. L. Heath and J. B. Schneewind; Cambridge and New York: Cambridge University Press, 2001), 208. On Kant's approach to almsgiving, see J. B. Schneewind, "Philosophical

That altruistic giving has unsavory attributes is likewise noted by Ralph Waldo Emerson, "The law of benefits is a difficult channel which requires careful sailing, or rude boats.... How dare you give them?... The hand that feeds us is in some danger of being bitten."[6] Marcel Mauss, following Emerson, wrote, "Charity is still wounding for him who has accepted it, and the whole tendency of our morality is to strive to do away with the unconscious and injurious patronage of the rich almsgiver."[7] Likewise, Mary Douglas writes that charity is meant to be a free gift and lauded as a virtue, yet "we know that it wounds."[8]

Charity is a problem because it can harm the recipient. Scholarship on gifts and gift exchange has been particularly helpful in this regard, as it illuminates how charity can deepen the recipient's sense of social exclusion.[9] Gifts, as Mauss and others have noted, generate an obligation for the recipient to give a gift in return.[10] Most societies, including those of the ancient Mediterranean, abide by the "norm of reciprocity," which entails an obligation to accept a gift when it is offered and to give something in return.[11]

The process of giving, receiving, and giving back creates relationships between the two parties and some forms of giving foster social cohesion.[12] Charity increases economic equity as it redistributes assets from rich to poor, reducing the gaps between the haves and have-nots. In its own way, however, charity also erodes solidarity.[13] Charity, whereby gifts are given and accepted

---

Ideas of Charity: Some Historical Reflections," in *Giving: Western Ideas of Philanthropy* (ed. J. B. Schneewind; Bloomington: Indiana University Press, 1996), 65–72.

[6] Ralph Waldo Emerson, "Gifts," in *Essays & Lectures* (ed. R. W. Emerson and J. Porte; New York: Viking Press, 1844 [repr. 1983]), 536.

[7] Marcel Mauss, *The Gift: The Form and Reason for Exchange in Archaic Societies* (trans. W. D. Halls; New York: W.W. Norton, 1990), 65.

[8] Mary Douglas, "Foreword: No Free Gifts," in *The Gift: The Form and Reason for Exchange in Archaic Societies*, by Marcel Mauss (trans. W. D. Halls; New York and London: W. W. Norton, 1990), vii.

[9] It is notable that many ancient Jewish writers (e.g., Ben Sira, Josephus), conflate gifts and charity; see Seth Schwartz, *Were the Jews a Mediterranean Society? Reciprocity and Solidarity in Ancient Judaism* (Princeton, N.J., and Oxford: Princeton University Press, 2010).

[10] Mauss, *The Gift*, see also Pierre Bourdieu, *The Logic of Practice* (Stanford, Calif.: Stanford University Press, 1990), 98.

[11] Alvin W. Gouldner, "The Norm of Reciprocity: A Preliminary Statement," *American Sociological Review* 25 (1960): 161–78. On the application of Mauss's ideas on gift exchange to antiquity, see Michael L. Satlow, ed., *The Gift in Antiquity* (Ancient World: Comparative Histories; Chichester, West Sussex, UK: Wiley-Blackwell, 2013).

[12] Gouldner, "Norm of Reciprocity," 162.

[13] A similar point is made in passing by Tzvi Novick concerning the gifts for the poor given on Purim mentioned in Esth 9:22. Novick rightly points out that this verse distinguishes the gifts given to "the poor" from those that are exchanged between "one another." The poor, therefore, are placed outside the boundaries of normal social intercourse; see Tzvi Novick, "Charity and Reciprocity: Structures of Benevolence in Rabbinic Literature," *HTR* 105 (2012): 34n. 3.

without the expectation of reciprocation or any kind of compensation in return, casts the recipient in an inferior light.[14] "There should not be any free gifts," writes Mary Douglas. "What is wrong with the so-called 'free gift' is the donor's intention to be exempt from return gifts coming from the recipient."[15] The lack of an expectation to reciprocate reflects and projects social and economic inequalities between the benefactor and beneficiary.[16] The gift itself – the piece of bread, the bronze coin – concretizes and indexes the hierarchical relationship between the wealthy donor and the poor recipient.

Similarly, charity can undermine social cohesion by creating relationships of personal dependency. Societies have long prized economic independence and scorned dependence upon others. "A poor man who begs is constantly depreciating his personhood and abasing himself," Kant writes, "he makes his existence dependent on other people, and accustoms others, but the sight of him, to the means whereby we neglect our worth."[17] Just as society looks down upon those who are dependent, the poor resent those on whom they are dependent. "We wish to be self-sustained," Emerson writes, "We do not quite forgive a giver.... We can receive anything from love, for that is a way of receiving it from ourself; but not from anyone who assumes to bestow."[18]

At the heart of the matter are the intentions of the giver, as it is not only the transfer of alms that can injure the poor, but also the very intention to do so. Especially insightful is Barry Schwartz's work on the social psychology of gifts, which can be applied to illuminate charitable giving. Schwartz shows that gifts impose identities upon the giver and recipient, as they reveal "an important secret: the idea which the recipient evokes in the imagination of the giver."[19] When a gift is offered without the expectation of a return, the giver identifies himself or herself as a benefactor and reveals his or her perception of the recipient as a charity case – the recipient is poor and willing to accept support from others. This perception may be created at the moment when a poor man asks for alms. It may also be based on the benefactor's perception or interpretation of the semiotic code projected by the poor man's appearance: perhaps he wore tattered clothes or ate poor quality food, which are signs of poverty. Whatever the case may be, offering alms can be a damaging unilateral

---

[14] Mauss, *The Gift*, 65.
[15] Douglas, "No Free Gifts," vii.
[16] Aafke E. Komter, *Social Solidarity and the Gift* (Cambridge: Cambridge University Press, 2005), 28–29.
[17] Kant, "Lectures," 431.
[18] Emerson, "Gifts," 536.
[19] Barry Schwartz, "The Social Psychology of the Gift," *American Journal of Sociology* 73 (1967): 2.

move, as the benefactor wounds an individual by identifying him or her as one willing to be dependent upon others. These otherwise intangible and ephemeral attitudes and ideas about the poor are concretized, objectified, and advertised by the things given.[20]

BEGGING IN LATE ANTIQUITY

The problems with begging were likewise apparent to the ancients. "My child, do not lead the life of a beggar; it is better to die than to beg," Ben Sira wrote in the second century B.C.E. "One loses self-respect with another person's food. In the mouth of the shameless begging is sweet, but it kindles a fire inside him."[21] Likewise, Philo observes that for many, begging is a "slavish state unbecoming the dignity of a freeman."[22] Begging breeds shame and indignity, and beggars are often suspected of deceit.[23] Yet, despite its problems, in the absence of organized charity in the ancient world, begging was the predominant way in which the poor could acquire what they needed.

Beggars were frequently seen in public soliciting alms and it was common to find them in and around religious spaces, such as Roman temples.[24] Jews were likewise known to beg near sacred spaces, such as the Temple compound in Jerusalem and synagogues.[25] The attraction of beggars to temples and other

---

[20] Komter, *Social Solidarity*, 7, drawing on the work of Erving Goffman, *Relations in Public: Microstudies of the Public Order* (New York: Basic Books, 1971), 138–237, writes, "Gifts as 'tie-signs' disclose the nature of the tie between giver and recipient. They reveal how we perceive the recipient while at the same time showing something about our own identity." This section reworks material from my article "Charity Wounds: Gifts to the Poor in Early Rabbinic Judaism," in *The Gift in Antiquity* (ed. M. L. Satlow: Wiley-Blackwell, 2013), 174–76.

[21] Sir 40:28–30; see Gary A. Anderson, *Charity: The Place of the Poor in the Biblical Tradition* (New Haven, Conn.: Yale University Press, 2013), 87–88.

[22] Philo, *Flaccus* 64.

[23] Begging also fosters pity, which was often viewed in negative terms (as fear and weakness) by Greek and Roman writers; see A. R. Hands, *Charities and Social Aid in Greece and Rome* (London: Thames & Hudson, 1968), 77–88; Anneliese Parkin, "An Exploration of Pagan Almsgiving," in *Poverty in the Roman World* (ed. M. Atkins and R. Osborne; Cambridge and New York: Cambridge University Press, 2006), 62–64.

[24] Parkin, "An Exploration," 66; Dominic Rathbone, "Poverty and Population in Roman Egypt," in *Poverty in the Roman World* (ed. M. Atkins and R. Osborne; Cambridge and New York: Cambridge University Press, 2006), 110.

[25] Acts 3:1–5; Susan R. Holman, *The Hungry are Dying: Beggars and Bishops in Roman Cappadocia* (New York: Oxford University Press, 2001), 49–50. Lysimachus (second-first century B.C.E.; as cited by Josephus in *Ag. Ap.* 1.305) claims that when the Jews were in Egypt, they were afflicted with diseases and begged for food at temples. Cleomedes (first–second century C.E.) mentions beggars in synagogue courtyards (*On the Circular Motions of the Celestial Bodies*, 2.1:91). Artemidorus (second century C.E.) also refers to Jewish beggars at synagogues (*Interpretation of Dreams* 3.53). On these texts, see Aryay B. Finkelstein, "Julian among Jews, Christians and 'Hellenes' in Antioch: Jewish Practice as a Guide to 'Hellenes' and a Goad to

religious locales was twofold. First, because the poor are often understood to be under the special care of the divine, it follows that they would seek protection and comfort at the deity's abode. Second, the poor improved their chances of receiving alms by begging in areas where people gathered. It was strategic to solicit alms from the stream of people coming from and going to sacred places. Likewise, it was common to find beggars milling about marketplaces and at junctions in the road.[26] While exposure to the public increases the chances that a beggar will receive alms, it also adds to the visibility of their poverty and draws attention to their begging. Thus, begging traps the poor in a dangerous cycle of humiliation.

While begging was shameful, giving to beggars was praiseworthy in ancient Jewish and Christian texts. "Help the poor for the commandment's sake," writes Ben Sira (29:9), "and in their need do not send them away empty-handed." Likewise, in Tobit 4:6–7 (early second century B.C.E.), "To all those who practice righteousness give alms from your possessions, and do not let your eye begrudge the gift when you make it. Do not turn your face away from anyone who is poor, and the face of God will not be turned away from you." The New Testament makes a similar point repeatedly, such as in Matthew (5:42), "Give to everyone who begs from you, and do not refuse anyone who wants to borrow from you."[27] Likewise in the *Didache* (1.5), an early work on Christian discipline, we read, "To all who ask you give, and do not ask back, for from their own gifts the father wishes to give to all."[28] Thus, a number of early Jewish and Christian texts not only find giving to beggars virtuous, but also caution against rejecting them.[29]

Christians" (Ph.D. diss., Harvard University, 2011), 134–36; Menahem Stern, *Greek and Latin Authors on Jews and Judaism* (3 vols.; Jerusalem: Israel Academy of Sciences and Humanities, 1974–1984), 2:157–58, 330.

[26] For sources on beggars in the Greco-Roman world, see Richard Finn, *Almsgiving in the Later Roman Empire: Christian Promotion and Practice (313–450)* (Oxford and New York: Oxford University Press, 2006), 19–20; Richard Finn, "Portraying the Poor: Descriptions of Poverty in Christian Texts from the Late Roman Empire," in *Poverty in the Roman World* (ed. M. Atkins and R. Osborne; Cambridge and New York: Cambridge University Press, 2006), 140–41; Bruce W. Longenecker, *Remember the Poor: Paul, Poverty, and the Greco-Roman World* (Grand Rapids, Mich.: Eerdmans, 2010), 97.

[27] See also Luke 6:30.

[28] As cited in Steven L. Bridge, "To Give or Not to Give? Deciphering the Saying of Didache 1.6," *JECS* 5 (1997): 555. Cf. Shepherd of Hermas, *Mandate* 2.4–6. Dates for the *Didache* range from the late first through the third century C.E.; see Jonathan A. Draper, "Didache," in *The New Interpreter's Dictionary of the Bible* (ed. K. D. Sakenfeld; Nashville, Tenn.: Abingdon, 2006), 120; Robert A. Kraft, "Didache," in *The Anchor Bible Dictionary* (ed. D. N. Freedman; New York: Doubleday, 1992), 2:197–98.

[29] It is notable that Jews were associated with begging and identified as beggars by a number of Greek and Latin authors, such as Martial and Juvenal; see Stern, *Greek and Latin Authors*, 1:529, 2:100–1.

In light of the early Jewish and Christian exhortations to give to beggars, as well as their warnings against turning panhandlers away empty handed, the early rabbinic approach to dealing with beggars is surprising:

> [If a poor man] went from door to door [begging, then] they [i.e., the householders] are not obligated to him in any way. (*t. Pe'ah* 4:8)

The Tosefta instructs the reader that if a beggar comes to the door, then one is not obligated to give him anything.[30] The Tannaim were not the only ones in the ancient world who warned against giving to beggars. One Greek dramatist wrote that you do no service to a beggar by giving him food or drink, because you lose what you give him and prolong his life of misery.[31] We see, however, no such reasoning in rabbinic texts. Rather, as I will show, the rabbis instruct their audience not to give to beggars because they seek to promote an alternative to begging: people should refuse beggars because they should give through the institutions of organized charity – the *tamhui* and *quppa*.[32] Later in this chapter I will discuss how organized charity can bring an end to begging.

THE PROBLEMS: BEGINNINGS AND ENDS

Two main issues have occupied scholarship on organized charity: its beginnings and ends. By "beginnings" I mean whether organized charity existed already in the Second Temple era and by the first century C.E. in particular. Exploring this issue will help us understand any possible background or predecessors to the earliest rabbinic discourses on the topic. By "ends" I mean the ends to which organized charity was put. Because the question of "ends" also illustrates the significance of organized charity (and, in turn, the significance

---

[30] By contrast, in *t. Pe'ah* 2:18 one must give at least a small amount to the poor in order to fulfill the poor tithe. It is common to read *t. Pe'ah* 4:8 through the apologetic lenses of later, traditional rabbinic interpretations, such as those in the Yerushalmi; see, amongst others, Ephraim Urbach, "Political and Social Tendencies in Talmudic Concepts of Charity [Hebrew]," *Zion* 16 (1951): 22. The image of the beggar at the door is also found in other early rabbinic texts, as well as extrarabbinic sources; see my discussion in Chapter 7.

[31] Plautus, *Trinummus* 339; on this text, see Longenecker, *Remember the Poor*, 107.

[32] On organized charity as an alternative to begging, see also the comments by the Roman Emperor Julian in 362 C.E.: "For it is disgraceful that, when no Jew ever has to beg, and the numerous impious Galileans [Christians] support not only their own poor but ours as well, all men see that our people lack aid from us [that is, from the pagan priesthood]." (Julian, *Ep.* 22; Stern, *Greek and Latin Authors*, 2:549). What has often been overlooked in Julian's comments is that he writes that no Jew has to *beg* – he does not say that no Jew was needy. This should be contrasted with early Greek and Latin writings, where Jews are often portrayed as beggars. On this text, see Finkelstein, "Julian among Jews, Christians and 'Hellenes' in Antioch," 134–36.

of the present study) for the broader history of religions, I will start with it here.

The Ends of Organized Charity

At first blush, the primary goal of organized charity is its most obvious – to support the poor. While there can be no doubt of this, in late antiquity organized charity also served the needs and objectives of the giver. When charity is organized, it can be controlled. This adds up to control over the funds given as charity as well as control over the selection of the recipients. The special properties of organized charity and the mechanisms that lie behind them have been taken for granted by scholars and insufficiently studied to date. I will return to this topic in Chapter 3. For now, I wish to emphasize that organized charity has been used to gain and consolidate economic, political, and religious power, most prominently by leaders of the church beginning in the fourth century.

Using charity for political purposes has been illuminated and discussed by a number of scholars, from Ephraim Urbach to Paul Veyne.[33] Most prominent is the work of Peter Brown, who writes that the bishops gained and consolidated their authority by presenting their actions as responses to the needs of the poor, for whom they claimed to speak.[34] The bishops' claims enabled them to control an entire segment of society, the poor, by controlling the assets given as charity. Moreover, control over charity enabled them to direct funds back to the church. By the fourth century, Brown finds, the bishops and their clergy expected to be supported by fellow believers. They formed a new category of individuals, alongside the poor, who required support. They accepted these offerings "in the name of the poor" and understood themselves as the stewards of the church. After covering their own expenses, the bishops and the clergy were to distribute what was left over to those in need.[35] "This wealth was to be used by the clergy for the benefit of the poor," Brown writes, "In some circles, even private almsgiving was discouraged: ideally, all gifts to the poor were to pass through the hands of the bishops and clergy, for only they knew who needed support."[36] Brown's work points to the importance of organized charity in the bishops' project: control over almsgiving and the poor could

---

[33] Urbach, "Political and Social Tendencies," 3–4; Paul Veyne, *Bread and Circuses: Historical Sociology and Political Pluralism* (trans. B. Pearce; London: Penguin, 1992).
[34] Peter Brown, *Poverty and Leadership in the Later Roman Empire* (Hanover, N.H.: University Press of New England, 2002), 8–9.
[35] Brown, *Poverty and Leadership*, 24–26.
[36] Brown, *Poverty and Leadership*, 24.

only be achieved if charity was organized. The church's control over the poor masses and over substantial economic resources were driving forces behind the bishops' consolidation of power and recognition by the state.[37]

The view that charity could be an instrument for obtaining and consolidating social, political, and religious authority is palpable in Palestinian Amoraic texts. *Leviticus Rabbah* and Yerushalmi *Pe'ah*, for example, depict rabbis as charity supervisors who collect contributions for, and distribute them to, other sages.[38] The Amoraim embed the texts with the terminology, structure, and imagery that is otherwise reserved for their discussions of organized charity for the poor.[39] That is, the Palestinian Amoraim self-consciously present the "collection of the sages" as a form of organized charity. This parallels the bishops, who cast themselves as "stewards" of charity and define "charity" to include contributions to clergy.[40]

While the confluence of authority and organized charity is palpable in late-antique Christian and Amoraic texts, it has yet to be investigated in Tannaitic texts. Did the Tannaim see organized charity as a means to promote their own authority? Or was this only a later, post-Tannaitic development? More generally, what are the objectives of the Tannaitic vision of organized charity, aside from supporting the poor? I will address these questions throughout this book. In general, I find that organized charity was not conceived by the

---

[37] Brown, *Poverty and Leadership*, 1–44; see also Peter Brown, *Through the Eye of a Needle: Wealth, the Fall of Rome, and the Making of Christianity in the West, 350–550 AD* (Princeton, N.J.: Princeton University Press, 2012), 53–90.

[38] *Lev. Rab.* 5:4; Mordecai Margulies, *Midrash Wayyikra Rabbah: A Critical Edition Based on Manuscripts and Genizah Fragments with Variants and Notes [Hebrew]* (New York and Jerusalem: Jewish Theological Seminary of America, 1953–1960 [repr. 1999]), 110–11; the parallel in *y. Horayot* 3:6 (in MS Leiden = 3:4 in Venice printed edition), 48a, and the discussion in Michael L. Satlow, "'Fruit and the Fruit of Fruit': Charity and Piety in Late Antique Judaism," *JQR* 100 (2010): 244–77. On *y. Pe'ah*, see my discussion in Chapter 8.

[39] The language in *Lev. Rab.* 5:4 that recalls organized charity includes the root *g-b-y* (*gabbai tsedaqah*); "to do a commandment" which is a locution for giving charity (Saul Lieberman, "Two Lexicographical Notes," *JBL* 65 [1946]: 69–72); *yarad m'nikhasav* ("he who lost his wealth") is common in a number of texts on charity (Alyssa M. Gray, "The Formerly Wealthy Poor: From Empathy to Ambivalence in Rabbinic Literature of Late Antiquity," *AJSR* 33 [2009]: 103–05); and the wife in the narratives is described as a "righteous [*tsadeket*] woman" recalling *tsedaqah*; and "fruit" or "rewards" [*perot*] are commonly promised for giving charity (cf. *t. Pe'ah* 4:18).

[40] Burton L. Visotzky, *Golden Bells and Pomegranates: Studies in Midrash Leviticus Rabbah* (Tübingen: Mohr Siebeck, 2003), 123–24, minimizes the importance of the similarities between the collections of the sages in *Leviticus Rabbah* and the church's use of organized charity by suggesting that organized charity played only a minor role in Palestinian Amoraic texts. I find, however, that organized charity is an important topic throughout Palestinian Amoraic texts (e.g., *y. Pe'ah*). Thus, the parallels between organized charity in Palestinian Amoraic texts and late-antique Christian works are substantial and warrant further examination; see my discussion in Chapter 8.

Tannaim as a means to enhance their own socioreligious authority. Rather, it was envisioned as a way to provide support while protecting the dignity of the poor.

The Beginnings of Organized Charity

The importance of organized charity for the study of late antiquity and the history of religions has prompted a number of scholars to inquire about its origins. Neither the *tamhui* nor *quppa* appear *as institutions* in the Hebrew Bible.[41] Nor do we find organized charity among the pagan societies of the Greek, Hellenistic, and Roman eras.[42] The absence of a systematic approach to poverty and charity is a consequence of Greco-Roman societies' failure to recognize the poor as a distinct social category, as noted by Hendrik Bolkestein, Brown, A. R. Hands, Urbach, Veyne, and others. In the Greco-Roman world, people were identified as either citizens or noncitizens. The reimagining of society along economic lines, whereby individuals were identified as rich or poor, would have to wait until the fourth century. Until then, however, "the poor" as a distinct social entity was invisible.[43]

At the heart of the matter is the important role that politics and civic identity played in pagan Mediterranean culture. The wealthy had a responsibility to

---

[41] Michael Hellinger, "Charity in Talmudic and Rabbinic Literature: A Legal, Literary, and Historical Analysis [Hebrew]," (Ph.D. diss., Bar-Ilan University, 1999), 205; Seth Schwartz, *Imperialism and Jewish Society, 200 B.C.E. to 640 C.E* (Princeton, N.J.: Princeton University Press, 2001), 229.

[42] For isolated instances of organized charity in the Greco-Roman world, such as in Rhodes in the first century C.E., see G. W. Bowersock et al., eds., *Late Antiquity: A Guide to the Postclassical World* (Harvard University Press Reference Library; Cambridge, Mass.: Belknap Press of Harvard University Press, 1999), 287–88; Longenecker, *Remember the Poor*, 85. Organized almsgiving, however, was mostly absent from Roman society; see M. I. Finley, *The Ancient Economy* (Berkeley: University of California Press, 1999), 40, and especially Greg Woolf, "Food, Poverty and Patronage: The Significance of the Epigraphy of the Roman Alimentary Schemes in Early Imperial Italy," *Papers of the British School at Rome* 58 (1990): 197–228, who demonstrates that the Roman empire's alimentary foundations (*alimenta*) for feeding children were not a form of poverty relief, as the recipients were selected due to their privileged status.

[43] Brown, *Poverty and Leadership*; Peter Brown, "Remembering the Poor and the Aesthetic of Society," *Journal of Interdisciplinary History* 35 (2005): 513–22; Brown, *Through the Eye*, 68–71; see also Hendrik Bolkestein, *Wohltätigkeit und armenpflege im vorchristlichen altertum; ein beitrag zum problem "moral und gesellschaft"* (Utrecht: A. Oosthoek, 1939), 101–48; Gregg E. Gardner, "Cornering Poverty: Mishnah *Pe'ah*, Tosefta *Pe'ah*, and the Reimagination of Society in Late Antiquity," in *Envisioning Judaism: Studies in Honor of Peter Schäfer on the Occasion of his Seventieth Birthday* (ed. R. S. Boustan et al.; Tübingen: Mohr Siebeck, 2013), 1.205–16; Gregg E. Gardner, "Who is Rich? The Poor in Early Rabbinic Judaism," *JQR* 104 (in press); Hands, *Charities and Social Aid*; Urbach, "Political and Social Tendencies," 1–27.

finance public works, including arranging for grain to be distributed during droughts and famines. However, benefactors directed acts of giving at their own cities and sought to aid their fellow citizens. Surely citizens who happened to be needy would benefit, though such benefactions were not meant for "the poor" per se. While Anneliese Parkin has rightly deconstructed the long-held view that Romans were incapable of expressing sympathy for the poor, it remains that these societies lacked systematic approaches to poverty.[44] Begging and giving to beggars was the predominant form of support for the poor in the ancient world.

Finding no organized charity among the Greeks and Romans, scholars have focused on early Jewish and Christian texts, including Hellenistic and Second Temple-era texts, the New Testament and other early Christian writings, and rabbinic literature. The discussion has centered on whether organized charity existed in the late Second Temple era (up to 70 C.E.), especially in the first century C.E. during the emergence of the Jesus movement. To be sure, scholarship on this issue often exudes an air of apologetics and modern-day religious competition. David Seccombe has observed that some scholars are interested in demonstrating that "the Christians did it first."[45] Other scholars have framed their discussions or focused on demonstrating the antiquity and priority of organized charity in Jewish sources.[46] Quite a few scholars find evidence of organized charity by the first century. These studies make the case for the pre-70 C.E. existence of organized charity by drawing on some or all of the following four sets of sources. The first is the House of Adiabene's distribution of provisions to Jerusalem during a famine in 46/47 C.E., as discussed by Josephus and other sources. The second is the hospitality provided by a certain first-century C.E. synagogue in Jerusalem, as outlined in the so-called Theodotos inscription. The third is the "chamber of secrets" in the Jerusalem Temple that, according to rabbinic texts, served as a locus of organized charity. The fourth is the Essenes' support of their own poor, as mentioned by Josephus and in the Dead Sea Scrolls. As I will show, the

---

[44] Parkin, "An Exploration," 60–82; cf. Finley, *Ancient Economy*, 39–40; Hands, *Charities and Social Aid*, 12–13, 77–88; Urbach, "Political and Social Tendencies," 3–4.
[45] David Seccombe, "Was there Organized Charity in Jerusalem before the Christians?," *JTS* 29 (1978): 140.
[46] For Jewish apologetics, see, e.g., Frank M. Loewenberg, *From Charity to Social Justice: The Emergence of Communal Institutions for the Support of the Poor in Ancient Judaism* (New Brunswick, N.J.: Transaction Publishers, 2001), 15–18; Ben Zion Rosenfeld and Haim Perlmutter, "Foundations of Charitable Organizations in Judea at the End of the Second Temple Period According to Tannaitic Sources [Hebrew]," *Judea and Samaria Research Studies* 20 (2011): 49n. 2.

evidence for organized charity before 70 C.E. is much thinner and more problematic than scholars have previously held.[47]

[47] Samuel Krauss, *Talmudische Archäologie* (3 vols.; Leipzig: G. Fock, 1910–1912), 3:67 traces organized charity to the First Temple era, suggesting that the existence of organized communal relief is presupposed by Deut 21:1–9. Ephraim Frisch, *An Historical Survey of Jewish Philanthropy: From the Earliest Times to the Nineteenth Century* (New York: Macmillan, 1924), 33–40, 100–1, draws upon the sources of Adiabene, Theodotos, the chamber of secrets, and the Essenes as evidence of organized charity in the first century and works backwards to link its origins to the emergence of the synagogue in the second century B.C.E. While Frisch is surely correct that organized charity would (eventually) be closely related to the synagogue, he does not adduce any prerabbinic sources. Judah Bergmann, *Ha-Tsedakah be-Yisra'el [Hebrew]* (Jerusalem: R. Mas, 1944; repr. 1974), 22–24, likewise argues that organized charity developed in correlation with the synagogue, whose emergence he dates to the return to Judah from the Babylonian exile in the sixth century B.C.E. He views the Theodotos inscription and the "chamber of secrets" as instantiations of organized charity, and generally reads rabbinic texts as transparent sources of history. Urbach, "Political and Social Tendencies," 12, presupposes the first-century existence of organized charity when he writes that the laws of the *tamhui* and *quppa* were reformulated after the destruction in 70 C.E., though he does not elaborate. Joachim Jeremias, *Jerusalem in the Time of Jesus: An Investigation into Economic and Social Conditions During the New Testament Period* (Philadelphia: Fortress Press, 1969), 129–34, has been influential and continues to frame scholarly discussions of early Jewish and Christian charity, and organized charity in particular; see, among others, Becknell, "Almsgiving," 515n. 608; Susan Sorek, *Remembered for Good: A Jewish Benefaction System in Ancient Palestine* (Sheffield: Sheffield Phoenix Press, 2010), 216–22. Jeremias draws upon sources on Adiabene, the Essenes, and the chamber of secrets – in addition to the New Testament – as evidence for organized charity before 70 C.E. He also imposes a modern conceptualization of charity onto the ancient sources. Some of the resultant conceptual difficulties have been pointed out by Seccombe, "Was there Organized Charity," 140–43, who notes that a woman's right to claim maintenance from the estate of her husband who went overseas (in *m. Ketubbot* 13:1–2) neither mentions the *quppa* nor constitutes an act of charity. Rather this text should be understood within the framework of the laws of marriage. While correct in this regard, Seccombe's own paper is not without problems as he draws upon rabbinic texts from the Mishnah through the Babylonian Talmud as sources for the Second Temple era. He questions Jeremias's use of *m. Pesahim* 10:1 for the pre-70 era, but Seccombe otherwise freely uses rabbinic texts as evidence for earlier eras. Gildas Hamel, "Poverty and Charity," in *The Oxford Handbook of Jewish Daily Life in Roman Palestine* (ed. C. Hezser; Oxford: Oxford University Press, 2010), 320–21, sees the Theodotos inscription, the chamber of secrets, and the Essenes as evidence of organized charity by the first century C.E. By contrast, in his earlier work, Gildas H. Hamel, *Poverty and Charity in Roman Palestine, First Three Centuries C.E.* (Berkeley: University of California Press, 1990), 218, writes in passing that rabbinic texts could not testify to the existence of organized charity in the first century – a position shared by Timothy J. M. Ling, *The Judaean Poor and the Fourth Gospel* (Cambridge and New York: Cambridge University Press, 2006), 174. Rosenfeld and Perlmutter, "Foundations of Charitable Organizations," 49–62, date the origins of organized charity to the "last generations" before the destruction of the Second Temple. Their findings are primarily based on Tannaitic texts (including those on the chamber of secrets), which they read as historically accurate sources for the pre-70 C.E. era – despite the authors' awareness of the methodological difficulties. They also draw upon Adiabene, Theodotos, and the New Testament as supporting evidence for organized charity in the first century C.E. Loewenberg, *From Charity to Social Justice*, 116–121, writes that communal poor relief emerged between the first century B.C.E. and the second century C.E., based mostly on the Dead Sea Scrolls, though the author also accepts the historicity of the chamber

HOUSE OF ADIABENE'S FAMINE RELIEF. The dynasty or House of Adiabene, including Queen Helena and her sons Izatus and Monobazus II, ruled a small area of Babylonia around the turn of the era. They famously converted to Judaism, which aroused the interest of Flavius Josephus, the first-century Jewish historian. Josephus recounts the various gifts that the family gave to the people of Jerusalem, especially in 46/47 C.E. when a drought struck. To relieve the famine that ensued, Adiabene arranged for the importation of grain from Egypt and dried figs from Cyprus. When the food arrived, it was distributed to the hungry by specially appointed individuals. There was a "memorial" to mark Abiabene's generosity.[48]

---

of secrets and the identification of Adiabene's benefactions as charity. Loewenberg's study also suffers from a number of other methodological difficulties in its handling of ancient religious texts. For example, he reads Deuteronomy as an accurate witness of the earliest times; states that David and Solomon authored Psalms and Proverbs, respectively; anachronistically uses the term "Jews" for the Israelites of the First Temple era; assumes that the commandments of the Hebrew Bible were uniformly followed by all through the end of late antiquity; and assumes that the Babylonian Talmud can accurately depict the first century B.C.E. (e.g., pp. 19–23, 30, 32). Also notable is the work of George Foot Moore, *Judaism in the First Centuries of the Christian Era* (Cambridge, Mass.: Harvard University Press, 1962), 2:174–79, who writes that evidence for charity institutions is "ample" for the second century C.E., while for the preceding period we have only "scanty intimations" (p. 174). His study, however, fails to discern between different kinds of giving, as Moore considers all forms of humanitarian aid as evidence for organized charity. Moore also uses later rabbinic texts for evidence of earlier eras (e.g., Amoraic texts and the Babylonian Talmud as evidence for the first and second centuries), and reads all rabbinic sources as transparent descriptions of social history. That is, for Moore, the *tamhui* and *quppa* existed and operated precisely as "described" in rabbinic literature. For a similar approach, see Becknell, "Almsgiving," 501–06; Zeev Safrai, *The Jewish Community in the Talmudic Period [Hebrew]* (Jerusalem: Zalman Shazar Center, 1995), 64–76.

[48] The principle account of the House of Adiabene's relief of the famine in Jerusalem is Josephus, *Ant.* 20:49–53. With regard to the famine relief, it is notable that Josephus styles it, as well as his other accounts of famines (e.g., *Ant.* 15.299–316, during the reign of Herod the Great) along the lines of the biblical narrative of Joseph's benefactions (they both acquire staples from Egypt, etc.). The story of Joseph, moreover, shapes other elements of Josephus's account of the Adiabene family. From a historical perspective, the famine may be the same one mentioned in Acts 11:27–30; see David J. Downs, *The Offering of the Gentiles: Paul's Collection for Jerusalem in its Chronological, Cultural, and Cultic Contexts* (Tübingen: Mohr Siebeck, 2008), 37–38. Later reflections on the famine and Adiabene's relief are included in highly stylized narratives in rabbinic texts, see *t. Pe'ah* 4:18; *y. Pe'ah* 1:1, 15b; and *b. Bava Batra* 11a. On the House of Adiabene, see Gregg E. Gardner, "Giving to the Poor in Early Rabbinic Judaism" (Ph.D. diss., Princeton University, 2009), 163–200; Gregg E. Gardner, "Competitive Giving in the Third Century CE: Early Rabbinic Approaches to Greco-Roman Civic Benefaction," in *Religious Competition in the Third Century C.E.: Jews, Christians, and the Greco-Roman World* (ed. N. DesRosiers et al.; Journal of Ancient Judaism: Supplements of: Vandenhoeck & Ruprecht, 2014), 81–92; Lawrence H. Schiffman, "The Conversion of the Royal House of Adiabene in Josephus and Rabbinic Sources," in *Josephus, Judaism, and Christianity* (ed. L. H. Feldman and G. Hata; Detroit, Mich.: Wayne State University Press, 1987), 293–312. It is possible that the "memorial" for the benefaction initially took an oral form, as opposed to plastic form, thus adapting *euergetism* to local Judean sensitivities; see the discussions in Seth Schwartz,

While this episode was certainly "organized," it was not "charity" per se. Rather, the philanthropic behavior of the House of Adiabene is an act of *euergetism* – a neologism created from the wording of Greek decrees that honor a benefactor (*euergetēs*).[49] Euergetism was a form of benefaction in which a benefactor gave a gift to a city and the citizens would reciprocate by giving a countergift to the benefactor. This informal institution was ubiquitous from the fifth century B.C.E. onward throughout the Greek-speaking world. Among other places, we find it in Hellenistic and Roman-era Palestine.[50] It was defined by a remarkably consistent set of features. From his or her own pocket, a benefactor would finance public works, games, fortifications or other forms of military assistance, or municipal services, or provide for the local cult. In return, the benefactor would receive a gift drawn from a fairly standardized set of rewards. The gift most characteristic of *euergetism* was an honorary decree passed by the local council that recounted the benefactor's contribution to the city and bestowed personal honors upon him or her. The honors set forth in the decree were accompanied by other gifts given to the benefactor, including statues in his or her image, crowns and other objects made of gold, and seats of honor at games and festivals. The gifts were awarded in public ceremonies that praised the benefactor, and the decrees themselves were inscribed and displayed in prominent locations. This served to publicize the benefaction, encourage others to contribute to the city, and elevate the social status of the benefactor.[51] It created a lasting memorial so that the benefaction, the benefactor, and the honors would be remembered as long as the stele with the inscription stood. Because these gifts either elevated or solidified the benefactor's social position, political standing, or both, *euergetism* provided a means to acquire or maintain authority. Royalty, therefore, were benefactors *par excellence*.[52]

"Euergetism in Josephus and the Epigraphic Culture of First-Century Jerusalem," in *From Hellenism to Islam: Cultural and Linguistic Change in the Roman Near East* (ed. H. M. Cotton: Cambridge University Press, 2009), 85–86; Schwartz, *Were the Jews*, 103–04.

[49] Veyne, *Bread and Circuses*, 10. For *euergetism* in Jewish sources, see Gregg Gardner, "Jewish Leadership and Hellenistic Civic Benefaction in the Second Century B.C.E.," *JBL* 126 (2007): 327–43; Gardner, "Competitive Giving," 81–92; Tessa Rajak, "Benefactors in the Greco-Jewish Diaspora," in *Geschichte-Tradition-Reflexion: Festschrift für Martin Hengel zum 70. Geburtstag* (ed. H. Cancik et al.; Tübingen: J. C. B. Mohr, 1996); Michael L. Satlow, "Giving for a Return: Jewish Votive Offerings in Late Antiquity," in *Religion and the Self in Antiquity* (ed. D. Brakke et al.; Bloomington: Indiana University Press, 2005), 91–108; Schwartz, *Imperialism and Jewish Society*, 284–87; Schwartz, "Euergetism in Josephus," 75–92; Schwartz, *Were the Jews*.

[50] Gardner, "Jewish Leadership," 327–43; Gardner, "Competitive Giving," 81–92.

[51] See Gardner, "Jewish Leadership," 327; Veyne, *Bread and Circuses*, 102–08.

[52] On kings as civic benefactors, see Klaus Bringmann, "The King as Benefactor: Some Remarks on Ideal Kingship in the Age of Hellenism," in *Images and Ideologies: Self-Definition in the Hellenistic World* (ed. A. Bulloch et al.; Berkeley: University of California Press, 1993), 7–24.

The famine relief provided by Adiabene falls within the framework of *euergetism*.[53] As Gary Anderson, Brown, Veyne, and other scholars have noted, however, *euergetism* was not charity. Famine relief was only one possible instantiation of *euergetism*, which included an array of acts that were understood as beneficial to a city, such as financing public games and building infrastructure. By contrast, charity entailed only material relief for the poor. Unlike charity, *euergetism* was meant to benefit the citizens of a particular town. These may have included needy individuals, but euergetism did not target "the poor" per se. Whereas charity lies in the moral realm, *euergetism* was a mechanism for the benefactor to capture honor and status.[54]

Adiabene's famine relief, therefore, cannot be considered evidence of charity – let alone organized charity – for the first century. Likewise, the individuals appointed to distribute provisions to the people of Jerusalem cannot be identified with the charity supervisors who would oversee the *quppa* at a later date. Rather, the episode of Adiabene's famine relief was an occasional instance of *euergetism*, Greek civic benefaction.

THEODOTOS SYNAGOGUE IN JERUSALEM. In 1913–1914, during excavations just south of the Temple Mount in Jerusalem, archaeologists uncovered a cistern filled with architectural fragments including a stone slab bearing an inscription. The inscription, which dates to the first century C.E., marks the founding of a synagogue and enumerates its functions:

> Theodotos son of Vettenos, priest and *archisynagogos*, son of an *archisynagogos*, grandson of an *archisynagogos*, built the synagogue for the reading of the Law and teaching of the commandments, and the guest-house and the (other) rooms and water installations (?) for the lodging of those who are in need of it from abroad, which (= the synagogue) his forefathers, the elders and Simonides founded.[55]

---

[53] To be sure, Adiabene's act of *euergetism* exhibited some idiosyncrasies; see the discussions in Schwartz, "Euergetism in Josephus," 85–86; Schwartz, *Were the Jews*, 103–4.

[54] On the differences between charity and *euergetism*, see Anderson, *Charity*, 15–16; Brown, *Poverty and Leadership*, 4–5; Brown, *Through the Eye*, 61–71; Longenecker, *Remember the Poor*, 71–73; Ilana F. Silber, "Neither Mauss Nor Veyne? Peter Brown's Interpretative Path to the Gift," in *The Gift in Antiquity* (ed. M. L. Satlow; Chichester, West Sussex, UK: Wiley-Blackwell, 2013), 205–08; Veyne, *Bread and Circuses*, 19–20; C. R. Whittaker, "The Poor in the City of Rome," in *Land, City, and Trade in the Roman Empire* (ed. C. R. Whittaker; Collected Studies Series; Aldershot, Hampshire, and Brookfield, Vt.: Variorum, 1993), 24.

[55] Translation according to Hannah M. Cotton et al., eds., *Corpus Inscriptionum Iudaeae/Palaestinae: Multi-lingual Corpus of the Inscriptions from Alexander to Muhammed* (Berlin and New York: De Gruyter, 2010), Vol. 1, Part 1, no. 9, p. 54. Theodotos son of Vettenos and the Simonides are otherwise unknown. The *archisynagogos* ("head of the synagogue") was a title held in high esteem, though the precise functions of this office are unclear; see

The inscription itself reflects another exercise in *euergetism*, in which the benefactor is rewarded for his construction of a synagogue with an honorific dedication in return. Funded by a certain Theodotos, probably from Italy, this synagogue was constructed for reading the Torah and studying the commandments. It also included a guest chamber with rooms, access to water, and an inn for Jews traveling from abroad.[56] The imperative for the synagogue to provide hospitality was prompted by religious obligations that require travel to Jerusalem. Foremost is the commandment that adult males make a pilgrimage to Jerusalem during Sukkot (Tabernacles), Passover, and Shavuot (Weeks). While this commandment is found in Deuteronomy, it was only in the late Second Temple period that Jews from outside of Judea – including the Galilee and points in the Diaspora such as Egypt – made pilgrimages en masse to Jerusalem.[57] The services that the inscription outlines are clear instances of hospitality. While elements of organized charity are related to customs of hospitality, charity and hospitality differ in significant ways. As I will discuss in more detail in Chapter 4, hospitality is provided under the assumption that the guest could or would return the favor to the host. Charity, on the other hand, is by definition given without the expectation of a return. The Theodotos inscription, therefore, does not constitute evidence for the existence of charity in the first century and surely not organized charity.

CHAMBER OF SECRETS. The earliest references to the chamber of secrets are found in Tannaitic texts:

> There were two chambers in the Temple. One was the chamber of secrets [or secret things] and the other was the chamber of utensils.[58] The chamber of secrets: Those who feared sin put their contribution into it, and the wellborn poor were maintained from it in secret. (*m. Sheqalim* 5:6)[59]

Lee I. Levine, *The Ancient Synagogue: The First Thousand Years* (2nd ed.; New Haven, Conn., and London: Yale University Press, 2005), 57–59.

[56] Levine, *Ancient Synagogue*, 58.

[57] On pilgrimage to Jerusalem, see Martin Goodman, "The Pilgrimage Economy of Jerusalem in the Second Temple Era," in *Jerusalem: Its Sanctity and Centrality to Judaism, Christianity, and Islam* (ed. L. I. Levine; New York: Continuum, 1999), 69–76; Shemuel Safrai, *Pilgrimage at the Time of the Second Temple [Hebrew]* (Tel-Aviv: Am Hassefer, 1965).

[58] In rabbinic traditions, the chamber of utensils collected items that could be used or sold for the Temple's upkeep; see *m. Tamid* 3:4.

[59] On this text and its parallel in *SifreDeut* 117, see Jacob Neusner, *A History of the Mishnaic Law of Appointed Times: Part Three, Sheqalim, Yoma, Sukkah* (Leiden: Brill, 1982), 40; Tzvi Novick, *What is Good, and What God Demands: Normative Structures in Tannaitic Literature* (Leiden and Boston: Brill, 2010), 140; Shmuel Safrai and Zeev Safrai, *Mishnat Eretz Israel: Tractate Skalim [Hebrew]* (Jerusalem: Liphshitz Publishing House College, 2009), 189–92.

This passage from the Mishnah is paralleled in the Tosefta, which adds the following:

> Just as there was a chamber of secrets in the Temple, so too there was such a chamber in every town, so that the wellborn poor could be maintained from it in secret. (*t. Sheqalim* 2:16)

In light of the Tosefta's references to "every town" and the "wellborn poor," it is reasonable to conclude that the text's redactors have the *quppa* in mind. The *quppa*, as I will discuss at greater length in Chapters 5 and 6, was envisioned as a civic institution that aimed to support the conjunctural poor, with a special focus on the wellborn poor – that is, those who were born wealthy, but have since fallen into poverty. The issue, then, becomes whether these rabbinic texts preserve accurate information from the time in which the Second Temple was still standing. Alternatively, do they reflect the ideas and prerogatives of the texts' authors and redactors who lived in the late second and early third century C.E., well after the end of the Second Temple era? This question goes to the very heart of important methodological issues in the modern, academic study of rabbinic literature, particularly if rabbinic texts can be used as historical sources for earlier periods.

Scholars who argue for the chamber of secrets as evidence for pre-70 C.E. organized charity take the historicity of these texts at face value. They likewise tend to cite rabbinic texts as chronologically and geographically diverse as the Mishnah (redacted in third-century Roman Palestine) and Babylonian Talmud (sixth-seventh century Mesopotamia) side-by-side in an effort to reconstruct the social and religious life of Judea in the first century and earlier.[60] These arguments, moreover, point to support for the pre-70 C.E. existence of the chamber of secrets as a locus of organized charity in passages from the New Testament and Apocrypha that mention the financial and commercial functions of the Jerusalem Temple. Like many other temples in the ancient world, the Jerusalem Temple served as a kind of bank that held deposits for individuals.[61] Similarly, these scholars conflate contributions to the Temple, such as those mentioned in Mark 12:41–44 and Luke 21:1–4, with

---

[60] Becknell, "Almsgiving," 505–06; Frisch, *Historical Survey*, 34–35, 37, 63; Jeremias, *Jerusalem in the Time of Jesus*, 133; Joseph Lehmann, "Assistance publique et privée d'après l'antique législation juive," *Revue des Études Juives* 35 (1897): xxii; Loewenberg, *From Charity to Social Justice*, 20–23, 119; Moore, *Judaism in the First Centuries*, 2:167; Safrai and Safrai, *Mishnat Eretz Israel: Tractate Skalim*, 190–91; Seccombe, "Was there Organized Charity," 140–41.

[61] Jeremias, *Jerusalem in the Time of Jesus*, 134. On the Temple treasury, see Gardner, "Jewish Leadership," 331–32.

giving charity to the poor.[62] These scholars further note that it was common for the poor to frequent temples and other holy sites to solicit alms.[63]

There are a number of problems, however, with this synthesis. Contributing to the Temple and the operation of the central cult, as we have in Mark 12:41–44 and Luke 21:1–4, was not the same as giving alms to the poor. These sources, which tell how both the wealthy and the poor contribute to the Temple, should be read in the exact opposite way – as a critique of society's failure to care for the needy.[64] The Temple treasury, moreover, had nothing to do with the *quppa*. Rather, the treasury held funds used to maintain the Temple and its cult. Depositing money into a bank, needless to say, should not be confused with giving charity to the poor. Contributing to the funding of religious activity, its personnel, and its institutions is an instance of religious patronage or what Ilana Silber calls "sacerdotal giving" (gifts to religious specialists or institutions) – but not charity.[65]

In the end, any argument that the origins of the *quppa* can be found in a "chamber of secrets" in or near the Temple must be based on a maximalist understanding of the historicity of material in the Mishnah and Tosefta. One would have to assume that they accurately preserve traditions from the Second Temple period – a presupposition that is highly questionable in the critical, academic study of rabbinic literature.[66] As I will discuss later in this chapter, rabbinic materials may not accurately depict social history in their own time – all the more so for an earlier age. While Tannaitic literature surely draws upon older sources, rabbinic texts do not preserve older material in ways that allow them to be recovered reliably.

This is not to say that the "chamber of secrets" was a rabbinic invention; there may have been a structure with that name in the Temple precincts at

---

[62] Safrai and Safrai, *Mishnat Eretz Israel: Tractate Skalim*, 190. See also J. N. Ford, "Another Look at the Mandaic Incantation Bowl BM 91715," *JANES* 29 (2002): 31–47, which raises the possibility that something like a *quppa* served as a public financial institution elsewhere in the ancient near east. I thank Daniel Potts for this reference.

[63] E.g., Acts 3:2; see also Holman, *Hungry are Dying*, 49–50. Likewise, beggars are known to loiter around Roman temples; see Parkin, "An Exploration," 66.

[64] Addison G. Wright, "The Widow's Mites: Praise or Lament – A Matter of Context," *CBQ* 44 (1982): 56–65. I thank David Downs for this reference.

[65] Ilana F. Silber, "Echoes of Sacrifice? Repertoires of Giving in the Great Religions," in *Sacrifice in Religious Experience* (ed. A. I. Baumgarten; Leiden and Boston: Brill, 2002), 300–08; Silber, "Neither Mauss Nor Veyne," 213.

[66] See most recently Naftali S. Cohn, *The Memory of the Temple and the Making of the Rabbis* (Philadelphia: University of Pennsylvania Press, 2013). While Cohn does not address passages on the "chamber of secrets" in particular, his broader conclusions (esp. pp. 55–56, 119–22) that depictions of the Temple in the Mishnah were constructed to support rabbinic claims to authority, cast further doubt on the reliability of these texts as sources for the Second Temple era.

some point. Rather, what I find is that its *function* as a charity institution akin to the *quppa* is unattested in prerabbinic writings and was likely applied by the Tannaim. It is possible that the authors and redactors of early rabbinic texts drew upon an earlier tradition of a structure with an obscure name, whose function was clouded in mystery (if not secrecy) or simply forgotten, and the Tannaim anachronistically assigned to it a post-Temple function. Thus, while early rabbinic texts on the chamber of secrets cannot be used as transparent windows into first century Judaism and do not preserve independent evidence for organized charity in the first century, they can (and will) help us understand the conceptualization of organized charity by the Tannaim in the late second and early third centuries. That is, these texts should be read within the contexts in which they are preserved, as opposed to contexts in which they are not.

ESSENES AND THE DEAD SEA SCROLLS. As discussed earlier, a number of scholars find evidence for organized charity by the first century C.E. in Josephus's writings on the Essenes and in the Dead Sea Scrolls.[67] Josephus writes that Essenes in each city would give clothes and food to other Essenes in need. As Josephus clearly indicates, however, this kind of almsgiving was left "to individual discretion" and Essenes could "of their own motion" help the needy.[68] Thus, this was not an example of organized charity, but rather the kind of individual almsgiving performed on an *ad hoc* and *ad loc.* basis that we find in other Second Temple era texts.[69]

A different form of poverty relief emerges from the *Damascus Document*, CD 14:12–16:

12. any kind of dispute or legal matter. *vacat* This is the rule of the general membership for meeting all their needs: a wage of
13. two days every month at least shall be given to the Overseer (*mevaqqer*). Then the judges
14. will give some of it for their [w]ounded, with some of it they will support the poor and needy, and the [sickly] elder,

---

[67] I follow the scholarly consensus that adheres to a modified version of the classic "Essene Hypothesis," whereby the authors of (at least some of) the Dead Sea Scrolls are identified as Essenes. The scholarship on this topic is voluminous; for recent overviews, see Jörg Frey, "Essenes," in *The Eerdmans Dictionary of Early Judaism* (ed. J. J. Collins and D. C. Harlow; Grand Rapids, Mich.: William B. Eerdmans, 2010), 599–602; Robert A. Kugler, "Dead Sea Scrolls," in *The Eerdmans Dictionary of Early Judaism* (ed. J. J. Collins and D. C. Harlow; Grand Rapids, Mich.: William B. Eerdmans, 2010), 520–24.

[68] Josephus, *War* 2.134.

[69] E.g., Tob 4, 12, 14, and their extensive discussion in Anderson, *Charity*.

15. the man with a skin-disease, whoever is taken captive by a foreign nation, the girl
16. with[out] a near kin[sm]an, the boy without an advocate; and the rest for the business of the entire community, so that (CD 14:12–16; trans. Cook)[70]

This Dead Sea Scroll fragment instructs each member to contribute two days wages to the "Overseer" or "Examiner" (*mevaqqer*), who functioned as the head of the community.[71] Based on the decisions of judges, these funds would then be distributed to members of the Qumran community who were in need, including the poor.[72] The compulsory nature of the contributions, the centralized intake of the funds, and the adjudication and distribution of these funds bears some similarities to the Tannaitic prescriptions for organized charity.

What, then, are we to make of these similarities between CD and the Tannaitic texts? The evidence is sparse and some 150 years separate the Qumran sectarians and the Tannaim. It is difficult to use CD as evidence for the existence of institutional charity throughout Jewish society in the Second Temple era, let alone as a "forerunner" to rabbinic approaches. Thus, it is probably too much to claim that CD represents some kind of precursor to the institutions discussed by the Tannaim, as a direct link is unlikely.

That being said, scholars have increasingly demonstrated that Tannaitic discourses draw upon vague or loosely defined traditions from the Second Temple era, which they then elevate to legal categories, flesh out, and discuss in encyclopedic detail.[73] Moreover, Aharon Shemesh and Steven Fraade, among

---

[70] Translation according to E. Cook in Timothy H. Lim et al., *The Dead Sea Scrolls Electronic Reference Library* (Oxford, New York, and Leiden: Oxford University Press and Brill, 1997), with my emendations.

[71] See the overview in James H. Charlesworth, "Community Organization in the Rule of the Community," in *Encyclopedia of the Dead Sea Scrolls* (ed. L. H. Schiffman and J. C. VanderKam; New York: Oxford University Press, 2000), s.v. Based on the surviving fragments of this passage, Charlotte Hempel, *The Laws of the Damascus Document: Sources, Tradition and Redaction* (Leiden: Brill, 1988), 138–40, suggests that the law underwent some development, as it was initially collected annually.

[72] See Joseph M. Baumgarten, "A Qumran Text with Agrarian Halakhah," *JQR* 86 (1995): 5; cf. Josephus *War* 2.125.

[73] Shaye J. D. Cohen, "Judaean Legal Tradition and the *Halakha* of the Mishnah," in *The Cambridge Companion to the Talmud and Rabbinic Literature* (ed. C. E. Fonrobert and M. S. Jaffee; New York: Cambridge University Press, 2007), 134–35; Gregg E. Gardner, "Let Them Eat Fish: Food for the Poor in Early Rabbinic Judaism," *JSJ* 45 (2014): 265–66; David M. Freidenreich, *Foreigners and their Food: Constructing Otherness in Jewish, Christian, and Islamic Law* (Berkeley: University of California Press, 2011), 48.

others, have increasingly highlighted the similarities of laws prescribed by the Tannaim and those found in the Dead Sea Scrolls.[74] While a direct link is unlikely, it seems possible that the Tannaim drew upon isolated developments in poverty relief from Second Temple era traditions, some of which were paralleled in CD 14.[75] They thoroughly rabbinized this handful of received traditions and added their own innovations. They brought all of this together into a single, coherent vision of what organized charity ought to look like – a vision whose comprehensiveness was unprecedented in Jewish traditions. We may conclude that the earliest rabbinic discourses on organized charity were not created entirely *ex nihilo*, but rather drew upon some ideas – however disparate, isolated, and possibly marginal – from an earlier age.

In short, contrary to previous scholarship, I find that there is little evidence for the widespread existence of organized charity before 70 C.E. Neither the House of Adiabene's famine relief nor the hospitality evidenced by the Theodotos inscription constitute charity, let alone organized charity. That a chamber of secrets served as a locus of organized charity is an anachronistic identification. That is, scholarship that argues for the widespread existence of organized charity in the first century suffers from two methodological problems: working within a misunderstanding of hospitality and certain kinds of giving as charity, and the misuse of rabbinic texts as sources for periods much earlier than when they were authored and redacted. Only the *Damascus Document* fragment indicates some form of organized charity. Thus, organized charity would have been carried out among a small group of marginalized sectarians. Yet, it may also suggest that the Tannaitic discourses on organized charity drew upon traditions of organized charity from the Second Temple era – however fragmentary and limited in scope they were. Whatever the case may be, it was the *Tannaitic* vision that would be carried forward and serve as the foundation of all future approaches to organized charity in rabbinic Judaism.

---

[74] Steven D. Fraade, *Legal Fictions: Studies of Law and Narrative in the Discursive Worlds of Ancient Jewish Sectarians and Sages* (Leiden and Boston: Brill, 2011); Aharon Shemesh, "Things That Have Required Quantities [Hebrew]," *Tarbiz* 73 (2004): 387–405; Aharon Shemesh, "The History of the Creation of Measurements: Between Qumran and the Mishnah," in *Rabbinic Perspectives: Rabbinic Literature and the Dead Sea Scrolls: Proceedings of the Eighth International Symposium of the Orion Center for the Study of the Dead Sea Scrolls and Associated Literature, 7–9 January, 2003* (ed. S. D. Fraade et al.; Studies on the Texts of the Desert of Judah 62; Boston and Leiden: Brill, 2006), 147–73.

[75] One possible, albeit speculative, reading is that the Tannaitic vision of organized charity constitutes a nonsectarian analogue to the sort of care for one's own that we see in the Dead Sea Scrolls. In which case, the Tannaim replace *the sect* with *the town* as the corporate structure that defined who received provisions.

THE REALITY OF ORGANIZED CHARITY

What can we say about the reality of organized charity in the time and place in which the Tannaim authored and redacted these texts? Were the *tamhui* and *quppa* inventions of the rabbis or were they real institutions? While there is ample evidence that the *tamhui* and *quppa* existed as household vessels, it is less clear if they existed *as institutions* (as a soup kitchen and charity fund, respectively) in Roman Palestine. Answering this question will help us frame and better understand the Tannaitic texts on organized charity that are the focus of this book.[76]

As I have just discussed, it is unlikely that organized charity has precursors before the Tannaim and there are no contemporaneous extra-Tannaitic sources.[77] Likewise, there is a dearth of sources for organized charity in the period immediately following the Tannaim. As I will discuss in Chapter 3, archaeologists have, at times, identified *quppot* at various synagogue sites. These include a "closet" installation built into a synagogue wall, which some have interpreted as a charity box constructed in a way that allowed the poor to anonymously collect the alms that were placed inside. Scholars have

---

[76] It will also contribute to broader scholarly discussions on the use of rabbinic literature as a historical source. The literature on this topic is vast; see, among others, David Goodblatt, "Towards the Rehabilitation of Talmudic History," in *History of Judaism: The Next Ten Years* (ed. B. M. Bokser; Chico, Calif.: Scholars Press, 1980), 31–44; Martin Goodman and Philip Alexander, eds., *Rabbinic Texts and the History of Late-Roman Palestine* (Proceedings of the British Academy; Oxford and New York: Oxford University Press for the British Academy, 2010); Catherine Hezser, "Correlating Literary, Epigraphical, and Archaeological Sources," in *The Oxford Handbook of Jewish Daily Life in Roman Palestine* (ed. C. Hezser; Oxford: Oxford University Press, 2010), 9–27; Seth Schwartz, "Historiography on the Jews in the 'Talmudic Period' (70–640 CE)," in *The Oxford Handbook of Jewish Studies* (ed. M. Goodman et al.; Oxford and New York: Oxford University Press, 2002), 79–114; Strack and Stemberger, *Introduction to the Talmud*, 45–61.

[77] One tantalizing, but ultimately disappointing, find is a Bar Kochva coin that was etched over in graffito with the words "encourage [?] *tsedaqah*" in Aramaic (written in Paleo-Hebrew characters). The inscription was probably applied after the end of the revolt in 135 C.E. It is notable that the coin is a *dupondius*, a denomination also mentioned in Tannaitic discussions on charity (*pondion* in m. Pe'ah 8:7; t. Pe'ah 4:8). Arie Kindler, who published the coin, argues that Bar Kochva coins had no value after the end of the second revolt and that this item was used as a "charity token." There is too much, however, that we do not know about the coin to draw any significant conclusions. The coin itself comes from a private collection as it is an unprovenanced artifact. In addition to bringing its authenticity into question, this also means that the coin is devoid of its archaeological context. Thus, we do not know where it was found and we cannot know how soon after 135 C.E. the graffito was applied, or for what purpose. Casting further doubt on the purpose and use of this coin, as Kindler himself notes, is that it is a unique item – no other "charity token" has survived from antiquity. On the coin, see Arie Kindler, "A Bar Kokhba Coin used as a Charity Token," *Israel Numismatic Journal* 12 (1992–1993): 73–75, plate 16; see also Satlow, "Fruit and the Fruit of Fruit," 272.

also identified coin hoards found under synagogue floors as evidence of the collection of charity. These interpretations, however, are far from certain and even the earliest finds postdate the redaction of Tannaitic compilations by a half century. Inscriptions recording donations to synagogues not only postdate the Tannaim, but also reflect a kind of giving that is very different from charity, which the Tannaim define as solely for the poor.[78]

Worthy of special mention is an inscription from Aphrodisias (Asia Minor) that lists the names of individuals who contributed funds for the establishment of a *patella*. Joyce Reynolds and Robert Tannenbaum initially dated the inscription to the third century C.E. and identified *patella* as a *tamhui* – dubbing it a "communal soup kitchen."[79] More recently, however, Marianne Bonz has redated the inscription to the fourth through sixth century, an interpretation that has gained widespread acceptance.[80] Scholars now also find the identification of the *patella* with the *tamhui* to be unlikely; among other reasons, the *patella* denotes a building – a meaning never conveyed by *tamhui* in late-antique rabbinic texts.[81]

What remains, then, is the possible evidence of the rabbinic texts themselves. Do rabbinic discussions on the soup kitchen and charity fund reflect some kind of reality? This question relates to a larger methodological issue, as scholars have pointed to a number of problems with the use of rabbinic texts as sources for social history and realia. There are problems related to dating and geography, which are closely related to the question of the reliability of attributions. How can we be sure that a tradition attributed to a rabbi known to have lived in second-century C.E. Roman Palestine has been accurately preserved by a text compiled in sixth- or seventh-century Sasanian Mesopotamia? Scholars have found that rabbinic traditions have been so heavily worked over during their transmission and redaction that we can no longer reliably recover information from them about social history. The problems of chronology and geography can be accounted for by focusing on specific compilations and reading them at the level of redaction. Thus, I read these texts as products of their redactors – individuals living in a specific time (the early third century) and place (Roman Palestine). This does

---

[78] See my discussions in the next section of this chapter and in Chapter 8.
[79] Joyce M. Reynolds and Robert Tannenbaum, *Jews and God-Fearers at Aphrodisias: Greek Inscriptions with Commentary* (Cambridge: Cambridge Philological Society, 1987), 22, 26–27.
[80] Marianne Palmer Bonz, "The Jewish Donor Inscriptions from Aphrodisias: Are They Both Third-Century, and Who Are the *Theosebeis*?," *HSCP* 96 (1994): 281–99.
[81] For a summary of recent scholarship, see Walter Ameling, *Inscriptiones Judaicae Orientis: Kleinasien* (Tübingen: Mohr Siebeck, 2004), 83–86. I add that the relevance of an archaeological find from Asian Minor to rabbinic texts from Roman Palestine is highly questionable.

not, however, resolve all the issues of using rabbinic literature as a historical source.

The problem that remains is more complex, as it involves issues of the authorship, biases and objectives, transmission, and literary character of rabbinic works. Rabbinic texts have a limited perspective, as they reflect only the views of the rabbis, a social and intellectual elite. The texts have ideological purposes, as the rabbis who redacted them sought to regulate the daily lives of Jews, even while they lacked the authority and influence to do so. Thus, rabbinic texts are prescriptive, not descriptive.[82] They were not intended as works of historiography or as a trove of data on every day social life in Roman Palestine. Rather, they are meant as legal and theological discourses that focus only on the aspects of life that are pertinent to the discussion at hand. They also exhibit literary qualities, indicating that these traditions have been heavily reworked.[83]

This does not, however, mean that rabbinic texts are useless for helping us understand the social history of Roman Palestine.[84] Some scholars reasonably argue that details of rabbinic discussions that do not directly serve prescriptive or polemical purposes can more or less reflect some kind of reality on the ground.[85] In the case at hand, the Mishnah mentions charitable institutions only in passing, without introduction or explanation, as it seems to assume their existence and the audience's familiarity with them.[86] As such, the Mishnah seems to presuppose the reader's knowledge of these institutions and, in turn, presupposes their existence.[87]

The discussion of the *tamhui* and *quppa* as institutions in the Tosefta is more elaborate and, as Michael Satlow notes, provides many more details than the Mishnah.[88] Thus, this could be included among those instances identified by Shamma Friedman and Judith Hauptman in which the Tosefta provides precisely the information that is presupposed by the Mishnah.[89] To

---

[82] Michael L. Satlow, *Jewish Marriage in Antiquity* (Princeton, N.J., and Oxford: Princeton University Press, 2001), xxiv–xxv.
[83] Martin Goodman, *State and Society in Roman Galilee, A.D. 132–212* (London and Portland, Ore.: Vallentine Mitchell, 2000), 6; Hezser, "Correlating," 10–13.
[84] For constructive ways forward, see Hezser, "Correlating," 16–23.
[85] Goodman, *State and Society*, 7–8, 13–14; David Kraemer, "Food," in *The Oxford Handbook of Jewish Daily Life in Roman Palestine* (ed. C. Hezser; Oxford: Oxford University Press, 2010), 404.
[86] As noted by Satlow, "Fruit and the Fruit of Fruit," 273.
[87] I have paraphrased the remarks by Kraemer, "Food, Eating, and Meals," 404. See also Goodblatt, "Towards the Rehabilitation," 31–44; Hezser, "Correlating," 12.
[88] Satlow, "Fruit and the Fruit of Fruit," 273.
[89] In Gardner, "Cornering Poverty," 1:205–16, I explore in further detail how these texts align with the relationships between the Mishnah and Tosefta that are explored in Shamma Friedman,

be sure, this is a highly subjective test and a reader could reasonably argue that even the Tosefta's discussions do not provide enough basic, introductory information for those without prior knowledge of these institutions.

We are left with two possibilities. The first is that these institutions did exist outside of the rabbinic mind, that they developed in extrarabbinic Jewish circles, and that they were a fact of life in late second- and early third-century Roman Palestine. If this is the case, it is important to note that the rabbinic portrayals cannot be taken at face value, as straightforward accounts of how these bodies actually worked. Rather, one must consider that their portrayals in rabbinic texts have been influenced by rabbinic interests and idiosyncrasies. The texts do not tell us how they were, but rather how the rabbis thought that they ought to be. They reflect the rabbis' efforts to legislate on these institutions, even though (and perhaps especially because) they did not invent or control them. As such, the Tannaim deigned to legislate about the soup kitchen and charity fund in much the same way that they deigned to legislate about synagogues, whose existence is presupposed by rabbinic texts, yet lay beyond rabbinic authority as they were controlled by nonrabbinic Jews.[90]

"The Primacy of Tosefta to Mishnah in Synoptic Parallels," in *Introducing Tosefta: Textual, Intratextual, and Intertextual Studies* (ed. H. Fox et al.; Hoboken, N.J.: KTAV, 1999); Judith Hauptman, *Rereading the Mishnah: A New Approach to Ancient Jewish Texts* (Tübingen: Mohr, 2005); Judith Hauptman, "The Tosefta as a Commentary on an Early Mishnah," *Jewish Studies Internet Journal* 4 (2005): 109–32.

[90] On Tannaitic approaches to synagogues, see Shaye J. D. Cohen, "The Rabbi in Second-Century Jewish Society," in *The Cambridge History of Judaism: Volume 3: The Early Roman Period* (ed. W. Horbury et al.; Cambridge: Cambridge University Press, 1999), 972–74; Steven Fine, *This Holy Place: On the Sanctity of the Synagogue during the Greco-Roman Period* (Notre Dame, Ind.: Notre Dame University Press, 1997), 35–59; Levine, *Ancient Synagogue*, 466–98. Taking this approach could contribute to discussions on the relationship between rabbis and nonrabbinic Jews. As Schwartz, *Imperialism and Jewish Society*, 129–61, notes, the Roman elite and imperial authorities surely exercised real control over the cities and towns of Palestine. Brown, *Through the Eye*, 4, rightly notes that the Roman empire maintained control of high justice and the army, but otherwise delegated other aspects of governance to local groups. Thus, it is highly unlikely that they would have been concerned with the organization of charitable giving. Since the Tannaim themselves did not control charitable giving (Schwartz, *Imperialism and Jewish Society*, 124), it follows that some wealthy nonrabbinic Jews would have exercised influence, perhaps the same Jewish elites who held significant sway over synagogues. The classical paradigm, such as that outlined by Adolf Büchler, *The Political and the Social Leaders of the Jewish Community of Sepphoris in the Second and Third Centuries* (London: Jews' College, 1909), suggests antagonism between the Tannaim and wealthy nonrabbinic Jews. This, however, is based on a now-antiquated use of rabbinic sources and must also be revised in light of the fact that the rabbis themselves were well-off and some were quite wealthy; see Gardner, "Who is Rich." This would explain the Tannaim's special empathy toward well-born individuals who fell into poverty; see Gray, "Formerly Wealthy Poor," 105–09. Yet, it is also reasonable to deduce that the rabbis' interest in influencing charitable giving would have been a source of tension. Indeed, just as the rabbis' attitudes toward other groups of nonrabbinic Jews (*amme ha'aretz*, holy men or wonder workers, Christians and

The second possibility is that the soup kitchen and charity fund are rabbinic inventions. This is based on the absence of extrarabbinic sources and the assessment that the problems of using rabbinic texts as sources for social history are too great to overcome. That is, we have no way of evaluating how *what ought to be* in the opinions of the rabbinic authors relates to *what is*.[91] Rabbinic texts on the *tamhui* and *quppa* are read as part of an idealized rabbinic worldview on how society should care for the poor.

Whether the soup kitchen and charity fund are rabbinic inventions or Jewish inventions rabbinized, the evidence in either direction is far from overwhelming. We have, perhaps, reached what Hezser calls the "limits of interpretability."[92] In either case what we have in these texts are charity institutions as the rabbis wanted them to be. That is, the early rabbis develop a system of organized charity that, while in conversation with their contemporary world, is uniquely their own. It is laced with distinctly rabbinic features and addresses characteristically rabbinic concerns. And it is these distinctly Tannaitic versions of the soup kitchen and charity fund that would be carried forward in later rabbinic Judaism. They were drawn upon by the Talmuds and form the basis of poverty relief from the middle ages onwards. Thus, regardless of the reality at the time of the Tannaim, the versions of these institutions as they are set forth in the Tannaitic texts that are examined in this book constitute the foundations and origins of organized charity in rabbinic Judaism.

TSEDAQAH AND "CHARITY": SOME DEFINITIONS

The term *tsedaqah* is found some 150 times in the Hebrew Bible, where it means "righteousness" – a broad concept, denoting right living or proper

---

heretics, etc.) are deeply ambiguous – at times they are inimical and advocate avoidance, at times they promote cooperation in varying degrees – so too their relationships with wealthy nonrabbinic Jews would have been highly complex. To be sure, the paucity and opaqueness of our sources cannot give us a clear indication of who controlled the *tamhui* and *quppa* (*if* they existed outside of the rabbinic mind) – let alone the Tannaim's relationship to these individuals over this issue. On rabbis, nonrabbinic Jews, and the Tannaim's lack of authority over broader Jewish society, see Cohen, "Rabbi in Second-Century," 942–43, 956–77; Christine Hayes, "The 'Other' in Rabbinic Literature," in *The Cambridge Companion to the Talmud and Rabbinic Literature* (ed. C. E. Fonrobert and M. S. Jaffee; New York: Cambridge University Press, 2007), 257–63; Richard L. Kalmin, *The Sage in Jewish Society in Late Antiquity* (London and New York: Routledge, 1999), 27–50; Schwartz, *Imperialism and Jewish Society*, 103–28.

[91] Kraemer, "Food, Eating, and Meals," 404.
[92] Hezser, "Correlating," 21.

behavior.⁹³ Nowhere in the Hebrew Bible does the Hebrew *tsedaqah* mean charity or almsgiving.⁹⁴ It is only in the Hellenistic era that we begin to find charity as a specific expression of righteous behavior. These include references in Tobit and the Dead Sea Scrolls, where charity/*tsedaqah* is understood as almsgiving.⁹⁵ These, however, amount to only a handful of instances and their significance should not be overstated, as *tsedaqah* predominantly denoted "righteousness" in prerabbinic texts. It is only in early rabbinic literature that "charity" becomes a common definition of *tsedaqah*. It would later become the predominant sense of the term and it remains so today.⁹⁶

Tannaitic texts mark a major turning point in the development of *tsedaqah* from righteousness to charity.⁹⁷ Following a thorough study of *tsedaqah* in Tannaitic compilations, Benno Przybylski concludes, "As a matter of fact, the primary meaning of the term *tsedaqah* in the Tannaitic literature is without doubt that of almsgiving as defined in T[osefta] *Pe'ah* 4:19."⁹⁸ Of the Tosefta's thirty-six "independent" uses of *tsedaqah* – where *tsedaqah* is not part of a quotation of Scripture – thirty-one refer to giving, receiving or administering alms. Of the Mishnah's six independent uses, four refer to charity.⁹⁹

The evolution of *tsedaqah* from "righteousness" to "charity" in early rabbinic texts is vividly illustrated in its "dependent" uses, where the word appears as part of citations of biblical verses. Here, we see Tannaitic texts interpreting

---

[93] The root *ts–d–q* occurs no less than 525 times in the Hebrew Bible, which includes over 150 instances of *tsedaqah* in particular.

[94] In later books of the Hebrew Bible, *tsedaqah* develops associations with material support for the needy, such as in Ps 37:21, 112:4–5; see Gary A. Anderson, "Redeem Your Sins by the Giving of Alms: Sin, Debt, and the 'Treasury of Merit' in Early Jewish and Christian Tradition," *Letter & Spirit* 3 (2007): 45–48; A. Hurvitz, "The Biblical Roots of a Talmudic Term: The Early History of the Concept of *tsedaqah* [= charity, alms] [Hebrew]," (1987): 155–60. To be sure, however, the only instance in which *tsedaqah* may denote charity is in Aramaic in Dan 4:24; see Ahuva Ho, *Sedeq and Sedaqah in the Hebrew Bible* (New York: P. Lang, 1991), 143; Franz Rosenthal, "Sedaka, Charity," *HUCA* 23 (1950/51): 411–30.

[95] 4Q424 or 4QWisd, and Qumran fragments of Tobit; see Anderson, "Redeem Your Sins," 45n. 28.

[96] On the history of the term *tsedaqah*, see the scholarship cited earlier and Eliezer Ben-Yehuda et al., *A Complete Dictionary of Ancient and Modern Hebrew: Thesaurus totius Hebraitatis et veteris et recentioris [Hebrew]* (8 vols.; New York and London: Thomas Yoseloff, 1960), s.v.; Avraham Even-Shoshan and Moshe Azar, *Milon Even-Shoshan: meḥudash u-me'udkan li-shenot ha-alpayim be-shishah kerakhim be-hishtatfut ḥever anshe mada'* [Hebrew] (Tel Aviv: ha-Milon he-ḥadash: Yorshe ha-meḥaber, 2003), 5:1571; Ya'akov Kena'ani, *Otsar ha-lashon ha-'Ivrit li-tekufoteha ha-shonot [Hebrew]* (18 vols.; Jerusalem and Tel-Aviv: Masadah, 1960–1989), s.v.

[97] Benno Przybylski, *Righteousness in Matthew and his World of Thought* (Cambridge: Cambridge University Press, 1980), 74–76. This is also noticed by Mauss, *The Gift*, 18.

[98] Przybylski, *Righteousness in Matthew*, 66.

[99] Przybylski, *Righteousness in Matthew*, 66–67.

tsedaqah in scripture as "charity." We see this, for example, in *SifreDeut* 47, which posits that *those who lead many to righteousness* (root: *ts-d-q*) in Daniel 12:3 refers to the charity supervisors. Also illustrative is the Tannaitic commentary on Deut 33:21:

A. *He executed the righteousness (tsidqat)*[100] *of the Lord* (Deut 33:21)
B. What *tsedaqah* did Moses perform for Israel?
C. Is it not true that all during those forty years that Israel was in the wilderness a well sprang up for them, manna came down for them, pheasants were available for them, and the clouds of glory encompassed them?
D. Rather, this refers to what Moses said: *If there be among you a needy man* (Deut 15:7). (*SifreDeut* 355)[101]

The rabbis' question in line C arises because they want to know what Moses could have possibly done if God had already provided for all of Israel's needs in the desert.[102] The rabbis indicate that they understand *tsedaqah* as material support for those in need, as God provides sustenance in manna and pheasants, and shelter with clouds. The answer, in line D, is that Moses performs *tsedaqah* by providing for the poor in accordance with Deuteronomy 15:7. This verse is couched as an imperative for one human to provide for another as opposed to God providing for all. It should be noted that *SifreDeut* quotes Deuteronomy 15:7 selectively, truncating the verse and taking it out of context. Within Deuteronomy, the verse exhorts individuals to extend loans to the poor in the years leading up to the Sabbatical year, when all debts are canceled. Within its biblical context, Deuteronomy 15:7 does not constitute almsgiving or charity.[103] In short, this passage from *SifreDeut* 355 projects late-antique concepts onto Deuteronomy, illustrating the principle that charity constitutes a specific way in which to perform righteousness. Likewise, numerous other texts from the Tannaitic corpus interpret *tsedaqah* in citations from the Hebrew Bible as "charity."[104] The interpretation of *tsedaqah* in

---

[100] It is notable that the Venice ed. reads *tsedaqot*, i.e., "charities," as the copyist projects the understanding of *tsedaqah* as charity onto the Hebrew of the biblical text itself. On the interpretation of this variant, see Przybylski, *Righteousness in Matthew*, 69; Hermann Leberecht Strack and Paul Billerbeck, *Kommentar zum Neuen Testament aus Talmud und Midrasch* (6 vols.; München: Beck, 1922), 3:163n. 1.

[101] Translation based on Reuven Hammer, *Sifre: A Tannaitic Commentary on the Book of Deuteronomy* (New Haven, Conn.: Yale University Press, 1986), 373, with my modifications.

[102] As explained in Przybylski, *Righteousness in Matthew*, 69.

[103] Cf. Rosenfeld and Perlmutter, "Foundations of Charitable Organizations," 51n. 5.

[104] E.g., *t. Pe'ah* 4:18; on this, see Gardner, "Giving to the Poor," 163–200; Gardner, "Competitive Giving," 81–92; for more examples, see Przybylski, *Righteousness in Matthew*, 39–76.

biblical passages as "charity" would steadily increase with time, as it becomes pervasive in the Babylonian Talmud.[105]

By understanding *tsedaqah* as "charity," the rabbis promote a finite and concrete way to fulfill the broader imperative to live a righteous life. It is critical, then, to gain an accurate understanding of what the rabbis mean by *tsedaqah* when they use it as "charity." The early rabbinic concept of "charity" is far more specific and narrow than modern understandings of the term. Today, "charity" has a broad range of meanings, which have been heavily influenced by Christianity – it can be understood as love, kindness, affection, generosity, spontaneous goodness, a lenient disposition, and benevolence.[106] It follows that charity could mean giving to institutions considered to be altruistic, philanthropic, or that serve the common good, civic needs, or religious groups, such as synagogues, churches, hospitals, or other nonprofit organizations. Charity, moreover, can be carried out with either money or personal service, such as volunteering or visiting the sick. These modern understandings of "charity" have been misapplied by scholars and retrojected onto ancient sources. The confusion between the early Jewish and Christian conceptualizations of charity with modern connotations has hindered scholarship on the topic, as almost any text that addresses beneficent or generally philanthropic behavior has been mistakenly brought into discussions of charity in general and organized charity in particular.[107]

In contrast to today's broad understanding of "charity," the late-antique rabbis had a narrower and more specific view. The key statement on charity, as noted by Przybylski in the earlier quotation, is *t. Pe'ah* 4:19. Here the Tannaim define *tsedaqah* as monetary support for the living poor:

> *Tsedaqah* and *gemilut hasadim* are equal in weight to all the commandments in the Torah. Except that *tsedaqah* is for the living; *gemilut hasadim* is for the living and the dead. *Tsedaqah* is for poor people; *gemilut hasadim* is for poor

---

[105] See, e.g., the reinterpretation of *tsedaqah* in Prov 10:2 as "charity" in *b. Shabbat* 156b (see the discussion in Gregg Gardner, "Astrology in the Talmud: An Analysis of Bavli Shabbat 156," in *Heresy and Identity in Late Antiquity* [ed. E. Iricinschi and H. Zellentin; TSAJ 119; Tübingen: Mohr Siebeck, 2008], 314–38). Likewise, Prov 10:2 (and similarly Prov 11:4, Isa 59:17) in *b. Bava Batra* 9b–10a; Prov 21:3 in *b. Sukkah* 49b; Gen 18:19 in *b. Yevamot* 79a. Biblical figures are also portrayed as carrying out acts of almsgiving as expressions of their righteousness. See, for example, *b. Yevamot* 79a where Abraham donates a small coin as an expression of his righteousness.

[106] *Oxford English Dictionary* (Oxford and New York: Oxford University Press, 2000), s.v. charity. In her study of pagan almsgiving, Parkin, "An Exploration," 61, observes that the modern understandings of *alms* and *charity* are often "thoroughly imbued with Christian connotations."

[107] E.g., Bergmann, *Ha-Tsedakah*; Jeremias, *Jerusalem in the Time of Jesus*, 126–34; see further Chapter 8.

people and rich people. *Tsedaqah* is with one's money; *gemilut hasadim* is with one's money and body.[108] (*t. Pe'ah* 4:19)

The context of this passage, within the rabbis' expansive discussion of charity in *t. Pe'ah* 4:8–21, indicates that *tsedaqah* can also be given in kind, including food, clothing, and shelter. Thus, the earliest conceptualization of charity in rabbinic Judaism defines *tsedaqah* as *material provisions for the living poor*. Likewise, in this book, "charity" will denote only relief for the living poor, to correlate directly with the rabbinic understanding of *tsedaqah*. I use terms and phrases such as *philanthropy*, *support for the poor*, and *beneficence* to denote acts that are altruistic, but do not qualify as *charity* per se.

Let us look closely at each aspect of Tannaitic texts' understanding of charity as *material provisions for the living poor*. First, material support means that personal services, such as visiting the sick, are excluded from the early rabbinic concept of *tsedaqah*. Instead, the rabbis placed these philanthropic acts under a different heading, within the broader category of *gemilut hasadim* – acts of kindness or piety. Second, charity is meant for the *living*. Thus, burial of the dead was not considered an act of *tsedaqah* in Tannaitic compilations.[109] Third, charity is for the *poor*, specifically. The rabbis understand the *poor* as adult men who lack the material resources to support themselves, maintain their household (which includes his wife, children, animals, and inanimate possessions), or both.[110] Rabbinic discussions of support for the poor do not necessarily include assistance to widows, orphans, and other needy individuals – rather, aid to them is covered under other areas of rabbinic law.[111] Similarly, while slaves are impoverished of the most basic human rights, treatment of slaves likewise falls under other areas of rabbinic law.[112]

Because it is exclusively for poor males, the Tannaim do not consider contributions to synagogues, rabbis, or schools as charity. Rather, these types of contributions would only be considered "charity" by later rabbis, beginning

---

[108] That is, providing some kind of personal service.
[109] Cf. Bergmann, *Ha-Tsedakah*, 23.
[110] See Gardner, "Who is Rich," and my discussion in Chapter 2.
[111] See, for example, the laws supporting orphans in *t. Ketubbot* 6:7–8. Support for women, which is addressed in the rabbinic laws on marriage, ultimately comes from her husband, father, or their estates. We see this, for example, in *m. Ketubbot* 13:1–2, which neither mentions the *quppa* nor constitutes an act of charity; see Seccombe, "Was there Organized Charity," 140–41.
[112] That slaves are distinct from the poor is evident in *t. Pe'ah* 4:10, where a poor man is given a slave; see my discussion in Chapter 5. On slaves in ancient Judaism and classical rabbinic literature, see Paul Virgil McCracken Flesher, *Oxen, Women or Citizens? Slaves in the System of the Mishnah* (Atlanta, Ga.: Scholars Press, 1988); Catherine Hezser, *Jewish Slavery in Antiquity* (Oxford and New York: Oxford University Press, 2005).

with the Amoraim. In an important move, the Amoraim would use the rhetoric, terminology, and conceptual architecture of *tsedaqah* to raise money for themselves.

It is also important to distinguish charity from other forms of support for the poor. Outside of charity, the other major category of poverty relief consists of agrarian laws associated with the harvest. These require leaving leftovers or marginal crops for the poor, such as *pe'ah*, produce standing in the "corner" of a field. Other items to be left for the poor are "gleanings" (sheaves that fell to the ground during the harvest), "forgotten things" (items overlooked by the harvester), and similar allocations of grapes and olives.[113] The laws of *pe'ah*, gleanings, and forgotten things, which I will call collectively "harvest-time allocations," draw directly from and elaborate upon commandments in the Torah (Lev 19:9–10, 23:22; Deut 14:28–29, 24:19–21). They are, however, not charity. The landowner or harvester does not *give* this produce to the poor. There is no agency on his part. Rather, the harvester's obligation is to refrain from interfering with the distribution of provisions to the poor *by God*. That is, God is the benefactor of *pe'ah*, gleanings, and so forth – not humans.

The misunderstanding of harvest-time allocations as charity can mistakenly lead one to conclude that the poor have a right to charity. All poor individuals have a right to claim and collect *pe'ah*, gleanings, and forgotten things. If harvesters fail to leave these items for the poor, the rabbis instruct, they have essentially stolen what rightfully belongs to the poor. Charity, however, entails no such right. Charity is an obligation for a non-poor individual to give – not a right for the poor to receive. In general, the laws governing harvest-time allocations are negative obligations which, in turn, are "perfectly" defined – the identities of the giver, recipient, and things given are all completely (i.e., "perfectly") determined. The laws of charity, by contrast, are positive duties and "imperfect," as key aspects of giving are left undefined and up to the personal discretion of the giver.[114]

Charity is also distinct from the poor tithe. Deuteronomy (14:28–29; 26:12) instructs that, once every three years, one should set aside a tithe of his produce for the Levites, strangers, widows, and orphans. The Tannaim expand upon and reorient this commandment, instructing that this tithe be devoted to "the poor" alone (*m. Pe'ah* 8:2–6; *t. Pe'ah* 4:1–7). The distinction between the poor tithe and charity is set out expressly in *t. Pe'ah* 4:16, where the Tannaim

---

[113] The key texts are *m. Pe'ah* and *t. Pe'ah* 1:1–4:7; see Gardner, "Giving to the Poor," 16–41.
[114] On perfect and imperfect obligations as they apply to poverty relief, see Schneewind, "Philosophical Ideas of Charity," 54–75.

instruct that *tsedaqah* cannot be taken out of the money designated for the poor tithe.¹¹⁵

In short, "charity" or *tsedaqah* in early rabbinic texts is a narrow concept, far more restricted than the modern sense of charity that has been misapplied to early rabbinic texts by previous scholars. The rabbis understand "charity" to be a specific way to fulfill the more general obligation to live righteously. In later rabbinic texts, *tsedaqah* would expand to denote a wide variety of endeavors understood to be altruistic or philanthropic. These would include donations to support rabbis and rabbinic disciples – sacerdotal giving as opposed to charitable giving.¹¹⁶ *Tsedaqah* would also later include contributions toward the salaries of teachers, gifts to synagogues, care for orphans, burying the dead, dowries for poor women, visiting and caring for the sick and elderly, and ransoming captives.¹¹⁷ For the Tannaim, however, charity was exclusively meant for poor men.

CHARITY AND OTHER FORMS OF SUPPORT

How do the Tannaim, who discuss charity (both individual and organized) in the midst of discourse on harvest-time allocations and the poor tithe, envision that all of these forms of support would work together? First, while the two categories (harvest-time allocations and charity) are distinct, they are also complementary as they address poverty in two different settings. The laws for allocations made at the harvest presume a rural setting and it is easy to see how *pe'ah,* gleanings, and forgotten things would be most accessible to poor peasants. Charity is an ideal solution for the poor living in towns. Soliciting alms from individuals is most effective in densely packed areas, as the poor can situate themselves in high-traffic locations (such as marketplaces and near temples) to increase their chances of receiving alms. Moreover, charity institutions (especially the *quppa*) are shaped by Greco-Roman civic culture, as they stand alongside other institutions in the urban landscape.¹¹⁸ Indeed, the

---

[115] As noted in Przybylski, *Righteousness in Matthew,* 67.
[116] Silber, "Echoes of Sacrifice," 300–08; Silber, "Neither Mauss Nor Veyne," 291–312.
[117] E.g., Maimonides, *Mishneh Torah, Hilkhot mattenot 'aniyyim* (Laws on Gifts to the Poor) 7–10; see also Aryeh Cohen, *Justice in the City: An Argument from the Sources of Rabbinic Judaism* (Boston: Academic Studies Press, 2011), 101–2; Mark R. Cohen, *Poverty and Charity in the Jewish Community of Medieval Egypt* (Princeton, N.J.: Princeton University Press, 2005); Mark R. Cohen, *The Voice of the Poor in the Middle Ages: An Anthology of Documents from the Cairo Geniza* (Princeton, N.J.: Princeton University Press, 2005); Jacob Katz, *Tradition and Crisis: Jewish Society at the End of the Middle Ages* (New York: New York University Press, 1993), 150–51.
[118] See my discussion in Chapter 6.

creation of solutions to urban poverty may have been prompted by increased urbanization during the Roman era.

Second, while the two forms of support for the poor complement one another, in certain respects they also overlap as they all target the same beneficiaries. *All* poor individuals are eligible for the harvest-time allocations as well as alms from the *tamhui*. It is conceivable that that a single poor man could collect *pe'ah*, gleanings, forgotten things, the poor tithe, and alms from the *tamhui* (and some could collect from the *quppa* as well). While each allocation provides the poor man with only a minimum amount of provisions (the *tamhui* and poor tithe each provide the poor man just enough to stay alive), combined they could provide a significant amount of support. That is, if a poor man collected everything for which he was eligible, he could consume well beyond the minimum amount of calories required for physical efficiency.

It can be said that the Tannaim multiplied the number of ways to support for the poor – Tannaitic texts elucidate more distinct commandments related to poverty relief than we find in the Hebrew Bible or Second Temple texts. For example, Josephus names only one type of allocation for the poor from the vineyard, while the Tannaim identify multiple categories of grapes for the poor.[119] Likewise, in an unprecedented move, the Tannaim expand the commandment of *pe'ah* to include grapes and fruit (i.e., olives), alongside cereals.[120] Thus, if each form of poverty relief is to provide only a small amount of alms, working together these allocations would go beyond merely keeping the poor alive. In combination, these forms of support could keep a poor individual reasonably well fed.

ORGANIZED CHARITY AS AN END TO BEGGING

Organized charity, as it is laid out in Tannaitic texts, is "organized" in the sense that it gives to the poor in a way that is collective, indirect, and institutionalized. I will take each feature in turn. First, organized charity is *collective*, as multiple individuals give alms to the poor in a coordinated fashion. This contrasts with giving to beggars, whereby an individual benefactor gives directly to an individual beneficiary. It also differs from *euergetism*, where there is

---

[119] Shemesh, "Things That Have," 389–92; Shemesh, "Creation of Measurements," 151–53, who also notes that 4Q270 3 ii 12–19 is more similar to Josephus (*Ant.* 4:231–232) than early rabbinic literature. Cf. Philo, *Virtues*, 90–94, who draws upon Lev 19:9 to identify two types of allocations (equivalent to *pe'ah* and *gleanings*) and extends them to include olives, which are mentioned in Deut 24:20.

[120] *t. Pe'ah* 2:13.

only one benefactor, as opposed to a community of benefactors. By enabling giving in a collective way, the rabbis promote almsgiving and care for the poor as a communal objective and virtue. The rabbinic vision was not limited to fellow sectarians, like the Essenes' support for their own poor during the Second Temple period. Rather, the Tannaim outline an ideal system in which everyone in Jewish society either gives or receives charity. In particular, the residents of each town should contribute to that town's charitable institutions. Also, if a poor man receives alms from the community as a whole, then he has received benefits from and is indebted to no one in particular.

Second, organized charity is *indirect* in that alms are funneled from benefactors to beneficiaries though institutions – the *tamhui* and *quppa*. They provide a framework for collecting contributions from the community and the supervisors of the *quppa* can serve as third-party enforcers who can pressure individuals to contribute. Indirect charity also supports giving in an anonymous fashion, whereby the benefactor and beneficiary do not meet, thereby protecting the poor from the indignity of begging on the streets.

Collective and indirect giving is made possible by the third feature of organized charity – it is *institutionalized*. To organize charity, one must create a means to transfer assets in an orderly and efficient way. The Tannaim structure this transfer by prescribing a series of laws and norms of behavior that together form an institution. "Institutions," the economist Douglass North writes, "are the rules of the game in a society, or more formally, the humanly devised constraints that shape human interaction ... they are the framework within which human interaction takes place."[121] While it is common to think of institutions in a tangible way, as buildings that house organizations, North's influential writings in the field of neoinstitutional economics have demonstrated that institutions are in essence rules that govern and constrain human behavior. The rabbis seek to do exactly that, as they lay out a framework to direct the ways that the poor and non-poor interact, regulating how well-off givers transfer assets to needy recipients. Another aspect of institutionalized charity is that the institutions are permanent and reliable sources of food, clothing, and shelter for the poor. *Euergetism*, by contrast, was an occasional act of giving.

The system of organized charity that was envisioned by the rabbis provided a way for the poor to acquire their necessities in a dignified fashion. Begging was a highly visible act in the ancient world, which exacerbated the shame and humiliation incurred by the poor. Organized charity is a way to support

---

[121] Douglass C. North, *Institutions, Institutional Change and Economic Performance* (Cambridge and New York: Cambridge University Press, 1990), 3–4.

the poor while avoiding feelings of shame – it is "charity with dignity" in Susan Holman's words.[122] Dignity and honor were essential values of rabbinic Judaism; they would play important roles in the formation of rabbinic charity.[123] Creating alternatives to begging and giving to beggars was advantageous not only for the poor, but also for the non-poor. While it would be "grotesque" to be overly concerned with the sensibilities of those offended by the sight of beggars, one cannot dismiss the fact that poverty has adverse effects on the non-poor as well as the poor.[124] "There is little doubt that the penury of the poor does, in fact, affect the well being of the rich," writes Amartya Sen.[125] Likewise, Kant bemoans the "sight" of beggars and suggests, "the state must therefore restrict open begging as much as possible, rather than encourage it."[126] Indeed, organized charity provides a means to exercise social control by prescribing precisely where, when, and how the poor should solicit alms. Moreover, organized charity assists the non-poor by outlining a specific and systematic way by which one could be sure that they have properly fulfilled the commandment of *tsedaqah*, of giving material aid to the living poor. Thus, organized charity benefits the community as a whole – poor and non-poor alike.

ORGANIZING CHARITY: THE STRUCTURE OF THIS BOOK

This book explores the discussions of organized charity in the earliest texts of rabbinic Judaism, the Tannaitic corpus. I place these texts and their ideas in their literary, social, and historical contexts, and find that, for the Tannaim, organized charity was a means to end begging in order to solve the problems created by giving alms directly to the poor. Early rabbinic texts discuss two charitable bodies that function as intermediaries between benefactors and beneficiaries. Instead of one individual handing over assets to another, people give to the *tamhui* and *quppa*, which in turn distribute provisions to the needy. These bodies became the most important institutions of poverty relief in classical rabbinic literature and served as the prototypes for later Jewish philanthropic efforts. Institutionalizing charity enables control over the almsgiving process, regulating what, when, to whom, and how provisions were given.

---

[122] Holman, *Hungry are Dying*, 47.
[123] E.g., *m. Avot* 2:10, 4:1; see further Chapter 6.
[124] Amartya Sen, *Poverty and Famines: An Essay on Entitlement and Deprivation* (Oxford and New York: Clarendon Press and Oxford University Press, 1982), 10.
[125] Sen, *Poverty and Famines*, 9.
[126] Kant, "Lectures," 431–32.

To understand the social, historical, and economic contexts in which the early rabbinic movement formulated their ideas on charity, in Chapter 2 I explore the nature of poverty in Roman Palestine. I use sources that are contemporaneous to the rabbinic corpus, but external to them, such as archaeology, epigraphy, and Greek and Latin writings, to sketch the socioeconomic realities of the time. I find that poverty manifested itself as a lack of assets with respect to two different thresholds. The first was physiological, as poverty was defined by a lack of basic necessities (food, clothing, and shelter) – a "biological" approach. The rabbis see the *tamhui* as a means to supply these to the poor while avoiding the problems that begging and other forms of direct almsgiving create.

The second form that poverty took in Roman Palestine was a dearth of assets that left one short of thresholds defined by social standards or conventions – a "value-judgment" approach. The food that one ate (or was seen eating), the quality of the clothes that one wore, and the kind of dwelling in which one lived indexed and concretized one's place in society. A failure to reach certain well-accepted thresholds marked one as poor. One who ate barley bread, which was undesirable in the ancient world, or legumes – the "poor man's meat" – was considered to be poor, even if these items met one's basic biological needs (e.g., minimum caloric intake). One was poor if he wore clothes that were undecorated, gray in color, or stitched together from tattered rags – even if these garments provided sufficient protection from the sun, wind, and rain. If a man had a roof over his head, but his dwelling was small, dark, or unadorned; if he ate or slept on the floor; or if he had little or no privacy, then he was surely considered to be poor by conventional standards. The poor man's sense of shame, moreover, would have been more acute if his poverty was conjunctural – that is, if he used to be wealthier and could afford to eat fine bread made of wheat, wear new clothes, and live in a nice house. The rabbis instruct that the *quppa* is a means to address this type of poverty while avoiding the problems created by direct charity, especially begging.

Begging was *ad hoc* and *ad loc.*; one could be approached for alms at any time and in any place, including one's own home. The poor, moreover, had no guarantee of receiving what they needed – or anything at all, for that matter. Institutional charity, by contrast, was conceived as a permanent, regular, and reliable way to give and receive alms. In Chapter 3, I explore the transformation of the *tamhui* from a household "dish" into a "soup kitchen" and the *quppa* from a "basket" to a "charity fund." I illuminate the process of institutionalization with ideas from economics, which help us understand how institutions provide a means to control human interactions, including when a benefactor gives a material or economic asset to a beneficiary. The *tamhui* and *quppa* also offer specific and systematic ways in which one could discharge the religious obligation to give *tsedaqah*. One who gives to the *tamhui* and *quppa* does so with the satisfaction of knowing that he or she has properly fulfilled the religious commandment of *tsedaqah*, so much so that if a poor man comes to the door, begging, then one is not obligated to give him anything. Directing charity through these institutions enables social, economic, and even religious control over the flow of assets from one individual to another. Resources could be directed to address the poor's needs, both biological and social, and allow the distribution to be carried out in a way that preserves the poor's dignity. With this conceptual infrastructure in place, the post-Tannaitic rabbis would employ these institutions to direct funds to the rabbinic movement itself, much like the Christian clergy did for the church.

I examine the *tamhui* in detail in Chapter 4. The *tamhui* is a soup kitchen and is open to all individuals, regardless of where they live. Because local residents were also eligible for the long-term support provided by the *quppa*, the *tamhui* was especially relevant for nonresidents, including individuals who wandered from town to town. I find that the depiction of the *tamhui* in Tannaitic texts is modeled on the treatment of guests, as it offers food and shelter to the itinerant poor. The rabbis also make special provisions for the *tamhui* to supply the poor with the material necessities for observing certain commandments. For example, observing the Sabbath in the rabbinically prescribed way requires eating three meals with special foods, which the *tamhui* would provide.

Attention to the itinerant poor, coupled with the kinds of provisions that the *tamhui* offers, suggests that the rabbis developed their thoughts on the *tamhui* from pan-Mediterranean customs of hospitality. At the same time, the Tannaim purposefully distinguish the *tamhui* from hospitality in important ways. First, whereas the goods and services provided through hospitality are subject to the host's personal discretion, the shelter and specific foods given by the *tamhui* are cast as rigid laws by the rabbis. Thus, the *tamhui* would be a reliable and consistent way for the poor to acquire the basic necessities. Second, whereas hospitality generates an obligation to reciprocate – either with a future act of hospitality in which the guest becomes host and vice versa, or with an expression of gratitude – the *tamhui* provides food and shelter without any expectation of reciprocation. It is a compensation-free means by which one can receive the food and shelter that would otherwise come from acts of hospitality, enabling a poor person to avoid subordinating himself into a position of debt and dependency to a human host. The *tamhui* supplies provisions without generating any personal relationship between giver and recipient, as the needy receive charity with their dignity intact. My findings coalesce with the recent work of Seth Schwartz and Tzvi Novick, who have illuminated the rabbinic tendency to avoid reciprocal arrangements and the vertical relationships of dependency that they create.

Whereas the *tamhui* supplies short-term, basic necessities to all, the *quppa* – which I explore in Chapters 5 and 6 – provides long-term care for the poor who live in the town in which the *quppa* is located. In Chapter 5, I examine the alms that the *quppa* offers. Whereas the *tamhui* offers the same items for everyone, the *quppa* furnishes alms that are individualized to meet each poor person's particular needs. The needs that the *quppa* addresses, moreover, are defined by semiotics and social status – in contrast to the *tamhui*, which provides for the poor's basic biological needs. Thus, the goal of the *quppa* is to restore each impoverished individual to his previous place in society by providing him with the kinds of clothes that he used to wear, the types of food that he used to eat, and so forth. The rabbis instruct that the *quppa* must restore the poor at any cost, which could entail expensive outlays if the poor individual used to be wealthy (the "wellborn poor"). To ensure that the *quppa* has the resources that it needs to restore each and every poor individual, it follows that the community must give prodigiously to the charity fund. Thus, the Tannaim hold that there should be no limit to the amount that one could give – a conclusion that challenges previous scholarship on charity in Judaism.

Underlying the rabbinic discussions of the *quppa's* alms is the image of the beneficiary. The *quppa* provides assistance for the conjunctural poor, individuals who used to be well-off but have fallen into poverty. This type of poverty carried a heightened sense of shame and indignity. In Chapter 6, I explore how the *quppa* addresses and elevates the dignity of the local, conjunctural poor. Conjunctural poverty, and the shame that it carried, was especially visible in the densely populated towns in which the Tannaim lived. I illustrate how the Tannaim model the *quppa* as a civic institution whose primary objective is to care for the local conjunctural poor. In doing so, the *quppa* benefits the community as a whole – the poor beneficiaries as well as the non-poor who considered beggars and poverty to be unsightly. Indeed, the *quppa* also played an important role in the emergence of the local community in rabbinic thought. Finally, the rabbis conceptualize the *quppa* as a mechanism for carrying out anonymous charity, whereby the benefactors and beneficiaries never meet. By enabling anonymous giving – which would become a hallmark of Jewish charity – the *quppa* provides another means by which the poor can preserve their dignity while receiving the provisions that they need. This process is facilitated, and in many ways made possible, by the charity supervisor.

The charity supervisor – the *gabbai tsedaqah* or *parnas* – whom I examine in Chapter 7, is the cornerstone of organized almsgiving. This official oversees the *quppa*, as his main tasks are collecting contributions from the town's residents and distributing them to the poor. In Tannaitic texts, the supervisor's collection duties are modeled along the lines of a tax collector, who has the authority and mandate to demand payments from all of the town's residents. Likewise, the supervisor ought to have the authority to compel people to contribute to the *quppa*, which the rabbis understood as a civic or communal obligation. In his distribution of alms, the supervisor is modeled after a judge, as he must first assess the claims of the poor before reaching a decision on which alms should be provided to which claimants.

The way that the supervisor handles the public's funds was crucial. He had to distinguish clearly between his own possessions, on the one hand, and the assets that had been entrusted to him by the community, on the other. The supervisor had to avoid even the suspicion that he would steal from the *quppa* or derive personal, material benefit from his duties. Rather, the supervisor was intended to be an agent of the entire community who carried out his responsibilities with honesty, transparency, and fairness. Only if the charity supervisor is trustworthy could organized charity approach its objectives of bringing an end to begging.

The rabbis' prescriptions for the behavior of the supervisor would set the stage, at a later date, to associate this office and its authority with the rabbinic movement. As I discuss in Chapter 8, Palestinian Amoraic texts present the rabbis themselves as charity supervisors and as those who appoint the supervisors. Moreover, the Palestinian Amoraim direct these funds to members of the rabbinic movement. The Amoraim, much like the leaders of the early church, understood how charity could be used for instrumental purposes. In particular, organized charity could promote the Amoraim's own social and religious authority and boost the economic position of fellow rabbis. Thus, the Palestinian Amoraim developed instrumental uses for organized charity that were never intended by the Tannaim – who, by contrast, focused on protecting the dignity of the poor by bringing an end to the shame and humiliation of begging.

APPENDIX: A BRIEF INTRODUCTION TO TANNAITIC LITERATURE

The Tannaitic or early rabbinic corpus is a collection of legal and exegetical compilations written in postbiblical Hebrew that address an array of topics including ethics, law, religion, and the interpretation of the Hebrew Bible. These texts, which took shape in the late second and early third centuries C.E.

in Roman Palestine, constitute the foundations of the Talmuds and all subsequent works of rabbinic Judaism – the preeminent form of Judaism today. These works are attributed to the early rabbinic movement or Tannaim – so named because they are said to have "repeated" the teachings of their teachers as a way to learn, memorize, and transmit them to their own disciples. The Tannaim were a loosely connected network of about one hundred rabbis, Jewish men who taught Torah, that emerged in the wake of the destruction of the Second Jerusalem Temple by the Romans in 70 C.E. Their traditions were collected by the last generations of the Tannaim (late second, early third century C.E.), who edited and redacted them into a handful of discrete – but voluminous – legal and exegetical compilations.[127]

The Mishnah is the earliest legal compilation, redacted around 220 C.E. While the Mishnah's overall purpose is not entirely clear, the most compelling suggestions are that it is a compendium of laws, a curriculum or textbook used for teaching rabbis and their disciples, or a combination of the two. Much of what has been said about the Mishnah likewise applies to the Tosefta, which took shape shortly after the Mishnah, perhaps around 220–230. The Tosefta's name, "addition," reflects the traditional understanding that it is a supplement to – and therefore dependent upon – the Mishnah. Modern scholars, however, have found the relationship between the two works to be far more complex.[128] While the Mishnah and Tosefta are organized by legal topic, other Tannaitic compilations are structured as line-by-line commentaries on and expansions of the Torah or Pentateuch. These Tannaitic midrashim (sing. midrash) or exegeses include the *Mekilta of Rabbi Ishmael* on Exodus; *Sifra* on Leviticus; *Sifre to Numbers*; and *Sifre to Deuteronomy*.[129] Because the selections from Exodus, Leviticus, Numbers, and Deuteronomy are mostly legal in genre, the

---

[127] Hayim Lapin, "The Origins and Development of the Rabbinic Movement in the Land of Israel," in *The Cambridge History of Judaism: Volume Four: The Late Roman-Rabbinic Period* (ed. S. T. Katz; Cambridge: Cambridge University Press, 2006), 206–29; Strack and Stemberger, *Introduction to the Talmud*, 1–5.

[128] On the complex relationships between the Mishnah and Tosefta, see among others Friedman, "Primacy of Tosefta," 99–121; Hauptman, *Rereading the Mishnah*; Alberdina Houtman, *Mishnah and Tosefta: A Synoptic Comparison of the Tractates Berakhot and Shebiit* (2 vols.; Tübingen: Mohr Siebeck, 1996), 7–19; Strack and Stemberger, *Introduction to the Talmud*, 152–55. In Gardner, "Cornering Poverty," 1:205–16, I demonstrate that *t. Pe'ah* 4:8–9 preserves the kind of elaborate and introductory discussions on organized charity that *m. Pe'ah* 8:7 assumes that its reader already knows. This suggests that these particular pericopae align with the more general findings by Friedman and Hauptman that the Tosefta preserves some material that may be earlier than that in the Mishnah.

[129] The following compilations cannot be confidently dated to the Tannaitic era: *Avot d'Rabbi Natan*; *Mekilta of Rabbi Shimon bar Yohai*, *Midrash Tannaim*, and *Sifre Zutta*; see Strack and Stemberger, *Introduction to the Talmud*, 225–27, 257–59, 268–70, 273–75.

APPENDIX: A BRIEF INTRODUCTION TO TANNAITIC LITERATURE   41

Tannaitic midrashim are also called the halakhic ("legal") midrashim. These exegetical works reached their final form by the middle of the third century.[130] Like other recent scholarship that focuses on the Tannaitic corpus, this book excludes traditions that are attributed to the Tannaim or Tannaitic times but only found in post-Tannaitic compilations (e.g., a *baraita*, a supposedly Tannaitic source that is "external" to – i.e., not included in – the Mishnah). These traditions are more likely to reflect the interests of the texts in which they are found (e.g., the Talmuds) than those in which they are not (i.e., Tannaitic compilations).[131]

Following the redaction of the Tannaitic texts, the next wave of rabbis emerged with their own distinct identity. The Amoraim (sing. Amora; "commentators" of the Tannaim) were active in Roman Palestine (until c. 360–370) and Babylonia under Sasanian rule (until c. 500). The Amoraim added to the teachings of the Tannaim, incorporating them into new legal and exegetical compilations, such as the Jerusalem Talmud or Yerushalmi, *Genesis Rabbah*, and *Lamentations Rabbah*. The Amoraim were succeeded by the Savoraim, who incorporated the teachings of both the Tannaim and Amoraim into the Babylonian Talmud or Bavli, which was redacted in the sixth or seventh century and remains the preeminent work of Jewish law.[132]

---

[130] Jay M. Harris, "Midrash Halachah," in *The Cambridge History of Judaism: Volume Four: The Late Roman-Rabbinic Period* (ed. S. T. Katz; Cambridge: Cambridge University Press, 2006), 336–68; Strack and Stemberger, *Introduction to the Talmud*, 247–73.

[131] Shaye J. D. Cohen, "The Place of the Rabbi in Jewish Society of the Second Century," in *The Galilee in Late Antiquity* (ed. L. I. Levine; New York and Jerusalem: Jewish Theological Seminary of America, 1992), 157–58; Cohen, "Rabbi in Second-Century," 922–90; Goodman, *State and Society*, 8–9; Jordan D. Rosenblum, *Food and Identity in Early Rabbinic Judaism* (New York: Cambridge University Press, 2010). On the question of the authenticity of these traditions, see Strack and Stemberger, *Introduction to the Talmud*, 104, 177–78, 198–99.

[132] Richard Kalmin, *Sages, Stories, Authors, and Editors in Rabbinic Babylonia* (Atlanta, Ga.: Scholars Press, 1994), 1; Richard Kalmin, "The Formation and Character of the Babylonian Talmud," in *The Cambridge History of Judaism: Volume Four: The Late Roman-Rabbinic Period* (ed. S. T. Katz; Cambridge: Cambridge University Press, 2006), 842; Hayim Lapin, "The Rabbinic Movement," in *The Cambridge Guide to Jewish History, Religion, and Culture* (ed. J. R. Baskin and K. Seeskin; Cambridge and New York: Cambridge University Press, 2010), 77; Jeffrey L. Rubenstein, *Talmudic Stories: Narrative Art, Composition, and Culture* (Baltimore, Md.: Johns Hopkins University Press, 1999), 18; Jeffrey L. Rubenstein, *The Culture of the Babylonian Talmud* (Baltimore, Md.: Johns Hopkins University Press, 2003), 3; Strack and Stemberger, *Introduction to the Talmud*, 165–224, 277–88.

2

ॐ

The Poor and Poverty in Roman Palestine

An examination of poverty and the socioeconomic realities of Roman Palestine at the time of the Tannaim will help us contextualize and shed new light on early rabbinic teachings on charity. This chapter sketches the contours of poverty in Roman Palestine by focusing on extrarabbinic sources, including archaeology, inscriptions, papyri, coins, the writings of Greek and Latin authors, and scholarship based on these sources.[1] By eschewing rabbinic texts as transparent windows into realia, I hope to avoid the pitfalls associated with the use of rabbinic literature as a historical source and to construct on firm ground the socioeconomic context in which the rabbinic authors and redactors lived.[2] As we will see, poverty in the ancient world was defined

---

[1] Poverty is difficult to track in the archaeological record, as the poor were defined by their lack of material possessions, leaving very few remains (Rosenfeld and Perlmutter, "Foundations of Charitable Organizations," 49; Inge Uytterhoeven, "Housing in Late Antiquity: Thematic Perspectives," in *Housing in Late Antiquity: From Palaces to Shops* [ed. L. Lavan et al.; Late Antique Archaeology 3.2 of; Leiden and Boston: Brill, 2007], 47). Wealth is more immediately discernible in the material record. It is evidenced by ornate mosaic floors; garments with fine, high-quality weaving and multicolored dyes; and vessels made of expensive metals, fine ware, or imported from other regions. The absence of extreme signs of wealth, however, cannot be taken as an indicator of extreme poverty. It is also important to keep in mind that literary sources from the ancient world were predominantly authored by those who were well-off or by the elite; see Gardner, "Who is Rich." We do not have any late-antique writings by the poor themselves like those for the middle ages found at the Cairo Geniza; see Cohen, *Voice of the Poor*. That being said, reading the late-antique sources in a critical light, combined with the archaeological finds that we do have (especially those from the Judean desert), will allow us to sketch the contours of poverty in Roman Palestine and inform our readings of rabbinic texts.

[2] On the problems of using rabbinic texts as a sources for economic history, see the discussions in Hayim Lapin, *Economy, Geography, and Provincial History in Later Roman Palestine* (Tübingen: Mohr Siebeck, 2001), 1–14; Schwartz, "Historiography," 91–95; Seth Schwartz, "Political, Social, and Economic Life in the Land of Israel, 66–c.235," in *The Cambridge History of Judaism: Volume Four: The Late Roman-Rabbinic Period* (ed. S. T. Katz; Cambridge: Cambridge University Press, 2006), 23–52.

by physiological or biological criteria as well as by social conventions. With regard to the latter, I have detected a "semiotic language" whereby certain objects signify status, wealth, and poverty. In subsequent chapters, I will show how the realities of poverty in Roman Palestine informed the rabbis' thoughts on organized charity.

ECONOMY AND POVERTY IN ROMAN PALESTINE

Agriculture was the foundation of the ancient Mediterranean economy and its most important sector.[3] Roman Palestine was no exception, as the majority of its population lived and worked as peasants, cultivating the land as tenants, sharecroppers, and hired laborers for landowners who lived in towns, away from their fields.[4] Cereals (especially wheat and barley), olives, grapes, and legumes were the most important crops in Roman Palestine.[5] Other produce included walnuts, palms, figs, and vegetables.[6] Cash crops, cultivated on a small scale, included balsam, and Pliny, Josephus, and other writers mention that these were grown in the Jericho area.[7] Papyri from the second century C.E. known as the Babatha archive refer to the cultivation of dates near the Dead Sea.[8]

Olives were widely cultivated and played a prominent role in multiple aspects of daily life.[9] The production and distribution of olive oil was especially important to the economy of Roman Palestine. Josephus remarks that the Galilee excelled in the cultivation of olives, which were marketed locally and

---

[3] Walter Scheidel et al., eds., *The Cambridge Economic History of the Greco-Roman World* (Cambridge and New York: Cambridge University Press, 2007).

[4] Hamel, *Poverty and Charity in Roman Palestine*, 125; Catherine Hezser, *The Social Structure of the Rabbinic Movement in Roman Palestine* (Tübingen: Mohr Siebeck, 1997), 260n. 12. On village life in Roman Galilee, see Goodman, *State and Society*. On tenancy, see the scholarship cited in Susan E. Alcock, "The Eastern Mediterranean," in *The Cambridge Economic History of the Greco-Roman World* (ed. W. Scheidel et al.; Cambridge and New York: Cambridge University Press, 2007), 678n. 21.

[5] Schwartz, "Political, Social," 38.

[6] Goodman, *State and Society*, 22–23.

[7] Pliny the Elder, *Natural History* 12.111–124; Josephus, *War* 1.138, 361; 4.468; *Ant.* 2.118; 14.54; 15.96. Balsam is also mentioned in the writings of Diodorus Siculus, Tacitus and others; see Zeev Safrai, *The Economy of Roman Palestine* (London: Routledge, 1994), 147–50. Balsam may be the substance contained in a Herodian-era juglet found at Qumran; see Joseph Patrich and Benny Arubas, "A Juglet Containing Balsam Oil (?) from a Cave Near Qumran," *IEJ* 39 (1989): 43–59.

[8] Schwartz, "Political, Social," 39. Such exotic goods caught the eye of ancient writers; thus, their impact on the overall economy may be overstated in modern scholarship based on these sources.

[9] Rafi Frankel, *Wine and Oil Production in Antiquity in Israel and Other Mediterranean Countries* (Sheffield, England: Sheffield Academic Press, 1999), 38.

to other regions.[10] Archaeological remains of oil presses have been uncovered all over the country.[11] "There was no ancient settlement in Palestine that did not have an olive press to produce oil," Shimon Dar writes, reflecting on the results of his archaeological field work, "and in areas where olives grew we found six or seven presses in every town and village."[12] The importance of olive oil production is also reflected in the names of places. The Garden of Gethsemane in Jerusalem, for example, derives its name from *gat shemanim* or "oil vat" in Hebrew.[13]

There was also a healthy nonagricultural sector of the economy, composed of services, marketing, and manufacturing. Significant was the production of ceramic wares such as bowls and other household vessels.[14] For the most part, however, the vast majority of livelihoods in Roman Galilee were tied directly to agriculture and the cultivation of crops for local consumption.

Agriculture was the engine of the economy; its successes were a source of wealth, and its failures were the major causes of poverty.[15] Palestine, however, was not blessed with optimal environmental conditions, which in turn restricted economic output – resulting in only modest successes but acute failures. The country is topographically diverse, as each region is characterized by varying altitudes, terrains, and soils; excluding the Negev desert in the south, only about one-fourth of the country is arable.[16] Because few rivers flow perennially and there is a dearth of springs, rainfall was of singular importance and often guided the fortunes of the country's inhabitants. It fell from October to April and the annual mean rainfall was sufficient to grow cereals and other staple crops.[17] Even when rainfall thresholds were

---

[10] Goodman, *State and Society*, 22–23; Schwartz, "Political, Social," 35–39, 46–47; cf. Safrai, *Economy*, 108, 118–136.

[11] Etan Ayalon et al., eds., *Oil and Wine Presses in Israel from the Hellenistic, Roman and Byzantine Periods* (BAR International Series; Oxford: Archaeopress, 2009).

[12] Shimon Dar, "Food and Archaeology in Romano-Byzantine Palestine," in *Food in Antiquity* (ed. J. Wilkins; Exeter: University of Exeter Press, 1995), 331.

[13] Rafael Frankel et al., *History and Technology of Olive Oil in the Holy Land* (Arlington, Va., and Tel Aviv: Olearius Editions and Eretz Israel Museum, Tel Aviv, 1994), 22.

[14] David Adan-Bayewitz, *Common Pottery in Roman Galilee: A Study of Local Trade* (Ramat-Gan, Israel: Bar-Ilan University Press, 1993); Jodi Magness, *Jerusalem Ceramic Chronology: Circa 200–800 CE* (Sheffield, England: JSOT Press, 1993).

[15] Schwartz, "Political, Social," 23–52. Lapin, *Economy, Geography*, 1–4 rightly notes that scholarship on the economy of Roman Palestine tends to fall along the fault lines of the broader "formalist/substantivist debate" on the nature of the economy of the ancient world.

[16] Jehuda Feliks and Shimon Gibson, "Agricultural Land-Management Methods and Implements in Ancient Erez Israel," in *Encyclopaedia Judaica*, 2nd ed. (ed. F. Skolnik and M. Berenbaum; Detroit: Macmillan Reference and Keter Publishing House, 2007), 471; Hamel, *Poverty and Charity in Roman Palestine*, 101–09.

[17] Feliks and Gibson, "Agricultural Land-Management Methods," 471, 481–82; Hamel, *Poverty and Charity in Roman Palestine*, 102–03.

met, however, the country's environmental conditions required dry farming, a labor-intensive method of cultivation that was low in productivity.[18]

Crop yields for wheat, the ratio of seeds to yield, measure the productivity of the country's most important crop and are the best available indicator of the performance of the overall economy. Rabbinic literature mentions crop yields as high as 1:45, an astronomical figure that has only been replicated in modern times, and thus is highly suspect for the ancient world.[19] By contrast, papyri, comparative evidence from elsewhere in the Roman world, and studies of the pre-industrial Mediterranean provide more reliable sources on crop yields for Roman Palestine.[20] They indicate that wheat yields in Roman Palestine were approximately 1:5, a low return compared with other areas of the Mediterranean.[21] Because cultivators reinvested one-fifth of the yield as seed and set aside an additional fifth for taxes, little was left over for consumption and as surplus.[22] Many people likely lived at or near subsistence levels and food shortages were common.[23] The economy of Palestine was characterized by low performance and surely created significant poverty even in normal times – that is, structural or permanent poverty.

Low productivity would have made individuals particularly vulnerable to disruptions in cultivation, brought about by environmental and sociopolitical factors. Such occasional crises or conjunctures cause temporary or "conjunctural" poverty, impoverishing individuals who would otherwise not be poor. Low crop yields limit the amount of surplus produce, so little cereal or other staples could be stored away as insurance for times of crisis.[24] The

---

[18] Hamel, "Poverty and Charity," 113.
[19] See Yehuda Feliks, *Agriculture in Erets-Israel in the Period of the Bible and Talmud [Hebrew]* (Jerusalem: Reuven Mas, 1990), 143; for a critical evaluation, see Schwartz, "Historiography," 91–95.
[20] Hamel, *Poverty and Charity in Roman Palestine*, 130–32.
[21] For example, 1:4 and 1:10 for Italy; 1:8 to 1:10 for Sicily alone; and 1:15 for Etruria; see Richard Duncan-Jones, *The Economy of the Roman Empire: Quantitative Studies* (Cambridge and New York: Cambridge University Press, 1982), 370–71; Hamel, *Poverty and Charity in Roman Palestine*, 131–32; Hamel, "Poverty and Charity," 310; Schwartz, "Political, Social," 41.
[22] Schwartz, "Political, Social," 42. Taxation by Rome included a poll tax, land tax, taxes for military or administrative purposes, duties on imports and tolls levied on various products or trades, and the *fiscus judaicus* levied following the Jewish Revolt of 66–73 C.E. Roman taxes totaled about 12.5 percent of one's income. Allocations given in accordance with Jewish laws are estimated at 20.6 percent of the one's income; see Arye Ben-David, *Talmudische Ökonomie: Die Wirtschaft des jüdischen Palästina zur Zeit der Mischna und des Talmud* (Hildesheim: Olms, 1974), 136, 297–98. Such "taxes" include tithes, though, as Schwartz rightly notes, tithing laws were probably not followed as stringently as Hamel assumes; see Seth Schwartz, "Review of G. Hamel, *Poverty and Charity in Roman Palestine, First Three Centuries C.E.*," *AJSR* 17 (1992): 295.
[23] See my following discussion on droughts and other crises.
[24] Schwartz, "Political, Social," 39–41. Lapin likewise finds that only a modest proportion of rural production was sold in the marketplace; see Lapin, *Economy, Geography*, 113.

economy was subject to a number of natural disturbances, including vermin, hail, wind, crop diseases, earthquakes, fertilizer shortages, and pests such as locusts, rodents, and birds.[25] Most significant, however, were problems with rainfall. While the rainfall per annum tended to be sufficient over the long run, the precise amount of rainfall from year to year – and even from month to month within the rainy season – varied considerably and could cause severe damage to the normal cultivation process.[26] Unexpectedly heavy rains eroded arable soil, which was already scarce, and washed away crops.[27] Too little rainfall would result in lower yields and food shortages. The most feared disruptions were severe shortages in rainfall. For the ancients, droughts were synonymous with economic downturns and famines, and were the cause of significant conjunctural poverty. Long-term climactic data suggest that they were frequent, as precipitation was insufficient to meet the needs of wheat crops about once every 12.5 years. Indeed, a number of droughts are mentioned by ancient writers such as Josephus.[28]

In addition to natural causes, human activity damaged the economy of Roman Palestine and impoverished many. Normal economic life was disrupted by military conflicts, as the country was rocked by multiple revolts.[29] The passage and stationing of troops, as well as the battles themselves, inflicted damage to the land.[30] The long-term productivity of the land was compromised by neglect during years of upheaval and by the short-term needs of commanders seeking immediate sustenance or supplies for their troops.[31] Such damage was profound, as it could take years of care, investing time

---

[25] Hamel, *Poverty and Charity in Roman Palestine*, 114; Kenneth W. Russell, "The Earthquake Chronology of Palestine and Northwest Arabia from the 2nd Through the Mid-8th Century A. D," *BASOR* (1985): 37–59.

[26] Hamel, *Poverty and Charity in Roman Palestine*, 102–03; Jack Pastor, *Land and Economy in Ancient Palestine* (London and New York: Routledge, 1997), 2–4.

[27] Hamel, *Poverty and Charity in Roman Palestine*, 103, 106–07.

[28] E.g., Josephus, *Ant.* 15.121. On droughts, see Pastor, *Land and Economy*, 3–4, 82–86, 115–127, 173n. 11; Hamel, *Poverty and Charity in Roman Palestine*, 44–52.

[29] Schwartz, "Political, Social," 23.

[30] Hamel, *Poverty and Charity in Roman Palestine*, 132.

[31] For example, forests would be cut down as a source of wood for troops – or to prevent one's enemies from obtaining wood; see Hamel, *Poverty and Charity in Roman Palestine*, 132; E. Mary Smallwood, *The Jews Under Roman Rule: From Pompey to Diocletian: A Study in Political Relations* (Leiden: Brill, 1981), 476. In a remarkable letter from the leader of the second Jewish revolt against Rome, Simeon bar Kochva instructs the addressee to confiscate the wheat of a certain Tanhum bar Yishmael and to bring it to Bar Kochva under guard. In another letter, Bar Kochva commands his charge to harvest the winter wheat that lies within his area of supervision; see Yigael Yadin, "New Discoveries in the Judean Desert," *BA* 24 (1961): 47, 49–50.

and resources, to restore the land to its previous productive capacity.[32] The economy was also harmed by a loss of population through casualties and enslavement. Migration during and after a conflict, including the migration of Jews northward from Judea to the Galilee, likewise destabilized the economy, at least in the short run, and was a cause of conjunctural poverty.[33]

Military conflicts also had important consequences on who controlled the land, the economy's most important resource. It was common for armies to seize land to house troops during a conflict and settle veterans on it afterwards. After the first revolt, for example, a Roman legion (Legio X Fretensis) was supplemented with auxiliary units and stationed permanently in Judea; land near Emmaus was appropriated for settling veterans; and in the 120s, Rome placed an additional legion (Legio VI Ferrata) in the Galilee, which was later removed.[34] The holdings of the losing side could be seized as booty, confiscated by the Romans.[35] The seized land would have been a cause of conjunctural poverty for those who had previously depended on it for their livelihoods. Minor conflicts, brigandage, and other disturbances also disrupted normal economic activity during this era.[36]

THE THIRD-CENTURY CRISIS

A word should be said about the economic crisis that plagued the Roman Empire for fifty years in the middle of the third century (c. 235–284). The so-called third century crisis was characterized by political and economic

---

[32] Vines and fruit trees take longer to recover their productive capacity than grains. It might take an olive tree up to twenty years to be productive again; see Smallwood, *Jews Under Roman Rule*, 477.

[33] Michael Avi-Yonah, *The Jews Under Roman and Byzantine Rule: A Political History of Palestine from the Bar Kokhba War to the Arab Conquest* (New York: Schocken Books, 1984), 18; Hamel, *Poverty and Charity in Roman Palestine*, 140; Fergus Millar, *The Roman Near East, 31 B.C. – A.D. 337* (Cambridge, Mass.: Harvard University Press, 1993), 368; Schwartz, "Political, Social," 37–38; Smallwood, *Jews Under Roman Rule*, 473.

[34] Avi-Yonah, *Jews Under Roman and Byzantine Rule*, 36–37; Millar, *Roman Near East*, 368; Zeev Safrai, "The Roman Army in the Galilee," in *The Galilee in Late Antiquity* (ed. L. I. Levine; New York and Jerusalem, 1992), 103–14; Schwartz, "Political, Social," 25; Smallwood, *Jews Under Roman Rule*, 331–32. To be sure, the permanent presence of the military had some positive impact on the economy. Roman soldiers earned a good salary, which was spent locally as they consumed local services and supplies, produced wares of their own, and prompted other positive economic externalities; see Safrai, "Roman Army in the Galilee," 110–13; Schwartz, "Political, Social," 28–29.

[35] Pastor, *Land and Economy*, 160–65.

[36] Pastor, *Land and Economy*, 2–3; Smallwood, *Jews Under Roman Rule*, 489–90.

instability, as well as widespread poverty.[37] Was this crisis ongoing while the Tannaim formulated their ideas on charity? Although the redaction of some Tannaitic compilations, particularly the Tannaitic midrashim, may have extended into the age of the crisis, the works very much reflect the world in which the last generations of the Tannaim lived – the late second and early third centuries.[38] That is, it reflects the era *before* the onset of the crisis. For this reason, Martin Goodman finds no evidence of the crisis in Tannaitic sources, including the midrashim.[39] Likewise, Alyssa Gray finds that statements reflecting the crisis's widespread misery, such as one attributed to Rabbi Ze'ora' that "poverty is common" in the Yerushalmi (*y. Nedarim* 9:4, 41c), are found only in post-Tannaitic texts – no such traditions are found in Tannaitic compilations.[40] It is highly unlikely, therefore, that the crisis of the mid-third century forms the backdrop to Tannaitic literature's discussions of poverty, let alone the Tannaim's impetus or motivation for their prescriptive discourses on charity. Poverty persists even in normal times. Any time during the late second and early third centuries could have provided the context for discussions of poverty and charity.

THE POOR AND POVERTY: REALIA

Having explored the causes of poverty, I now seek to describe it. What did it mean to be poor in Roman Palestine? What did the poor eat, what did they wear, and where did they live? In general, it can be said that the poor were

---

[37] Alcock, "Eastern Mediterranean," 671–97; Mireille Corbier, "Coinage, Society and Economy," in *Cambridge Ancient History, Volume 12* (ed. A. K. Bowman et al.; Cambridge: Cambridge University Press, 2005), 393–439; John Drinkwater, "Maximus to Diocletian and the 'Crisis,'" in *Cambridge Ancient History, Volume 12* (ed. A. K. Bowman et al.; Cambridge: Cambridge University Press, 2005), 28–66; Daniel Sperber, *Roman Palestine, 200–400: Money and Prices* (Ramat-Gan: Bar-Ilan University Press, 1991), 128–31; Günter Stemberger, *Jews and Christians in the Holy Land: Palestine in the Fourth Century* (Edinburgh: T&T Clark, 2000), 12–17. Most scholars hold that the third-century crisis was felt in Palestine; see Gray, "Formerly Wealthy Poor," 101–33; Visotzky, *Golden Bells*, 121–22; Hamel, *Poverty and Charity in Roman Palestine*, 132–33. Cf. Doron Bar, "Was There a 3rd-c. Economic Crisis in Palestine?," in *The Roman and Byzantine Near East: Some Recent Archaeological Research* (ed. J. H. Humphrey; Journal of Roman Archaeology Supplementary Series; Ann Arbor, Mich.: Journal of Roman Archaeology, 1995), 43–54; Doron Bar, "The 3rd Century Crisis in the Roman Empire and its Relevance to Palestine During the Late Roman Period [Hebrew]," *Zion* 66 (2001): 143–70, who finds no archaeological evidence of an economic decline during the period. Brown, *Through the Eye*, 9, characterizes it as less of a catastrophe and more as a "return to reality after a period of extraordinary good fortune."

[38] Gray, "Formerly Wealthy Poor," 118n. 62.

[39] Goodman, *State and Society*, 179–80.

[40] Gray, "Formerly Wealthy Poor," 117–19.

mostly peasants who worked on land owned by others through tenancy, sharecropping, and other arrangements characterized by dependency. As already suggested, the combination of low crop yields, taxes, and rents made it difficult for many peasants to make ends meet and they were often in debt or on the cusp of poverty.[41] Below tenants and sharecroppers on the socioeconomic hierarchy were hired laborers, whose employment was defined by short-term arrangements that could be seasonal, daily, or even hourly. These individuals were needed for the large, labor-intensive stages of cultivation, such as plowing and harvesting.[42] Between periods of employment, hired laborers were likely to have been poor, joining those who were regularly unemployed and reduced to penury. In times of crisis, tenants, sharecroppers, and hired laborers who were paid in kind enjoyed some security as they could simply consume what they owned or earned. Laborers paid in fix sums, however, would be vulnerable to the spikes in food prices that came with crises.[43]

Food

All segments of society consumed cereals, olives, grapes, and legumes, the staples of the Mediterranean diet. Each came in many varieties, whose individual quality, price, and desirability were determined by where they were cultivated and how they were prepared. The poor, needless to say, were compelled to consume the least expensive – and therefore least desirable – varieties, which had both physiological and social consequences. This could be seen, for example, in the type of bread that one ate. Wheat and barley were the most common cereals and the main sources of calories. Those living in Roman Palestine, as well as the Greco-Roman world in general, consistently preferred wheat to barley. Wheat was desirable because it contained gluten, enabling bread to rise; had more nutrients than the equivalent amount of barley; and was considered more palatable. Wheat was more expensive to cultivate, requiring a greater input of labor, and was more vulnerable to shortages of rain than barley, which remained abundant in dry climates.[44] In the end, the low

---

[41] Hamel, *Poverty and Charity in Roman Palestine*, 154–63.
[42] In towns, they would be hired for construction, maintenance, and transportation; see Hamel, *Poverty and Charity in Roman Palestine*, 142–63.
[43] Sen, *Poverty and Famines*, 4.
[44] Pastor, *Land and Economy*, 5; Rosenblum, *Food and Identity*, 25–28; Robert Sallares, "Ecology," in *The Cambridge Economic History of the Greco-Roman World* (ed. W. Scheidel et al.; Cambridge and New York: Cambridge University Press, 2007), 27–34. On the nutritional value of cereals, see Willem M. Jongman, "The Early Roman Empire: Consumption," in *The Cambridge Economic History of the Greco-Roman World* (ed. W. Scheidel et al.; Cambridge and New York: Cambridge University Press, 2007), 598–600.

supply combined with high demand to ensure that wheat was consistently more expensive than barley.[45] The poor, therefore, were compelled to consume more barley than most as a proportion of their diets. The lower nutrient content and palatability left the poor malnourished and with a bad taste in their mouths. Socially, eating bread made of barley marked one's limited economic means and lower standing. Josephus, for example, notes that the poor ate barley while the rich ate wheat.[46] The way in which bread was made likewise influenced its price and the social standing of its consumer. While the well-off ate bread of finely sifted white wheat flour, the poor ate bread made of barley that often contained inclusions or other impurities.[47]

The semiotic values of bread were likewise shared by the wider Mediterranean world. Athenaeus, the second-century C.E. Egyptian writer, names seventy-two different types of bread.[48] The anthropologist Jack Goody finds that each kind of bread marked out a unique position in the social hierarchy.[49] Roland Barthes's observation that "We are... justified in considering the *varieties* of bread... as units of signification" is likewise apt for the ancient world.[50]

What has been said about bread likewise can be said about the other staples of the Mediterranean diet. Olives, grapes, and legumes were all produced in a variety of qualities, some of which were available to all but others of which could only be consumed by those who were well-off.[51] Moreover, many foods were simply beyond the means of the poor. They ate few onions, garlic, leeks, squashes, cabbages, radishes, beets, and other vegetables. Instead, the poor would substitute wild mushrooms, grasses, and edible roots.[52] The poor rarely ate animal proteins such as fish, foul, and dairy products.[53] Above all, meat was widely recognized as the most expensive food in the region. For many,

---

[45] See the sources cited in Pastor, *Land and Economy*, 174n. 31.
[46] Josephus, *War* 5.427.
[47] Hamel, *Poverty and Charity in Roman Palestine*, 22–23, 39.
[48] On Athenaeus, see Peter Garnsey, *Food and Society in Classical Antiquity* (Cambridge and New York: Cambridge University Press, 1999), 9, 116–27.
[49] Jack Goody, *Cooking, Cuisine and Class: A Study in Comparative Sociology* (Cambridge: Cambridge University Press, 1982), 103.
[50] Roland Barthes, "Toward a Psychosociology of Contemporary Food Consumption," in *Food and Drink in History: Selections from the Annales, économies, sociétés, civilisations, volume 5* (ed. O. A. Ranum and R. Forster; Baltimore, Md.: Johns Hopkins University Press, 1979), 168; with my emphasis.
[51] There are, for example, several different kinds of olive oil, which could be prepared and consumed in a number of different ways; see Rosenblum, *Food and Identity*, 28–30.
[52] It was not uncommon for the wealthy to have dessert as well, which may have included roasted ears of wheat with almonds, honey, and spices; Hamel, *Poverty and Charity in Roman Palestine*, 17–18, 32.
[53] Rosenblum, *Food and Identity*, 20–21.

it was a delicacy and eating it regularly marked extreme wealth and status.[54] Needless to say, the poor rarely ate meat.

Economic constraints compelled the poor to eat foods that were low in quality, taste, and nutrients. This had negative physiological implications and lowered their overall quality of life. There were also social implications of what one ate. Those who ate fish and vegetables regularly would be known as well-off, while drinking old wine and eating meat on a regular basis were emblematic of significant wealth and status.[55] Certain legumes were known as the "poor man's meat," while eating wild carobs was synonymous with living in poverty.[56] "You are what you eat" holds true here, as scholars have demonstrated that food and eating played important roles in identity construction, including the construction of one's religious identity. Eating pig, for example, was an identity marker of non-Jewishness.[57] Likewise, eating barley bread or wild carobs advertised one's limited economic means. The foods that the poor ate left them not only malnourished, but also stigmatized.

That food was used to distinguish between various strata of society is perhaps best illustrated by Pliny the Elder, the first-century C.E. Latin naturalist:

> of the bakers' shops – one kind of bread for my lords and another for the common herd, the yearly produce graded in so many classes right down to the lowest of the low: but have distinctions been discovered even in herbs, and has wealth established grades even in articles of food that sell for a single copper? The ordinary public declares that even among vegetables some kinds are grown that are not for them. Even a kale being fattened up to such a size that there is not room for it on a poor man's table. Nature had made asparagus to grow wild, for anybody to gather at random: but lo and behold! Now we see a cultivated variety, and Ravenna produces heads weighing three to a pound. Alas for the monstrosities of gluttony! It would surprise us if cattle were not allowed to feed on thistles, but thistles are forbidden to the lower orders! Even the water supply is divided into classes, and the power of money has made distinctions in the very elements. (Pliny the Elder, *Natural History* 19.53–55)[58]

---

[54] Hamel, *Poverty and Charity in Roman Palestine*, 24–25.
[55] Hamel, *Poverty and Charity in Roman Palestine*, 8–56.
[56] Hamel, *Poverty and Charity in Roman Palestine*, 15–16, 47; Joshua J. Schwartz, "The Material Realities of Jewish Life in the Land of Israel, c. 235–638," in *The Cambridge History of Judaism: Volume Four: The Late Roman-Rabbinic Period* (ed. S. T. Katz; Cambridge: Cambridge University Press, 2006), 442.
[57] Rosenblum, *Food and Identity*.
[58] Translation according to Pliny the Elder and H. Rackham, *Natural History* (Cambridge, Mass.: Harvard University Press, 1938). On Pliny, gardens, and vegetables, see Michael Beer, *Taste or Taboo: Dietary Choices in Antiquity* (Totnes, Devon: Prospect Books, 2010), 22–23; James Lawson, "The Roman Garden," *Greece & Rome* 19 (1950): 97–105.

Clothing

The poor were also identified by the clothing that they wore.[59] The most common clothes throughout the ancient Mediterranean world, including Roman Palestine, were tunics and mantles.[60] It was common to wear multiple tunics, loose-fitting garments that extend to the knees, with the lowest layer serving as an undergarment.[61] Mantels – large, rectangular, sleeveless garments – wrapped around the body and served as outerwear.[62] Tunics and mantels were accompanied by belts, head coverings, and sandals or occasionally shoes.[63] They were usually made of wool, which came in a variety of grades, ranging from fine to coarse. The garments themselves could be prepared in a number of ways depending on how the wool was washed, spun, woven, and dyed. If the wool were thoroughly processed, embodying a significant investment of time and expertise, it would be white in color; poor-quality clothes were brown or gray. Garments could be decorated with vertical stripes, notched bands, gamma patterns, and dyes, especially red and purple. Material remains of tunics and mantels from the era include the second-century C.E. finds from the Cave of Letters and Wadi Murabba'at in the Judean desert. In addition to fragments of garments, the finds include one specimen that is nearly intact.[64]

The cloaks and tunics used by the poor were of low-grade wool, with a brown or gray color, as opposed to white.[65] It was common for the tunics and mantles of the poor to be worn and tattered, due to overuse or because used clothing was less expensive, if not free. They might show signs of mending, such as a tunic from the Cave of Letters that has three patches that do not

---

[59] The following addresses clothes for poor men, as the rabbis understood "the poor" as exclusively male (see my discussion in Chapter 5). To be sure, clothes were gendered in Roman Palestine and a study of poor women's dress is a desideratum.

[60] Jews, for the most part, wore the same clothes as non-Jews; see Shaye J. D. Cohen, *The Beginnings of Jewishness: Boundaries, Varieties, Uncertainties* (Berkeley: University of California Press, 1999), 30–34; Jodi Magness, *Stone and Dung, Oil and Spit: Jewish Daily Life in the Time of Jesus* (Grand Rapids, Mich.: Eerdmans, 2011), 107–11; Schwartz, "Material Realities," 449–52.

[61] Hamel, *Poverty and Charity in Roman Palestine*, 60–62.

[62] Hamel, *Poverty and Charity in Roman Palestine*, 58–64; Yigael Yadin, *The Finds from the Bar Kokhba Period in the Cave of Letters* (Jerusalem: Israel Exploration Society, 1963), 219–21.

[63] Hamel, *Poverty and Charity in Roman Palestine*, 58–72.

[64] On wool, see Hamel, *Poverty and Charity in Roman Palestine*, 59–60, 78–92; Johannes Renger, "Wool," in *Brill's New Pauly: Encyclopaedia of the Ancient World* (ed. H. Cancik et al.; Leiden and Boston: Brill, 2002), s.v. wool. Many of the tunics and tunic sheets found at the Cave of Letters are dyed; see Yadin, *Finds from the Bar Kokhba Period*, 204–18 plates 60–69.

[65] Hamel, *Poverty and Charity in Roman Palestine*, 81.

match the color of the rest of the garment.[66] It was also desirable to have multiple sets of garments, to wear simultaneously in layers or as a change of clothing.[67] The poor, however, likely had few garments and their continuous wear would accelerate their disintegration into rags. The poor also tended to wear shorter clothing. Made from less fabric, this reflected their limited economic means as well as their need to perform manual labor, as shorter garments allowed for greater mobility. Long garments, which restricted movement, were marks of leisure.[68] The poor were also distinguished by their lack of accessories such as belts, head coverings, and sandals. A lack of clothing left the destitute exposed to the sun, cold, rain, and wind. In addition to physiological harm, the poor may have also suffered from the shame of exposure or nakedness.[69]

Shelter

Our sources for where the poor would have lived are meager. Surely, many were homeless or lived in temporary structures that left few (if any) traces in the archaeological record.[70] To be sure, some of the poor were able to secure permanent housing. Dwellings for the poor could consist of small

---

[66] Hamel, *Poverty and Charity in Roman Palestine*, 72–73; Yadin, *Finds from the Bar Kokhba Period*, 212–13, no. 7, plate 76. Tunic no. 8 (p. 213, plate 75) also has patches.

[67] Hamel, *Poverty and Charity in Roman Palestine*, 61; Schwartz, "Material Realities," 450.

[68] Hamel, *Poverty and Charity in Roman Palestine*, 76–77.

[69] Hamel, *Poverty and Charity in Roman Palestine*, 73–76.

[70] There are a number of problems inherent in identifying the housing of the poor. First, by definition of their material poverty, the poor left relatively few traces in the archaeological record. Second, excavators tend to focus on monumental, public architecture, or the lavish abodes of the wealthy; see Uytterhoeven, "Housing in Late Antiquity: Thematic Perspectives," 26; notable exceptions are Katharina Galor, "Domestic Architecture in Galilee and Golan During the Roman and Byzantine Periods: First Century B.C. to Seventh Century A.D.," (Ph.D. diss., Brown University, 1996); Yizhar Hirschfeld, *The Palestinian Dwelling in the Roman-Byzantine Period* (Jerusalem: Franciscan Printing Press and Israel Exploration Society, 1995). Third, all material culture was reused, recycled, and repurposed in antiquity, perhaps none more so than housing; see Joshua Schwartz, "'Reduce, Reuse and Recycle' Prolegomena On Breakage and Repair in Ancient Jewish Society: Broken Beds and Chairs in Mishnah Kelim," *Jewish Studies Internet Journal* 5 (2006): 147–80. Fourth, and most problematic, are the problems associated with interpreting the finds. As Goodman, *State and Society*, 31, notes, it is difficult to distinguish exterior walls from interior dividers in rooms/units that abut one another; see further Galor, "Domestic Architecture," Katharina Galor, "The Roman-Byzantine Dwelling in the Galilee and the Golan: 'House' or 'Apartment'?," in *Miscellanea Mediterranea* (ed. R. R. Holloway; Providence, R.I.: Brown University, 2000), 109–24; Katharina Galor, "Domestic Architecture," in *The Oxford Handbook of Jewish Daily Life in Roman Palestine* (ed. C. Hezser; Oxford: Oxford University Press, 2010), 420–39. On the poor reduced to homelessness, see Philo, *Embassy* 123.

units arranged in rows, opening out to noisy thoroughfares.[71] These shops may have been purpose-built for the poor families who operated and lived in them, while others were originally constructed for commercial purposes alone but later repurposed as housing.[72] Other dwellings for the poor consisted of small "apartments" that were organized around a central, shared courtyard.[73] A unit consisted of one or two rooms of 15 to 20 sq m each and housed an individual family. Multiple families would share a central courtyard. The boundaries between these "apartments" were permeable as privacy came at a premium that the poor could not afford. While some units were divided by walls, others were separated only by wooden boards, cloth curtains, other removable dividers, or arranged to obscure sightlines from one room to another.[74]

The dwellings of the poor were crowded, dark, and uncomfortable.[75] The poor lacked furniture such as the couches and sofas that were found in the abodes of the wealthy and probably even simple chairs, stools, and seats. In the absence of furniture, the poor sat on the floor while they ate. Sitting on the floor was a sign of poverty and hindered, if not precluded, dining

---

[71] Simon Ellis, *Roman Housing* (London: Duckworth, 2000), 80; Peter Richardson, "Towards a Typology of Levantine/Palestinian Houses," *JSNT* 27 (2004): 57–60.

[72] The poor may have also lived in one-room dwellings, such as those at Khorazin; see Goodman, *State and Society*, 31. Also notable is a fourth–fifth century C.E. structure in the Galilean town of Khirbet Shema (Eric M. Meyers et al., *Ancient Synagogue Excavations at Khirbet Shema'*, *Upper Galilee, Israel, 1970–1972* [Durham, N.C.: Published for the American Schools of Oriental Research by Duke University Press, 1976], 107–13), which Hirschfeld, *Palestinian Dwelling*, 34, has identified as a dwelling for a poor family. We should be skeptical of Hirschfield's identification, as the dwelling covers some 40 square meters, which would have been large for a single poor family. I thank Franco De Angelis for this observation.

[73] Galor, "Domestic Architecture," 71–74; Galor, "Roman-Byzantine Dwelling," 114–16; Galor, "Domestic Architecture," 420–39; Richard Saller, "Poverty, Honor, and Obligation in Imperial Rome," *Criterion* 37 (1998): 19. As already noted earlier, it is difficult to distinguish exterior walls from interior dividers. Adding to the complexity is that domestic architecture developed organically and haphazardly, as units were subdivided or expanded over time. The initial layout of doorways and dividers, as well as floor levels, often changed, as did the functions of the room and the structure as a whole; see Galor, "Roman-Byzantine Dwelling," 110–11; Richardson, "Towards a Typology of Levantine/Palestinian Houses," 48. Further compounding the problem is that most archaeological remains are only partially preserved, excavated, or both. This makes dwellings resistant to classification and also introduces the possibility that a structure could house a single wealthy family in one era and multiple poor families in the next; see Cynthia M. Baker, *Rebuilding the House of Israel: Architectures of Gender in Jewish Antiquity* (Stanford, Calif.: Stanford University Press, 2002), 36–37; Galor, "Roman-Byzantine Dwelling," 110, 114.

[74] Baker, *Rebuilding the House of Israel*, 42–47.

[75] This was exacerbated if the area was unsafe and the owner had to bring his domestic animals inside at night; see Schwartz, "Material Realities," 436.

and other social activities.[76] The floors themselves were indicators of one's socioeconomic standing. While those of the wealthy were paved with hewn or polished stones, or even colorful mosaics, modest dwellings had floors made of compacted earth.[77] Likewise, the poor lacked proper bedding and would have slept on the floor or on simple mats, which provided minimal protection against the rough, cold, and damp ground.[78]

All dwellings in antiquity were dimly lit by modern standards, though those of the poor were especially dark. During the day, natural lighting was restricted to doorways and windows; the latter were often located only on the upper story for security.[79] After sunset, oil lamps were the most common source of artificial lighting. In well-off households, lamps were placed around the room with care to maximize illumination as well as a form of decoration that expressed one's personal tastes.[80] The best lamps, however, were those made of expensive materials, such as bronze and glass, and even ceramic lamps were considered fine ware. Most significantly, lamps burned olive oil. Lighting a lamp was akin to burning food, as sustenance was sacrificed for illumination – a trade off that would have been difficult for the poor to make.[81]

Joshua Schwartz aptly describes residential life in late-antique Palestine as "bleak" by modern western standards.[82] All the more so, I would say, for the poor. The homes that the poor could afford were small, unadorned, crowded, dark, and cold. Such conditions were not only physically uncomfortable, but also limited social activities and fostered exclusion. To be sure, many individuals lacked housing altogether, though it is impossible to know how many. They lacked shelter and protection for themselves, their households, and their possessions, and they suffered from the stigma of homelessness.[83]

---

[76] Schwartz, "Material Realities," 438.
[77] Katharina Galor, "Domestic Architecture in Roman and Byzantine Galilee and Golan," *NEA* 66 (2003): 54; Galor, "Domestic Architecture," 420–39.
[78] Cam Grey and Anneliese Parkin, "Controlling the Urban Mob: *The colonatus perpetuus of CTh* 14.18.1," *Phoenix* 57 (2003): 287; Schwartz, "Reduce, Reuse and Recycle," 154–55; Schwartz, "Material Realities," 437–38.
[79] Galor, "Domestic Architecture (NEA)," 53; Goodman, *State and Society*, 31.
[80] Unlike today, artificial lighting in antiquity did not blanket an entire room. Rather, the best that one could do is to provide spot lighting to illuminate various areas of the room. The placement of lamps became a form of expression and decoration; see Simon Ellis, "Shedding Light on Late Roman Housing," in *Housing in Late Antiquity: From Palaces to Shops* (ed. L. Lavan et al.; Late Antique Archaeology 3.2; Leiden and Boston: Brill, 2007), 283–302.
[81] Frankel, *Wine and Oil Production*, 44.
[82] Schwartz, "Material Realities," 439.
[83] E.g., Philo (*Embassy* 123) mentions formerly wealthy individuals who became impoverished and compelled to dwell in the open air, endangering them to death by exposure to the sun during the day and the cold at night.

Richard Saller's remarks on Rome are likewise apt for Roman Palestine: "A man's house was a central symbol of status: in Rome the hundreds of the wealthiest had their grand *domus*... while the hundreds of thousands of poor passed a squalid existence in single dark rooms... in apartment buildings."[84]

TWO POVERTIES

Poverty in ancient Palestine was defined by a failure to meet two different thresholds. Useful in this regard is the typology of poverty set out by economist Amartya Sen in his *Poverty and Famines* (1982).[85] The first type of poverty that I have identified in Roman Palestine can be classified as Sen's "biological" approach, whereby the poor are those who are unable to obtain the minimum provisions needed to maintain physical efficiency.[86] They live below subsistence levels, in want of the basics needed to survive. If one did not have enough food to eat, lacked clothing for protection from the elements, or was without shelter, he or she would fall into this category. "The necessities of life," Ben Sira writes, "are water, bread, and clothing, and also a house to assure privacy."[87] Those who lacked these items lived in absolute destitution and were in constant danger of death.

Biological poverty was an acute problem in the ancient world, as large swaths of the inhabitants of the Roman Empire lived at or near the subsistence level, with barely enough to stay alive. It is conspicuous, then, that Hellenistic and Roman societies offered few systematic solutions to poverty. There were no Poor Laws, there was no social welfare, no safety net that would catch individuals before they fell into danger. There was no permanent, reliable way for indigents to obtain necessities. Concern for the poor was itself in poverty, as it was common for emperors, notables, and those at middling levels to ignore the poor at best and despise them at worst. The rabbis were acutely aware of humanity's basic needs and, as we will see, the *tamhui* provides subsistence in ways that allow the poor to avoid the shame of begging.

The second type of poverty can be classified as Sen's "value-judgment" approach, which is a failure to meet thresholds established by social

---

[84] Saller, "Poverty, Honor," 19.
[85] Sen, *Poverty and Famines*, which has been applied to antiquity by Garnsey, *Food and Society*, 5, 42; Walter Scheidel, "Stratification, Deprivation and Quality of Life," in *Poverty in the Roman World* (ed. M. Atkins and R. Osborne; Cambridge and New York: Cambridge University Press, 2006), 40–59.
[86] Sen, *Poverty and Famines*, 11–14.
[87] Sir 29:21. See also 1 Tim 6:8: "but if we have food and clothing, we will be content with these."

conventions.[88] A useful, illustrative example of this type of poverty can be found in Adam Smith's classic *Wealth of Nations*:[89]

> By necessaries we understand not only the commodities which are indispensably necessary for the support of life, but whatever the custom of the country renders it indecent for creditable people, even the lowest order, to be without. A linen shirt, for example, is, strictly speaking, not a necessary of life. The Greeks and Romans lived, we suppose, very comfortably though they had no linen. But in the present times, through the greater part of Europe, a creditable day-labourer would be ashamed to appear in public without a linen shirt, the want of which would be supposed to denote that disgraceful degree of poverty which, it is presumed, nobody can well fall into without extreme bad conduct. Custom, in the same manner, has rendered leather shoes a necessary of life in England. The poorest creditable person of either sex would be ashamed to appear in public without them.[90]

Those who lack leather shoes are not necessarily impoverished from a physiological standpoint. Rather, they are poor because they do not meet thresholds that are defined by conventions specific to the English society in which they live.[91]

Returning to ancient Palestine, those who were poor according to the value-judgment approach had the means to subsist, yet were considered poor because of the way that they subsisted. A man who ate barley bread, certain types of legumes, or other foods was considered poor, even if he consumed sufficient calories and nutrients to stay alive. One who wore clothes that were undecorated, gray in color, or made of a patchwork of tattered rags was considered to be poor, even if these garments provided sufficient protection from the elements. If he had a roof over his head, but his dwelling was small, dark, or unadorned; he ate or slept on the floor; or he had little or no privacy, then a man was surely considered to be poor. One who lived below what was considered to be acceptable social conventions was identified by others as poor, resulting in shame and a loss of dignity.

Because poverty was defined by the clothes that one wore and the foods that one ate, semiotics plays a central role in the value-judgment approach to poverty. Helpful in this regard is the work of anthropologists who have

---

[88] Scheidel, "Stratification, Deprivation," 57; Sen, *Poverty and Famines*, 17–19.
[89] See the treatments in Sen, *Poverty and Famines*, 18; Scheidel, "Stratification, Deprivation," 57–58.
[90] Adam Smith, *An Inquiry into the Nature and Causes of the Wealth of Nations* (Chicago, Ill.: University of Chicago Press, 1776 [repr. 1976]), 399–400.
[91] Sen, *Poverty and Famines*, 17–19.

observed that food serves both "food and non-food" uses. Claude Levi-Strauss, for example, understands food to be a kind of language or code, whose elucidation reveals the deep structures of a society.[92] Similarly, Roland Barthes writes, "For what is food? It is not only a collection of products that can be used for statistical or nutritional studies. It is also, and at the same time, a system of communication, a body of images, a protocol of usages, situations, and behavior... it signifies."[93] Likewise, Mary Douglas writes, "If food is treated as a code, the messages it encodes will be found in the pattern of social relations being expressed. The message is about different degrees of hierarchy, inclusion and exclusion, boundaries and transactions across the boundaries... the taking of food has a social component, as well as a biological one."[94]

For the Roman world, Peter Garnsey writes that a language of foods developed that indexed and communicated differences in social class and status.[95] As I discussed earlier, the same can be said about clothing and shelter. Indeed, the peoples of the ancient Mediterranean shared in what Webb Keane terms a "semiotic ideology," defined as the "basic assumptions about what signs are and how they function in the world."[96] Applying Keane's work to late antiquity, Ra'anan Boustan finds that the "various religious communities that made up the world of late antiquity constituted a broad 'semiotic community' that enabled mutual intelligibility across specific boundaries of creed and ritual practice."[97]

As we will see throughout the following chapters of this book, the Tannaim participated in the Mediterranean semiotic community. Tannaitic compilations demonstrate a thorough understanding of how material culture produces and broadcasts one's social status. For example, we see repeatedly in rabbinic texts an association between meat and wealth, on the one hand, and legumes and poverty on the other. Likewise, the rabbis instruct their students on what they should eat, how to dress, and the type of housing in which to live.[98] Semiotics would play an important role in the Tannaim's discourse

---

[92] Claude Levi-Strauss, "The Culinary Triangle," *Partisan Review* 33 (1966): 595.
[93] Barthes, "Toward a Psychosociology of Contemporary Food Consumption," 167–68.
[94] Mary Douglas, "Deciphering a Meal," *Daedalus* 101 (1972): 61.
[95] Garnsey, *Food and Society*, 5–7, 113–27.
[96] Webb Keane, "Semiotics and the Social Analysis of Material Things," *Language & Communication* 23 (2003): 410, as cited in Ra'anan S. Boustan, "Jewish Veneration of the 'Special Dead' in Late Antiquity and Beyond," in *Saints and Sacred Matter: The Cult of Relics in Byzantium and Beyond* (ed. C. Hahn and H. Klein; Washington, D.C.: Dumbarton Oaks Papers, forthcoming). I thank the author for sharing his forthcoming paper with me.
[97] Boustan, "Jewish Veneration."
[98] I discuss further the semiotic values of legumes, meat, and clothing in Chapters 4 and 5. On housing in rabbinic literature, see Alan Webber, "Building Regulation in the Land of Israel in the Talmudic Period," *JSJ* 27 (1996): 263–88; Alan Webber, "A Consideration of the

on organized charity, as they envision the *quppa* as way to elevate the social standing of the poor by providing them with alms that are defined by the status that they signify.

URBANIZATION AND URBAN LIFE

Urbanization and urban living were also important aspects of socioeconomic life in Roman Palestine that will help us better understand poverty and early rabbinic approaches to charity. While ancient Palestine has been dotted with urban centers from (seemingly) time immemorial, urbanization significantly increased in the wake of Alexander the Great's conquest of the Near East in 332 B.C.E.[99] New cities were founded and existing settlements were expanded, as they became important centers of Greek culture.[100] The subsequent wave of urbanization was initiated by Herod the Great (37–4 B.C.E.) and continued by his sons. Of particular note, Herod Antipas transformed the Galilee by founding Tiberias in 20 C.E. and expanding Sepphoris, both of which would later become important centers to the rabbinic movement.[101] Another wave of urbanization followed the end of the first Jewish revolt in 70 C.E., as the Flavians established military colonies in strategic locations as part of an effort to integrate Palestine into the eastern Roman Empire.[102] Urbanization reached its peak in the second century under Hadrian and the Severans, as urban life and culture became essential and unavoidable aspects of the socioeconomic fabric of Roman Palestine; this would have important implications for both the poor and the Tannaim.[103]

Dimensions of Walls Contained in Mishnah Bava Batra 1:1," *JSJ* 39 (1998): 92–100. Wearing certain clothes and eating special foods were highly visible acts that could be readily emulated. Thus, I suggest that these instructions can be understood within the framework of what Martin S. Jaffee, "A Rabbinic Ontology of the Written and Spoken Word: On Discipleship, Transformative Knowledge, and the Living Texts of Oral Torah," *JAAR* 65 (1997): 525–49, calls "transformative knowledge" whereby rabbinic disciples are trained to reconceive their own human perfection through the emulation of their masters.

[99] In this section, "urbanization" and "urban centers" refer to all cities and large towns, regardless of whether they had the official designation of *polis*. Scholars have demonstrated that the cultural differences between city and town were not as readily apparent as the legal distinctions might suggest; see Jürgen K. Zangenberg and Dianne van de Zande, "Urbanization," in *The Oxford Handbook of Jewish Daily Life in Roman Palestine* (ed. C. Hezser; Oxford: Oxford University Press, 2010), 180.

[100] Such as Greek language, customs, education, institutions; festivals, etc.; see Zangenberg and van de Zande, "Urbanization," 166–68.

[101] M. H. Jensen, *Herod Antipas in Galilee: The Literary and Archaeological Sources on the Reign of Herod Antipas and Its Socio-Economic Impact on Galilee* (Tübingen: Mohr Siebeck, 2006), 126–86; Zangenberg and van de Zande, "Urbanization," 175.

[102] Zangenberg and van de Zande, "Urbanization," 176–77.

[103] At least until the Byzantine age; see Benjamin Isaac, *The Limits of Empire: The Roman Army in the East (Revised Edition)* (Oxford: Clarendon Press, 1992), 352–61; Zangenberg and van de

Urban layout and civic architecture played important roles in the lives of the poor. The homeless, for example, could take shelter in the gaps between the columns of porticoes and in shanty towns built up or on top of permanent structures such as workshops or public buildings.[104] Marketplaces, the hearts of Greek, Hellenistic, and Roman cities, were central locations for communication, display, and commerce. They were places in which the poor could locate and approach well-off individuals and solicit them for alms. Begging in public locations brought the poor out of the shadows, ensuring that even the elites were aware of their existence but also laying bare the shame of their poverty.[105] Urban life also included *euergetism*. As discussed earlier, in times of famine a benefactor would be called upon to sustain the population. As this was provided to rich and poor alike, the poor would have been fed as well as others among the general populace – at least until the famine passed.

The administration of Roman cities also played an important role in urban settlements. Public life and public order were overseen by a number of civic officials, usually drawn from the upper classes. These officials oversaw commercial activities, served as judges, collected taxes, kept birth records, and performed a number of other essential services. Their presence would have been readily apparent to the residents; indeed rabbinic texts include numerous references to the *agoranomos*, who would police the markets.[106] As I will show later, Greco-Roman civic officials would provide important models for the rabbinic instructions on how charity supervisors should carry out their duties.

Increased urbanization also meant an increase in the population density. As I discussed earlier, archaeological remains of domestic structures can be interpreted as either single-family dwellings with rooms surrounding a private

---

Zande, "Urbanization," 176–77. Benjamin Isaac, "Roman Administration and Urbanization," in *Greece and Rome in Eretz Israel: Collected Essays* (ed. A. Kasher et al.; Jerusalem: Yad Izhak Ben-Zvi, 1990), 158–59, argues that the expansion of existing cities was a product of local policies and endeavors – not the product of an imperial policy. Cf. A. H. M. Jones, "The Urbanization of Palestine," *JRS* 21 (1931): 78–85, who views the urbanization of Palestine as an imperial policy.

[104] Daniel Caner, *Wandering, Begging Monks: Spiritual Authority and the Promotion of Monasticism in Late Antiquity* (Berkeley: University of California Press, 2002), 57–65; Goodman, *State and Society*, 39; Grey and Parkin, "Controlling the Urban Mob," 287.

[105] On the urban layout, see Arthur Segal, *From Function to Monument: Urban landscapes of Roman Palestine, Syria, and Provincia Arabia* (Oxford and Oakville, Conn.: Oxbow Books, 1997), 5–81; Zangenberg and van de Zande, "Urbanization," 169–70.

[106] On the *agoranomos* in ancient Palestine, see Gardner, "Jewish Leadership," 330–32; for references to rabbinic texts, see Daniel Sperber, *The City in Roman Palestine* (New York: Oxford University Press, 1998), 32–47.

courtyard or individual family apartments that share a common courtyard. In either case, what is striking is the proximity of domestic units and the fact that they were rarely closed off with rigid boundaries – allowing for fluidity and sociality between dwellings.[107] The rich, well-off, and poor were living cheek-by-jowl, as encounters between the poor and non-poor must have been regular. The deleterious effect of urban poverty on the non-poor is noted succinctly by the economist Alfred Marshall, "the conditions which surround extreme poverty, especially in densely crowded places, tend to deaden the higher faculties."[108] Marshall's observation on the arresting visibility of poverty in urban settings was no less true in the ancient world. C. R. Whittaker writes of ancient Rome, "It is the urban poor and the conditions of urban living, which always attract the attention of writers and the fears of the rich."[109] These problems were prominent in the towns of Roman Palestine as well, where rich and poor lived in close proximity, as attested by archaeological remains of domestic dwellings from the Galilee in the Roman era.[110] This, in turn, would impact early rabbinic literature.

The Tannaim were active in the major cities and towns of northern Palestine, as elements of urban life penetrated the rabbis' thoughts and find expression in their writings.[111] Life in Roman cities presented certain challenges to rabbinic ideals and generated creative solutions. The Tannaim had to formulate ways to cope with Hellenistic and Roman market days, which often coincided with pagan festivals. They also coped with bathing culture and the general "sculptural environment" of Greco-Roman cities – which posed challenges

[107] Baker, *Rebuilding the House of Israel*, 35–42; Galor, "Roman-Byzantine Dwelling," 114–15; Richardson, "Towards a Typology of Levantine/Palestinian Houses," 47–49. The notion of shared, domestic spaces is presupposed in a number of rabbinic discussions – from interaction with Gentiles to legal discourses on the rights of joint-holders; see Baker, *Rebuilding the House of Israel*, 37.
[108] Alfred Marshall, *Principles of Economics* (London: Macmillan, 1961), 2, and the evaluation by William T. Ganley, "Poverty and Charity: Early Analytical Conflicts between Institutional Economics and Neoclassicism," *Journal of Economic Issues* 32 (1998): 433–40.
[109] Whittaker, "Poor," 8.
[110] Baker, *Rebuilding the House of Israel*, Galor, "Roman-Byzantine Dwelling," 109–24; Galor, "Domestic Architecture," 420–39; Hirschfeld, *Palestinian Dwelling*.
[111] Hayim Lapin, *Early Rabbinic Civil Law and the Social History of Roman Galilee: A Study of Mishnah Tractate Baba' Mesi'a'* (Atlanta, Ga.: Scholars Press, 1995), 233–34; Hayim Lapin, "Rabbis and Cities in Later Roman Palestine: The Literary Evidence," *JJS* 1 (1999): 187–207; Hayim Lapin, "Rabbis and Cities: Some Aspects of the Rabbinic Movement in its Graeco-Roman Environment," in *The Talmud Yerushalmi and Graeco-Roman Culture II* (ed. P. Schäfer and C. Hezser; TSAJ 79; Tübingen: Mohr Siebeck, 2000), 51–80. For the rabbinic movement in the cities of northern Palestine in the Amoraic period, see Stuart S. Miller, *Sages and Commoners in Late Antique 'Erez Israel: A Philological Inquiry into Local Traditions in Talmud Yerushalmi* (Tübingen: Mohr Siebeck, 2006).

to the prohibition of idolatry.[112] In order to coexist, the rabbis deliberately misinterpreted pagan culture, what Seth Schwartz calls "misprision," whereby the rabbis defined pagan religiosity as consisting exclusively of cultic activity. Thus, activity that was noncultic – however religious it was – was deemed acceptable aspects of urban culture. This enabled the rabbis to live and work in cities, which were best suited to meet their goal of promoting their socioreligious influence.[113] Indeed, as Lapin has shown for early rabbinic texts, the rabbis were deeply entrenched in cities and urban life played an important role in rabbinic law.[114]

Likewise, I find that urban culture shaped rabbinic views of the poor and charity.[115] The semiotics of poverty were more readily apparent in urban locations, where rich and poor lived so close together. This may be reflected in early rabbinic traditions on face-to-face encounters with the poor.[116] The urbanization of Palestine during the Roman era may have constituted the broad, socioeconomic undercurrent that contextualizes rabbinic approaches to poverty and poverty relief.

CONCLUSION

Poverty was defined in two ways in Roman Palestine, by approaches that were biological and value-judgment in nature. Both of these approaches are reflected in Tannaitic compilations and they played important roles in the rabbis' approach to organized charity. The *tamhui* aims to provide the poor with the basic, physiological necessities. The *quppa*, by contrast, is concerned with semiotic poverty and its social ramifications, as it aims to restore the poor to their previous standing in society by providing them with the objects (and the status that they projected) that they had lost. The *tamhui* saves the poor from biological death, while the *quppa* saves the poor from a social death. The Tannaim, moreover, envision that these alms would be provided in ways that forestall begging and the humiliation that it carries.

---

[112] Yaron Z. Eliav, "Viewing the Sculptural Environment: Shaping the Second Commandment," in *The Talmud Yerushalmi and Graeco-Roman Culture* (ed. P. Schäfer; Tübingen: Mohr Siebeck, 1998–2002), 411–33; Zangenberg and van de Zande, "Urbanization," 181.
[113] Schwartz, *Imperialism and Jewish Society*, 164
[114] Lapin, *Early Rabbinic Civil Law*, 238–39; Lapin, "Rabbis and Cities in Later Roman Palestine," 187–207; Lapin, "Rabbis and Cities: Some Aspects," 51–80.
[115] These complemented modes of poor relief that presupposed agricultural settings, such as the laws of *pe'ah*, gleanings, etc. in *m. Pe'ah* and *t. Pe'ah* 1:1–4:7.
[116] E.g., *m. Shabbat* 1:1.

3

From Vessels to Institutions

INTRODUCTION

The study of organized charity in Judaism is inextricably intertwined with the study of material culture. Poverty in Roman Palestine was defined in material terms, the poor are identified by the fabric and condition of their possessions, and the rabbis define charity as money or material support for the poor. The *tamhui* and *quppa* both began their careers, so to speak, as mere household vessels – the *tamhui* was a dish, usually made of earthenware, while the *quppa* was a wicker basket. The multiple meanings of *tamhui* and *quppa* as both vessels and institutions have strongly influenced scholarship on the origins of organized charity. A typical line of reconstruction is that the *tamhui* and *quppa* happened to be the containers used for collecting and distributing alms and that they simply *became* institutions.[1] This genealogy presents the transition of ceramic dishes and wicker baskets into sophisticated institutions of beneficence as simplistic and inevitable processes. It fails to account for the fact that the majority of uses of the *tamhui* and *quppa* in early rabbinic sources had nothing to do with the poor or charity; they are merely employed as containers. Such scholarship oversimplifies what it means to be an institution and the process of institutionalization. It presupposes that the laws pertaining to charitable collections and distributions simply *existed* and that these vessels happened to be the means to carry them out. Above all, the existing body of scholarship has failed to account for institutions as complex social, economic, and legal entities, and institutionalization as a complex process. Surely, not every cup, bowl, or jar laying around one's house in Roman Palestine evolved into an economic and legal entity. In fact, only two did, and this chapter aims

---

[1] E.g., Frisch, *Historical Survey*, 50; Hellinger, "Charity in Talmudic," 198–214; Moore, *Judaism in the First Centuries*, 2:176; Sorek, *Remembered for Good*, 216–17.

to explore how and why this happened. The previously discussed question of the reality behind these institutions is pertinent. Are the rabbis responsible for transforming these vessels into institutions or do rabbinic texts reflect extrarabbinic processes, albeit in a distinctly rabbinic and rabbinized way? Because there are no extrarabbinic sources on the *tamhui* and *quppa qua* institutions, we are left to examine the vessels' transformations as they are depicted in rabbinic sources. Whether this is a rabbinic invention or an invention rabbinized, the result is the same – what we have are laws that define institutions in a way that reflects rabbinic concerns, objectives, and ideals.

In this chapter, I take a closer look at the transformation of the *tamhui* from a dish into a soup kitchen and the *quppa* from a basket into a charity fund. I aim to account for how these entities were transformed from concrete objects for domestic use into laws and norms of social and economic behavior – that is, institutions. This chapter devotes special attention the material attributes and functions of these vessels within rabbinic discourse. Extrarabbinic sources on these vessels, including archaeological finds, are also brought into the conversation to add texture and context to the materiality of these items. I find that the *tamhui* and *quppa* held certain properties that made them unique and attractive choices to be the concrete manifestations of charitable institutions. Their names, how they were made, and their semiotic properties help us understand why these vessels – as opposed to the hundreds of others that were used in Roman Palestine – would embody ideals about communal obligations and poverty relief.

VESSELS AND INSTITUTIONS

In 1960–1961, during two seasons of excavations in caves in the Judean desert, Israeli archaeologist Yigael Yadin discovered a number of extraordinary artifacts.[2] Excavating the caves of Nahal Hever, which were located on a cliff face and could only be reached by rope ladder, was challenging but rewarding. The first season produced a number of artifacts dating to the

---

[2] The finds from the excavations have been published in Yadin, *Finds from the Bar Kokhba Period*; Naphtali Lewis et al., *The Documents from the Bar Kokhba Period in the Cave of Letters* (Jerusalem: Israel Exploration Society, 1989); Yigael Yadin et al., *The Documents from the Bar Kokhba Period in the Cave of Letters: Hebrew, Aramaic and Nabatean-Aramaic Papyri* (Jerusalem: Israel Exploration Society, Hebrew University of Jerusalem, and Shrine of the Book, 2002). See the overviews in Yohanan Aharoni et al., "Judean Desert Caves: The Historical Periods," *The New Encyclopedia of Archaeological Excavations in the Holy Land*: 3:821; Hannah Cotton and Hanan Eshel, "Hever, Nahal," *Encyclopedia of the Dead Sea Scrolls*: 1:357–61.

second century C.E., including a leather flask that held papyri letters from Shimon bar Kochva, the leader of the second Jewish revolt against Rome. Returning to the so-called Cave of Letters for a second season, the excavators uncovered pottery, utensils made of glass and bronze, coins, and, perhaps most significantly, another cache of documents belonging to an otherwise-unknown woman named Babatha. The documents, as well as some of the other more spectacular finds such as incense shovels and coins, have been the subjects of extensive scholarship, which has produced fresh insight into daily life during the period.[3] Of particular interest for understanding institutionalized charity are the seemingly mundane wicker baskets in which many of these items were found.[4]

Very few baskets from ancient Palestine have been uncovered in archaeological excavations, as items made from organic materials such as palm fronds, straw, and reeds usually perish. The caves of the Judean desert, however, sheltered these baskets from the elements over the millennia in much the same way that they protected and preserved the Dead Sea Scrolls.[5] While some of the specimens were only fragmentary, the cave preserved others so well that they could be mistaken for baskets made today.[6] Some baskets held letters and others contained valuable bronze vessels. Those found in burial niches contained human remains as they were perhaps pressed into service as makeshift ossuaries, receptacles for human remains that were otherwise made of limestone.[7] Yadin, based on comparisons of the finds with early rabbinic texts, identifies this type of basket as the *quppa* (pl. *quppot*) that is mentioned throughout rabbinic literature.[8]

---

[3] See the references in Catherine Hezser, ed., *The Oxford Handbook of Jewish Daily Life in Roman Palestine* (Oxford: Oxford University Press, 2010); Schwartz, "Material Realities," 431–56.
[4] Yadin, *Finds from the Bar Kokhba Period*, 136–56 plates 43–49.
[5] Other evidence from this era includes the depiction of a wicker basket with a handle that is full of figs on ceramic oil lamps from the late first to second centuries C.E. Similar motifs are known from ossuaries from Jerusalem, on Judean coins, and in a graffito at Masada; see Varda Sussman, *Ornamented Jewish Oil-Lamps: From the Destruction of the Second Temple through the Bar-Kokhba Revolt* (Warminster and Jerusalem: Aris & Phillips and the Israel Exploration Society, 1982), 39. A miniature gold basket attached to a necklace (second–third century C.E.) and worn as jewelry was uncovered from a sarcophagus in Jerusalem; see A. De Ridder, "Parure de Jérusalem au Musée du Louvre," *Syria* 1 (1920): 102–03; Galor, "Jewelry," 396. Earlier examples of basketry, from Palestine in the Chalcolithic era, were uncovered at the "Cave of the Treasure" in the Judean desert. At Jericho, Megiddo, and other sites, archaeologists found impressions of basketry pressed into the bases of pottery vessels while the clay was still wet; see Pessah Bar-Adon, *The Cave of the Treasure: The Finds from the Caves in Nahal Mishmar* (Jerusalem: Israel Exploration Society, 1980), 190–97.
[6] See especially Yadin, *Finds from the Bar Kokhba Period*, 143 nos. 3–4, plates 43–44.
[7] Yadin, *Finds from the Bar Kokhba Period*, 136.
[8] Yadin, *Finds from the Bar Kokhba Period*, 140–41.

Nearly half a century earlier, a *quppa* of an entirely different sort had been uncovered in excavations at Arbel, located just east of the Sea of Galilee.[9] Following earlier American and British surveys of the ruins of an ancient synagogue, in 1905 German archaeologists Heinrich Kohl and Carl Watzinger came upon an unusual find.[10] In the northeast corner of the wall of the synagogue, probably constructed in the fourth century, they discovered an installation that they initially described as a kind of closet. It consisted of a rectangular limestone chest (1.48 m wide, 1.35 m high, and 1.1 m deep) standing upright, with a door attached on one side by a hinge. The installation's orientation and construction allowed its contents to be accessed from outside the synagogue itself, perhaps allowing items to be placed inside and retrieved anonymously.[11] Scholars have identified this receptacle as a box for collecting, holding, and distributing charity, which is termed *quppa* in rabbinic literature.[12] Hoards of coins found underneath the floors of ancient synagogues (from the fourth century onwards) have also been identified by scholars as evidence of *quppot*.[13] At the sixth-century synagogue at Bet Alpha, for example, Eleazar Sukenik found a small cavity in the floor, about 80 cm deep, one meter long, and 80 cm wide. Its interior was plastered to prevent small items from falling through and it was covered with flagstones. Inside were thirty-six bronze coins dating to the Byzantine era.[14] A *quppa* has also

---

[9] Zvi Ilan, *Ancient Synagogues in Israel [Hebrew]* (Tel-Aviv: Ministry of Defence Israel, 1991), 116–17; Zvi Ilan and Avraham Izdarechet, "Arbel," *The New Encyclopedia of Archaeological Excavations in the Holy Land*: 1:87–89, 5:2087.

[10] Ilan and Izdarechet, "Arbel," 1:88–89; Heinrich Kohl and Carl Watzinger, *Antike Synagogen in Galilaea* (Osnabrück: O. Zeller, 1916 [repr. 1975]), 59–70.

[11] Z. Ilan and A. Izdarechet, "Arbel – An Ancient Town in the Eastern Lower Galilee [Hebrew]," *Qadmoniot* 22 (1989): 115; Ilan and Izdarechet, "Arbel," 1:88; Kohl and Watzinger, *Antike Synagogen in Galilaea*, 62.

[12] Ilan and Izdarechet, "Arbel – An Ancient Town," 115; Ilan, *Ancient Synagogues in Israel*, 117; Ilan and Izdarechet, "Arbel," 1:88; Levine, *Ancient Synagogue*, 283.

[13] Examples include the synagogues at Bet Alpha, Hammat Tiberias, and Meroth; see M. Dothan, *Hammath Tiberias* (Jerusalem: Israel Exploration Society, 1983), 1:31; Hamel, "Poverty and Charity," 320–21; Arie Kindler, "Donations and Taxes in the Society of the Jewish Villages in Eretz Israel During the 3rd to 6th Centuries CE," in *Ancient Synagogues in Israel: Third-Seventh Century C.E.: Proceedings of Symposium, University of Hafia (i.e., Haifa), May 1987* (ed. R. Hachlili; BAR International Series 499; Oxford, England: British Archaeological Reports, 1989), 55–59; Levine, *Ancient Synagogue*, 397; Emil Schürer et al., *The History of the Jewish People in the Age of Jesus Christ (175 B.C. – A.D. 135)* (3 vols.; Edinburgh: Clark, 1973–1987), 2: 72n. 241, 2:437; Eleazar Lipa Sukenik, *The Ancient Synagogue of Beth Alpha: An Account of the Excavations Conducted on Behalf of the Hebrew University, Jerusalem* (Piscataway, N.J.: Gorgias Press, 1932 [repr. 2003]), 13.

[14] M. Narkis, "The Snuff-Shovel as a Jewish Symbol," *JPOS* 15 (1935): 25 suggests that this was a container for alms, while Sukenik, *Ancient Synagogue of Beth Alpha*, 13, interprets it as a treasury for storing funds to finance repairs for the synagogue.

been identified by some at the synagogue complex at Meroth, where archaeologists uncovered a storeroom that contained nearly five hundred coins.[15] Yet another *quppa*, some suggest, is depicted in the mosaic pavement of the synagogues at Bet Alpha and Gerasa.[16] To be sure, we cannot be certain of the identities of any of these finds. What they illustrate, however, is that an installation built into a synagogue wall, a storage room, a treasury of coins hidden under a floor, and a box depicted in a mosaic floor *could* all plausibly be identified as *quppot*. Yet none of them are wicker baskets.

The word *quppa* can denote two very different things in early rabbinic literature. On the one hand, it was a simple wicker basket that was common to most households, like those found in the Judean desert. On the other hand, it could be an institution of beneficence, a charity fund for the poor, which could take any number of material forms. This fund is overseen by a team of charity supervisors – specially appointed individuals or administrators who supervise the collection of provisions from the community and their distribution to the poor. The charity fund also had a companion. The *tamhui* (pl. *tamhuyim*) was both a tangible vessel and a less tangible institution. In early rabbinic sources, the term *tamhui* predominantly marked a common household ware, a bowl or dish that was usually made of clay. In a handful of sources, however, *tamhui* denotes an organization of beneficence that provides immediate sustenance to all those in need – a "soup kitchen." Together, the soup kitchen and the charity fund embody the ideals that supporting the poor should be an organized effort and a communal responsibility.

TAMHUI: FROM DISH TO SOUP KITCHEN

In most early rabbinic texts, the *tamhui* had no particular association with the poor or charity. Rather, more often than not, it is nothing more than a household vessel – a dish. The *tamhui* is mentioned in discussions on purity, particularly how and when certain vessels can transmit impurities, as well as in instructions on preparing and serving food on the Sabbath. In these contexts, the *tamhui* is mentioned alongside other culinary utensils including a kettle for heating water and a cup for allowing it to cool. Likewise, the rabbis discuss how a wide-mouth pan and a cooking pot are used to prepare

---

[15] Ilan and Izdarechet, "Arbel – An Ancient Town," 115; Zvi Ilan, "Meroth," *The New Encyclopedia of Archaeological Excavations in the Holy Land*: 1:87–89.

[16] This is proposed by S. Klein and dismissed in Narkis, "Snuff-Shovel as a Jewish Symbol," 25; Sukenik, *Ancient Synagogue of Beth Alpha*, 32n. 3; E. L. Sukenik, "Designs of the Lectern in Ancient Synagogues in Palestine," *JPOS* 13 (1933): 224, though their reasons are not altogether convincing.

the food, after which the food is transferred to a *qe'arah* (a type of bowl) and a *tamhui*, from which it is eaten.[17] In terms of its shape, the *tamhui* was an open vessel with concave sides, similar to the *qe'arah* but larger.[18] Some *tamhuyim* are said to have had internal partitions, dividing the vessel into a number of compartments, an example of which was uncovered in the excavations of the Jewish Quarter of Jerusalem.[19] It is notable that this find was made of stone, which is impervious to impurities – resonating with the aforementioned rabbinic discussions that link the *tamhui* with purity laws.[20] The partitions allowed the user to separate different foods or portions for different individuals. Form was the defining characteristic of a *tamhui*, as it could be made from any number of materials, including wood, stone, glass, bronze, and silver, though the vast majority of *tamhuyim* were ceramic.[21]

The shape and size of the *tamhui* made it useful to perform a number of functions. The *tamhui* was used for washing in discourses on ritual baths and elsewhere holds sacrifices for priests to eat.[22] Primarily, however, the *tamhui* is a serving dish, a receptacle for food that is ready to eat, as opposed to a storage or cooking vessel.[23] Because it was so large, the *tamhui* could hold enough food for several individuals and the rabbis talk about passing it around the table. For example, in a Tannaitic discussion on vows the rabbis explore a scenario in which one individual is bound by vow not to benefit at the expense of another. If and when the two parties eat together, the former can only take food from the latter's *tamhui* if the dish is first passed around to someone else at the table. This ensures that the vow-bound individual does not benefit

---

[17] *t. Kelim Bava Batra* 7:10; *t. Mikwa'ot* 6:15, 16; *m. Shabbat* 3:5. Other vessels found alongside the *tamhui* include a pan (*m. Ma'aserot* 1:7; *t. Ma'aserot* 1:7) and *unfil* (*t. Kelim Bava Metzi'a* 5:10), a wooden vessel for collecting refuse; see Yehoshua Brand, *Ceramics in Talmudic Literature [Hebrew]* (Jerusalem: Mosad ha-Rav Kuk, 1953), 539; Marcus Jastrow, *A Dictionary of the Targumim, the Talmud Babli and Yerushalmi, and the Midrashic Literature with an Index of Scriptural Quotations* (London and New York: Luzac & Co. and G. P. Putnams Sons, 1903), 29. On these vessels, see further Adan-Bayewitz, *Common Pottery*; Schwartz, "Material Realities," 439–41.

[18] *m. Kelim* 17:2; *m. Nedarim* 4:4; Brand, *Ceramics*, 541–42.

[19] *m. Kelim* 16:1; Nahman Avigad, *Discovering Jerusalem* (Nashville: Thomas Nelson, 1983), 176, 181 no. 208; Brand, *Ceramics*, 541–42.

[20] On stone vessels and their relationship to purity laws, see Magness, *Stone and Dung, Oil and Spit*.

[21] *m. Kelim* 16:1, 30:2; Brand, *Ceramics*, 540–41; Uzah Zevulon and Yael Olenik, *Function and Design in the Talmudic Period [Hebrew]* (Tel-Aviv: Haaretz Museum, 1978), 24.

[22] *t. Hagigah* 3:4; *m. Keritot* 3:9; Brand, *Ceramics*, 540. On the characterization of the priests in early rabbinic literature, see Peter Schäfer, "Rabbis and Priests, or: How to Do Away with the Glorious Past of the Sons of Aaron," in *Antiquity in Antiquity: Jewish and Christian Pasts in the Greco-Roman World* (ed. G. Gardner and K. L. Osterloh; TSAJ 123; Tübingen: Mohr Siebeck, 2008), 155–72.

[23] *m. Nedarim* 4:4; *m. Shabbat* 3:5; *m. Kelim* 16:1, 17:2, 30:2; Brand, *Ceramics*, 542–43.

directly from the other.[24] The *tamhui* often appears at communal meals and banquets.[25] Yehoshua Brand, in his massive study of the ceramic vessels mentioned in classical rabbinic texts, has called the *tamhui* the "banquet vessel par excellence."[26]

The form and function of the *tamhui*, as it is presented in rabbinic texts, suggest that it should be identified with a certain type of vessel known from a number of archaeological sites, including Beth Shearim, Jerash, and Nazareth.[27] It is likewise identified with the Greek *tryblion* and Latin *paropsis*, whose uses parallel those we find in rabbinic texts.[28] Just as it was associated with washing in the Mishnah so too in the Gospels it holds water used for hand washing.[29] As in rabbinic texts, in extrarabbinic sources it is prominent at meals, including two of the most famous feasts in the literature of the ancient world – the banquet of Trimalchio in Petronius's *Satyricon* and the Last Supper in the New Testament.[30] An open vessel, providing access ready-to-eat provisions, the *tamhui* would be an ideal choice for a charitable institution that provides immediate sustenance to any and all in need. It is for these reasons that this particular vessel was transformed into the physical manifestation of the soup kitchen, an institution that would provide ready-to-eat food and other immediate necessities.

QUPPA: FROM BASKET TO CHARITY FUND

Quppa is mentioned 101 times in Tannaitic compilations. Only six of these references, which are concentrated into four pericopae, understand the *quppa* as an institution; I will examine these in close detail in Chapters 5 and 6.[31] For now, it is important to highlight that the nearly all of the references to the *quppa* in Tannaitic compilations indicate vessels and appear in the

---

[24] While they are allowed to eat together, the two individuals alone cannot share food from the same *tamhui*, as one might hold back, allowing the other to benefit by eating more than his allocation and thus violate the vow; see Neusner, *History of the Mishnaic Law – Nedarim, Nazir*, 40.

[25] m. Nedarim 4:4; m. Pesahim 10:1.

[26] My translation of Brand, *Ceramics*, 542, whose remarks are echoed in Zevulon and Olenik, *Function and Design*, 24. On commensality, see Rosenblum, *Food and Identity*.

[27] Zevulon and Olenik, *Function and Design*, 24–25, 107, in addition to the stone vessel discussed earlier from Jerusalem.

[28] Frederick W. Danker et al., *A Greek-English Lexicon of the New Testament and Other Early Christian Literature* (= BDAG) (Chicago, Ill.: University of Chicago Press, 2000), no. 7454. See also Josephus, *Ant.* 3.220–221; 12.117; Sir 31:14; Brand, *Ceramics*, 540.

[29] Matt 26:23; Mark 14:20.

[30] Matt 26:23; Mark 14:20; Petronius, *Satyricon* 34; see Brand, *Ceramics*, 540.

[31] m. Pe'ah 8:7; t. Pe'ah 4:9 (twice); t. Pe'ah 4:10 (twice); t. Demai 3:16.

Mishnah and Tosefta, with only a handful in the Tannaitic midrashim.[32] The preponderance of references to the *quppa* in legal compilations is due to the rabbis' interest in the laws of purity, how they applied to daily life in general and household wares in particular (especially tractate *Kelim*), as well as the laws related to preparing food and carrying on the Sabbath. In these sources, the *quppa* is frequently mentioned alongside other vessels, such as the *qe'arah* (bowl), amphora, pots, and a jar.[33] It is most frequently paired with *sal*, a basket similar to but smaller than a *quppa*, as well as a *saq* (sack), suggesting that they are from the same family of vessels. That is, they are similar in shape and the ways in which they are used.[34]

In Tannaitic texts, the *quppa* is presented as a wicker basket made of palm fronds.[35] It was woven in a distinctive pattern, which is mentioned in a discussion of purity laws:

> Small food-baskets and hand baskets [become susceptible to uncleanness] after their rims are bound round and the rough ends smoothed off; large food-baskets and large hampers, after two circling bands have been made around their sides; the container of a sifter or sieve and the cup for balances, after one circling band has been made around their sides; a *quppa*, after two twists have been made around its sides; a rush basket, after one twist has been made around its sides. (*m. Kelim* 16:3)[36]

This text also indicates the rabbis' interest in the form of the *quppa*.[37] The weave was tight enough to allow it to hold small objects, which could include coins.[38] At the same time, liquids could easily pass through, as rabbinic texts speak of the moisture of an olive leaking out and water flowing in when the basket is submerged.[39] The handle of the *quppa* was made from rope and

---

[32] The breakdown is as follows: Mishnah 37; Tosefta 57; *Sifra* 2; *SifreNum* 1; *SifreDeut* 4.

[33] *m. Makhshirin* 4:3–6, 8; *m. Ohalot* 6:2; *t. Nazir* 1:3. Many of these vessels have been identified with archaeological finds; see Adan-Bayewitz, *Common Pottery*; Brand, *Ceramics*; Krauss, *Talmudische Archäologie*, 2:271–99; Schwartz, "Material Realities," 439–41; Zevulon and Olenik, *Function and Design*.

[34] *m. Terumot* 1:7; *m. Ma'aserot* 3:2; *m. Betzah* 4:1; *m. Kelim* 28:6; *t. Kelim Bava Qamma* 6:6; *t. Kelim Bava Batra* 6:2; *t. Kelim Bava Batra* 6:6; *m. Kil'ayim* 9:10; *m. Bava Metzi'a* 2:8; *m. Mikwa'ot* 6:5; *SifreDeut* 232.

[35] *m. Kelim* 16:2–3; *t. Kelim Bava Batra* 3:1.

[36] Translation based on Herbert Danby, *The Mishnah: Translated from the Hebrew with Introduction and Brief Explanatory Notes* (London: Oxford University Press, 1933), with my emendations. It is on the basis of this text that Yadin identifies his finds as *quppot*; see Yadin, *Finds from the Bar Kokhba Period*, 140–41. See also *t. Kelim Bava Metzi'a* 5:13.

[37] See also *t. Kelim Bava Qamma* 6:6, where the *quppa* is a utensil.

[38] *m. Sheqalim* 3:2; *t. Sheqalim* 2:1.

[39] *m. Teharot* 9:1. After olives are harvested, they are placed into baskets where they produce moisture while they are carried to the olive press; see the discussion in Jacob Neusner, *A*

could be tied to or sewn into the basket's body.[40] Tears in the *quppa* would be patched up.[41] Tannaitic texts depict the *quppa* as relatively large, up to ten handbreadths high (approximately 85 cm) and 24 pints in volume.[42] Again, it was large enough to carry a significant amount of goods, yet small enough to be carried by one person, usually slung over the shoulder.[43]

Based on the way that it appears and functions in rabbinic discussions, we can find close parallels to the *quppa* in extrarabbinic sources, including Greek and Latin texts and archaeological finds. The Hebrew term *quppa* is equivalent to the Greek *kophinos* and the Latin *cophinus*, which appear in a number of sources.[44] Pollux, the second-century C.E. grammarian from Alexandria, includes the *kophinos* in a list of woven utensils in his *Onomasticon*.[45] The second-century column of Trajan in Rome depicts workers using a *kophinos* to move earth.[46] Archaeological evidence includes the aforementioned remains of *quppot* from the Judean desert caves, dating to the second century C.E. They were made of palm fronds, which are common to the region. Both the depiction on Trajan's column and the finds from the Judean desert indicate that the basket was tightly woven, with a distinctive style of plaiting. The rim was fashioned around a cord to increase its strength. The basket had two large, arched handles made of palm-fiber rope, which were likewise inlaid with a

---

History of the Mishnaic Law of Purities: Part Eleven, Tohorot (Leiden: Brill, 1976), 203–08. On its use in a ritual bath, see *m. Mikwa'ot* 6:5. See also *t. Shabbat* 5:14, which suggests that a *quppa* is too porous to protect one from the rain.

[40] *m. Mikwa'ot* 10:5; *m. Shabbat* 8:2.
[41] *m. Kelim* 28:6; *t. Kelim Bava Batra* 6:2; *t. Parah* 8:4.
[42] *t. Teharot* 7:2; *t. Shabbat* 10:10. See also *t. Kelim Bava Metzi'a* 5:1, where the *quppa* holds 40 *seahs* in liquid measure, which is two *kor* in dry measure.
[43] *Sifra, Qedoshim, Parashah* 2, *Pereq* 4 (Weiss, *Sifra*, 89a–b); *SifreDeut* 232.
[44] For the identification of *quppa* as *cophinus*, see Eduard Lohse and Günter Mayer, *Die Tosefta, Seder I: Zeraim, 1.1: Berakot – Pea* (eds. G. Kittel et al.; Stuttgart, Berlin, and Köln: Kohlhammer, 1999), 150n. 74; Nathan ben Jehiel of Rome et al., *Aruch completum [Hebrew]* (Vienna, 1878), 7: 160; cf. Samuel Krauss, *Griechische und lateinische Lehnwörter im Talmud, Midrasch und Targum* (2 vols.; Berlin: S. Calvary, 1898–1899), 516–17. It is notable that *quppa* is absent from the Hebrew Bible; see Hellinger, "Charity in Talmudic," 205; Schwartz, *Imperialism and Jewish Society*, 229. In the New Testament, see Matt 14:20; Mark 6:43; 8:19; Luke 9:17; John 6:13. On these verses, see Adela Yarbro Collins, *Mark: A Commentary* (Minneapolis, Minn.: Fortress Press, 2007), 326, 387; W. D. Davies and Dale C. Allison, *A Critical and Exegetical Commentary on the Gospel According to Saint Matthew* (Edinburgh: T. & T. Clark, 1988), 2: 492; Ulrich Luz et al., *Matthew 8–20: A Commentary* (Minneapolis, Minn.: Fortress Press, 2001), 315; Joel Marcus, *Mark: A New Translation with Introduction and Commentary* (New York: Doubleday, 2000), 1: 411, 414, 421, 514. Cf. Henry George Liddell et al., *A Greek-English Lexicon (Revised and Augmented Edition)* (Oxford and New York: Clarendon Press and Oxford University Press, 1996), 1019.
[45] As cited in F. Hort, "A Note by the Late Dr Hort on the Words," *JTS* 10 (1909): 569.
[46] Graham Webster and John Updike, *The Roman Imperial Army of the First and Second Centuries A.D* (Norman: University of Oklahoma Press, 1998), 130.

cord, whose ends were woven into the body to form a strong attachment. The bases of the baskets varied, as they could be round, oval, or pointed.[47] When they were torn or worn, they would be repaired with swatches of plaiting from unusable baskets or mats, or repaired with leather patches.[48] The smallest example found at Nahal Hever was 15 cm in height and 90 cm in circumference, while the largest measured over 70 cm in height and some three meters in circumference at its rim.[49] Based on epigraphic sources, scholars have estimated that an average *kophinos* could hold between 7.5 and 10 kilograms of wheat.[50] As in the rabbinic texts discussed earlier, so too in extrarabbinic sources the *quppa* varied in size, was large enough to hold a significant amount of items, and yet small enough to be carried by a single individual.

The form of the *quppa/kophinos* largely determined its function. Extrarabbinic sources indicate that it was useful for holding and carrying dry goods. Those found at Nahal Hever held an individual's personal belongings, including metal utensils, a tunic and other textiles, knives, a sickle, keys, wooden objects including a box and a bowl, sandals, papyri (e.g., Babatha archive), and water skins.[51] One basket held a cache of valuable personal items, including incense shovels, bowls, and jugs all made of bronze.[52] The Roman satirist Juvenal (c. 60–130 C.E.) notes that the Jewish poor in Rome would use it (*cophinus*), alongside a truss of hay, to hold and carry their possessions.[53] In addition, Josephus writes that each Roman legionnaire would be equipped

---

[47] Yadin, *Finds from the Bar Kokhba Period*, 136–51.

[48] Yadin, *Finds from the Bar Kokhba Period*, 144 no. 8; 147 no. 15. For the basket repaired with leather, see p. 145, no. 13, plate 46.

[49] Smallest basket: Yadin, *Finds from the Bar Kokhba Period*, 144, no. 7; largest basket: Yadin, *Finds from the Bar Kokhba Period*, 145 no. 14, plate 45.

[50] A second-century B.C.E. inscription from Thessaly (Greece) indicates that the *kophinos* carries about 7.5 kilograms of wheat; see Peter Garnsey et al., "Thessaly and the Grain Supply of Rome during the Second Century B.C," *JRS* 74 (1984): 39n. 40, 43. Cf. the ten liters in volume estimated by Luz et al., *Matthew 8–20: A Commentary*, 315. In an inscription from Boeotia (Greece; *IG* 7.2712.65), the *kophinos* is equivalent to about two gallons; see Liddell et al., *Greek-English Lexicon*, 988. To be sure, the size of these baskets varied; see L. William Countryman, "How Many Baskets Full: Mark 8:14–21 and the Value of Miracles in Mark," *CBQ* 47 (1985): 643–55; Hort, "A Note," 567–71.

[51] Yadin, *Finds from the Bar Kokhba Period*, 23–41. Notably, just as a sickle was found in a *quppa* (p. 39), so too these two items are paired in *m. Menahot* 10:1, 10:3; *t. Menahot* 10:23.

[52] Yadin, *Finds from the Bar Kokhba Period*, 37, 143. A similar usage is reflected in rabbinic texts; see *m. Betzah* 4:1, where the *quppa* holds jugs of wine.

[53] See Juvenal, *Saturae* III, 10–18; VI, 542–547; see Susanna Morton Braund, *Juvenal: Satires: Book I* (Cambridge and New York: Cambridge University Press, 1996), 176–77; Susanna Morton Braund, *Juvenal and Persius* (Cambridge, Mass.: Harvard University Press, 2004), 168–69; Stern, *Greek and Latin Authors*, 2:97–98, 100–1, nos. 296, 299. Stern associates these references to the Jewish custom of keeping food warm on the Sabbath, though this was only one of many uses of the *quppa*.

with a *kophinos* to carry various provisions and equipment, to negate the need for a pack-mule.[54] These baskets could also hold skulls and bones, as some in the Judean desert caves did, perhaps as makeshift ossuaries for burial inside a cave – a use that is also reflected in the Mishnah.[55] The *kophinos* could carry earth, as depicted in the Column of Trajan.[56] Likewise, the basket could be employed in agriculture, used for carrying dung as fertilizer, as noted by Plutarch, Xenophon, and Aristophanes.[57]

Above all, the *kophinos* was used for holding and carrying food.[58] Pollux notes that it was used in the harvest, while the Athenian Strattis writes that it carried corn.[59] It is this understanding that leads the Septuagint to translate the Hebrew *sal* into *kophinos* in Judges 6:19, where Gideon uses the vessel to hold and carry meat. In an inscription from Thessaly, it is used to hold and distribute wheat.[60] In the Gospels, after the five thousand men were fed with five loaves and two fish, the leftover pieces were gathered into twelve *kophinoi*.[61]

Similarly, in early rabbinic literature, the *quppa* was especially useful for holding and carrying dry goods. It held and carried cloth and clothing, and was even used to transport wine jars and other vessels.[62] Like the *kophinos/cophinus* in Greek and Latin sources, the *quppa* in Tannaitic texts was especially useful for food. In its laws on transporting objects during the Sabbath, for example, the Mishnah mentions a *quppa* that is full of fruit.[63] A *quppa* holding legumes is mentioned in a discussion on how liquids can transform the purity status

---

[54] Josephus *War* 3.95.
[55] Yadin, *Finds from the Bar Kokhba Period*, 31–32, 36, 136, 141, 143, 145. See *t. Ohalot* 4:2, where the *quppa* is used to bring buckets of bones from Kefar Tabya to the synagogue in Lod. It is interesting to note that *kophinos/cophinus* would develop into the English "coffin"; see *Oxford English Dictionary*, s.v. coffin, nos. 2–3.
[56] Webster and Updike, *Roman Imperial Army*, 130.
[57] Hort, "A Note," 568.
[58] See the references in Danker et al., *BDAG*, no. 4379. For using *quppot* at harvests, see Feliks, *Agriculture In Eretz-Israel*, 200.
[59] See the sources cited in Hort, "A Note," 568.
[60] Garnsey et al., "Thessaly and the Grain Supply," 39n. 40, 43.
[61] Matt 14:20, 16:9; Mark 6:43, 8:19; Luke 9:17; John 6:13. The New Testament juxtaposes the *kophinos* with another basket, the *spuris*, seven of which were used to feed the four thousand and which was large enough to use to lower Paul down from the walls of Damascus (Matt 15:37, 16:10; Mark 8:8, 8:20; Acts 9:25; Marcus, *Mark*, 411). For a discussion of the differences, see Robert C. Horn, "Use of the Greek New Testament," *Lutheran Quarterly* 1 (1949): 301, who distinguishes between the two based on size. Cf. Hort, "A Note," 567, who argues that the difference between the *kophinos* and the *spuris* is not based on size, but rather on material, consistency, and use: the *kophinos* is a stiff wicker basket, while the *spuris* is a flexible mat-basket made of rushes and used for carrying fish or other food.
[62] Textiles: *t. Kelim Bava Batra* 6:6; *Sifra, Qedoshim, Parashah* 2, *Pereq* 4 (Weiss, *Sifra*, 89a–b); *SifreDeut* 232; Wine jars: *m. Shabbat* 4:2, *m. Betzah* 4:1.
[63] *m. Shabbat* 10:2.

of dry foods from clean to unclean.[64] In multiple passages, the *quppa* is used to hold and carry straw.[65] It was useful for gardeners and it was common to use *quppot* to hold vegetables.[66] In the same way the *quppa* also holds olives, dates, mustard seed, and figs.[67] The *quppa* often carries food in bulk, as the rabbis frequently note that a *quppa* is "full of" any number of things – "*quppa* full of mustard-seed" in one text, "*quppa* full of legumes" in another, and "*quppa* full of fruit" in *m. Shabbat* 10:2.[68] A similar expression is found in the New Testament, as Mark 6:43 reads "baskets (*kophinos*) full of broken pieces and of the fish."

The form of the *quppa* and its ability to carry dry goods, especially food, leant itself well to fulfilling religious obligations that required holding, carrying, collecting, or distributing produce. Alongside a sickle, for example, a *quppa* is required for fulfilling the commandment of reaping the *omer* ("sheaf").[69] Following its harvest, which is cast as a public and collective act in which the harvester's calls must be met by the appropriate responses from the gathered crowd, the *omer* itself was then carried in *quppot* to be processed into flour, a tenth of which was then distributed to the priests.[70] Likewise, if one has finished expressing oil from olives, but had set aside a full *quppa* of olives, it is to be given to a poor priest who would express the oil himself for the purposes of taking the priest's dues.[71] It is permissible, under certain restrictions, to use a *quppa* to separate and hand over the heave offering.[72] A *quppa* may also be used to hold and carry a tithe.[73]

To sum up, throughout early rabbinic literature, the *quppa* was predominantly a basket. In an overwhelming number of instances, it is very clearly a tangible, hand-held receptacle, as the rabbis discuss its physical attributes, the ways in which it held certain goods, as well as the fact that *quppot* are frequently grouped together with other vessels or utensils.[74] As a vessel, it was

---

[64] *m. Makhshirin* 4:6.
[65] *m. Shabbat* 18:1; *m. Betzah* 4:1; *m. Kelim* 17:1; *m. Ohalot* 6:2; *t. Shabbat* 14:4; *t. Betzah* 3:10; *t. Bava Qamma* 2:6.
[66] *m. Kelim* 17:1; *m. Demai* 2:5; *t. Demai* 3:12.
[67] Olives: *m. Teharot* 9:1, 9:4; *t. Eruvin* 6:9; *t. Terumot* 3:13; *t. Teharot* 10:9. Dates: *t. Eruvin* 6:9. Mustard seed: *m. Nazir* 1:5. Figs: *m. Ma'aserot* 3:2.
[68] Legumes: *m. Makhshirin* 4:6. Mustard seed: *m. Nazir* 1:5. Fruit: *m. Shabbat* 10:2.
[69] *m. Menahot* 10:1; 10:3; *t. Menahot* 10:23. Literally a "sheaf," the *omer* is a biblically prescribed donation to the priests consisting of a portion of the flour made from the first barley harvested (Lev 23:10).
[70] *m. Menahot* 10:3–4.
[71] *m. Teharot* 9:4.
[72] *m. Terumot* 1:7.
[73] *m. Demai* 5:7.
[74] Physical attributes: *m. Shabbat* 8:2; *m. Kelim* 16:3, 27:4 (2), 28:6 (3); *m. Mikwa'ot* 10:5; *t. Kelim Bava Qamma* 6:6; *t. Parah* 8:4; *t. Teharot* 7:2. Understood as a basket: *m. Shabbat* 4:2, 10:2

useful for carrying dry goods, especially food and other produce. The Tannaitic understanding of the form and function of *quppot* finds close parallels in extrarabbinic sources, in both archaeological finds and Greek and Latin texts. From these sources, it emerges that a *quppa/kophinos* is a wicker basket, made from palm fronds, tightly woven but also porous, which varied in size but was probably nine to fourteen liters in volume. Its handles and rims were inlaid with rope or cord to provide strength and the *quppa/kophinos* could be repaired with other pieces of woven materials (i.e., basketry including baskets and mats). This understanding of the *quppa* is common to both the way that the *quppa* is presented and how it functions within the vast majority of rabbinic texts and extrarabbinic sources.

These qualities made the *quppa* a particularly apt choice for embodying the rabbis' vision of a charity fund. The *quppa* was a large vessel, useful for holding a significant amount of provisions. Unlike the *tamhui*, the *quppa* could be closed, allowing one to control access to its contents. Likewise, as a charity fund, the *quppa* held a significant amount of provisions – enough to support an individual for a week at a time. Its contents were tightly controlled by the charity supervisor, as only select individuals were eligible for the *quppa*. As a basket, moreover, the *quppa/kophinos* had a particular association with the poor and poverty. For these reasons, it was an ideal fit to serve as the physical manifestation of their charity fund.

INSTITUTIONS

Throughout early rabbinic literature, *tamhui* and *quppa* predominantly denote common, household vessels. In a handful of passages, however, they are much more. In these passages, they are charitable institutions. The key texts that outline the *tamhui* and *quppa* are *t. Pe'ah* 4:8–9 and *m. Pe'ah* 8:7; I will examine each in turn, beginning with the passages from the Tosefta:[75]

A. They do not [give] to a poor person, who travels from place to place, less than a loaf of bread worth a *pondion*, [made from grain valued at] four *seahs* per *sela*.[76]

---

(2); *m. Sheqalim* 3:3; *m. Nazir* 1:5 (2); *m. Menahot* 10:1, 10:3 (2); *m. Kelim* 17:4; *t. Demai* 3:12; *t. Shabbat* 10:10, 14:4; *t. Eruvin* 6:9; *t. Betzah* 3:10; *t. Sotah* 14:6; *t. Bava Qamma* 2:6; *t. Menahot* 10:23; *t. Ohalot* 4:2; *t. Teharot* 10:9; *Sifra, Qedoshim, Parashah* 2, *Pereq* 4 (Weiss, *Sifra*, 89a–b); *SifreNum* 6; *SifreDeut* 232. Appears alongside other vessels or receptacles: *m. Kil'ayim* 9:10; *m. Terumot* 1:7; *m. Ma'aserot* 3:2; *m. Betzah* 4:1 (2); *m. Bava Metsi'a* 2:8; *m. Kelim* 8:2; *m. Ohalot* 6:2; *m. Teharot* 9:1, 9:4; *m. Mikwa'ot* 6:5.

[75] See also *t. Demai* 3:16.

[76] That is, bread worth a *pondion* made from wheat that costs at least one *sela*, for four *seahs* of wheat (one *seah* = 800.9 cubic inches = 13,222 cubic centimeters). This works out to a

B. [If] he lodges overnight, [then] they give him provisions for lodging, oil, and beans.
C. [If he lodges over] the Sabbath, [then] they give him food for three meals, oil and beans, fish and a vegetable.
D. Under what circumstances does this apply?
E. In instances in which they do not know him.
F. But in instances in which they do know him, then they also clothe him.[77]
G. [If a poor man] went from door to door [begging, then] they are not obligated to him in any way. (*t. Pe'ah* 4:8)

A. The *tamhui* [provides for] the entire day.[78]
B. The *quppa* [provides] from Sabbath eve to Sabbath eve.
C. The *tamhui* [provides] for every man.
D. The *quppa* [provides] for poor individuals of the same town. (*t. Pe'ah* 4:9)

The discussion opens by exploring what should be given to vagrants, poor individuals who wander from one town to another seeking support. The rabbis instruct that a vagrant should be provided with a loaf of bread weighing roughly 500 grams and made from a certain quality of wheat.[79] If he needs a place for the night, then the poor man should be given "maintenance for lodging," which includes the basic necessities of shelter and a bed or mattress, as well as additional foods – olive oil and beans.[80] During the Sabbath, the vagrant is also provided with enough food for three meals, the requisite number of meals that one must eat to keep the Sabbath in accordance with

---

500-gram loaf of bread; see the calculations and discussion in Hamel, *Poverty and Charity in Roman Palestine*, 39–42, 243–48.

[77] Cf. Roger Brooks, *Support for the Poor in the Mishnaic Law of Agriculture: Tractate Peah* (Chico, Calif.: Scholars Press, 1983), 147, who reads *ksy* as "shelter" instead of "clothing." Understanding this as clothing, however, seems more likely as the local, resident poor are entitled to clothing through the *quppa* (*t. Pe'ah* 4:9–10), while vagrants are not. Moreover, this passage indicates that shelter is provided through the *tamhui*.

[78] This is likewise the reading in the *editio princeps*, as noted by Brooks, *Support for the Poor*, 200n. 31. Cf. MS Erfurt, which reads *bkl ywm* "on every day." That is, on a daily basis. For the manuscript variants, see Lieberman, *The Tosefta*, 1:57.

[79] Hamel, *Poverty and Charity in Roman Palestine*, 39–42, 243–48.

[80] Saul Lieberman, *Tosefta Ki-Fshutah: A Comprehensive Commentary on the Tosefta [Hebrew]* (8 vols.; New York: Jewish Theological Seminary of America, 1955–1988), 1: 183. On bedding in antiquity and classical rabbinic literature, see Joshua Schwartz, "Material Culture and Rabbinic Literature in the Land of Israel in Late Antiquity: Beds, Bedclothes, and Sleeping Habits [Hebrew]," in *Continuity and Renewal: Jews and Judaism in Byzantine-Christian Palestine [Hebrew]* (ed. L. I. Levine; Jerusalem: Dinur Center for Jewish History, Yad Ben-Zvi Press, and the Jewish Theological Seminary of America, 2004), 197–208.

rabbinic instructions.[81] By contrast, during the week it was customary to eat only two meals per day.[82] In addition to the oil and beans provided during a weeknight, the meals on the Sabbath must also include fish and a vegetable. The provisions given to a vagrant, therefore, are arranged in a hierarchy: bread for the day; oil, beans, and shelter if he stays overnight; plus fish, vegetables, and enough food for three meals if he stays over the Sabbath. Following these instructions, an anonymous rabbinic voice asks: Under what circumstances does this apply? This question is commonly used to limit the application of the law. In this case, it applies to instances in which one does not "know" the poor individual. Some scholars have interpreted this to mean that the poor man is not a local, while others understand this to mean that they do not know if he is genuinely poor.[83] The two suggestions are not, however, mutually exclusive and may point in a similar direction: eligibility for the *quppa* depends on one's residential status as well as the state of one's need. If one is "unknown" because he is not local, then surely his financial claims cannot be verified. However, when the poor man is known or recognized, then he is also entitled to receive clothing. As we will see, provisions for nonlocals are provided through the soup kitchen, while those for locals are given through the charity fund.

The passage (*t. Pe'ah* 4:8) ends on a surprising note. If a poor man comes begging at the door of one's house, then one is not obligated to give him anything. Taken on its own and at face value, this line could be understood to suggest that the rabbis advocate rejecting a beggar's plea for alms. Contrast the Tosefta's position, for example, to Matt 5:42, "Give to everyone who begs from you, and do not refuse anyone who wants to borrow from you." The Talmuds offer apologetic interpretations, positing that the householder should give at least a small amount of alms to the beggar.[84] A different line of apologetics is taken by later rabbinic interpreters, who limit the application of this instruction to begging at doorways alone, while one is obligated to give when encountering beggars in other places such as the streets and other public areas.[85] The line's simplest and most straightforward meaning, however, is

---

[81] See also *m. Shabbat* 16:2.
[82] *m. Pe'ah* 8:5, 8:7; *m. Eruvin* 8:2; *m. Kelim* 17:11; *m. Sukkah* 2:6; *t. Eruvin* 6:9.
[83] The former opinion is expressed by Brooks, *Support for the Poor*, 147–48, while the latter is held by Lieberman, *Tosefta Ki-Fshutah*, 1:183–84; Lohse and Mayer, *Die Tosefta*, 149n. 68.
[84] *y. Pe'ah* 8:7, 21a; *b. Bava Batra* 9a. The Talmuds' interpretations are followed by Frank M. Loewenberg, "On the Development of Philanthropic Institutions in Ancient Judaism: Provisions for Poor Travelers," *Nonprofit and Volunteer Sector Quarterly* 23 (1994): 201; Sperber, *Roman Palestine, Money and Prices*, 154. See also the summary of the Talmuds and traditional commentaries in Lieberman, *Tosefta Ki-Fshutah*, 1:184.
[85] Michael Hellinger, "Quppat ha-tzedakah ve-ha'aniyyim ha-machzarim al ha-petachim [Hebrew]," *Shema'tin* 174 (2009): 93–100. The beggar at the doorway was a common motif

that one need not give to a beggar at all. A lack of obligation to give to beggars, however, should not be mistaken for the absence of a duty to give charity to the poor. Indeed, the last line of *t. Pe'ah* 4:8 should be read in conjunction with the discussion of the *tamhui* and *quppa* in *t. Pe'ah* 4:9:[86] the alms should be given through the *tamhui* and *quppa*, instead of through personal solicitations.[87] The rabbis' institutionalization of almsgiving enables a degree of social control, as they aim to eliminate begging.

The text goes on to prescribe rules for providing alms through the *tamhui* and *quppa*. The *tamhui* should give enough alms to sustain an individual for a full day. The *quppa*, by contrast, maintains the poor for a full week, from the eve of one Sabbath to the next. The *quppa* provides alms only to locals, only to individuals from the town in which the *quppa* is located. The *tamhui*, by contrast, provides alms to anyone, regardless of their place of origin or civic affiliation. The implication is that the poor man who wanders from place to place would be given bread, lodging, oil, beans and (on the Sabbath) fish and vegetables through the *tamhui*, because he would not be eligible for the *quppa*.

The Mishnah adds important restrictions on who is eligible for alms from the *tamhui* and *quppa*:

> One who has food for two meals may not take from the *tamhui*.
> One who has food for fourteen meals may not take from the *quppa*.
> And the *quppa* is collected by two people and distributed by three people. (*m. Pe'ah* 8:7, D–F)

The Mishnah instructs that no one who has enough food for two meals (or, presumably, enough money to acquire two meals worth of food) may take from the soup kitchen. Two meals was, at least to the rabbis, the minimum number of meals that one should eat during the day. The *quppa* provides only to those individuals who have fewer than fourteen meals – that is, a week's worth of food. The *quppa*, moreover, is to be closely supervised, as provisions should be collected by two individuals and distributed by three. This was a team of specially appointed administrators, charity supervisors who held the title of *gabbai tsedaqah* or *parnas*. Charity supervisors, whom I examine in more detail in Chapter 7, would go from neighborhood to neighborhood collecting alms, though pledges to give were also made in public at synagogues.

In these passages, the *tamhui* and *quppa* are clearly more than mere vessels. They may still be receptacles for holding things. But now the rabbis attach

---

in rabbinic literature and extrarabbinic sources in the ancient world; see my discussion in Chapter 7.
[86] Rashi and the Tosefot read them together, as noted by Lieberman, *Tosefta Ki-Fshutah*, 1:184.
[87] Brooks, *Support for the Poor*, 147–48.

various rules to them, instructing that the *tamhui* and *quppa* hold certain items, such as certain foods and clothing, as well as "hold" access to shelter. The rabbis also define access to the *tamhui* and (more so) the *quppa*, as the collection and distribution of alms is regulated by certain rules that govern their operation. The rules applied to the *tamhui* and *quppa* constrain the way that the non-poor give alms and how the poor receive them. The *tamhui*, then, is more than a dish as it provides immediate support and sustenance to all those in need – it is a soup kitchen. The *quppa* is likewise more than a basket, as it is institutionalized into a communal charity fund for the benefit of the local poor. These institutions place limits on the way that alms are given, so as to deincentivize begging and discourage giving to beggars.

FROM VESSELS TO INSTITUTIONS

How were the *tamhui* and *quppa* transformed from a dish and a basket into the central institutions of organized charity? On one level, the physical attributes of these vessels bear important similarities to the conceptual architecture of the institutions themselves. The *tamhui* was an "open" vessel, as its widest part was the opening at the top. This made it well suited for serving food, whereas cooking, preparing, or storing food was relegated to vessels with a narrower opening – that is, "closed" vessels. The *tamhui* held provisions that were ready to consume, a function that likewise matches the soup kitchen's objective to provide immediate sustenance. Just as the open-shaped dish allowed for free access to its contents, so too all individuals – regardless of their civic affiliation – were eligible to take from the soup kitchen. As a relatively large dish, the *tamhui* could serve multiple meals; likewise, the soup kitchen provided two meals per day to the poor.

The *tamhui*, however, was not unique in its capacity to serve food and have open access to its contents. There are a number of vessels known from ancient Palestine and mentioned in rabbinic texts that were equally well suited. The aforementioned *qe'arah*, for example, was similar to the *tamhui* in shape and was also a serving vessel. What made the *tamhui* unique and apt to represent the "soup kitchen" may have been its name. *Tamhui* is a relatively new word in the history of the Hebrew language, as it is unattested in the Hebrew Bible. Rather, it was created in Roman times, drawing upon the biblical root *m-h-y*, or "sustenance,"[88] which in the Hebrew Bible is used to refer to the most basic

---

[88] *Tamhui* consists of the biblical Hebrew root *m-h-y* inflected into a nominal pattern with *t–* as a prefix; see Chaim E. Cohen, "Masculine Nouns with Prefixed t- in Tannaitic Hebrew [Hebrew]," in *Sha'are lashon: Studies in Hebrew, Aramaic and Jewish Languages Presented to Moshe Bar-Asher [Hebrew]* (ed. A. Maman et al.; Jerusalem: Bialik Institute, 2007), 2:166–82.

provisions needed for the preservation of life.[89] This aligns nicely with the primary function of the soup kitchen, which we will see in Chapter 4 is to provide basic provisions to those in immediate need. The *tamhui*'s form was a perfect match for the soup kitchen, while its name may point to the reason why this was the serving dish that was transformed into a charity institution.

In a similar vein, as a basket the *quppa* had physical attributes that matched the nature of the charity fund. It was a fairly large vessel, with the capacity to hold, carry, and store a large amount of dry goods. Likewise, the charity fund's goal is to provide enough provisions to support an individual for a full week. Unlike the *tamhui*, which was an open vessel, the *quppa* could be closed by pulling its handles together. It could even be sealed and the finds from Nahal Hever illustrate how this was done: its two handles were tied together by a rope, one end of which was fastened to a large bowl placed just inside the basket's opening. The rope cinched together the two sides of the *quppa* and also held the bowl in place, which blocked access to the basket's contents.[90] Just as the basket was closed, so too the charity fund was similar to a closed vessel, as access to its valuable contents was tightly controlled by charity supervisors. It may also be significant that the *quppa/kophinos/cophinus* is associated by some ancient writers with poor individuals, Jews, or both. This may also help us understand why it was chosen above other vessels to be a centerpiece of the rabbis' approach to organized charity.[91]

An interesting parallel to the transformation of the *tamhui* and *quppa* may be found in the *sportula*, known from Greco-Roman sources. The *sportula* was a basket, probably similar to the *kophinos*.[92] Sources indicate that it could be used to hold money that was given to clients by their patrons. *Sportula* could also indicate a public feeding or a portion of food given by a host to a guest.[93] It differs, however, from the *tamhui* and *quppa* in that the *sportula* constituted a direct transfer between individuals, whereas the *tamhui* and

---

[89] E.g., Gen 45:5; Judg 6:4, 17:10; 2 Chr 14:12.
[90] Yadin, *Finds from the Bar Kokhba Period*, 37 plate 11–12.
[91] The poor: Nicolaus of Damascus in Stolebaeus, *Flor.* xliv 41; see Hort, "A Note," 568; David Kovacs, *Euripidea* (Leiden and New York: E.J. Brill, 1994), 31; Liddell et al., *Greek-English Lexicon*, 988. Jewish poor: Juvenal, *Saturae* III, 10–18; VI, 542–547; see Stern, *Greek and Latin Authors*, 2:97–98, 100–1, nos. 296, 299. The basket was also a symbol of the Jews in Sidonius Apollinaris, *Epistulae*, VII, 6 (fifth century, Gaul); see Stern, *Greek and Latin Authors*, 2:98n. 14.
[92] Hort, "A Note," 567–71.
[93] Hubert Cancik et al., eds., *Brill's New Pauly: Encyclopaedia of the Ancient World* (Leiden and Boston: Brill, 2002), s.v. sportula; Duncan-Jones, *Economy of the Roman Empire*; Novick, "Charity and Reciprocity," 42; Andrew Wallace-Hadrill, ed., *Patronage in Ancient Society* (Leicester-Nottingham Studies in Ancient Society 1; London and New York: Routledge, 1989), 209–15; Woolf, "Food, Poverty and Patronage," 197–228.

quppa facilitated indirect transfers from the community as a whole to poor individuals. The *sportula*, moreover, was part of reciprocity-based exchanges, such as hospitality, whereas the *tamhui* and *quppa* were meant to circumvent reciprocity.

Understanding the *tamhui* and *quppa* in *m. Pe'ah* 8:7 and *t. Pe'ah* 4:8–9 as simply the dish and basket used for collecting and distributing charity, as many scholars do, does not adequately capture the significance of what they had become. It simply assumes and presupposes the existence of a complex and sophisticated set of rules and norms of behavior that govern the distribution of their alms. That is, it fails to appreciate their character *as institutions*. It also fails to appreciate the rabbis' conscious efforts to flesh out their terms of use. The rabbis prescribe and instruct what the *tamhui* and *quppa* should hold and how their contents are to be distributed, presenting instructions as normative law in the Mishnah and Tosefta. This, indeed, is characteristic of the broader rabbinic project to elevate concepts to legal categories and discuss them in encyclopedic detail.[94] They are more than mere collection vessels, as the *tamhui* and *quppa* represent forms of conduct expressed by a system of rules that organize and control activities. That is, they become institutions.[95] As rules of the game and systems of constraints, institutions can exist independently of their physical manifestations.[96] A charity fund, for example, is no less a charity fund if its provisions are collected in a limestone chest, such as the one found at the Arbel synagogue, or in wicker baskets.

An institution, as scholars of neoinstitutional economics hold, is a web of rules and norms of behavior that facilitate and control economic processes such as the transfer of assets. Institutions establish and enforce the terms of an exchange, controlling the transaction.[97] In the case at hand, the *tamhui*

---

[94] See the broader discussion in Cohen, "Judaean Legal Tradition," 121–43.

[95] On institutions, see Thráinn Eggertsson, *Economic Behavior and Institutions* (Cambridge and New York: Cambridge University Press, 1990); Claude Ménard and Mary M. Shirley, eds., *Handbook of New Institutional Economics* (Dordrecht: Springer, 2005); North, *Institutions*. On philanthropic institutions, see Allen Buchanan, "Charity, Justice, and the Idea of Moral Progress," in *Giving: Western Ideas of Philanthropy* (ed. J. B. Schneewind; Bloomington: Indiana University Press, 1996), 98–116; S. N. Eisenstadt, "Institutionalization and Change," *American Sociological Review* 29 (1964): 235–47; S. N. Eisenstadt, "Social Institutions: The Concept," in *International Encyclopedia of the Social Sciences* (ed. D. L. Sills; New York: Macmillan, 1968), s.v. social institutions; John Rawls, *A Theory of Justice*, revised edition (Cambridge, Mass.: Belknap Press of Harvard University Press, 1999), 47–52.

[96] Rawls, *Theory of Justice*, 48.

[97] On neoinstitutional economics, see R. H. Coase, *The Firm, The Market, and the Law* (Chicago, Ill.: University of Chicago Press, 1988); Eggertsson, *Economic Behavior*; Claude Ménard and Mary M. Shirley, "Introduction," in *Handbook of New Institutional Economics* (ed. C. Ménard and M. M. Shirley; Dordrecht: Springer, 2005); Douglass C. North, *Structure and Change in Economic History* (New York: Norton, 1981); North, *Institutions*.

and *quppa* are institutions that control the way that assets or alms are transferred from one individual to another, from giver to recipient. It provides an alternative to begging that would otherwise result in undesirable externalities. These include the loss of dignity incurred by the beggar, the sense of invasion that individuals feel when a beggar comes to the door, and the suspicion of giving alms to an imposter, one who pretends to be poor.

As institutions, the *tamhui* and *quppa* control and structure the process of almsgiving. They stand between giver and recipient in an attempt to prevent the formation of direct, hierarchical relationships between the two. This saves the poor from shame and removes them from the doorways of the non-poor. The charity supervisors are tasked to assess those who request alms, so as to minimize the uncertainty created by imposters – those who pretend to be poor. Likewise, the rabbis instruct charity collectors to distribute provisions according to certain principles, ensuring what the rabbis believe to be the ideal allocation of a community's resources. This also instills givers with a sense of confidence that their contributions will be put to their intended purposes, which would encourage further giving. These institutions ensure fairness in the collection of charity and provide benefactors with a specific way in which to discharge their obligation to give *tsedaqah*.

Institutions also reflect political values, as the institutions that people choose to construct and maintain reflect what they believe a society should do collectively.[98] The rabbinic discussions indicate that the rabbis hold charity to be a priority in Jewish society and that care for the poor is an obligation incumbent upon the community as a whole. As I will show, rabbinic literature's rules and instructions point to the rabbis' interest in issues of fairness, honesty, impartiality, equality of opportunity, and dignity.

CONCLUSION

My analysis of the *tamhui* and *quppa* in Tannaitic texts and extrarabbinic sources suggests that they had qualities that made them particularly apt to represent charitable institutions. The *tamhui* is defined by its capacity to serve food, provide immediate sustenance, and offer entitlements to the poor. These functions, indeed, could be performed in different ways by both a "dish" and a "soup kitchen." The *quppa* stores provisions in the long term, operates on behalf of the community, provides entitlements, and is associated with the Sabbath – functions that could be carried out by both a basket and a charity

---

[98] That is, the "desirability question" of institutions; see the overview in Philip Pettit, "Institutions," *Encyclopedia of Ethics*: 2:858–63.

fund. As institutions, the *tamhui* and *quppa* in rabbinic texts embody the norms of behavior for what the rabbinic authors and redactors deemed to be the proper way to give alms. Through them, assets are transferred from the giver, to the *tamhui* and *quppa*, and finally to the poor. This constitutes a means to control economic assets in general and the process of giving alms in particular. Whereas the institutionalization of charity would be used by others in subsequent years for instrumental purposes to gain and maintain social and religious authority, it was designed by the Tannaim as a systematic means for discharging one's obligation to give charity in a way that protects the poor from the indignity of begging. In the following chapters, I will examine in close detail those Tannaitic passages in which the rabbis discuss the *tamhui* and *quppa* as charity institutions, reflecting the rabbinic perceptions of what these entities ought to be and how they ought to operate.

4

Tamhui, The Soup Kitchen

INTRODUCTION

The *tamhui* and *quppa* are the centerpieces of the Tannaitic vision of organized charity. As I discussed in the previous chapter, the early rabbis transformed the *tamhui* from a dish into a soup kitchen and the *quppa* from a basket into a charity fund by attaching to them a series of laws that define them and regulate their operation. They control and constrain how charity is given and received. I will investigate the origins and nature of these entities by examining the key legal texts, some of which were introduced in Chapter 3, that treat the *tamhui* and *quppa* as institutions. This chapter on the *tamhui*, as well as Chapters 5 and 6 on the *quppa*, will illuminate in detail how the Tannaim envisioned the operation of these institutions, shedding light on how they were perceived as alternatives to giving to beggars.

What were the nature and origins of the *tamhui*? How did the rabbis envision its role in society and in supporting the poor? An institution, as I have discussed, is defined by the rules that govern its behavior. The Tannaim prescribe a number of rules for the *tamhui*, by defining it in terms of *to whom*, *when*, and *what* goods and services should be provided. The first two questions have already been addressed in the previous chapter: *to whom* – the *tamhui* gives to any individual in need, whereas the *quppa* gives only to local residents. *When* – the *tamhui* provides alms on a regular basis, every day of the week, while the *quppa* doles out provisions once a week. The question of *what* the *tamhui* ought to give is of particular interest to the Tannaim, who address this issue in some detail. As I will discuss in this chapter, during the week the *tamhui* provides a loaf of bread; if the poor individual wishes to stay overnight, then the *tamhui* gives maintenance for lodging, oil, and legumes. Additional alms are provided for holy days, as the *tamhui* gives the poor enough fish and vegetables for three meals on the Sabbath and four cups of wine on Passover.[1]

What is the significance of these alms? Why were these items selected by the Tannaim and what can their choices tell us about the way that they envision the *tamhui*? I find that the primary objective of the *tamhui* is to provide immediate and short-term support to any individual who claims to be in need. The foods that the *tamhui* provides are staples of the Mediterranean diet, while maintenance for lodging supplies the poor with adequate bedding and shelter. Together, these alms constitute the minimum – no more, no less – that an individual would need in order to survive a full day and night. The goal is simply to keep a poor individual alive for twenty-four hours at a time. Thus, the *tamhui* addresses the "biological" poverty that I discussed in Chapter 2. It was only on special occasions, the Sabbath and Passover, that the rabbis instruct the *tamhui* to provide more than mere subsistence. On these days, the *tamhui* gives the poor the foods necessary for proper – that is, *rabbinic* – religious observance. By providing permanent and reliable access to the necessities of life, the *tamhui* was unlike anything else in the ancient world and may be characterized in modern terms as a dole or soup kitchen, an entity that serves food and provides other necessities to the destitute.

A close examination of the *tamhui* will also illuminate the origins of the institution. I find that the *tamhui* was an adaptation of long-standing customs of hospitality. It differs from hospitality in that the *tamhui* assists only the poor and the items that it provides are explicitly defined. Moreover, whereas hospitality is undergirded by expectations of reciprocity, where guests are expected to return the favor to their hosts, the rabbinic vision of the *tamhui* purposefully obviates the assumption of a reciprocal return. My findings coalesce with the broader rabbinic ethos that has been illuminated by Seth Schwartz and Tzvi Novick, who have highlighted the rabbinic tendency to avoid reciprocal structures, which create relationships of dependency between Jews. Such vertical or hierarchical relationships are anathema to ideals of equality and shame the poor.[2] Thus, the *tamhui* plays an important role in the rabbis' vision of organized charity as an alternative to begging that provides for the poor while protecting their dignity.

DAILY ALMS

Tannaitic texts stipulate that anyone who has less than two meals worth of food per day is eligible to receive the following alms from the *tamhui*.

---

[1] m. Pe'ah 8:7; m. Pesahim 10:1; t. Pe'ah 4:8–10.
[2] Novick, "Charity and Reciprocity," 33–52; Schwartz, *Imperialism and Jewish Society*, 227–28; Schwartz, *Were the Jews*, 110–65.

Bread

The first item that the rabbis instruct the *tamhui* to provide is a loaf of bread. Cereals were the most important foods in the ancient world and they comprised up to half of an individual's daily diet. They were high in calories and, because cereals were cultivated on a massive scale and could be stored for long periods, they were abundant and inexpensive relative to other foods. They were the most common means to prevent starvation, as in times of crisis dry grains were distributed to the masses. Likewise, it was common to give a beggar a piece of bread.[3] By instructing the *tamhui* to give bread, then, the rabbis offer the poor an alternative to begging.

Aware that bread could be made in seemingly infinite ways, the rabbis specify that the *tamhui* provide a loaf of bread worth a *pondion*, made from grain valued at one *sela* per four *seah* of grain.[4] Quantification is a characteristic of rabbinic approaches to law. By answering perceived questions of how much, how long, and how far, the rabbis added precision to the way in which their instructions should be carried out. Things without measure are rare and warrant special treatment.[5] These measurements for bread are also found in other early rabbinic texts, where they are used to indicate minimum amounts.[6] Although the precise value of the measures found in rabbinic texts is uncertain, the best scholarship estimates that they work out to a loaf of bread weighing roughly 500 grams, which would provide the recipient with sufficient calories for a full day.[7]

Nevertheless, the Tannaim fail to specify the type of grain from which the loaf of bread should be made. There is a great deal at stake, as the type of

---

[3] On cereals in the ancient Mediterranean, see Garnsey, *Food and Society*, 13–17. On cereals as a staple of the diet of Roman Palestine, see Magen Broshi, *Bread, Wine, Walls and Scrolls* (London: Sheffield Academic Press, 2001), 121–26; Dar, "Food and Archaeology," 326–35; Kraemer, "Food, Eating, and Meals," 405–6; Rosenblum, *Food and Identity*.

[4] *Pondion* and *sela* refer to bronze coins, while *seah* was a measure of volume.

[5] See e.g., *m. Pe'ah* 1:1; concern about a lack of measurement might underlie *m. Avot* 1:16. On rabbinic interests in quantification and their possible roots, see Cohen, "Judaean Legal Tradition," 121–43; Yitzhak D. Gilat, *Studies in the Development of the Halakha [Hebrew]* (Ramat Gan, Israel: Bar-Ilan University Press, 1992), 63–71; Shemesh, "Things That Have," 387–405; Shemesh, "Creation of Measurements," 147–73.

[6] *m. Kelim* 17:11; *m. Shevi'it* 8:4; *m. Eruvin* 8:2.

[7] Hamel, *Poverty and Charity in Roman Palestine*, 39–42, 243–48. Similar conclusions are reached by Pastor, *Land and Economy*, 5; Safrai, *Economy*, 105, all of which conform to the calculations by Garnsey, *Food and Society*, 19–20 that 490–600 grams of bread per day would satisfy one's minimum caloric intake; see also Jongman, "Early Roman Empire: Consumption," 598–99. To be sure, measures in rabbinic texts are internally inconsistent and difficult to convert into modern units; see Ben-David, *Talmudische Ökonomie*, 331–43; Broshi, *Bread*, 121–23; Kraemer, "Food, Eating, and Meals," 404–05.

grain was the most important determinant of the bread's quality, which in turn indexed the social position of its consumer. Unlike the *quppa*, the *tamhui* demonstrates no interest in elevating the social status of the poor man. Rather, the *tamhui* is focused, laser-like, on providing just enough to keep the poor man alive.

Legumes

If an itinerant poor man stayed overnight, then he received legumes from the *tamhui*. Scholars have increasingly recognized the importance of legumes to the region's diet and economy, suggesting that the classic "Mediterranean triad" of cereals, olives, and grapes be expanded to a quartet to include legumes.[8] Legumes, which could be eaten raw, cooked, or dried, were an inexpensive source of calcium, vitamin C, and other nutrients.[9] The writings of Greek and Latin authors, from Galen (second century C.E.) to Macrobius (fifth century C.E.), attest that the ancients were aware of the nutritional aspects of legumes.[10] Above all, legumes are rich in protein and could replace expensive animal proteins, such as fish or meat.[11] By giving the poor legumes, the *tamhui* addresses the poor man's basic biological needs, providing the nutrients needed to stay alive.

It should be noted, however, that providing the poor with legumes also reinforces the signs of poverty. As an inexpensive source of essential nutrients, legumes became closely associated with the poor and known as "the poor man's meat."[12] Those who were well-off avoided legumes, which affirmed

---

[8] For a classic statement of the Mediterranean triad, see Fernand Braudel, *The Mediterranean and the Mediterranean World in the Age of Philip II* (London: Collins, 1972), 236. More recently, however, scholars have argued that the concept of a "Mediterranean triad" has masked the existence of local variations of cereals, olives, and grapes, as well as overlooked the widespread cultivation of legumes; see Peter Garnsey and Walter Scheidel, *Cities, Peasants, and Food in Classical Antiquity: Essays in Social and Economic History* (Cambridge and New York: Cambridge University Press, 1998), 221–22; Garnsey, *Food and Society*, 13–17; A. Sarpaki, "The Palaeobotanical Approach: The Mediterranean Triad or is it a Quartet?," in *Agriculture in Ancient Greece: Proceedings of the Seventh International Symposium at the Swedish Institute at Athens, 16–17 May, 1990* (ed. B. Wells; Stockholm: Svenska Institutet i Athen, 1992), 61–76.

[9] Broshi, *Bread*, 126; Garnsey and Scheidel, *Cities, Peasants, and Food*, 219.

[10] Galen 6.529; Macrobius. *Sat.* 1.12.33; as cited in Garnsey and Scheidel, *Cities, Peasants, and Food*, 218–19.

[11] Broshi, *Bread*, 126; Garnsey and Scheidel, *Cities, Peasants, and Food*, 214–225; Hamel, *Poverty and Charity in Roman Palestine*, 17–19; Schwartz, "Material Realities," 442.

[12] Pliny the Elder, *Natural History* 18.50, 101, 119; 22.154; Mireille Corbier, "The Broad Bean and the Moray: Social Hierarchies and Food in Rome," in *Food: A Culinary History from Antiquity to the Present* (ed. J. L. Flandrin et al.; New York: Columbia University Press, 1999), 128, 132–33; Garnsey, *Food and Society*, 15, 116.

their distinction and superiority over the lower elements of society.[13] The first-century B.C.E. Roman poet Martial, for example, writes that broad beans are exclusively for the poor and Pliny the Elder and Petronius likewise associate legumes with the poor.[14] A typical dish for poor people in Greece, for example, was lentil soup, while the poor in Rome ate bean or lupine porridge.[15]

That legumes were both a dietary staple and associated with poverty is likewise reflected in early rabbinic texts. Tannaitic compilations mention some twenty different kinds of legumes, the most prominent of which are lentils, beans, peas, chickpeas, and lupines.[16] Eaten fresh or dried, legumes were understood by the rabbis to be a staple of the daily diet.[17] The Tannaim prescribe that legumes and bread constitute the simplest complete meal that an employer is obligated to provide his employees.[18] That the rabbis consider legumes to be a basic dietary staple is likewise reflected in their discussions of a husband's minimum obligations toward his wife, which includes a half-kab of legumes every week.[19] Rabbinic texts also reflect the use of legumes as a symbol, especially their association with poverty. In Mishnah *Shabbat* 18:1, the rabbis identify dried lupines as "food for the poor." Tosefta *Bava Metzi'a* 3:9 discusses charity supervisors who search for "poor folk among whom to distribute beans."[20] That the charity supervisor cannot find anyone to take them might indicate that he has completed his task, that all the poor are satisfied. Alternatively, it indicates that legumes are an inferior good: not even the poor would take them due to their stigma.

There is no intention that the *tamhui* should give to the poor, on a regular basis, meat or other prestige foods that would elevate their place in society. What the poor would otherwise have eaten out of economic and physiological necessity, the Tannaim institutionalize and codify as religious law. Thus, the provision of legumes highlights the rabbis' intentions that the *tamhui* provide the poor with physiological necessities. In doing so, however, they also

---

[13] Garnsey and Scheidel, *Cities, Peasants, and Food*, 225.
[14] Corbier, "Broad Bean," 128–130.
[15] Hor., *Sat.* 2,3,182; Pliny the Elder, *Natural History* 18.50; 101; 119; 22.154; Andreas Gutsfeld, "Vegetables," *Brill's New Pauly: Encyclopaedia of the Ancient World* (ed. H. Cancik and H. Schneider; Leiden: Brill, 2002–2010), s.v.
[16] Broshi, *Bread*, 126; Yehuda Feliks, *Plants and Animals of the Mishna [Hebrew]* (Jerusalem: Institute for Mishna Research, 1982), 138; Kraemer, "Food, Eating, and Meals," 404–05.
[17] m. *Ma'aserot* 1:6; m. *Nedarim* 7:1; and the other rabbinic sources that I discuss in this section.
[18] m. *Bava Metzi'a* 7:1; see Lapin, *Early Rabbinic Civil Law*, 210.
[19] m. *Ketubbot* 5:8.
[20] Translation based on Jacob Neusner, *The Tosefta: Translated from the Hebrew with a New Introduction* (Peabody, Mass.: Hendrickson, 2002), 2:1037, with my modifications. The rabbis' lowly opinion of legumes is likewise reflected in its use as animal fodder; see *t. Terumot* 8:3; Feliks, *Plants*, 138; cf. *Sifra, Behar, Pereq* 1 (Weiss, *Sifra*, 106b).

replicate, produce, and reproduce the recipient's identity as "poor." Indeed, it would be left to the *quppa* to address the social aspects of poverty and tend to those who are poor according to Sen's value-judgment approach.

Olive Oil

As I discussed in Chapter 2, the cultivation of olives and the production of olive oil were essential components of the economy of Roman Palestine. Because they were important sources of calories and fats, they were a dietary staple, as adults consumed 17–20 kilos of olive oil per year as food, or about 50–55 grams per day. Olives and olive oil were also used in cosmetics and as fuel for ceramic lamps.[21]

Tannaitic texts reflect the significance of olives. They are a standard of measure, as one is counted in the quorum needed to recite the grace after meals (*birkat ha-mazon*) if he has eaten an amount of food equivalent to the size of an olive.[22] Olives warrant their own legal category in rabbinic discourse, especially in the laws of agriculture.[23] The instructions to leave produce that was overlooked or "forgotten" during the harvest for the poor, for example, can be suspended for certain olive trees that are particularly productive.[24] Olive trees served as boundary markers to define the size of a field, and in turn, one's obligations with respect to fulfilling the laws of *pe'ah*.[25]

Above all, the Tannaim take special interest in the oil that olives produce, discussing it throughout their texts.[26] It is emblematic that the Mishnah refers to the Mount of Olives – the hill that borders Jerusalem on the east – as the "Mount of Oil."[27] A particular olive tree could even be singled out for special treatment, as some were "famous" for their prolific yield.[28] In rabbinic texts, olive oil appears in discussions of cooking, as an accompaniment to bread, and as a preservative for other foods.[29] Like legumes, olive oil is among the provisions that a husband must provide for his wife.[30] The Tannaim were also

---

[21] Broshi, *Bread*, 127; Dar, "Food and Archaeology," 331; Frankel, *Wine and Oil Production*, 44.
[22] E.g., *m. Berakhot* 7:1–2; *m. Kil'ayim* 8:5; *m. Terumot* 7:3; *m. Hallah* 1:2; *m. Shabbat* 10:5.
[23] E.g., the sources cited in Feliks, *Plants*, 55.
[24] *m. Pe'ah* 7:1; see also *m. Pe'ah* 2:4 where Gamaliel's father used to designate one portion of *pe'ah* on behalf of all his olive trees, regardless of where they were located.
[25] *m. Pe'ah* 3:1; *m. Pe'ah* 7:1–2. On *pe'ah*, see my discussion in Chapter 1.
[26] E.g., *m. Pe'ah* 3:1; *m. Pe'ah* 7:1–2; *m. Menahot* 8:3–4; *t. Menahot* 9:5. *t. Terumot* 4:3; *Sifra, Emor, Parashah* 13 (Weiss, *Sifra*, 103a).
[27] *m. Parah* 3:6.
[28] *m. Pe'ah* 7:1.
[29] *m. Avodah Zarah* 2:6; *m. Shevi'it* 8:7; Rosenblum, *Food and Identity*, 18–19; Safrai, *Economy*, 218–22.
[30] *m. Ketubbot* 5:8.

interested in the socioreligious aspects of producing olive oil. For example, they devote special attention to the production of oil during the Sabbatical year.[31] Oil was unsuitable if it was expressed from an olive cultivated with manure, by irrigation, or if the olive had fallen into water or was pickled or boiled.[32] Elsewhere, the Mishnah discusses laws for the sale of an olive oil plant, while the Tosefta explores the application of purity laws to an oil press.[33]

Olive oil is singled out for special treatment, the Mishnah says, by no less an authority than Rabbi Judah the Prince, who is traditionally credited with redacting the Mishnah. In a discussion on interactions with Gentiles and Jewish dietary laws, the Mishnah points to a long-standing prohibition against consuming olive oil that was produced by non-Jews. This prohibition seems to be presupposed by the text and, indeed, is discussed in earlier sources from the Second Temple period. In this Mishnah, however, Judah the Prince repeals the prohibition.[34] His move is extraordinary, as it runs counter to the Tannaim's broader tendency to add – rather than subtract – restrictions on the way that food should be prepared.[35] Judah the Prince's move may also be part of an effort to make olive oil more affordable, as it was needed for both biological and religious purposes.[36]

Olive oil was privileged over other oils for fulfilling religious obligations. The Tannaim express great interest in the kind of oil used for offerings at the Temple.[37] Olive oil was also the fuel of choice for lighting lamps on the Sabbath. While other oils could have provided illumination, such as sesame oil, nut oil, radish-seed oil, and fish oil, "Rabbi Tarfon says, 'They do not light with any oil except olive oil.'"[38] The exclusivity of olive oil for lighting lamps on the Sabbath is emphasized by the Tosefta:

> R. Tarfon said, "They light [lamps for the Sabbath] only with olive oil."
> R. Yohanan b. Nuri [got up] on his feet and said, "What will the people in Babylonia do, who have only sesame oil? What will the people in Media do, who have only nut oil? What will the people in Alexandria do, who have

---

[31] *m. Shevi'it* 8:6; cf. *t. Shevi'it* 6:27.
[32] *m. Menahot* 8:3–5; *t. Menahot* 9:5–8; *Sifra, Emor, Parashah* 13 (Weiss, *Sifra*, 103a); on these, see Frankel et al., *History and Technology of Olive Oil*, 79–84.
[33] *m. Bava Batra* 4:5; *t. Avodah Zarah* 8:3; *t. Teharot* 11:16; on these texts, see the discussion in Frankel et al., *History and Technology of Olive Oil*, 79–84.
[34] *m. Avodah Zarah* 2:6.
[35] Martin Goodman, "Kosher Olive Oil in Antiquity," in *Tribute to Geza Vermes: Essays on Jewish and Christian Literature and History* (ed. P. R. Davies and R. T. White; Sheffield: Sheffield Academic Press, 1990), 227–45.
[36] Jordan D. Rosenblum, "Kosher Olive Oil in Antiquity Reconsidered," *JSJ* 40 (2009): 356–65.
[37] *m. Menahot* 8:3–5; *t. Menahot* 9:5–8; *Sifra, Emor, Parashah* 13 (Weiss, *Sifra*, 103a).
[38] *m. Shabbat* 2:2.

only radish oil? What will the people of Cappadocia do, who have neither one nor the other?"[39]

Olive oil was an irreplaceable commodity for the proper observance of the Sabbath, one of the cardinal commandments of Judaism. More broadly, the rabbis understood it to be among the "things upon which life depends" in *t. Avodah Zarah* 4:1–2. Olive oil was essential for poor individuals who stay in town overnight. During the week, it was an important source of sustenance, as the poor would have used it to complement bread and legumes for cooking, and also as a source of illumination. During the Sabbath, it served as a form of sustenance (though cooking was not permitted) and to fulfill the religious obligation to light the Sabbath lamps.

Biological Poverty

The combination of bread, legumes, and olive oil provides the necessary calories, protein, and nutrients needed to survive. The primary purpose of the *tamhui*, then, can be said to address Sen's "biological poverty," which I outlined in Chapter 2. An adult male, for example, requires about 2600 calories per day to survive in decent health.[40] The half-kilogram loaf of bread given by the *tamhui* would approach this calorie count, while oil and legumes would push it over the threshold and provide complementary fats and proteins. The *tamhui*, as it is laid out by the rabbis, is a means to provide the poor – regardless of who they are or where they came from – with their most immediate biological needs. The Tannaim's strategy can be thought of in terms of John Rawls's "difference principle," whereby the objective is not to solve poverty per se, but rather to make the position of the least advantaged members of society as good as possible.[41]

PROVISIONS FOR THE SABBATH AND PASSOVER

On a regular basis, the *tamhui* provides the bare minimum, which sustains the poor but also reinforces their lowly social position. On two occasions,

---

[39] *t. Shabbat* 2:3. Novick, *What is Good*, 208–09, writes that this passage is typical of the representation of Tarfon in Tannaitic texts as "the rabbi in error."

[40] Jongman, "Early Roman Empire: Consumption," 598–600, notes that men who were particularly tall, lived in cold climates, or engaged in heavy physical labor required more calories than the average man. While men are the focus of Tannaitic discussions on charity, it is notable that adult women between the ages of 20 and 40 required only 2,117–2,285 calories per day. One's overall health depends on one's "energy balance" – whether one consumes more calories than one expends.

[41] John Rawls and Erin Kelly, *Justice as Fairness: A Restatement* (Cambridge, Mass.: Belknap Press of Harvard University Press, 2001), 137–40.

however, the *tamhui* doles out much more. If the poor man stays in town for the Sabbath, then the rabbis specify that he should receive enough food for three meals (*t. Pe'ah* 4:8). On Passover, the *tamhui* is to provide the poor with four cups of wine for the Seder (*m. Pesahim* 10:1). Religious obligations often had material requirements – one needs certain goods in order to fulfill certain commandments. The rabbis' instructions for the *tamhui* reflect the material requirements of the Sabbath and Passover, providing the poor with what they need to properly observe these days in the rabbinically prescribed way.

Three Meals

For the Sabbath, the *tamhui* is to provide enough food for three meals, which must include fish and a vegetable. Eating three meals has been and continues to be an important aspect of Sabbath observance. The first meal is eaten after the start of the Sabbath, after sundown on Friday evening; the second during the day on Saturday, possibly in the late morning; and the third meal is eaten in the late afternoon and completed before the Sabbath ends at sundown on Saturday.[42] A number of texts indicate that the rabbis assumed that people normally ate only two meals a day.[43] Thus, to fit three meals into the Sabbath, one would delay the Friday evening meal until after sunset and ensure that the Saturday evening meal concluded before sunset. Fulfilling the obligation also required additional planning, as all three meals had to be prepared before the start of the Sabbath.

The origin of the imperative to eat three meals during the Sabbath is unclear. The earliest sources are Tannaitic texts, where it was probably a way to elevate the Sabbath above the weekday, when it was customary to eat only two meals.[44] We see the obligation to eat three meals, for example, in a Tannaitic discussion on what may be carried out of a burning house on the Sabbath.[45]

> They save food for three meals. For human beings, [they save food] sufficient for a human being. For a beast, [they save food] sufficient for a beast. How so

---

[42] Gilat, *Studies*, 116n. 44; Joseph Tabory, "Jewish Festivals in Late Antiquity," in *The Cambridge History of Judaism: Volume Four: The Late Roman-Rabbinic Period* (ed. S. T. Katz; Cambridge: Cambridge University Press, 2006), 561–62. In Geonic times, the Sabbath morning meal was divided into two meals; see Yaakov Gartner, "The Third Sabbath Meal: *Halakhic* and Historical Aspects [Hebrew]," *Sidra* 6 (1990): 5–24.

[43] *m. Eruvin* 8:2; *t. Eruvin* 6:9; *m. Kelim* 17:11; *m. Pe'ah* 8:5; *m. Pe'ah* 8:7; Tabory, "Jewish Festivals," 562.

[44] *t. Shabbat* 13:7–8; *Mekilta*, *Vayyisa* 4, posits exegetical roots for the law, see Gilat, *Studies*, 115–16.

[45] *m. Shabbat* 16:1–3; *m. Shabbat* 22:1; *t. Shabbat* 13:1–6; on these passages, see Jacob Neusner, *A History of the Mishnaic Law of Appointed Times: Part One, Shabbat* (Leiden: Brill, 1981), 146.

[i.e., in what manner]? [If] a fire starts on Sabbath night [i.e., Friday night,[46] then] they save food for three meals. [If a fire starts] in the morning, [then] they save food for two meals. [If a fire starts] in the afternoon, [then they save] food for one meal. R. Yose says, "They may always save food for three meals."[47] (*m. Shabbat* 16:2)

This Mishnah instructs the reader to save only those foods necessary to feed a human and an animal on the Sabbath. For a human, this is defined as the minimum needed for three meals. As such, the food needed for three meals is placed into an elite category of objects, on par with other important objects such as Torah scrolls, that may be carried out of a burning building on the Sabbath.[48] Food for three meals is a religious staple, absolutely necessary in the rabbinic mind for the proper observance of the Sabbath. Thus, the rabbis prescribe that the *tamhui* should give the alms necessary to allow the poor man to properly observe the Sabbath.

Fish

The rabbis' instruction that the *tamhui* provide fish reflects a wider, extrarabbinic custom for Jews to eat fish on the Sabbath. This is apparent even to non-Jewish onlookers such as Persius, the first-century C.E. Italian satirical poet:

> But when the days of Herod come round,[49] and the lamps, wearing violets and arranged along the greasy window, spew out a fatty fog, when the tail of tuna fish swims coiling round the red bowl, when the white pitcher is bulging with wine, you silently move your lips and turn pale at the circumcised Sabbath. (Persius, *Saturae* 5.179–184)[50]

His demeaning tone aside, Persius provides an important characterization of the role of food and particularly fish on the Sabbath. In addition to wine, he notes the inclusion of special foods, in this case tuna fish. The importance of fish is suggested by its juxtaposition with the lamps, another object needed

---

[46] Before the meal has taken placed; see the commentary in Hanoch Albeck, *Shishah Sidrei Mishnah = The Mishnah [Hebrew]* (6 vols.; Jerusalem and Tel Aviv: Bialik Institute and Dvir Publishing House, 1952–1958 [repr. 1988]), 2:54.

[47] That is, they can save up to three meals worth of food at any point during the Sabbath, regardless of when the fire started.

[48] Neusner, *History of the Mishnaic Law – Shabbat*, 146.

[49] The "day of Herod" refers to the Sabbath; see Peter Schäfer, *Judeophobia: Attitudes toward the Jews in the Ancient World* (Cambridge, Mass.: Harvard University Press, 1997), 90–91; Stern, *Greek and Latin Authors*, 1:436–37.

[50] Translation according to Braund, *Juvenal and Persius (LCL)*, 111–13.

for Sabbath observance. Fish is cast as a special food for the Sabbath, as Goldenberg notes, embodying the holiness of the day.[51] Likewise, certain Tannaitic texts presuppose a custom of eating fish on the Sabbath.[52] For example, *m. Shabbat* 22:2 discusses how salted fish and Spanish tuna fish should be prepared for the Sabbath. Just as in Persius, so too in early rabbinic texts fish is juxtaposed with lighting lamps on the Sabbath. For example, *t. Sukkah* 4:11 instructs that one could not enter into the Sabbath limits until they have lit the Sabbath lamps and roasted a fish. In short, fish was a special food to mark a special meal. While less expensive and prestigious than meat, fish was nevertheless considered a delicacy that was normally beyond the means of the poor.[53]

Vegetables

In addition to fish, the rabbis also instruct that the *tamhui* should provide the poor with a vegetable. Vegetables are mentioned throughout early rabbinic texts, including legal discussions on tithing and whether they may be imported during the Sabbatical year.[54] The most common vegetables are onions, leeks, squashes, cabbages, radishes, beets, and garlic.[55] Vegetables are also needed to complete a proper meal, as they are mentioned as appetizers and accompaniments to the main course in rabbinic discussions of banquets.[56] Likewise, other texts suggest that the inclusion of a vegetable alongside a main dish (e.g., meat, fish) is what defined a proper meal, as opposed to a random

---

[51] Robert Goldenberg, "The Place of the Sabbath in Rabbinic Judaism," in *The Sabbath in Jewish and Christian Traditions* (ed. T. C. Eskenazi et al.; New York: Crossroad, 1991), 31–44.

[52] For rabbinic texts on fish, see Broshi, *Bread*, 134; Krauss, *Talmudische Archäologie*, 1:110–12.

[53] Broshi, *Bread*, 134–35; Garnsey, *Food and Society*, 16–17; Krauss, *Talmudische Archäologie*, 1:110–12; cf. Justin Lev-Tov, "'Upon What Meat doth this our Caesar feed...?' A Dietary Perspective on Hellenistic and Roman Influence in Palestine," in *Zeichen aus Text und Stein: Studien auf dem Weg zu einer Archäologie des Neuen Testaments* (ed. S. Alkier et al.; Tübingen: Francke, 2003), 420–46. Later traditions in the Babylonian Talmud tell of the difficulties that poor men had in acquiring fish for the Sabbath; see *b. Shabbat* 119a; Broshi, *Bread*, 134; S. Safrai, "Home and Family," in *The Jewish People in the First Century: Historical Geography, Political History, Social, Cultural and Religious Life and Institutions* (ed. S. Safrai and M. Stern; Compendia rerum Iudaicarum ad Novum Testamentum Section 1; Assen and Philadelphia: Van Gorcum and Fortress Press, 1974), 2:747.

[54] *m. Demai* 5:7; *t. Shevi'it* 4:16, 19; see Safrai, *Economy*, 386–87.

[55] Feliks, *Plants*; Hamel, *Poverty and Charity in Roman Palestine*, 17–18; Samuel Krauss, *Kadmoniyot ha-Talmud 'al pi ha-hakirot yeha-tagliyot ha-hadashot [Hebrew]* (2 vols.; Odessa: Moriyah, 1914–1929 [repr. 1945]), 2:233–43. Perhaps most prominent were onions and garlic, which some texts suggest were as important as any other food; see *t. Avodah Zarah* 4:11. Garlic may have been an identity marker of Judaism, as *m. Nedarim* 3:10 refers to Jews as "garlic eaters."

[56] *m. Pesahim* 10:3; *t. Berakhot* 4:8.

snack.[57] However, as I noted in Chapter 3, extrarabbinic sources suggest that the poor normally could not afford to acquire or eat vegetables. Instead of proper vegetables, the poor were compelled to substitute less expensive wild mushrooms, grasses, and edible roots.[58]

In short, the rabbis prescribe that the *tamhui* provide the poor with fish and a vegetable on the Sabbath for two interrelated reasons. First, fish and vegetables were foods that the poor would normally not be able to afford, elevating the quality of the poor man's diet, at least temporarily, perhaps in an effort to sanctify the Sabbath above weekdays and make it a day of delight.[59] Mishnah *Kelim* 17:11 notes that food for the weekday is different from food for the Sabbath. Second, fish and vegetables rounded out the minimum requirements for a complete meal, three of which were necessary to properly observe the Sabbath. Thus, the *tamhui* aims to provide the poor's basic necessities – addressing their biological needs during the week and their religious needs during the Sabbath.[60]

Wine at the Passover Seder

Grapes were also widely considered to be an essential component of daily life. Wine, usually mixed with water at a ratio of one-to-two, was the most common beverage in the country, as the ancients drank roughly a liter of wine per day.[61] "The basic necessities of life," Ben Sira writes, included the "blood of the grape" (Sir 39:26). The significance of grapes and wine is likewise reflected in early rabbinic texts. They discuss mundane aspects of the grape economy, addressing topics such as selling fresh grapes in the market and turning dried grapes into raisins.[62] The Hebrew equivalent of the amphora,

---

[57] m. *Berakhot* 6:8; Safrai, *Economy*, 105; Tzvee Zahavy, *Studies in Jewish Prayer* (Lanham, Md.: University Press of America, 1990), 23–24.

[58] Hamel, *Poverty and Charity in Roman Palestine*, 18; Hamel, "Poverty and Charity," 317.

[59] On sanctifying the Sabbath, see Gen 2:3; Exod 20:8–11; Deut 5:12–14; Ezek 20:20; 44:24. On using food to make the Sabbath a day of delight, see Isa 58:13; Goldenberg, "Place of the Sabbath," 36–41.

[60] See further Gardner, "Let Them Eat Fish," 250–70.

[61] Broshi, *Bread*, 129; Kraemer, "Food, Eating, and Meals," 405; Zeev Safrai, "Agriculture and Farming," in *The Oxford Handbook of Jewish Daily Life in Roman Palestine* (ed. C. Hezser; Oxford: Oxford University Press, 2010), 253–54. The significance of viticulture is reflected in the archaeological record, especially in the ubiquity of wine presses and amphorae; see Ayalon et al., eds., *Oil and Wine Presses in Israel*; Frankel, *Wine and Oil Production*; Uzi Leibner, "Arts and Crafts, Manufacture and Production," in *The Oxford Handbook of Jewish Daily Life in Roman Palestine* (ed. C. Hezser; Oxford: Oxford University Press, 2010), 286–88.

[62] t. *Ma'aserot* 2:4; t. *Teharot* 11:7; see Safrai, "Agriculture and Farming," 254.

havit, is mentioned almost three hundred times in Tannaitic texts, more than any other vessel.[63] The wine press is likewise mentioned in the sources and the rabbis were particularly interested in it with respect to purity laws.[64] In some texts, the winepress itself takes on holiness.[65] Wine and grapes are the subject of intense and extended *halakhic* discussions, such as which kind of wine was used for cultic purposes in Temple rites, and, perhaps most prominently, on the restrictions against wine made by Gentiles.[66] Wine is a necessity for the performance of certain obligations. For example, the rabbis formulate a special blessing, *qiddush*, to be recited before drinking wine. Wine was also needed for *havdalah*, at weddings, circumcisions, funeral meals, and festivals.[67] Wine, the Tosefta notes, stands alongside olive oil and cereals, as one of the "things upon which life depends."[68] The rabbis understood that a typical meal would include two cups of wine.[69]

In light of the centrality of wine in daily life, its absence from the *tamhui*'s daily distribution is conspicuous. The reasons for this omission are unclear. It is possible that the rabbis assumed that the poor would receive wine through allocations of the poor tithe.[70] To be sure, the ancient rabbis' treatments of wine are less uniform than modern scholars would like. While some rabbinic texts acknowledge its usefulness in daily life, others understand wine as a prestige food that is reserved for special occasions. We see this, for example, in *m. Sanhedrin* 8:2, where wine is paired with meat, and in *t. Ketubbot* 5:8, where wine is excluded from the provisions that a husband is obligated to give his wife because "she has no claim for wine, for the wives of the poor do not drink wine."

The idea that wine was reserved for special occasions finds further support in instructions for the *tamhui* to provide wine to the poor on Passover. Mishnah *Pesahim* 10:1, at the beginning of its discussion of the Seder, declares

---

[63] Brand, *Ceramics*, 111–73.
[64] E.g., *t. Terumot* 7:15, and the sources in Frankel, *Wine and Oil Production*, 186–96.
[65] *t. Sukkah* 3:15. The wine press was also employed in polemics against Christian traditions; see Joshua Schwartz, "A Holy People in the Winepress: Treading the Grapes and Holiness," in *A Holy People: Jewish and Christian Perspectives on Religious Communal Identity* (ed. M. Poorthuis and J. Schwartz; Jewish and Christian Perspectives 12; Leiden and Boston: Brill, 2006), 45–49.
[66] Temple: *m. Menahot* 8:6–7. Gentile-made wine: *m. Avodah Zarah* 2:3–7; *t. Avodah Zarah* 1:21, 3:11, 3:16, and passim; see Freidenreich, *Foreigners*, 57–61; Kraemer, "Food, Eating, and Meals," 412; Rosenblum, *Food and Identity*.
[67] Safrai, "Home and Family," 2:747.
[68] *t. Avodah Zarah* 4:1–2.
[69] *t. Berakhot* 4:8.
[70] *m. Pe'ah* 8:5.

that all participants must consume at least four cups of wine, including a poor person:

> On the eve of Passover, close to [the time of] *minhah* [the daily afternoon offering], a person should not eat until it gets dark. Even the poorest person in Israel should not eat until [he] reclines. They should not give him fewer than four cups of wine even if [it is provided] from the *tamhui*. (*m. Pesahim* 10:1)[71]

While it is unclear exactly where the poor would attend a Seder, from this passage we learn that the *tamhui* should provide enough wine for the requisite four cups.[72] This is similar to the rabbis' direction that the soup kitchen provide the foods necessary to eat three meals on the Sabbath, including fish and a vegetable.

Conclusion

In short, the rabbis instruct that the *tamhui* should provide additional alms on the Sabbath and Passover. In the case of the Sabbath, the poor receive foods that they could otherwise not afford to consume. This adds variety to their normal diet, elevating, if only briefly, the quality of their lives. With regard to the Sabbath and Passover, the rabbis prescribe that the poor are to receive some of the dietary requirements needed for their proper observance. The poor are given the wine necessary for the Passover Seder, as well as enough fish and vegetables needed for three meals on the Sabbath. I find that the rabbis shape charity so as to enable the poor to observe certain religious obligations that have material requirements. It should be noted that these prescriptions suggest control over the poor and their diets. Whether real or imagined, the *tamhui* serves as a means to control the ways that the poor observe the

---

[71] Translation is based on Baruch M. Bokser, *The Origins of the Seder: The Passover Rite and Early Rabbinic Judaism* (Berkeley: University of California Press, 1984), 29, with my emendations. Bokser's understanding that the *tamhui* finances the provision of wine, however, is inconsistent with Tannaitic sources where the *tamhui* only provides aid in kind and only the *quppa* provides monetary support; see my discussion in Chapter 5. On this text, see further Shamma Friedman, *Pesah Rishon: Synoptic Parallels of Mishna and Tosefta [Hebrew]* (Ramat Gan: Bar-Ilan University, 2002).

[72] The four cups of wine, each accompanied by a benediction, give the Seder its structure; see Bokser, *Origins of the Seder*, 50 66; Friedman, *Pesah Rishon*, 405–09, 415; Judith Hauptman, "How Old is the Haggadah?," *Judaism* 51 (2002): 5–18; Joshua Kulp, "The Origins of the Seder and Haggadah," *Currents in Biblical Research* 4 (2005): 109–34; Joseph Tabory, *Jewish Festivals in the Time of the Mishnah and Talmud [Hebrew]* (Jerusalem: Magness Press, 1995), 84–130. I note that the *tamhui* is absent from the Tosefta's version of the Seder.

Sabbath and Passover – though a distinction should be made between these subtle forms of control and the overt use of charity to gain authority in later Amoraic and Christian sources.[73]

LODGING FOR THE POOR

In addition to food, the *tamhui* also provides maintenance or arrangements for lodging to the itinerant poor who intend to lodge overnight. This would consist of bedding and shelter, which the rabbis understood as basic necessities.[74] Bedding in the ancient world typically consisted of a mattress atop a bed frame, pillow, and blanket.[75] Needless to say, the poor would have to make do with less and the rabbis had an understanding of what the minimum should be. They did not consider pillows to be a necessity, as they instruct that "the wives of the poor do not sleep on pillows."[76] Instead, the husband is required to provide only a straw or rush mat, possibly something similar to those found in the Judean desert caves alongside the baskets (*quppot*) that I discussed in Chapter 3.[77] While some probably placed these mats on the ground, for the most part the rabbis assumed that even the poor would have had a bed frame, with cords stretched across it, on which the mats could be placed.[78] This minimum bedding would protect the individual from insects, snakes, and other creatures on the ground, as well as from cold, damp, or rough floors.[79]

Maintenance for lodging included shelter as well.[80] Tannaitic texts, however, do not specify where the poor would have stayed. One possibility is that the poor were expected to stay at someone's home. This, however, would be in fundamental tension with a central objective of organized charity, to provide alms in an indirect and impersonal manner in order to obviate the creation of hierarchical relationships of personal dependency. The language "maintenance" for lodging suggests another possibility: that the *tamhui* arranged or

---

[73] See my discussion in Chapter 8.
[74] E.g., *m. Ketubbot* 5:8; *t. Ketubbot* 6:8; see further Safrai, "Home and Family," 2:735–36.
[75] *m. Shabbat* 20:5; Krauss, *Talmudische Archäologie*, 1:62–66; Schwartz, "Beds, Bedclothes, and Sleeping Habits," 204–08; Schwartz, "Material Realities," 437–38.
[76] *t. Ketubbot* 5:8.
[77] Yadin, *Finds from the Bar Kokhba Period*, 150–51.
[78] Schwartz, "Beds, Bedclothes, and Sleeping Habits," 197–208.
[79] Rabbinic texts do not advocate sleeping on the ground, except during Sukkot when individuals slept in booths to mark the festival. By contrast, sleeping on the ground was common among Christian monks; see the discussion in Schwartz, "Beds, Bedclothes, and Sleeping Habits," 206–08.
[80] Lieberman, *Tosefta Ki-Fshutah*, 1:183 cf. Brooks, *Support for the Poor*, 146, 200n. 26.

paid for poor individuals to stay at an inn or to rent a dwelling.[81] Similarly, the rabbis instruct that a home should be rented for an orphan boy who wishes to marry but could not support a family.[82] Another possibility is that the Tannaim presumed that the poor would stay at a local synagogue, which may have had been constructed with rooms for hospitality. Indeed, the similarities between the customs of hospitality for travelers and the *tamhui* are numerous and warrant a closer examination, to which I now turn.

Hospitality

As I discussed in Chapter 1, there are no pre- or nonrabbinic sources on the soup kitchen. Some of the attributes of the soup kitchen, however, find important parallels in long-standing customs of hospitality, as they both provide food and lodging to those in need. In Jewish sources, moreover, hospitality was at times a communal and collective venture. The affinities between the soup kitchen and hospitality suggest that the two were closely related; indeed, I find that the origins of the *tamhui* can be traced to Jewish customs of hospitality. While other scholars (e.g., Becknell, Bolkestein, and Loewenberg) have suggested similar origins for the *tamhui* and charity in general, the relationship between hospitality and the *tamhui* has yet to be fleshed out with a critical approach to the sources, reading them within their historical and literary contexts. Moreover, important differences between the *tamhui* and hospitality have been overlooked, as the two are often conflated or understood in evolutionary terms.[83] By contrast, I find that there are significant differences between them, particularly concerning the issue of reciprocity. In hospitality, a guest is expected to reciprocate for the provisions received from the host. With the *tamhui*, however, there is no expectation that the recipient will reciprocate or provide any kind of compensation in return. The *tamhui*, I find, was conceived by the Tannaim as an adaptation of hospitality – one did not replace the other; rather the two coexisted and performed similar but distinct social and economic functions.[84]

The word "hospitality" has a broad sense in modern usage, as it can denote any kind of cordial or generous reception for anyone identified as a guest.

---

[81] Inns are mentioned throughout Tannaitic sources; e.g., *m. Gittin* 8:9; *m. Eduyyot* 4:7; *m. Yevamot* 16:7; *t. Yevamot* 1:10; *m. Qiddushin* 4:12; see also the Tannaitic sources cited in Ben-Zion Rosenfeld, "Innkeeping in Jewish Society in Roman Palestine," *JESHO* 41 (1998): 133–58.
[82] *t. Ketubbot* 6:8.
[83] Cf. Becknell, "Almsgiving," 71–78; Bolkestein, *Wohltätigkeit*, 102; Loewenberg, "Development of Philanthropic Institutions," 193–207.
[84] Cf. Bolkestein, *Wohltätigkeit*, 102; Loewenberg, "Development of Philanthropic Institutions," 193–207.

Hosting a meal for a friend or neighbor, for example, would be included within today's understanding of hospitality. In the ancient world, however, hospitality (*xenia*) had a narrower focus.[85] It constituted temporary assistance in the form of provisions and protection for travelers or strangers.[86] A host might offer baths, clothes, entertainment, an opportunity to worship deities, medical care, and perhaps even burial in case of death. Above all, the host provides a guest with food and lodging.[87] It was dangerous to be a stranger or traveler in the ancient world, as they were easy prey for bandits along the roads, would be exposed to inclement weather, and might not be able to procure sufficient food.[88] Hospitality entailed a commitment by the host to protect his guest from others, the environment, and hunger.

There were a number of motivations for one to host a guest. These included an attempt to disarm a stranger's ill will, earn favor with deities, and promote one's own social standing and reputation.[89] Above all, hospitality was motivated and undergirded by the expectation of a return.[90] It was a form of gift exchange between strangers, whereby a gift from one party generates an obligation for the other party to reciprocate. A guest was expected to return the favor by giving a counter-gift, offering personal service, expressing gratitude,

---

[85] Andrew E. Arterbury, *Entertaining Angels: Early Christian Hospitality in its Mediterranean Setting* (Sheffield: Sheffield Phoenix, 2005), 1–4.

[86] This definition is based on Arterbury, *Entertaining Angels*, 6, 15–28, 57, 131–32; John Koenig, *New Testament Hospitality: Partnership with Strangers as Promise and Mission* (Philadelphia: Fortress Press, 1985), 8; Gustav Stahlin, "xenos," in *Theological Dictionary of the New Testament* (ed. G. Kittel et al.; Grand Rapids, Mich.: Eerdmans, 1964–1976), 5:2–4.

[87] Ladislaus J. Bolchazy, "From Xenophobia to Altruism: Homeric and Roman Hospitality," *Ancient World* 1 (1978): 59–60; Koenig, *New Testament Hospitality*, 6; Longenecker, *Remember the Poor*, 70–71.

[88] Loewenberg, "Development of Philanthropic Institutions," 199; Beate Wagner-Hasel, "Hospitality: Greece and Rome," *Brill's New Pauly: Encyclopaedia of the Ancient World* (ed. H. Cancik and H. Schneider; Leiden: Brill, 2002–2010), s.v.

[89] Ladislaus J. Bolchazy, *Hospitality in Early Rome: Livy's Concept of its Humanizing Force* (Chicago, Ill.: Ares Publishers, 1977), 1–34; Bolchazy, "From Xenophobia to Altruism," 45–64; Longenecker, *Remember the Poor*, 70–71; Stahlin, "xenos," 5:1–6.

[90] Hospitality is closely related with gift exchange, see Mauss, *The Gift*; Beate Wagner-Hasel, "Egoistic Exchange and Altruistic Gift: On the Roots of Marcel Mauss' Theory of the Gift," in *Negotiating the Gift: Pre-modern Figurations of Exchange* (ed. G. Algazi et al.; Veröffentlichungen des Max-Planck-Instituts für Geschichte 188; Gottingen: Vandenhoeck & Ruprecht, 2003), 156–59. On hospitality's expectation to reciprocate, see Arterbury, *Entertaining Angels*, 15–54; Bolchazy, *Hospitality in Early Rome*, 11–12; M. I. Finley, *The World of Odysseus* (Harmondsworth and New York: Penguin, 1979); Aafke Komter, "Women, Gifts and Power," in *The Gift: An Interdisciplinary Perspective* (ed. Aafke E. Komter; Amsterdam: Amsterdam University Press, 1996), 122; Novick, "Charity and Reciprocity," 33–52; Marshall David Sahlins, *Stone Age Economics* (London and New York: Routledge, 1972 [repr. 2004]), 193–94; Stahlin, "xenos," 5:2–4.

or eventually providing accommodations to the initial host.[91] Hospitality could be a calculated exchange (even a form of contract), more so than an act of altruism. While a meritorious host was expected to assist any traveler, it is inevitable that hosts and guests would select one another based on their potential for personal benefit.[92] Such calculations, however, would leave out in the cold individuals who had little to offer in return, or whose return (such as a token or expression of gratitude) was not particularly valuable to the host. Thus, while hospitality was extended to the poor, it did not focus on the poor per se.

These characteristics of hospitality are likewise reflected in Jewish writings of the Hellenistic and Second Temple age.[93] The New Testament is filled with exhortations to extend hospitality to strangers, where hosts provide food, drink, festive meals, and shelter.[94] That hospitality is a meritorious act is seen in the Wisdom of Solomon and the writings of Josephus.[95] Ben Sira, whose work was known to the rabbis, writes extensively on hospitality, outlining proper behavior for hosts and guests.[96] Noteworthy is the expectation that a guest will reciprocate by thanking, blessing, or praising the host.[97]

Postbiblical attitudes toward hospitality are grounded in precepts and narratives from the Hebrew Bible. Leviticus 19:34 posits that a stranger should have the rights of a citizen, while Deuteronomy 10:17–19 sees hospitality as *imitatio dei* – one should imitate God, who is the host par excellence.[98] Above all, these verses instruct that one should provide hospitality because Israel

---

[91] E.g., Cicero, *Off.* 1, 139 and the sources cited in Wagner-Hasel, "Hospitality." See also Joel Allen, *Hostages and Hostage-taking in the Roman Empire* (Cambridge and New York: Cambridge University Press, 2006), 67; Sahlins, *Stone Age Economics*, 194–95; Longenecker, *Remember the Poor*, 70–71.

[92] Arterbury, *Entertaining Angels*, 132; Bolchazy, *Hospitality in Early Rome*, 11–12.

[93] Andrew E. Arterbury, "Abraham's Hospitality Among Jewish and Early Christian Writers: A Tradition History of Gen 18:1–16 and its Relevance for the Study of the New Testament," *Perspectives in Religious Studies* 30 (2003): 359–76; Koenig, *New Testament Hospitality*; John Koenig, "Hospitality," *The Anchor Bible Dictionary*, 3:299–301.

[94] E.g., Matt 25:31–46; Luke 24:13–35; Acts 10:23, 28:7–8; Rev 3:20; Rom 12:13; Heb 13:2; 1 Tim 3:2; 1 Pet 4:9; see Arterbury, *Entertaining Angels*; Koenig, *New Testament Hospitality*; Koenig, "Hospitality," 3:299–301.

[95] Wis 19:14–17; Josephus, *Ant.* 1.246–255.

[96] Sir 29:20–27, 31:12–32:13. On rabbinic uses of Ben Sira, see Jenny R. Labendz, "The Book of Ben Sira in Rabbinic Literature," *AJSR* 30 (2006): 347–92.

[97] See especially Sir 31:23: "On a person generous with food, blessings are invoked, and this testimony to his goodness is lasting." Cf. *t. Berakhot* 6:2.

[98] On these verses, see Jacob Milgrom, *Leviticus 17–22: A New Translation with Introduction and Commentary* (New York: Doubleday, 2000), 1704–07; Moshe Weinfeld, *Deuteronomy 1–11: A New Translation with Introduction and Commentary* (New York: Doubleday, 1991), 438–40. Cf. Exod 12:49, 22:20–22, 23:9; Lev 19:18, 24:22; Num 15:16, 29; Ps 146:9.

itself was once a stranger and in need.[99] Postbiblical writings draw upon biblical narratives as models for hospitality. They extol Rebecca, Lot, Job, and others for their hospitality, contrasting them with Israel's enemies, who are punished for their lack of hospitality.[100] Hellenistic Jewish texts see Abraham, who provided for three strangers in Genesis 18:1–18, as the human host par excellence.[101] The reciprocal aspects of the biblical narrative are drawn out by Philo, who writes that the guests bestow upon Abraham "a reward beyond his expectation, the birth of a legitimate son in a short time."[102]

The rabbis drew upon and further developed these biblical and postbiblical traditions on hospitality. While the classic rabbinic term for hospitality, *hakhnasat orehim* ("bringing in guests"), would not come into use until after the Tannaim, its underlying principals are already apparent in Tannaitic compilations.[103] We see this in *t. Berakhot* 4:8:

> What is the order of a meal [at a banquet]? Guests enter and they are seated on benches and on chairs until [all of the guests] are gathered [and seated]. [Once] all of them are gathered, [and the servants] have given them [water] for their hands, every [guest] washes one hand.[104]

The passage instructs that guests are an integral part of an ideal banquet. Hospitality is also addressed in Tannaitic narratives on kings who invite

---

[99] Sir 32:13; *1 En.* 62:14; cf. Ps 23, 104.

[100] Lot: Gen 19:1–3; Josephus, *Ant.* 1.200–201; *1 Clement* 11.1. Rebecca: Gen 24:10–61; Josephus, *Ant.* 1.249–252; Job 31:32; *Testament of Job* 10:1–3; Sodomites: Gen 19:4–11, Josephus, *Ant* 1.194. The Egyptians are also disparaged for their failure to provide hospitality; see the sources cited in Stahlin, "xenos," 5:19.

[101] On Abraham as an ideal host in postbiblical writings, see, among others, *Testament of Abraham* 1.1–2, 5 and passim; Philo, *Abraham* 107–18. Josephus, *Ant.* 1.196–197; *1 Clement* 10.7. On Abraham as host, see Arterbury, "Abraham's Hospitality," 359–76; Arterbury, *Entertaining Angels*, 59–71.

[102] Philo, *Abraham* 110. *1 Clement* 10.7 also understands a son as a reward for Abraham's hospitality.

[103] On *hakhnasat orehim*, see *b. Shabbat* 127a, *b. Shevu'ot* 35b. On the history of the term, see Ben-Yehuda et al., *Complete Dictionary*, 2:1084; Kena'ani, *Otsar ha-lashon ha-'Ivrit*, 3:769–70; Rome et al., *Aruch completum*, 3:204–5. See also *akhsaniya*, which derives from the Greek *xenia* for "strangers," while *xenizein* often denotes extending hospitality toward strangers. The New Testament uses *philoxenos* "love for strangers" for one who extends hospitality. On *akhsaniya*, see the sources listed here and Jastrow, *Dictionary*, 65; Rome et al., *Aruch completum*, 1:81. On hospitality, see also *Lamentations Rabbah*, in Salomon Buber, *Midrasch Echa Rabbati: Sammlung aggadischer Auslegungen der Klagelieder [Hebrew]* (Hildsheim, 1899 repr. 1967), 46–47, where a host in Athens handles a complex inheritance issue upon the death of his guest from Jerusalem. Linguistic aspects of this text are discussed in Galit Hasan-Rokem, "An Almost Invisible Presence: Multilingual Puns in Rabbinic Literature," in *The Cambridge Companion to the Talmud and Rabbinic Literature* (ed. C. E. Fonrobert and M. S. Jaffee; New York: Cambridge University Press, 2007), 233–36.

[104] Translation based on Rosenblum, *Food and Identity*, 31, with my emendations.

guests to meals.[105] Rabbinic texts often portray a host providing a guest with extravagant foods, such as meat. In *SifreDeut* 116, for example, a guest in the Upper Galilee is given a pound of meat every day.[106] Likewise, in *m. Me'ilah* 6:1, the rabbis discuss scenarios in which a host provides meat to his guests.[107] Meat is used to illustrate the principle that a host ought to be unstinting, sparing no expense.

Hospitality is important enough for the rabbis to prescribe legal leniency, as produce from the Sabbatical year can be given to guests, but not to others.[108] Likewise, *Sifra* instructs that this produce may be used to feed gentile boarders.[109] Guests should be treated as if they are members of the host's own household. An exegesis on *[those] who live with you* (Leviticus 25:6), for example, is expounded by the Tannaim as "this serves to encompass guests."[110]

In light of the restrictions against carrying, the Sabbath and festival days present special opportunities for one to extend hospitality to travelers.[111] In their discussion on what may or may not be moved on the Sabbath, the rabbis make an exception to facilitate hospitality, rendering it permissible for a householder to move four or five baskets of straw or grain in order to make room for a guest. By contrast, one may not move baskets sitting in a storeroom, presumably because their location would not hinder one's ability to host guests.[112] Likewise, special attention is given to hospitality extended during a festival.[113]

The expectation for a guest to reciprocate is evident in early rabbinic literature, just as it was in Greek, Latin, and Hellenistic Jewish texts. An

---

[105] *t. Sanhedrin* 8:9; *SifreDeut* 53. On the use of kings in rabbinic parables to symbolize God, see David Stern, *Parables in Midrash: Narrative and Exegesis in Rabbinic Literature* (Cambridge, Mass.: Harvard University Press, 1991), 19–21.

[106] On this text and its parallel in *t. Pe'ah* 4:10, see my discussion in Chapter 5.

[107] On hospitality in the Mishnah, see also *m. Sotah* 9:6 and the sources cited in Loewenberg, "Development of Philanthropic Institutions," 199–201.

[108] *t. Shevi'it* 5:21; cf. Lieberman, *The Tosefta*, 1:189, who interprets "boarders" as Roman soldiers billeted in Jewish homes.

[109] *Sifra, Behar, Pereq* 1 (Weiss, *Sifra*, 106b); on this passage, see Howard L. Apothaker, *Sifra, Dibbura deSinai: Rhetorical Formulae, Literary Structures, and Legal Traditions* (Cincinnati, Ohio: Hebrew Union College Press, 2003), 57–58.

[110] *Sifra, Behar, Pereq* 1 (Weiss, *Sifra*, 106b); cf. Lev 19:34. Similarly, see *m. Avot* 1:5, where the poor are to be welcomed and treated like members of one's own household.

[111] See also Luke 14:1.

[112] *m. Shabbat* 17:1–18:1. In these texts, *quppot* has its usual sense of "baskets." See Neusner, *History of the Mishnaic Law – Shabbat*, 155–65. On the concept of "four or five," see Tzvi Novick, "Crafting Legal Language: *Four or Five* in the Mishnah and the Tosefta," *JQR* 98 (2008): 289–304.

[113] *m. Betzah* 5:7; on this text, see Novick, "Charity and Reciprocity," 42.

expression of gratitude is found in a parable where Israel's election is likened to a choice portion served at a meal hosted by a king. In return, Israel gives praise and thanks, a show of gratitude that signals satisfaction.[114] Likewise, the expectation to reciprocate is seen in *t. Berakhot* 6:2, where Ben Zoma instructs:

> What does a good guest say? May my host be remembered [by God] for good. How many kinds of wine did he bring before us? How many cuts [of meat] did he bring before us! How many kinds of cakes did he bring before us! And he prepared all this just for me! (*t. Berakhot* 6:2)[115]

Communal Hospitality and the Synagogue

Hospitality in ancient Mediterranean (including Jewish) sources generally features a series of direct transactions between individuals, where a host provides food and lodging and the guest is expected to reciprocate. Hellenistic Jewish sources also depict a form of hospitality that is collective and communal in nature, where synagogues provided the necessary organizational and physical infrastructure. As an institution, the synagogue housed and facilitated the provision of an array of communal services, including courts of law, communal meetings, and instruction. There is also ample evidence that the synagogue provided hospitality services – a venue for communal meals and lodging for travelers.[116] Archaeologists have identified guest quarters at the fourth-century synagogues in Hammat Tiberias and Khirbet Shema in the Galilee.[117] Likewise, synagogues in the Diaspora include installations for eating and sleeping.[118] The clearest evidence of an ancient synagogue hosting

---

[114] *SifreDeut* 53.

[115] Translation based on Tzvee Zahavy, "Berakhot," in Neusner, *The Tosefta*, with my emendations. It should be noted that "remembered for good" is also found in dedicatory inscriptions inlaid into mosaic floors in late antique synagogues; see Satlow, "Giving for a Return," 91–108; Sorek, *Remembered for Good*, 72–104.

[116] Levine, *Ancient Synagogue*, 2nd ed., 381–411; Ben-Zion Rosenfeld and Joseph Menirav, *Markets and Marketing in Roman Palestine* (Leiden and Boston: Brill, 2005), 211–34.

[117] Dothan, *Hammath Tiberias*, 32, whose finds have be re-dated by Jodi Magness, "Heaven on Earth: Helios and the Zodiac Cycle in Ancient Palestinian Synagogues," *Dumbarton Oaks Papers* 59 (2005): 8–13; A. Thomas Kraabel et al., eds., *Ancient Synagogue Excavations at Khirbet Shema, Upper Galilee, Israel, 1970–1972* (The Annual of the American Schools of Oriental Research 42; Durham, N.C.: Published for the American Schools of Oriental Research by Duke University Press, 1976), 85–87.

[118] E.g., Stobi, Ostia, and Priene; see A. Thomas Kraabel, "The Diaspora Synagogue: Archaeological and Epigraphic Evidence Since Sukenik," in *Ancient Synagogues: Historical Analysis and Archaeological Discovery* (ed. D. Urman and P. V. M. Flesher; StPB 47; Leiden and Boston: Brill, 1998), 107–09, 112–15.

guests comes from the Theodotos synagogue (Jerusalem), which I introduced in Chapter 1. Notably, the very founding of this synagogue is based on reciprocity, as Theodotos's benefaction is duly rewarded with a monumental inscription that publicizes his munificence.[119] The inscription tells how the synagogue was constructed for reading the Torah, studying the commandments, and providing accommodations for Jews visiting from afar.[120] That synagogues were understood as venues for providing food and shelter is likewise reflected in Tannaitic texts. For example, in *t. Ma'aserot* 2:20:

> A synagogue or a house of study – if they include living quarters one does not make a random snack [of untithed produce] within [the entire building]. But if not [i.e., if there is no dwelling], one makes a random snack [of untithed produce] within them.[121]

Synagogues provided basic necessities to travelers, the same kinds of necessities that would be provided through acts of hospitality. And it did so in an indirect, impersonal way, as opposed to the direct, personal transfers that were typical of hospitality. The synagogue, moreover, represented the community as a whole, as hospitality was a communal ideal and collective venture.

HOSPITALITY AND THE ORIGINS OF THE *TAMHUI*

While hospitality was often extended to the poor, it did not focus on the poor per se in pre- and nonrabbinic sources. It is notable, then, that Tannaitic approaches to hospitality include provisions for the poor.[122] In Mishnah *Avot* 1:5, Yose ben Yohanan of Jerusalem instructs, "Let your house be opened wide and let the poor be members of your household."[123] The similarities between

---

[119] On *euergetism* in early Judaism, see Gardner, "Jewish Leadership," 327–43; Schwartz, *Were the Jews*, 45–109.

[120] Such as those visiting Jerusalem on pilgrimage; see Levine, *Ancient Synagogue*, 58–59. On pilgrimage, see Goodman, "Pilgrimage Economy of Jerusalem," 69–75; Allen Kerkeslager, "Jewish Pilgrimage and Jewish Identity in Hellenistic and Early Roman Egypt," in *Pilgrimage and Holy Space in Late Antique Egypt* (ed. D. Frankfurter; Religions in the Graeco-Roman World 134; Leiden and Boston: Brill, 1998), 99–225; Safrai, *Pilgrimage*.

[121] Translation based on Martin S. Jaffee, "Maaserot," in *The Law of Agriculture in the Mishnah and the Tosefta: Translation, Commentary, Theology* (ed. J. Neusner; Handbook of Oriental Studies 79/1; 3 vols.; Boston and Leiden: Brill, 2005), 3:2278–79. Each room had a purpose in the ancient synagogue. The prayer hall, for example, was for reading scripture, but not for "frivolous" activities such as eating, drinking, or sleeping; see *t. Megillah* 2:18. The latter activities were reserved for their designated annexes; see Rosenfeld and Menirav, *Markets and Marketing*, 225.

[122] See also Matt 25:35–45; cf. Isa 58:7.

[123] This dictum finds an interesting parallel in the *Sibylline Oracles* (2.84), "Receive the homeless into your house and lead the blind," translation by James H. Charlesworth, ed., *The Old*

charity and hospitality in early rabbinic texts are further strengthened by *m. Pe'ah* 5:4, which views travelers and the poor in similar terms:

> "If a householder was travelling from place to place and wants [for provisions, then] he may take gleanings, forgotten things, and *pe'ah*, and the poor-man's tithe. But when he returns to his dwelling he should repay them," the words of R. Eliezer. But the sages say, "[No restitution is necessary because] he was a poor man at that time."

An individual, regardless of his personal wealth or holdings, is considered to be poor when he travels.[124] Thus, the traveler is eligible to take agricultural allocations reserved for the poor, including gleanings, forgotten things, and *pe'ah*. It is significant that the pericope's precise terminology "travelling from place to place" is also used to denote the itinerant poor in *m. Pe'ah* 8:7 and *t. Pe'ah* 4:8, key texts on the *tamhui* and *quppa*. The principal that he is presently in need and, therefore, qualifies as "poor" is emphasized in the pericope by the sages, who instruct that the householder is not required to provide restitution when he returns home because he was considered to be poor at the time when he received the allocations.[125] The principle is that anyone who is presently in want – either because he is generally needy or because resources are inaccessible at that moment – qualifies as "poor." The provision of food and lodging; the communal, collective approach to allocating these provisions; and an elevated interest in assisting the poor, all these suggest a strong connection between hospitality and the *tamhui*.

While there are important similarities between the *tamhui* and hospitality, there are also differences that have been overlooked by scholars. First, the goods and services provided by hospitality and the *tamhui*, as described earlier, are similar but also different in important ways. The food and shelter

---

Testament Pseudepigrapha (2 vols.; New York: Doubleday, 1983–1985), 1:347, who dates this section of the text to the second century C.E. See also the parallels in *Ps. Phocylides* 1.22–41 and the *Didache*, and their discussion in Bridge, "To Give or Not to Give," 566–68.

[124] On this pericope, see Moshe Weiss, "The Arrangement of the Mishna in Tractate Peah and its Relationship to the Tosefta [Hebrew]," (Ph.D. diss., Bar-Ilan University, 1978), 219–20. See also the writings of Aristides, the second-century C.E. Athenian philosopher and Christian apologist, "[the Christians] give ungrudgingly; if they see a travelling stranger, they bring him under their roof, and treat him like a brother" (*Apology of Aristedes* 15; translation by Longenecker, *Remember the Poor*, 61–62).

[125] Brooks, *Support for the Poor*, 93, writes that *m. Pe'ah* 5:4 seems out of place and is better suited for Chapter 8 of tractate *Pe'ah*, which discusses the definition of a poor man. Weiss, "Arrangement," 219, however, rightly notes that each major discursive unit in tractate *Pe'ah* ends with a short collection of miscellaneous traditions that provide a transition to the next unit. In this case, this pericope provides a transition or bridge from a discussion of gleanings to forgotten things.

that the *tamhui* provides would also normally be provided through customs of hospitality. The difference, however, is that the rabbis carefully define the kinds of items that the poor are to receive through the *tamhui*. While they do not address the specific measurements or quantities of the items (except for bread), the Tannaim at least identify them – bread, olive oil, legumes, and on certain occasions fish, vegetables, and wine. By contrast, the items provided by hospitality are entirely subject to the personal discretion of each individual host, who was under no obligation to provide any particular food. Hospitality can be said to be a weak institution, while the rabbis envision the *tamhui* as a rigid or strong institution that was undergirded by a sense of religious obligation – it is a permanent and reliable source of basic necessities.

The second important difference between hospitality and the *tamhui* is the latter's focus on the poor. Hospitality aims to provide for travelers and wayfarers. To be sure, individual hosts surely cared for the poor and the communal hospitality provided through synagogues exhibits an elevated interest in supporting the poor. Nevertheless, hospitality was not focused on the poor per se. By contrast, the *tamhui* and *quppa* were entities exclusively for the poor. Likewise, in the fourth century, we begin to see *xenodocheia/ptochotropheia* – places to feed, nurture, and patronize the destitute poor – and other Christian institutions purpose-built to care for the poor.[126] Whereas hospitality could support travelers who happened to be poor, the *tamhui* focuses on the poor alone.

The third important distinction between the *tamhui* and hospitality is the *tamhui's* lack of reciprocity. Hospitality is characterized as "generalized reciprocity," in anthropologist Marshall Sahlins's words, whereby the obligation to reciprocate is weak and indefinite, as it is not defined by time, quantity, or quality.[127] For example, the guest could reciprocate by hosting the host – if and when the opportunity arose. The guest could also reciprocate with a show of gratitude by thanking or blessing the host. The expectation for a guest to reciprocate in this manner was known to the Tannaim and is reflected in the texts discussed earlier.

By contrast, the rabbis do not instruct the recipients of the *tamhui* to reciprocate in this generalized way, as it would have been inconsistent with the provision of alms in a collective and indirect way. For whom would the poor return the favor? Who would the poor thank or bless? Because the alms

---

[126] Brown, *Poverty and Leadership*, 33–44; Demetrios J. Constantelos, *Byzantine Philanthropy and Social Welfare* (New Rochelle, N.Y.: A.D. Caratzas, 1991), 113–207; Holman, *Hungry are Dying*, 74–76.
[127] Sahlins, *Stone Age Economics*, 193–94.

were given by the community as a whole, the poor man is indebted to no one in particular. Likewise, it would have been inappropriate to thank or bless the charity supervisor, as the Tannaim go to great lengths to distinguish this communal official from an individual benefactor.[128]

Unable to verbally thank or bless the *tamhui*, perhaps the poor would be expected to reciprocate by contributing to the *tamhui*? The Tosefta addresses this very issue:

> [If] a poor person gave a *perutah* to the *quppa* and a piece of bread to the *tamhui*, [then] they accept them from him. If he did not give, [then] they do not obligate him to give. [If] they give him new garments but he returns old garments to them, [then] they accept them from him. If he did not give, [then] they do not obligate him to give. (*t. Pe'ah* 4:10)

Tosefta *Pe'ah* 4:10 instructs the reader that when a piece of bread or a small coin – a *perutah*[129] – is given to the soup kitchen and the charity fund (respectively), they should be accepted. That one gives bread to the *tamhui* and a small coin to the *quppa* is consistent with other rabbinic prescriptions for these institutions, as the same principle applies to clothing that is collected and distributed by the *quppa*.[130] Moreover, *t. Pe'ah* 4:10 instructs that if a poor man gives nothing at all, then he cannot be obligated to give. Thus, this passage instructs that while the poor are certainly welcomed to contribute to the *tamhui*, as well as the *quppa*, they are not obligated to do so. They do not need to give even a token amount – a scrap of bread or a small coin – in order to receive provisions.

While it would make little sense to us today to expect or compel the poor to give charity, the issue was not so clear-cut in the ancient Mediterranean, where reciprocity was the norm. Longenecker and Parkin, for example, argue that it was common for the lower strata of society to give to those who were even poorer.[131] The issue was complicated for the rabbis, for whom giving *tsedaqah* was a religious obligation presumably incumbent upon everyone. The question of whether the poor should be exempt from fulfilling this commandment was a real dilemma that was taken up by the Talmud and subsequent rabbinic interpreters. In the Babylonian Talmud, for example, Mar Zutra insists that even those who require charity themselves are obligated

---

[128] See my discussion in Chapter 7.
[129] The *perutah*'s value diminished until it ceased to be minted in the third-fourth century C.E. In rabbinic texts, it indicates worthlessness – like "pennies" or *gerushim* in modern Hebrew. In *t. Pe'ah* 4:10, therefore, the authors use a *perutah* to represent a monetary gift of little or no value.
[130] *t. Pe'ah* 4:10 and my discussion in Chapter 5.
[131] Longenecker, *Remember the Poor*, 77–80; Parkin, "An Exploration," 69, 73–74.

to give charity.[132] Thus, the Tannaim found it necessary to make the point that the poor are not obligated to give to the *tamhui* and *quppa* in order to receive alms. As such, I find here that the *tamhui* is devoid of what Sahlins would call "balanced reciprocity," the simultaneous exchange of goods of equal value.[133]

My findings on the nonreciprocal nature of the *tamhui* resonate with the recent work of Seth Schwartz and Tzvi Novick on reciprocity in ancient Judaism. Schwartz has shown how the Torah, Second Temple era texts, and Amoraic rabbinic literature make conscious efforts to avoid reciprocal transactions because they create hierarchical relationships of dependency.[134] Such vertical relationships are anathema to ideals of equity. Novick has recently shown that Tannaitic understandings of *tsedaqah*, unlike the similar category of *gemilut hasadim*, are devoid of social reciprocity.[135] Likewise, I find that the *tamhui* provides the same goods and services that are normally provided through hospitality, but it does so in a way that purposefully lacks hospitality's assumption of reciprocity.

To sum up, a close examination of the sources indicates that the *tamhui*'s origins can be found in conventions of hospitality. A lack of attention to their differences, however, has obscured the innovative nature of the *tamhui* as well as some of its basic tenets. I find that the *tamhui* has roots in customs of hospitality, but was adapted and altered by the Tannaim to fit within broader rabbinic ethics. Ephraim Frisch has characterized the transfer of care for the poor from hospitality to the *tamhui* as a move from the "domestic hearth" to a "colder environment."[136] I find, however, that the Tannaim themselves would have held very different sentiments on this development. It allowed the poor to avoid the discomfort of going into one's home and becoming dependent upon the host.[137] The *tamhui*, as an indirect and impersonal means of transferring assets, was a way to uphold and protect the dignity of the poor recipients.

CONCLUSION

The *tamhui* is institutionalized by the laws and instructions that govern its behavior. This primarily means defining the kinds of alms that it gives and the ways that it gives them. Aside from the Sabbath and Passover when the poor

---

[132] *b. Gittin* 7b. Cf. Maimonides, *Mishneh Torah, Hilkhot mattenot ʿaniyyim* (Laws on Gifts to the Poor) 7.11–12, who exempts the poor; see Frisch, *Historical Survey*, 78–79.
[133] Sahlins, *Stone Age Economics*, 194–95; see further Zeba A. Crook, "Fictive Giftship and Fictive Friendship in Greco-Roman Society," in *The Gift in Antiquity* (ed. M. L. Satlow; Chichester, West Sussex, UK: Wiley-Blackwell, 2013), 66.
[134] Schwartz, *Imperialism and Jewish Society*, 227–30; Schwartz, *Were the Jews*.
[135] Novick, "Charity and Reciprocity," 33–52.
[136] Frisch, *Historical Survey*, 145.
[137] See, likewise, the sentiments expressed in Sir 29:22.

received additional alms to meet certain religious obligations, the *tamhui* was meant to provide basic sustenance and shelter, and to do so in an indirect way. This encompassed a certain tension. On one hand, the alms provided on a regular basis (especially legumes) advertised and communicated a humble if not poor lifestyle, thereby reinforcing the recipients' lowly social position. On the other hand, the *tamhui* preserved the biological health of the poor. It also allowed the poor man to avoid the indignity of subordinating himself to dependency upon a host. This is the same sort of vertical social relationship that would form between a beggar and an individual almsgiver or benefactor. Providing for the poor in a way that protects their dignity is an important attribute of the rabbinic vision of organized charity and is addressed extensively by the *quppa* – the subject of the next two chapters.

5

Quppa, The Charity Fund

INTRODUCTION

Complementing the *tamhui* or soup kitchen was the *quppa* or charity fund, which would become the centerpiece of the rabbinic vision of organized charity. To understand the nature of the *quppa*, it is helpful to examine it in comparison with the *tamhui*. The *tamhui* gives alms based on biological criteria, giving the same food and shelter to all, regardless of each poor man's individual circumstances. By contrast, the rabbis envision the *quppa* as a way to address the relative, individual, and social needs of the poor. The *quppa* is a form of restorative charity, as it aims to restore to each individual precisely what he used to have before he became poor. The *quppa*'s alms are also defined by social conventions, as the rabbis are particularly attuned to the semiotic values of material possessions. Whatever the poor man used to have, even if it was an expensive prestige possession such as a horse, the *quppa* should provide to restore the poor man to his former place in society.

As I will show, the rabbis instruct the *quppa*'s supervisors and contributors to give prodigiously. This is a necessary outcome of the *quppa*'s objective to restore all poor men to their previous standard of living. The rabbis illustrate their point with the extreme case of a wellborn poor man – one who was born wealthy but has fallen into poverty. Restoring these individuals to their previous status would require an extensive outlay of resources. There is conceivably no limit to the amount of capital that would be needed in order to provide for a wellborn poor man's needs. It follows that contributions to the *quppa* must likewise be limitless. The Tannaim illustrate and exemplify prodigious giving in narratives in which the poor are given expensive gifts to restore them.

CLOTHING, MONEY, AND FOOD

The Tannaim instruct that the supervisors of the *quppa* should provide the poor with a number of provisions, including clothing, money, and food. The rabbis instruct that the quality of each item should be defined by what the poor man used to have, before his impoverishment:

> E. [If]he used to use garments made of *meilat* (wool), [then] they give him garments made of *meilat*.
> F. [If he used to have] a *ma'ah* (silver coin), [then] they give him a *ma'ah*.
> G. [If he used to have] dough (*isah*), [then] they give him dough (*isah*).
> H. [If he used to have] a piece of bread (*pat*), [then] they give him a piece of bread (*pat*).[1]
> I. [If he used] to have [bread] fed into his mouth, [then] they feed it into his mouth. (*t. Pe'ah* 4:10, E – I)[2]

If the poor man was once accustomed to eating a certain kind of bread or wearing a garment made of a certain kind of fabric, then the supervisors of the *quppa* should provide him with exact replacements. The implication is that the rabbis here envision a man who is "conjuncturally" poor – he was not always poor and used to be accustomed to a higher standard of living. The rabbis instruct that the alms given are defined by the particular needs of the individual and tailored to his personal circumstances. By contrast, the *tamhui* dispenses alms that are one-size-fits all, as everyone is entitled to and receives the same quality and quantity of bread and shelter.

Clothing

Just as it does in extrarabbinic sources, so too in rabbinic texts clothing carries semiotic values.[3] In particular, the old clothes mentioned by the Tosefta in the passage quoted earlier are associated with poverty and low status. In

---

[1] In MS Erfurt, the sequence reads: bread, *ma'ah*, dough.
[2] For specificity, I have enumerated the lemmata of *t. Pe'ah* 4:10 as A–O.
[3] On clothing in rabbinic literature, see Krauss, *Talmudische Archäologie*, 1:127–207; Joshua Schwartz, "Material Culture in the Land of Israel: Monks and Rabbis on Clothing and Dress in the Byzantine Period," in *Saints and Role Models in Judaism and Christianity* (ed. J. Schwartz and M. Poorthuis; Jewish and Christian Perspectives Series 7; Leiden and Boston: Brill, 2004), 121–37; Schwartz, "Material Realities," 49–52; Dafna Shlezinger-Katsman, "Clothing," in *The Oxford Handbook of Jewish Daily Life in Roman Palestine* (ed. C. Hezser; Oxford: Oxford University Press, 2010), 362–81; Daniel Sperber, *Material Culture in Eretz Israel during the Talmudic Period [Hebrew]* (2 vols.; Ramat-Gan, Israel: Bar-Ilan University Press, 1993–2006), 1:132–40.

m. Kelim 28:8, the rabbis discuss the application of purity laws to clothes knitted together from smaller bits of cloth or rags – what they call "the garments of the poor." One could not fully participate in communal and religious life if he wore old, ragged clothing. Mishnah *Megillah* 4:6, for example, prohibits one who wears rags from appearing before the ark in the synagogue or reading the Torah.[4] Wearing clothing that was extremely tattered was close to nakedness, which carried a great deal of shame.[5] While rags are a mark of shame and low standing, fine dress and new clothes are marks of distinction in early rabbinic literature. Similarly, in *SifreDeut* 343: "And thus Sages are recognized: by their walk, by their speech and their attire in the market."[6]

That clothing has semiotic value in rabbinic literature helps us understand the provisions given by the *quppa*. In Tosefta *Pe'ah* 4:10, the rabbis instruct that a poor man is entitled to receive new clothes from the *quppa*, as replacements for his worn, shabby clothing. The alternative, to allow the poor to wear rags, or repair their clothing, is not offered by the rabbis. If the color of the patches or their pattern of weave did not perfectly match the rest of the garment, the patches themselves drew attention to the garment's worn state. This was common wisdom in the ancient world, as we read in Luke 5:36, "No one tears a piece from a new garment and sews it on an old garment; otherwise the new will be torn, and the piece from the new will not match the old." This is also evident from the archaeological finds that I discussed in Chapter 2, as a number of garments found in the Judean desert from the second century include patches and other repairs that are rather conspicuous.[7] By contrast, the Tannaim specify that the *quppa* provide new clothes only, which would elevate the recipient's status.

Of particular significance is the fabric that the rabbis choose to make their point. Tosefta *Pe'ah* 4:10 instructs that if an impoverished individual was once accustomed to wearing garments made of *meilat*, a specific type of wool, then the *quppa* should provide him with a new garment made of the exact same fabric. The rabbis' choice of this particular wool is significant. Wool

---

[4] On this text, see Hamel, *Poverty and Charity in Roman Palestine*, 73–75; Michael L. Satlow, "Jewish Constructions of Nakedness in Late Antiquity," *JBL* 116 (1997): 429–54.

[5] *t. Megillah* 3:27, for example, instructs that one who wears ragged clothing while serving liturgical functions at the synagogue should be mindful not to be exposed through the rags. The rabbis' condemnation of nakedness is palpable in *SifreDeut* 320, "for there is none more despised and contemptible than one who goes about naked in the market place," see Satlow, "Jewish Constructions of Nakedness in Late Antiquity," 429–54.

[6] Translation according to Hammer, *Sifre*.

[7] Yadin, *Finds from the Bar Kokhba Period*, 212–13. Patches improved a garment's functionality only temporarily and may have made them even more prone to tearing; see Matt 9:16; Mark 2:21.

was the most common fabric in the Mediterranean world and Tannaitic texts themselves employ multiple terms for the various grades and types of wool that were available, such as *tsemer* and *'udeda*.[8] The rabbis choose *meilat*, which refers to material from Miletus, a town in Asia Minor that was praised for its wool.[9] That is, the Tosefta instructs that when providing the poor with new clothing, the garments should precisely match the quality that he once owned, restoring the poor man to the place in society that is communicated by that particular grade of clothing. Nothing is harder for the poor to endure than the ridicule attracted by one's torn or soiled clothing, Juvenal wrote.[10] The rabbis' prescription that the *quppa* provide new clothes made from *meilat* reflects their interest in the social aspects of poverty as well as restoring a poor man's dignity – as defined and communicated by his material possessions, including the clothes on his back.

Money

Giving money to the poor was an essential component of organized charity. Tosefta *Pe'ah* 4:10 instructs that if the man had been accustomed to having a *ma'ah* before his impoverishment, then the *quppa* should give him a *ma'ah*. Likewise, in *t. Sheqalim* 2:8 the rabbis address how supervisors should handle any *me'ot* left over after the distribution to the poor is complete.

Ma'ah (pl. *me'ot*) is the Hebrew term for a silver coin otherwise known as an *obolus*, probably referring to those minted in Tyre that circulated throughout the region. How much was the *ma'ah* worth and what can its value tell us about the *quppa* and charity? Straightforward answers to questions related to the coins mentioned in rabbinic texts are elusive. Because a coin could remain in use for centuries, a number of different currencies simultaneously circulated in Roman Palestine. These coins were minted at different times and by different minting authorities, each of which had their own standards in determining a coin's weight and the purity of its metal. The values of these coins, in terms of their purchasing power, differed by region and could fluctuate over time. Adding to this uncertainty is that aggregate figures and quantities mentioned by ancient authors are notoriously unreliable. Above all, attempts to pinpoint price levels and the value of coins are complicated – if not precluded – by a paucity of sources as well as their reliability for the

---

[8] For the various terms used for wool in rabbinic literature, see Jastrow, *Dictionary*, 775; Kena'ani, *Otsar ha-lashon ha-'Ivrit*, 9:2855.

[9] Simon Hornblower and Antony Spawforth, *The Oxford Classical Dictionary* (Oxford and New York: Oxford University Press, 2003), s.v. wool.

[10] *Saturae* III.152, as cited in Saller, "Poverty, Honor," 19.

study of economic history.[11] Determining an accurate price level is complex enough in the present day, all the more so for the ancient world where sources are sparse and unreliable.

I propose, then, a different approach to the study of money in rabbinic literature. Instead of trying to determine the historical, absolute value of a certain coin, it will be more fruitful to read the coin within the literary context in which it appears and bring to light its "value" by understanding the ways that it is used in rabbinic texts. That is, understanding why the rabbinic redactors chose a *ma'ah* for the passage at hand, as opposed to other coins – instead of trying to determine its purchasing power or the exchange rate. The significance of the *ma'ah* to the rabbis can be understood by looking to see how it is used throughout the Tannaitic corpus.

In these texts, coins function as standards of measure, where each denomination indicates a relative value.[12] The *ma'ah* was near the top of this pecuniary hierarchy, just below the *dinar*.

> Six silver *ma'ah* are a *dinar*.
> A silver *ma'ah* is two *pondions*.
> A *pondion* is two *issars*.
> An *issar* is two *mismasin*.
> A *mismas* is two *quntronin*.
> A *quntron* is two *perutot*.
> Rabban Shimon b. Gamaliel says, "The *perutah* of which they
>   have spoken is one of six *perutot* to the *issar*."
> There are three *hadrasin* to a *ma'ah*,
> Two *hanassin* to a *hadras*,
> Two *shemanin* to a *hannas*,
> Two *perutot* to a *shemen*. (*t. Bava Batra* 5:12)[13]

This text presents the *ma'ah* as twice as valuable as a *pondion*, but only one-sixth the value of a *zuz* or *dinar*, which tops the hierarchy. The relationship of the *ma'ah* to the *dinar* is important, as the *dinar* is the denomination found most frequently in rabbinic texts. It is the standard by which we can measure the relative value of other denominations. For example, the redactors frequently use the figure of 200 *zuz* or *dinar* to indicate the minimum amount that an individual needs to support himself and his household for a full year.[14]

---

[11] For the state of research on the use of rabbinic literature for economic history, see Schwartz, "Historiography," 91–95.
[12] See the summary discussion in Jacob Neusner and William Scott Green, eds. *Dictionary of Judaism in the Biblical Period: 450 B.C.E. to 600 C.E* (Peabody, Mass.: Hendrickson, 1999), 436.
[13] Translation based on Neusner, *The Tosefta*, with my emendations.
[14] Most prominently, see *m. Pe'ah* 8:8.

If the Tannaim understood one *zuz* or *dinar* to be equivalent to six *me'ot*, it follows that one would require about twenty-three *me'ot* per week to survive. The single *ma'ah* given through the *quppa*, therefore, is understood by the rabbis to be a modest sum.[15]

Bread

In addition to clothing and money, the Tosefta instructs the supervisors of the *quppa* to provide the poor with food, specifically bread or the dough used to make bread:

E. [If he used to have] dough (*isah*), [then] they give him dough (*isah*).
F. [If he used to have] a piece of bread (*pat*), [then] they give him a piece of bread (*pat*).
G. [If he used] to have [bread] fed into his mouth, [then] they feed it into his mouth. (*t. Pe'ah* 4:10, E – G)

As already discussed, bread was a staple of the daily diet and the preeminent form of aid for the poor. Likewise, giving bread to the poor is prominent in the biblical tradition. In Prov 22:9, for example, "Those who are generous are blessed, for they share their bread with the poor."[16] The essential nature of bread is likewise reflected in rabbinic texts, where *pat* or "piece of bread" expands into a metonym for "sustenance" in general.[17] Bread could vary both in its ingredients and in the way in which it was prepared. As do other writings from the ancient world, rabbinic texts mention numerous types of bread.[18]

The Tosefta instructs that if an individual who became poor used to have an *isah* then supervisors of the *quppa* must provide him with exactly that, an *isah*. The choice of dough is significant, as Tannaitic texts frequently distinguish between various types of dough. *Isah* is "started" dough that is made of finely sifted flour and used to make white bread. Elsewhere, in *m. Makhshirin* 2:8, the Tannaim contrast *isah* with *qiber*, dough used to make the black bread that is considered less desirable.[19] The kind of bread that one eats, as

---

[15] That the *ma'ah* is modest in value is supported by *m. Ketubbot* 5:8, where a husband is obligated to provide his wife with a *ma'ah* per week. The coin is meant as pocket money to cover only incidentals, as her food, clothing, and shelter are provided by the husband in kind.

[16] See also Isa 58:7.

[17] See the references in Jastrow, *Dictionary*, 1249–50.

[18] See my discussion in Chapters 2 and 4.

[19] Even lower quality dough might entail mixing in legumes; see Hamel, *Poverty and Charity in Roman Palestine*, 13.

previously noted, broadcasts one's status, as this Mishnah divides the world into those who eat bread made from *isah* and those who eat coarse bread made from *qiber*. Thus, the *quppa* must take care to restore to the impoverished individual the precise dough that he used to use and the social position that it communicated.

The Tosefta is not only interested in the ingredients of the bread that these individuals ate before their impoverishment, but also in the way that they procured their bread. The rabbis illustrate this point with three examples. First, if the poor man had been used to making bread from dough, then he should be given dough. The choice of the word *isah* indicates "started dough," that is, dough that is in its early stages. It requires more labor and preparation than *batseq* or "risen dough," let alone *pat* – a fully baked and ready-to-eat piece of bread.[20] That is, the Tosefta is interested not only in restoring to the poor the basic commodity that he once had, but also his lifestyle – as defined by the way that he procured his daily bread.

The next example is a man who had been accustomed to buying fully baked bread. Whereas the previous individual prepared his bread from dough, this one acquires bread that is ready to eat. It reflects an elevated lifestyle in which one can afford to pay for the labor of others, or at least properly support members of his household who could bake.[21] The third example is a poor man who used to have others feed bread into his mouth; likewise, the supervisors of the *quppa* should arrange to have him spoon-fed.[22] Attention to the way that the bread is prepared and consumed – what one eats *and* how one eats it – indicates an interest in the social, more so than the nutritional, value of the food. "The more the social aspect takes precedence over the strictly alimentary," Claude Levi-Strauss wrote, "the more emphasis is given to the style both of food and of the way in which it is presented."[23]

The restorative, relative, and semiotic nature of the alms given by the *quppa* is cast into high relief when compared to the *tamhui*. Whereas the bread given by the *tamhui* is defined by its weight and size, intended to provide just enough calories to keep the poor alive, the *quppa* is concerned with what the bread signifies and its social implications.

---

[20] On *batseq*, see e.g., *m. Pesahim* 3:2. On *isah*, compared to other types of dough, see the references in Jastrow, *Dictionary*, 1072–73, 1354. On the ways that bread was prepared, see Hamel, *Poverty and Charity in Roman Palestine*, 11–14.
[21] This is supported by *t. Berakhot* 4:15, where bread made by a professional baker is superior to bread that one makes himself, in his own home.
[22] See Lieberman, *Tosefta Ki-Fshutah*, 1:58; Lohse and Mayer, *Die Tosefta*, 151.
[23] Claude Levi-Strauss, "The Principal of Reciprocity," in *Sociological Theory* (ed. L. A. Coser and B. Rosenberg; New York: Macmillan, 1957), as reprinted in Komter, *The Gift*, 20.

WIVES, SLAVES, AND HORSES

The principle that the *quppa* provide the impoverished man with the possessions that he used to have, and the social standing that they communicated, is rigidly upheld by the rabbis. We see this clearly in lemmata K – M of *t. Pe'ah* 4:10:

> K. As it is said: *[Rather, you must open your hand and lend] him (lo) sufficient for whatever his needs (mahsoro)* (Deut 15:8)
> L. Even a servant, even a horse.
> M. *him* [in Deut 15:8 indicates] a wife, as it is said: *I will make a fitting helper for him (lo)* (Gen 2:18).[24] (*t. Pe'ah* 4:10, K – M)[25]

Lemma K makes the point that needs are missing (*haser*), as the language implies for the Tanna that the poor man in question formerly enjoyed wealth, but now lacks it, and that the point of the charity is to supply him with what he is now missing. The text then illustrates the principle of restorative charity by instructing that all of the poor man's missing needs are met, even if this implies providing him with a wife, a servant, and a horse. Such an individual presumably once had all three, but fell into poverty and could no longer support them or had to sell them off.

Wife

What, exactly, do the Tannaim mean when they instruct the supervisors of the *quppa* to give a wife to a poor man? Perhaps as part of an effort to

---

[24] Eliezer Segal, *Sanctified Seasons* (Calgary: Alberta Judaic Library, 2008), 3, commenting on the parallel version in the Bavli, writes that this exegesis seems "contrived." Indeed, the word "him" is found throughout the Hebrew Bible, as it is just as likely to refer to Gen 2:18 as to the 1,150 or so other verses in which it appears. This would be a case, common in rabbinic literature, in which legal traditions precede exegesis – as opposed to the other way around; see Cohen, "Judaean Legal Tradition," 138–39. To be sure, however, one could argue for a stronger connection between the two verses. In Gen 2:18, God supplies Adam with something that he does not have, just as Deut 15:8 envisions the addressee supplying the poor man with something he lacks. Thus the link to Gen 2:18 depends not only on the word *lo*, but also on a more substantive connection.

[25] Lemma M is absent from MS Erfurt, though Lieberman's edition of the Tosefta (which I follow here and throughout this book) continues to be the standard version of the text; see Paul Mandel, "The Tosefta," in *The Cambridge History of Judaism: Volume Four: The Late Roman-Rabbinic Period* (ed. S. T. Katz; Cambridge: Cambridge University Press, 2006), 332–33; Ronen Reichman, "The Tosefta and Its Value for Historical Research: Questioning the Historical Reliability of Case Stories," in *Rabbinic Texts and the History of Late-Roman Palestine* (ed. M. Goodman and P. Alexander; Oxford and New York: Oxford University Press for the British Academy, 2010), 117–18; Peter Schäfer, "Once Again the Status Quaestionis of Research in Rabbinic Literature: An Answer to Chaim Milikowsky," *JJS* 40 (1989): 92; Strack and Stemberger, *Introduction to the Talmud*, 158–60.

illustrate their case with an extreme example, if not hyperbole, the Tannaim may be playing on a transcultural notion that a wife could be "given" to an individual. This is part of a wider attitude evident in Tannaitic texts, whereby women can be transferred from one man to another. This understanding is assumed in a number of texts where the rabbis prescribe ways to regulate these transactions.[26] Judith Wegner's careful study of sources from the Mishnah demonstrates that, in many contexts, the rabbis view women as chattel.[27] This attitude is the product of the patriarchal society in which the Tannaim lived as these texts were redacted by men and for men.[28] The rabbis instruct that the *quppa* should provide the poor with a wife in much the same way that it provides clothing, money, food, and other assets. That a woman could be given as a gift was seen in ancient Jewish literature in general. Ben Sira calls a good wife a "gift to her husband" (Sir 26:3) – a statement that would be cited approvingly in the Babylonian Talmud centuries later.[29] Giving a woman as a gift was, moreover, typical of many premodern societies, as noted by Levi-Strauss:

> Not so long ago it was the custom in our society to "ask for" a young girl in marriage; the father of the betrothed woman "gave" his daughter in marriage; in English the phrase is still used, "to give up the bride." And in regard to the woman who takes a lover, it is also said that she "gives herself." The Arabic word, *sadaqa*, signifies the alm, the bride's price, law and tax. In this last case, the meaning of the word can be explained by the custom of wife buying. But marriage through purchase is an institution which is special in form only; in reality it is only a modality of the fundamental system as analyzed by Mauss, according to which, in primitive society and still somewhat in ours, rights, goods and persons circulate within a group according to a continual mechanism of services and counter-services.[30]

Building upon Marcel Mauss's classic *The Gift*, Levi-Strauss posits that marriage is a form of gift exchange – the "giving" of a wife – which in turn is based upon the principle of reciprocity.[31] Levi-Strauss's comments are useful

---

[26] Jacob Neusner, *Method and Meaning in Ancient Judaism* (Missoula, Mont.: Scholars Press, 1979), 79–100.

[27] Judith Romney Wegner, *Chattel or Person? The Status of Women in the Mishnah* (New York: Oxford University Press, 1988).

[28] Hayim Lapin, "The Construction of Households in the Mishnah," in *The Mishnah in Contemporary Perspective* (ed. A. J. Avery-Peck and J. Neusner; Handbook of Oriental Studies 87; Leiden and Boston: Brill, 2006), 55–80; Neusner, *Method and Meaning in Ancient Judaism*, 79–100.

[29] *b. Yevamot* 61b–64a. Gift giving was also an essential aspect of marriage in ancient Judaism; see Satlow, *Jewish Marriage*, 10–11, 162–81.

[30] Levi-Strauss, "Principal of Reciprocity," as reprinted in Komter, *The Gift*, 24.

[31] Recently, Lygia Siguad has cast a spotlight on the significance of Levi-Strauss's endorsement and interpretation of Mauss's classic *The Gift*, suggesting that Levi-Strauss diverged from

for understanding the uniqueness of rabbinic views. On the one hand, the Tosefta's discussion of the *quppa* is typical of premodern views in that women are treated as chattel. On the other hand, whereas Levi-Strauss views marriage and the giving of a wife as a form of gift exchange and the reciprocity that goes with it, the rabbis instruct that the *quppa* should be devoid of reciprocity.[32] Indeed, the *quppa*, like the *tamhui*, gives provisions to a poor man without expecting the recipient to provide any compensation in return. That is what made it a charitable institution and truly unique in the ancient world, and perhaps why the rabbis felt that it required further explication.

There are a number of underlying principles at work here, which are illuminated by exploring rabbinic attitudes toward marriage and the household. The household was the basic building block of Greco-Roman society and likewise was the focus of the ideal Jewish society envisioned by the rabbis.[33] It was a unit of domestic, ritual, and economic activities, consisting of a family, home and living space, possessions (land, animals, capital, etc.), and possibly nonrelatives such as slaves. It was mapped out in a patriarchal fashion, where the householder, who was male by definition, maintained his dependents and managed the household's factors of production.[34] Viewed in a strictly economic sense, the wife embodied the household's ability to reproduce.[35] The sentiment expressed in *m. Yoma* 1:1, where *his house* in Lev 16:17 is interpreted as "his wife," is characteristic of Tannaitic understandings of the importance of women for constructing a household.[36] Because a household was unimaginable without its capacity to reproduce, a wife was synonymous with the household itself. To be sure, the Tannaim participated in widespread sentiments about the importance of marriage. A salient example is found in the writings of the Stoic philosopher Antipater of Tarsus, who surely expressed broadly held views when he wrote, "The wellborn ... being, moreover, a product of civilization and a political being, perceiving that one's home or life cannot otherwise be complete except with a wife and children."[37]

Mauss's original intent; see Lygia Sigaud, "The Vicissitudes of *The Gift*," *Social Anthropology* 10 (2002): 335–58.

[32] *t. Pe'ah* 4:10.

[33] Lapin, "Construction of Households," 55; Jacob Neusner, *The Economics of the Mishnah* (Chicago, Ill.: Chicago University Press, 1990), 50–71.

[34] That is, the householder was at the center, with obligations and dependents extending outward to the subordinate members of the household.

[35] Satlow, *Jewish Marriage*, 26–36.

[36] Baker, *Rebuilding the House of Israel*, 34–76.

[37] Antipater of Tarsus, *SVF* 3.254.23–257.10 (Stobaeus 4.507.6–512); translation by Will Deming, *Paul on Marriage and Celibacy: The Hellenistic Background of 1 Corinthians 7* (Cambridge and New York: Cambridge University Press, 1995), 226; see also Satlow, *Jewish Marriage*, 13–14.

To be sure, the instruction to provide a wife is a hyperbolic exemplar to illustrate the principle that the *quppa* restore to the poor man precisely what he used to have. In practical terms, the Tannaim probably intended that the Tannaim provide the poor man with sufficient assets in order to marry, maintain his wife, or both. By enabling the poor man to have and maintain a wife, the *quppa* provides him with an essential component of a household and restores him to the status of householder. Status as a householder was inextricably intertwined with maleness and was necessary to fully participate in and contribute to society. He alone was empowered to farm out the household's factors of production and interact with other householders, as the Tannaim envision society as a web of social and economic interactions between householders. Without a household, a poor man lacked maleness and was excluded from society – thereby adding to his sense of shame and loss of personal dignity.[38] The *quppa* restores to the poor both maleness and his place among the householders, and couches this move as derivative of the Hebrew Bible, adding authenticity and authority to their instructions.

Slave and a Horse

In addition to clothing, food, money, and a wife, the Tosefta instructs the *quppa* to provide the poor man with a slave and a horse. I will examine each in turn. While attitudes toward slavery varied, its existence was taken for granted during this age.[39] Slavery was considered to be a normal part of life for all peoples of the ancient world – Greeks, Romans, and Jews alike. Slaves performed essential tasks and were an important component of the economy, including that of Roman Palestine. This is likewise reflected in Tannaitic texts, which address legal and religious aspects of slaves and slavery. Some of the Tannaim are said to have been slave owners, such as Rabban Gamaliel, who appears together with his slave Tabi. Hezser finds that early rabbinic texts view slavery from the perspective of a slave owner.[40]

---

[38] Lapin, "Construction of Households," 55–80; Satlow, *Jewish Marriage*, 3–41. On the social exclusion of the poor in the Roman world, see Neville Morley, "The Poor in the City of Rome," in *Poverty in the Roman World* (ed. M. Atkins and R. Osborne; Cambridge and New York: Cambridge University Press, 2006), 33–35.

[39] Hezser, *Jewish Slavery in Antiquity*, 1; Dale B. Martin, "Slavery and the Ancient Jewish Family," in *The Jewish Family in Antiquity* (ed. S. J. D. Cohen; BJS 289; Atlanta, Ga.: Scholars Press, 1993), 113–16.

[40] On Gamaliel and Tabi; see *m. Berakhot* 2:7; *m. Sukkah* 2:1; *m. Pesahim* 7:2; *t. Pesahim* 2:15. In *t. Mo'ed Qatan* 2:16, the sons of R. Yehudah and Hillel own slaves. On these texts, see Catherine Hezser, "The Impact of Household Slaves on the Jewish Family in Roman Palestine," *JSJ* 34 (2003): 375–424; Hezser, *Jewish Slavery in Antiquity*, 157–61, 294.

While slaves were primarily employed in agricultural activities in earlier eras, by Roman times it was common for them to perform domestic tasks. Slaves were considered nonrelative members of their master's household, as the householder maintained them and managed their output.[41] Likewise, in rabbinic texts slaves performed many of the tasks that would otherwise have fallen to the master (i.e., householder), his wife, or their children.[42] For example, they portray slaves as cooking, baking, shopping, transporting, performing secretarial or administrative duties, advising their masters on business matters and household management, and nursing and supervising the householder's children. Providing the master and his family with leisure time, slaves were also expensive to acquire and maintain.[43] Owning a slave was a mark of prestige for the master, as slave ownership was possible for only the upper strata of society.[44]

In addition to a wife and a slave, the Tosefta (*Pe'ah* 4:10) instructs that a poor man should be given a horse if he was once accustomed to owning and exercising on one. Much of what has been said about slaves can likewise be applied to horses. Like slaves, horses were symbols of wealth and prestige as they were expensive to purchase and maintain, and demonstrated one's ability to control another living being. Learning to ride a horse required leisure time that only the wealthy could afford and demonstrated discipline and self-mastery, which were important virtues in the Greco-Roman world.

---

[41] See Flesher, *Oxen, Women or Citizens*; Paul V. M Flesher, "Slaves, Israelites, and the System of the Mishnah," in *Literature of Early Rabbinic Judaism: Issues in Talmudic Redaction and Interpretation* (ed. A. J. Avery-Peck; Lanham, Md.: University Press of America, 1989), 104–05; Lapin, "Construction of Households," 57–58; Martin, "Jewish Family in Antiquity," 113–29; Solomon Zeitlin, "Slavery During the Second Commonwealth and the Tannaitic Period " *JQR* 53 (1963): 185–218.

[42] E.g., *m. Ketubbot* 5:5 which instructs that a slave can perform any of the labors typically assigned to a married woman, except for wool work, which Peskowitz finds becomes a symbol of marital piety for Jewish women. To be sure, the rabbis also warn against excess leisure time for women, which would result in "lifelessness." On this pericope, see Judith Hauptman, *Rereading the Rabbis: A Woman's Voice* (Boulder, Colo.: Westview Press, 1998), 61–62; Miriam Peskowitz, *Spinning Fantasies: Rabbis, Gender, and History* (Berkeley: University of California Press, 1997), 97–103, 106–08.

[43] Hezser, *Jewish Slavery in Antiquity*, 125, 247–52. See also K. R. Bradley, *Slavery and Society at Rome* (Cambridge and New York: Cambridge University Press, 1994), 10–30, esp. p. 14; Flesher, *Oxen, Women or Citizens*; Flesher, "Slaves, Israelites, and the System of the Mishnah," 104–05; Keith Hopkins, "Slavery in Classical Antiquity," in *Caste and Race: Comparative Approaches* (ed. A. V. S. De Reuck and J. Knight; London: Churchill, 1968), 172.

[44] Hezser, *Jewish Slavery in Antiquity*, 294–95. A slave could also increase the honor of his master by absorbing any shame that might otherwise be projected onto the master; Bradley, *Slavery and Society at Rome*, 10–30; Hezser, "Impact of Household Slaves," 401, 404.

In ancient Palestine, likewise, horses were seen as symbols of status and power.[45]

The understanding of horses as marks of prestige is likewise reflected in early rabbinic literature. Mishnah *Sanhedrin* 2:5, for example, punctuates its discourse on ideal kingship with a discussion of proper behavior toward a king:

> One may not ride on [a king's] horse. And one may not sit on his throne. And one may not use his scepter. And one may not see him naked, except when he has his haircut,[46] but not in the bathhouse. As it is said: *you shall be free to set a king over yourself* (Deut 17:15) – that his awe shall be over you. (*m. Sanhedrin* 2:5)

To fulfill the Deuteronomist's dictum *you shall be free to set a king over yourself*, the Mishnah instructs the reader to revere his king. Deference is conveyed by refraining from looking at the king while he is undressed, sparing him the shame of nakedness. The Mishnah, moreover, prohibits its audience from using the king's possessions, notably those that mark and define his unique status, including a scepter, throne, and horse. That a horse is closely associated with nobility is likewise reflected in other early rabbinic texts.[47]

Just as the acquisition and ownership of a horse and a slave broadcasts one's high social standing, so too their loss or surrender advertises a fall in the owner's status. A slave and horse were conspicuous in their absence. Economic distress or outright impoverishment could force an owner to abandon or sell his horse or slave. Because slaves and horses are treated by the rabbis as chattel, they could be transferred from one individual to another, or simply given to a poor man.[48] If providing the poor man with a wife restored him to the status of a householder, than giving him a slave and a horse restored him to the status

---

[45] Moshe Beer, "The Attitude of the Sages Toward Riding Horses [Hebrew]," *Cathedra* 60 (1991): 23–24. However, the sources I discuss in the following bring into question Beer's claim that the rabbis purposefully wished to distance themselves from such status symbols.

[46] According to the printed edition, one may not view the king while his hair is being cut.

[47] E.g., *m. Sanhedrin* 2:4 and *t. Bava Metzi'a* 7:9, where horses are prized above all other animals. The Tannaim were surely aware of biblical traditions in which horses convey status. For example, Deut 17:16 prohibits an Israelite king from acquiring too many horses, as they represent self-aggrandizement and encourage the king to feel that he is self-sufficient and not dependent upon God; see the explanation in Jeffrey H. Tigay, *The JPS Torah Commentary: Deuteronomy* (Philadelphia: Jewish Publication Society, 1996), 167. In Esth 6:9, Haman advises the king to bestow honor by adorning a man with royal clothes and providing him with a horse, which should be worn and ridden in the town square – that is, conspicuously consumed. See also 1 Kgs 1:5, 10:28–29.

[48] Hezser, *Jewish Slavery in Antiquity*, 55–68, 252–60.

of a wealthy householder. Thus, the *quppa* is required to provide an individual with all the trappings of a prestigious and wealthy life, if that is what the poor man had enjoyed before his impoverishment. It also demonstrates that the *quppa* ought to restore the poor to his previous standard of living, regardless of the cost.

These principals are illustrated by the Tosefta with a *ma'aseh* (pl. *ma'asim*; literally "deed" or "event"), a short narrative that establishes a legal precedent. Because it is couched as a historical anecdote, a *ma'aseh* also provides the rabbinic redactors with an opportunity to illustrate their legal principles with storylines and characters who serve as exemplars.[49]

> N. Another event (*ma'aseh*): Hillel the Elder bought, for a wellborn poor man, a horse he used to exercise on, and a slave who used to serve [him]. (*t. Pe'ah* 4:10, N)

In this narrative, the renowned Hillel the Elder provides a horse and servant for a "wellborn poor man" – one who was born into a wealthy family but has become impoverished.[50] By restoring a horse and slave to the wellborn poor, Hillel likewise restores to him the high social status that these items communicated.

There is some tension between the narrative and the principles that it is supposed to support. The problem lies in that the narrative portrays a transfer of assets to a poor man in a manner that is direct and personal – which is at odds with the objective that organized charity provides for the poor in an indirect and impersonal way. This tension was later recognized and papered over by medieval rabbinic interpreters, who posit that Hillel serves as a charity supervisor and draws upon funds from the *quppa*.[51] To be sure, ancient texts are never as consistent as we would like them to be and here some consistency on one point (avoiding direct almsgiving) comes at the expense of illustrating another – namely, that the *quppa* should address the poor's needs regardless of the expense.[52] In turn, the members of the community who fund the *quppa* must give unstintingly in order to uphold this principle.

---

[49] See Arnold Goldberg's classic study of the *ma'aseh*, reprinted in Margarete Schlüter and Peter Schäfer, eds., *Rabbinische Texte als Gegenstand der Auslegung: Gesammelte Studien II* (TSAJ 73; Tübingen: Mohr Siebeck, 1999), 22–49; see also Moshe Simon-Shoshan, *Stories of the Law: Narrative Discourse and the Construction of Authority in the Mishnah* (New York: Oxford University Press, 2012).

[50] On other terms for the wellborn or formerly wealthy poor in rabbinic literature, see Gray, "Formerly Wealthy Poor," 103–05.

[51] E.g., Meiri to *b. Ketubbot* 67b.

[52] While the Tannaim prefer giving alms through institutions, they also acknowledge and address the ongoing existence of personal, direct charity (e.g., *m. Shabbat* 1:1). One did not replace

Alyssa Gray has shown that Tannaitic compilations show empathy for the wellborn poor, far more than that found in later rabbinic writings.[53] I suggest that this is due to the Tannaim's own socioeconomic position, as they tended to be well-off and wealthy themselves. Not one Tanna was poor, as Shaye Cohen has noted.[54] Wellborn men, whose existence is evidenced by extrarabbinic sources, would have been the social peers of the Tannaim.[55] The wellborn poor, then, evoke a special empathy from the rabbis, as well as a fear among the rabbis that they would fall into poverty. In this sense, the Tannaim envision the *quppa* as a kind of safety net for themselves – if a Tanna were to become poor, then the *quppa* would restore him to his former standing.

The principle that one should return the poor to their previous standard of living, even if it means giving him a horse and a slave, relates back to the Tannaim's overarching ideal of charity with dignity. In the case at hand, charity is a means to stave off shame by restoring an individual to his previous standing, which is indexed by material culture. It is, essentially, charity *for* dignity. These principles, moreover, should be upheld even if an expensive outlay is required, as further illustrated by the next narrative that I will discuss.

THE POOR'S NEEDS

As we have seen, *t. Pe'ah* 4:10 instructs that the *quppa* should provide a poor man with the kinds of clothes that he used to wear, the amount of money

---

the other, but rather they coexisted side by side; cf. Loewenberg, *From Charity to Social Justice*, 122–23. On these tensions and ambiguities, see further my discussion in this chapter on prodigious giving. The Tannaitic preference for institutional, over personal, giving would continue through the Bavli; see Alyssa Gray, "Redemptive Almsgiving and the Rabbis of Late Antiquity," *JSQ* 18 (2011): 170–174, 180–183. Kalmin, *Sage in Jewish Society*, 43, suggests that this may be due to the desire of Babylonian rabbis to avoid direct encounters with lowly non-rabbis.

[53] Gray, "Formerly Wealthy Poor," 101–33.
[54] Cohen, "Rabbi in Second-Century," 935; see further Gardner, "Who is Rich."
[55] The existence of aristocrats in Roman Galilee is attested in an array of sources from late-antique Palestine, such as Josephus on the first century C.E. and dedicatory inscriptions in synagogue floors from the fourth and fifth centuries and beyond. In short, these individuals were Jewish, non-rabbis, landowners, and held some authority as they staffed the town's *boule*. In addition to the "wellborn," they are referred to in rabbinic literature as *gedolim* or "great ones." The relationship between these individuals and the rabbis has been the subject of a number of studies. Little tension between the two can be detected in Tannaitic compilations. As I suggest, moreover, rabbis and aristocrats likely stemmed from similar socioeconomic circles. Later rabbinic sources, such as the Babylonian Talmud, tend to project onto the earlier Tannaitic era an air of enmity between rabbis and local aristocrats. The study by Büchler, *Political and the Social Leaders*, provides a useful collection of sources, but his conclusions should be viewed with skepticism in light of the methodological advancements made in the study of rabbinic texts over the last century.

that he used to spend, and dough or bread in the way in which he had been accustomed. He also receives a wife, slave, and horse if he used to have them. These are arranged in a hierarchy that increase in expense and prestige, from the essentials of clothing, money, and bread (which itself is arranged in a hierarchy from started dough to baked bread to being spoon-fed); to a wife (making the poor man a householder); to a slave and a horse (symbols of leisure and prestige). That is, to restore the poor man to his previous standard of living and spare no expense in doing so.

The Tosefta grounds its instructions as derivative of scripture:

> K. As it is said: *[Rather, you must open your hand and lend] him sufficient for whatever he needs* (Deut 15:8).
> L. Even a servant, even a horse. (*t. Pe'ah* 4:10, K – L)

The exegetes see their discourse as the fulfillment of the commandment to satisfy the "needs" of the poor. That the Tannaim understand a poor man's needs to include a horse and a slave is illustrated and emphasized in the parallel text from *Sifre to Deuteronomy*:[56]

> *[Rather, you must open your hand and lend] him sufficient* (Deut 15:8) – you are not commanded to make him rich. *For whatever he needs* (Deut 15:8) – even a horse and even a slave. (*SifreDeut* 116)

SifreDeut 116 differs from the Tosefta in that it contains an additional gloss that interprets *[Rather, you must open your hand and lend] him sufficient* (Deut 15:8) as "you are not commanded to make him rich." It then parallels the Tosefta by glossing *for whatever he needs* as "even a horse and even a slave." The first gloss seems to acknowledge to the reader that what follows, a horse and slave, may be perceived as excessive and an effort to make a poor man rich. At the same time, *SifreDeut* reassures that, despite perceptions to the contrary, providing a poor man with a horse and slave that he used to have does not make him rich.[57] Rather, it merely restores him to his proper place in society.

That the Deuteronomist, however, would have understood the poor's needs to include a horse and a servant is highly unlikely. Deuteronomy 15, a key chapter in the book's discourse on social justice, discusses regulations for

---

[56] For the problem, meaning, and significance of parallels between Tannaitic works, see Shaye J. D. Cohen, ed., *The Synoptic Problem in Rabbinic Literature* (BJS 326; Providence, R.I.: Brown Judaic Studies, 2000).

[57] Similarly, one could read *SifreDeut* 116 as emphasizing that the commandment is the *restoration* – not the *enrichment* – of the poor. If the poor become rich in the process, then so be it, but the commandment is not to *enrich* the poor. I thank Moulie Vidas for this observation.

loans. Deut 15:7–8 exhorts the reader to lend to the poor even in the time leading up to the remission of debts every seventh year:[58]

> If, however, there is a needy person among you, one of your kinsmen in any of your settlements in the land that the Lord your God is giving you, do not harden your heart and shut your hand against your needy kinsman. Rather, you must open your hand and lend him sufficient for whatever he needs. (Deut 15:7–8)

It is important to understand the function and meaning of loans in Deuteronomy.[59] In the Hebrew Bible, loans are extended exclusively to the poor, as lending for commercial and investment purposes was unknown.[60] Loans, especially those that were canceled or forgiven, were an important form of aid to the needy. They tended to be given only in times of distress, such as droughts and crop failures.[61] As a remedy for temporary poverty in the Hebrew Bible, this proof text is a particularly apt choice for the Tosefta, as it shares its interest in conjunctural poverty. And yet, within its biblical context, Deut 15:8 reads as an exhortation to provide the poor with basic, alimentary needs. Indeed, to interpret a poor man's "needs" to include a slave and a horse is a stretch, to say the least. It seems, again, that rabbinic exegesis is presupposed by existing legal traditions.

David Hamilton's observation, "Status defines what is adequate expenditure not vice versa," may be somewhat extreme but nevertheless proves useful for understanding what the rabbis considered one's "needs" to be.[62] A wellborn poor man's pedigree served as an economic constraint, as it dictated the possessions that he should have and the foods that he should consume. What some see as unnecessary, wasteful, or conspicuous spending and consumption would be necessary to the wellborn poor. Useful here are economist and sociologist Thorstein Veblen's observations on the leisure class and conspicuous consumption:

> Many items of customary expenditure prove on analysis to be almost purely wasteful, and they are therefore honorific only, but after they have once been incorporated into the scale of decent consumption, and so have become an

---

[58] See Deut 15 and the commentary in Tigay, *JPS Torah Commentary: Deuteronomy*.
[59] The Tosefta, by contrast, primarily advocates providing aid as a gift without any expectation of compensation in return; in some instances, the aid can be provided as a forgivable loan; see t. Pe'ah 4:12 and my discussion in "Charity Wounds," 173–88.
[60] Exod 22:25–28, 23:19–20; Deut 24:6, 24:10–13; 2 Kgs 4:1–7; Neh 5:1–13; see Robert Gnuse, "Debt, Debtor," *The New Interpreter's Dictionary of the Bible* 2:2:76–77.
[61] Tigay, *JPS Torah Commentary: Deuteronomy*, 146–47, 217.
[62] David B. Hamilton, "Institutional Economics and Consumption," in *Evolutionary Economics* (ed. M. R. Tool; Armonk, N.Y.: 1988), 124, as quoted in Ganley, "Poverty and Charity," 436.

integral part of one's scheme of life, it is quite as hard to give up these as it is to give up many items that conduce directly to one's physical comfort, or even that may be necessary to life and health. That is to say, the conspicuously wasteful honorific expenditure that confers spiritual well-being may become more indispensable than much of that expenditure which ministers to the "lower" wants of physical well-being or sustenance only.[63]

Poverty is relative. It is relative to social standards, relative to physiological needs, and relative to one's own expectations or personal history. Seneca's idea of being poor was to have to make do with *only* a few slaves. The Stoic philosopher also tells us of a certain Apicius, whose taste for exotic foods caused him to squander a massive fortune. When he discovered that he had only ten million sesterces left, he considered himself in poverty and committed suicide to avoid a depressed living standard.[64] So too the rabbis understood a horse and a slave as "necessary" for the wellborn poor.

That the social conventions that define poverty were uniform was a principle assumed by many, from Karl Marx to Adam Smith. Later, however, economists Mollie Orshansky and Amartya Sen would question the uniformity of the social conventions that defined poverty, introducing an important corrective.[65] "Counting the poor," Orshansky wrote, "is an exercise in the art of the possible. For deciding who is poor, prayers are more relevant than calculation because poverty, like beauty, lies in the eye of the beholder."[66] The same holds true for the rabbis, who fully participated in the social conventions of the world in which they lived. But it should be noted that their understanding of poverty is uniquely their own and reflects rabbinic values. Above all, these are the values of the rabbis – who were not poor.[67] It must remain an open question as to how, if given the opportunity, the poor would have envisioned the *quppa* differently.

UNLIMITED GIVING

The principal that the *quppa* should give in accordance with one's needs raises the question of how much each member of the community ought to contribute to the *quppa*. While the Tannaim instruct that one should give money to the

---

[63] Thorstein Veblen, *The Theory of the Leisure Class: An Economic Study of Institutions* (New York: Macmillan, 1912), 102–03.
[64] Seneca, *Consolatio ad Helviam* 10.10, as cited in Saller, "Poverty, Honor," 13–14.
[65] Sen, *Poverty and Famines*, 17.
[66] Mollie Orshansky, "How Poverty is Measured," *Monthly Labor Review* 92 (1969): 37.
[67] Gardner, "Who is Rich."

quppa (and bread to the *tamhui*), no Tannaitic text specifies how much.[68] I contend that the rabbis intentionally leave this obligation open-ended, as part of an effort to encourage individuals to give as much as possible in order to meet the needs of the poor. While they stop short of Christian exhortations to impoverish oneself for the sake of charity, the Tannaim nevertheless do not specify an upper limit to the amount of charity that one should give. My findings challenge the historicity of the so-called Usha ordinance (supposedly enacted by the Tannaim in 140 C.E.), which prohibited individuals from giving more than one-fifth of one's annual income to charity. Rather, as I will show, these limits on charitable giving are post-Tannaitic, as Tannaitic compilations instruct that giving should be commensurate with the poor's needs – not in accordance with the benefactors' means.

Prodigious Giving

Tannaitic texts do not focus on how much one should give to the *quppa*, but on how much the *quppa* should allocate to the needy. This amount, in turn, is determined by each poor man's particular needs. Because a poor man's "need" could be seemingly unlimited, it follows that the amount allocated by the *quppa* – and provided by the community – must likewise be unlimited. That one individual should give generously in order to finance a *quppa* that is capable of restoring any poor man's previous lifestyle is illustrated in a narrative:

> They said: The family of the House of Navtalah was in Jerusalem, and they used to claim pedigree with the descendants of Ornan the Jebusite. The sages provided them (*'ly*) [with] three hundred[69] shekels of gold, for they did not want them to be removed from Jerusalem. (*t. Pe'ah* 4:11, lemmata D – E)

In this narrative, the House of Navtalah is in economic straits that would compel them to leave their home in Jerusalem. The source of their difficulties is not specified, though it is common for the rabbis to set narratives like

---

[68] By contrast, we find broad guidelines for how much one should give in Tob 4:8, "If you have many possessions, make your gift from them in proportion; if few, do not be afraid to give according to the little you have." On this text, see Gary A. Anderson, "You Will Have Treasure in Heaven," in *New Approaches to the Study of Biblical Interpretation in Judaism of the Second Temple Period and in Early Christianity: Proceedings of the Eleventh International Symposium of the Orion Center for the Study of the Dead Sea Scrolls and Associated Literature, Jointly Sponsored by the Hebrew University Center for the Study of Christianity, 9–11 January, 2007* (ed. G. A. Anderson et al.; Studies on the Texts of the Desert of Judah 106; Leiden and Boston: Brill, 2013), 150.

[69] MS Erfurt reads 600 pieces of gold, in accordance with 1 Chr 21:25.

these against the backdrop of crises that are drawn from the Jewish collective consciousness, such as droughts, famines, and the siege of Jerusalem in 70 C.E. by the Romans.[70] The overall narrative arc is familiar in the ancient world, as Seneca writes that impoverishment is often coupled with exile from Rome.[71]

The Tosefta traces the genealogy of the House of Navtalah to Ornan (i.e., Araunah) the Jebusite.[72] In the Hebrew Bible, the Jebusites are the pre-Israelite inhabitants of Jerusalem. Ornan is said to have owned a threshing floor on a small hilltop, a plot of land on which Solomon would later build the First Temple. After rejecting Ornan's offer to give the land to him as a gift, David instead purchases it for a large sum – 50 shekels of silver according to 2 Sam 24:24, which increases to 600 shekels of gold in 1 Chr 21:25. David then builds an altar on the land and offers sacrifices to avert God's destruction of Jerusalem. As the owner of the land that would become the Temple Mount, Ornan embodies a locus of traditions on sacred geography and status in Jerusalem, which endows the Navtalah family with prestige.[73] The significance of the Tannaim's choice of Navtalah for this narrative extends to the family name itself, as its root *btl* plays on "wealthy individual" (*batlan*)[74] and the family's removal from Jerusalem would "negate" (*btl*) its prestige. The stakes, then, are particularly high as Navtalah's standing and identity are inextricably intertwined with their residence in Jerusalem.[75]

---

[70] For a drought, see the narrative on Munbaz in *t. Pe'ah* 4:18; on this text, see Gardner, "Giving to the Poor," 163–200; Gardner, "Competitive Giving," 81–92. On the siege of Jerusalem as a backdrop for rabbinic narratives, see the narrative on the removal of Yohanan ben Zakkai from Jerusalem in *Avot d'Rabbi Natan* and *b. Gittin* 56; see Rubenstein, *Talmudic Stories*, 139–75; Peter Schäfer, "Die Flucht Johanan b. Zakkais aus Jerusalem und die Gründung des 'Lehrhauses' in Jabne," in *Aufstieg und Niedergang der Römischen Welt* II.19.2 (ed. H. Temporini and W. Haase; Berlin and New York: de Gruyter, 1979), 43–101. On collective memory among Jews, Christians, Greeks, and Romans in late antiquity, see Gregg Gardner and Kevin L. Osterloh, eds., *Antiquity in Antiquity: Jewish and Christian Pasts in the Greco-Roman World* (TSAJ 123; Tübingen: Mohr Siebeck, 2008).

[71] See the discussion in Saller, "Poverty, Honor," 16; cf. Philo, *Embassy* 123.

[72] He is Ornan in 1 Chr 21:15–28 and 2 Chr 3:1, and Araunah in 2 Sam 24:20–25.

[73] See also Josh 15:63; Judg 1:21; 2 Sam 5:6; 1 Chr 11:4. The name Ornan, philologists have shown, is synonymous with "lord" or "aristocrat"; see Richard D. Nelson, "Araunah (Person)," in *The Anchor Bible Dictionary* (ed. D. N. Freedman; New York: Doubleday, 1992), 1:353; A. Heath Jones, "Araunah," in *The New Interpreter's Dictionary of the Bible* (ed. K. D. Sakenfeld; Nashville, Tenn.: Abingdon, 2006), 1:230.

[74] Lee I. Levine, *The Rabbinic Class of Roman Palestine in Late Antiquity* (Jerusalem and New York: Yad Izhak Ben-Zvi and The Jewish Theological Seminary of America, 1989), 163.

[75] The idea that biological genealogy can be superseded by socially constructed genealogies in rabbinic literature is demonstrated for the Bavli in Moulie Vidas, "The Bavli's Discussion of Genealogy in *Qiddushin* IV," in *Antiquity in Antiquity: Jewish and Christian Pasts in the Greco-Roman World* (ed. G. Gardner and K. L. Osterloh; TSAJ 123; Tübingen: Mohr Siebeck, 2008), 285–326.

Heroically, the rabbis come to the rescue. They provide Navtalah with three hundred gold shekels, recalling the large sums paid by King David. Just as David's spending would forestall a crisis, so too the rabbis prevent the crisis of uprooting an important line of Jerusalemites. It should be noted that this narrative implies a responsibility to aid impoverished Gentiles – a point the Tannaim also make elsewhere.[76] Above all, the hundreds of gold shekels that the rabbis provide are meant to denote an extraordinary sum.[77] Just as in *t. Pe'ah* 4:10 where the Tosefta advocates giving a horse and a slave to the wellborn poor, so too the Navtalah narrative instructs one to give prodigiously so as to meet the needs of the poor – regardless of the cost.

The principle that the supervisors of the *quppa* – as well as those who contribute to it – should give liberally to the poor is also illustrated by another narrative:

> O. Another event (*ma'aseh*): The men of the Galilee used to provide (*'ly*) a pound (*litra*) – according to the standards [used in] Sepphoris – of meat for an elder every day.[78] (*t. Pe'ah* 4:10, O)

A similar tradition is found in *SifreDeut* 116:

> Another event (*ma'aseh*): In the Upper Galilee, a guest was served a pound of meat every day. (*SifreDeut* 116)[79]

There are a number of important differences between these two parallel traditions. First, in the Tosefta, the meat is given by the "men of the Galilee," while in *SifreDeut* the agent is not named, as the meat is simply served to the individual "in the Upper Galilee" – a subregion of the Galilee.[80] It is notable

---

[76] *t. Gittin* 3:13.

[77] The root *'ly* also denotes *to offer up* – namely, a sacrifice (e.g., *m. Zevahim* 14:3). This is a particularly apt allusion to the David-Ornan narratives in the Hebrew Bible, which end with David offering up a sacrifice to God on the land that he had just bought from Ornan (2 Sam 24:25; 1 Chr 21:28). The use of the root *'ly* also connects the Navtalah narrative to the two narratives at the end of *t. Pe'ah* 4:10, where it indicates "to provide" in the traditions on Hillel and the men of the Galilee.

[78] On this passage, see Brooks, *Support for the Poor*, 149; Lieberman, *The Tosefta*, 1:58; Lieberman, *Tosefta Ki-Fshutah*, 1:185–86. The Bavli's version of this tradition (*b. Ketubbot* 67b) reads *b'zipori* ("in Sepphoris") as *b'ziporin* ("in birds" or "in poultry") which points to the Stammaim's distance from the realia of Roman Palestine. Indeed, that Sepphoris had its own standards of weights and measures is illustrated in the following. On giving meat in *t. Pe'ah* 4:10–11, see also Safrai, *Jewish Community*, 76n. 103.

[79] Translation based on Hammer, *Sifre*, with my emendations.

[80] See the treatment of *'anshei* in Tannaitic, as well as Palestinian Amoraic, literature in Miller, *Sages and Commoners*, 163–78. It is also noteworthy that, centuries later, the Babylonian Talmud would combine and harmonize these traditions, reading "men of the Upper Galilee" (*b. Ketubbot* 67b).

that the word "provide" in the Tosefta and "upper" in *SifreDeut* share the same root (*'ly*). Second, the recipients differ. In the Tosefta, the meat is given to an "elder," presumably one in need.[81] In *SifreDeut*, the recipient is a "guest." Third, the Tosefta specifies that the meat should weigh a pound according to the system of weights and measures used in the city of Sepphoris. The version in *SifreDeut* omits this detail.

The overarching contexts and functions of the two traditions also differ. *SifreDeut* 116, where a guest visits the Upper Galilee, is a straightforward case of hospitality as it is common for a host to provide a guest with meat in early rabbinic discussions of hospitality. We only connect the narrative in *SifreDeut* 116 to giving to the poor because it is included within a midrash on Deut 15:8. Hospitality, as I discussed in Chapter 4, is very different from charity and on its own *SifreDeut* 116 has nothing to do with charity. By contrast, the narrative in the Tosefta is explicitly about charity. Its language ("elder") recalls Hillel the Elder in the narrative on the wellborn poor, which precedes this passage and functions as support for the Tannaim's instructions on how the *quppa* should operate. In particular, it supports the notion that the *quppa* (and its contributors) should give prodigiously – a point made by the provision of a pound of meat every day.

As I touched upon in Chapters 2 and 4, meat was expensive in the ancient world and a prestige food that marked its consumer as wealthy and with a high social standing.[82] It would have been exceedingly rare for an individual to eat meat on a regular basis, let alone every day. It follows that a pound of meat every day serves a rhetorical function in rabbinic texts to denote extreme wealth and status. We see this, for example, in *t. Arakhin* 4:27:

And so did R. Eleazar b. 'Azariah say,
"He who has ten *maneh*[83] suffices with a vegetable in a cooking pot every day.
"[He who has] twenty *maneh* suffices with a vegetable in a cooking pot and a wide-mouth cooking pot.

---

[81] The "elder" may also be a reference to a rabbi; for example, see the statement, "a *zaqen* is none other than a sage" in *Sifra, Qedoshim, Parashah* 3, *Pereq* 7 (Weiss, *Sifra*, 91a). If so, then the beneficiary of the meat in *t. Pe'ah* 4:10 is not necessarily an elderly man, but rather a respected sage – a possibility suggested by Cohen, "Rabbi in Second-Century," 935n. 63.

[82] Hamel, *Poverty and Charity in Roman Palestine*, 19–21, 31–34, 55. Cf. Lev-Tov, "Upon What Meat," 420–46, and the daily diet of meat consumed by Theophanes, a fourth-century traveler to Antioch, as discussed in John Matthews, *The Journey of Theophanes: Travel, Business, and Daily Life in the Roman East* (New Haven, Conn., and London: Yale University Press, 2006), 163–79.

[83] *Maneh* is a weight in gold or silver; see following discussion.

"[He who has] fifty *maneh* suffices with a pound (*litra*) of meat from Sabbath eve to Sabbath eve.

"[He who has] a hundred *maneh* suffices with a pound (*litra*) of meat every day." (*t. Arakhin* 4:27)[84]

Note that the language of *t. Arakhin* 4:27 features a number of parallels to the discussion of the *quppa* in *t. Pe'ah* 4:8–10, including a vegetable (*yrq*), "from Sabbath eve to Sabbath eve," and a pound (*litra*) of meat every day. This passage is constructed as a hierarchy indexed by one's income, from ten to twenty to fifty to a hundred *maneh*. Likewise, the value and prestige of the foods increases from vegetables, which are first provided in a cooking pot, then in a cooking pot and a wide-mouth cooking pot; to meat, which increases in frequency from once a week (i.e., from one Friday evening to the next) to every day. Consuming a pound of meat, every day, is at the apex of the hierarchy and is associated with an income of one hundred *maneh*. As previously discussed, it is highly unlikely that we can recover the absolute, historical values of currencies mentioned in rabbinic texts. What is clear, however, is that a hundred *maneh* is intended to denote an extraordinary sum – perhaps equivalent to 10,000 *dinars*.[85] By comparison, the rabbis elsewhere hold that 200 *dinars* is sufficient to maintain a household for an entire year.[86] In short, eating a pound of meat every day would elevate the elder's quality of life. The elder is lifted to a higher social plane, placed among those who can afford to eat meat on a daily basis.[87]

The Tosefta's inclusion of the detail that the meat should be a pound according to the Sepphoran standards is also significant. In the ancient Mediterranean, it was common for regions or towns to use their own standards of weights and measures. Sepphoris played a prominent role in the economy of the Galilee and was home to a number of members of the early rabbinic movement.[88] The significance of Sepphoran weights and measures is illuminated by an archaeological find from the city, a lead weight whose obverse reads "half *litra*," employing the same word for "pound" – *litra* – as that

---

[84] Translation is based on Neusner, *The Tosefta*, with my emendations. On the cooking pot (*qedera*) and wide-mouth cooking pot (*ilpas*), see Adan-Bayewitz, *Common Pottery*, 32–35.
[85] S. Applebaum, "Economic Life in Palestine," in *The Jewish People in the First Century: Historical Geography, Political History, Social, Cultural and Religious Life and Institutions* (ed. S. Safrai and M. Stern; Compendia rerum Iudaicarum ad Novum Testamentum: Section 1; Assen and Philadelphia: Van Gorcum and Fortress Press, 1974–1976), 699.
[86] *m. Pe'ah* 8:8.
[87] There may be a play on the word *ma'alin* ("they provide"), which can also be rendered "they elevate": the people of the Galilee elevate the elder by purchasing meat for him.
[88] On Sepphoris in rabbinic literature, see Stuart S. Miller, *Studies in the History and Traditions of Sepphoris* (Leiden: E.J. Brill, 1984).

chosen by the redactors of *t. Pe'ah* 4:10.[89] The reverse side of the lead weight reads "under the market inspection of Simon."[90] Similar lead weights have been found throughout the Greco-Roman world, including Roman Palestine, where they were used by officials such as the *agoranomos* (supervisor of the markets) to check the accuracy of the weights used by merchants in the marketplace.[91] The inclusion of the name of the supervisor, Simon, lends further accountability to the office and its work, suggesting that Sepphoran standards were well policed.[92] By mentioning the Sepphoran pound, the Tosefta adds specificity to the quantity of meat given, indexing it as a tangible and substantial gift. That is, the Sepphoran pound adds weight to the Galileans' munificence. Moreover, the "men of the Galilee" serve as exempla that this munificence should be a collective effort – an ideal to be followed by those obligated to contribute to the *quppa*.[93]

The "Usha Ordinance"

In order to restore the conjunctural poor, even those who used to be particularly wealthy, the *quppa* would require enormous resources. It follows that the well-off should would be encouraged to contribute as much as possible. Yet, almost uniformly, traditional interpreters and academic scholars alike have

---

[89] It is notable that a "half *litra*" is also mentioned in *t. Bava Batra* 5:9.

[90] For the lead weight and the inscription, see Ya'akov Meshorer in Eric M. Meyers et al., "Sepphoris: 'Ornament of All Galilee,'" *BA* 49 (1986): 16–17. It is notable, moreover, that a weight found in the Judean desert dating to the time of the Bar Kochva Revolt (132–135 C.E.) identifies the supervisor over the weights as *parnas*. On the one hand, it is significant because *parnas* also indicates a charity supervisor in Tannaitic compilations (see my discussion in Chapter 7). On the other hand, this source is unique, as no other source (epigraphic, rabbinic, etc.) from the period suggests that the *parnas* oversaw weights and measures. See the discussions in Steven D. Fraade, "Local Jewish Leadership in Roman Palestine: The Case of the *Parnas* in Early Rabbinic Sources in Light of Extra-Rabbinic Evidence," in *Halakhah in Light of Epigraphy* (ed. A. I. Baumgarten et al.; Journal of Ancient Judaism. Supplements 3; Göttingen: Vandenhoeck & Ruprecht, 2011), 169–73; Daniel Meir, "The *Parnas* in Israel: Identity, Status, and Authority [Hebrew]," (M.A. thesis, Hebrew University of Jerusalem, 2007), 3, 16–18.

[91] On the *agoranomos* in ancient Palestine, see Gardner, "Jewish Leadership," 329–32.

[92] A number of weights from the ancient world bear only the supervisor's title, *agoranomos*, without giving his name. See, for example, the weights uncovered in the Jewish Quarter of Jerusalem dating to the first century C.E. published in Ronny Reich, "Stone Scale Weights of the Late Second Temple Period from the Jewish Quarter," in *Jewish Quarter Excavations in the Old City of Jerusalem: Conducted by Nahman Avigad, 1969–1982* (ed. H. Geva; Jerusalem: Institute of Archaeology of the Hebrew University of Jerusalem and the Israel Exploration Society, 2000), 3:329–88.

[93] This may mitigate, somewhat, the tension that was also evident in the Hillel narrative (*t. Pe'ah* 4:10), as the transfer of assets from benefactor to beneficiary is direct. The *quppa*, by contrast, is an indirect transfer that is mediated by a disinterested third party.

held that the Tannaim limited the amount that one could give to charity to one-fifth of one's annual income. This is based on the assumed dating to the Tannaitic period of the "Usha ordinance," which legislated that one may use only up to one-fifth of one's assets toward fulfilling commandments, including charity.[94] However, a few scholarly voices have expressed concerns about the historicity of the ordinance, most notably and recently Alyssa Gray.[95] Indeed, in light of the influence that the Usha ordinance has had on scholarship on charity, it deserves as fresh look.

The earliest references to the Usha ordinance are found in the Palestinian Talmud, redacted by the Amoraim in the fourth century:

> [These are things that have no measure....] acts of kindness. (*m. Pe'ah* 1:1)
> That means with his person.[96] But with his money it has a measure.
> This parallels what Rabbi Simeon bar Laqish said in the name of Rabbi Yehudah ben Hanina, "They voted at Usha that a person may give a fifth of his property for fulfilling commandments."
> ... It happened that Rabbi Yeshebab went and let his entire property be distributed to the poor.
> Rabban Gamaliel sent word to him, "Did they not say one-fifth of one's property for commandments?"
> And was not Rabban Gamaliel before Usha?
> Rabbi Yose ben Rabbi Abun [said in the name of] Rabbi Levi, "That was the current practice, they forgot it, but the later ones got up and agreed to the opinion of the earlier ones, to teach you that everything the court insists on will come to be in the end." (*y. Pe'ah* 1:1, 15b)[97]

The reasoning behind limiting limitless or "heroic" almsgiving is to prevent benefactors from falling into poverty themselves, suffering shame, adding to

---

[94] *y. Ketubbot* 4:6 (= 4:8 in Venice ed.), 28d; *b. Ketubbot* 49b–50a; *b. Ketubbot* 67b; *b. Arakhin* 28a; and the ninth (?) century compilation *Pesikta Rabbati* 25:2. See also *Mishneh Torah, Hilkhot mattenot 'aniyyim* (Laws on Gifts to the Poor) 7.5. The historicity of the Usha decree is assumed by Becknell, "Almsgiving," 491–497, 504, 516–17, 543–44, 580–84, 590, 604; Bergmann, *Ha-Tsedakah*, 27; Frisch, *Historical Survey*, 126n. 2; Loewenberg, *From Charity to Social Justice*, 116; Moore, *Judaism in the First Centuries*, 170; Sorek, *Remembered for Good*, 230, 233; Urbach, "Political and Social Tendencies," 15.

[95] Gray, "Redemptive Almsgiving," 148–49. In an largely overlooked article in Hebrew, H. Mantel, "The Date of the Usha Ordinances [Hebrew]," *Tarbiz* 34 (1965): 281–83, ascribes the ordinance to the Amoraim.

[96] That is, in services provided, as opposed to money or material goods.

[97] Translation based on Heinrich W. Guggenheimer, *The Jerusalem Talmud: First Order, Zeraim: Tractates Peah and Demay* (Berlin and New York: Walter de Gruyter, 2000), 19, with my emendations. See also Schäfer and Becker, eds. *Synopse zum Talmud Yerushalmi*, 1:1–2, pp. 262–65; Gerd A. Wewers, *Der Jerusalemer Talmud in deutscher Übersetzung: Pea, Ackerecke* (Tübingen: Mohr, 1986), 7–9.

the roles of the *quppa*, and increasing the burden upon the community that supports it. The prohibition against giving away all of one's possessions has also been interpreted as a way to distinguish Jewish attitudes toward charity from the kind of voluntary poverty that we see in early Christian texts.[98] The Yerushalmi dates and locates the prohibition against giving more than one-fifth of one's possession to the "synod" of Usha – a small town in the Lower Galilee that was a locus of rabbinic activity in the years following the failed Bar Kochva Revolt and the expulsion of the Jews from Jerusalem, around 140 C.E.[99]

That the Usha ordinance dates to the Tannaitic era, however, is highly questionable. First, as I have already discussed in the methodological comments in my introductory chapter, it is highly suspect that post-Tannaitic writings accurately preserve Tannaitic traditions that are otherwise absent from Tannaitic compilations. Increasingly, critical investigations of the Tannaim, their ideas, and their age exclude those traditions that are ascribed to Tannaitic times but found only in the Talmuds or other post-Tannaitic compilations.[100] Along these lines, it is significant that although Tannaitic compilations devote extensive space to the issues of poverty and charity, nowhere do they indicate an awareness of this "ordinance." Rather, we find it only in later works, from the Amoraic period onwards.[101] Second, the earliest versions of the Usha ordinance, those found in the Yerushalmi, attribute the tradition to Rabbi Yehudah b. Hanina – an Amora.[102] That is, the versions in the Yerushalmi attribute the tradition to a figure living perhaps a century after the supposed vote in 140 C.E. It would only be later, in the Babylonian Talmud, that the tradition would be placed in the mouth of a Tanna: Bavli *Ketubbot* 67b, for example, reads, "And did not Rabbi Ilai say, 'In Usha they ordained....'"[103] Rabbi Ilai would have been active in 140 C.E. when the supposed vote took

---

[98] As suggested by Urbach, "Political and Social Tendencies," 15; see also Gary A. Anderson, *Sin: A History* (New Haven, Conn.: Yale University Press, 2009), 178–81; Anderson, *Charity*, 152–56.

[99] On the location of Usha, as well as references to it in rabbinic literature and a bibliography of archaeological finds, see Yoram Tsafrir et al., *Tabula Imperii Romani. Iudaea-Palestina: Eretz Israel in the Hellenistic, Roman and Byzantine Periods: Maps and Gazetteer* (Jerusalem: Israel Academy of Sciences and Humanities, 1994), 255–56.

[100] E.g., Cohen, "Rabbi in Second-Century," 922–90; Goodman, *State and Society*; Novick, *What is Good*; Rosenblum, *Food and Identity*.

[101] The absence of parallels to the "Usha ordinance" in Tannaitic compilations is confirmed by Leib Moscovitz, *Database of Sources and Parallels to the Yerushalmi [Hebrew]* (Bar-Ilan University http://www.biu.ac.il/js/tl/yerushalmi/, 2008).

[102] *y. Pe'ah* 1:1, 15b; *y. Ketubbot* 4:6 (= 4:8 in Venice ed.), 28d.

[103] The tradition is likewise attributed to Ilai in the other two versions in the Bavli, *b. Ketubbot* 50a and *b. Arakhin* 28a.

place. Those who trust the Bavli's attribution use it to further support the authenticity of the Usha ordinance. The Bavli's attributions, however, cannot be taken at face value.[104]

More broadly, not only is the so-called Usha ordinance conspicuously absent from Tannaitic compilations, but there is no hint of agreement with its sentiments. That is, no text from a Tannaitic compilation suggests a limit to charitable contributions. In fact, the opposite appears to be the case. We see this especially in *t. Pe'ah* 4:18, a narrative on how Munbaz the King gives away all of his fortunes to the needy in a time of famine. The Tannaim present Munbaz as an exemplar of proper behavior, dubbing him a "righteous individual" and his deeds as acts of "righteousness."[105] Surely, these are not terms of disapproval.[106] That is, the Usha ordinance seems to express an approach to charity that is foreign to Tannaitic compilations. Indeed, the Usha ordinance should be read within the context of the compilations in which it is found, instead of those in which it is not – that is, within the context of Amoraic, rather than Tannaitic, compilations.[107] In short, in light of the most recent methods for dating rabbinic materials, I find that the Usha ordinance cannot be used reliably as evidence that the Tannaim sought to limit the amount that one could give as charity. Rather, generous giving would be needed in order to finance the *quppa*, which sought to restore the conjunctural poor – even those who used to be particularly wealthy – to their previous positions.

CONCLUSION

Alongside the *tamhui*, the *quppa* is a centerpiece of organized charity. They play complementary roles, as the *tamhui* provides alms based on immediate, physiological needs, while the *quppa* addresses the poor's social needs. In particular, the *quppa* restores to the conjunctural poor their former possessions and the status that they convey. Of particular note, the quppa should even provide expensive marks of prestige, such as a horse and a slave, to those who used to be particularly wealthy. As such, the Tannaim encourage the *quppa*

---

[104] On the problem of attributions, see Strack and Stemberger, *Introduction to the Talmud*, 57–59.

[105] On this text, see Gardner, "Competitive Giving," 81–92. Indeed, the idea that charity has an upper limit may be the result of category confusion with *pe'ah*, which is defined quantitatively (*m. Pe'ah* 1:1; *t. Pe'ah* 1:1–2). On the differences between *pe'ah* and charity, see my discussion in Chapter 1.

[106] Likewise, it is notable that the dangers of heroic almsgiving – that the benefactor would become poor and dependent upon the community – are reflected only in Amoraic texts; see *Lev. Rab.* 5:4 and my discussion in Chapter 8.

[107] Goodman, *State and Society*, 8–9.

and the community that funds it to give prodigiously, in order to restore even the most extreme cases of conjunctural poverty. The Tannaim's interest in the social aspects of poverty, and particularly the dignity of the poor, was unique to the ancient world and will be explored in further detail in the next chapter.

6

Charity with Dignity

Having addressed *what* the *quppa* provides in Chapter 5, in this chapter I examine *to whom* and *how* it provides these alms.[1] In doing so, I illuminate several important attributes of the *quppa*, uncovering its underlying objective to give to the poor while protecting their dignity. I show that the recipients of the *quppa* are envisioned as "conjuncturally" poor – individuals who were not always poor but have fallen into poverty. Conjunctural poverty carried a great deal of shame in the ancient world, which was amplified in urban settings where the signs of poverty were particularly visible and arresting. Because poverty adversely affects everyone, both poor and non-poor alike, I demonstrate how the *quppa* functions as a local, civic, and communal institution that assists the conjunctural poor in the town in which the *quppa* is located. I bring these findings into conversation with the works of Peter Brown on the development of giving in late antiquity and Seth Schwartz on the emergence of towns and local communities as meaningful religious entities in rabbinic thought. Finally, I discuss how the rabbis see the *quppa* as a mechanism for giving and receiving alms in an anonymous fashion, whereby benefactors and beneficiaries never meet – an alternative to face-to-face begging. Thus, the *quppa* protects the dignity of the local conjunctural poor.

THE CONJUNCTURAL POOR

While the *quppa* certainly supports the poor, it is more accurate to say that it supports the impoverished. The beneficiaries of the *quppa* are not those who were born poor, but rather those who were born wealthy or well-off and have fallen into poverty for one reason or another. As the texts discussed in the

---

[1] I owe the title "charity with dignity" to Holman, *Hungry are Dying*, 47.

previous chapter indicate, the *quppa* provides alms in accordance with what individuals *used to* have, as it seeks to restore the recipients to their previous standards of living.[2] Tannaitic texts instruct that the *quppa* should go to great lengths to restore these individuals – even if it meant giving them expensive items that are marks of prestige, such as a horse and a slave.

It is worthwhile to explore this image of the poor in greater depth, in order to understand the implications of perceiving the needy in this way. Helpful in this regard is a taxonomy of the poor that has been employed by social historians, who distinguish between structural and conjunctural poverty. The structural poor are those who are unable to participate fully in the economy due to a lack of ability or other barriers to entry into the labor force. In ancient society, the structural poor typically included widows, the elderly, the disabled, orphans, aliens, and simply those who were born into poverty so deep that they could not escape. No amount of training or environmental change could lift them from poverty and they remain poor even when everyone else prospers. For the structural poor, poverty was long term and often permanent.[3]

By contrast, conjunctural poverty is the result of a change. It is a sudden impoverishment brought about by a conjuncture – an extraordinary crisis or series of crises. Such events include anything that can disrupt the economic status quo, such as droughts, changes in civil law (such the landholding structure), military conflicts, and demographic shifts. Unlike the structural poor, the conjunctural poor possess the skills, abilities, and, perhaps most important of all, access and social connections to reenter the matrix of the economy and lift themselves up from their downtrodden state. Conjunctural poverty was a particular concern in ancient texts, whose authors tended to be well-off themselves.[4] Seeing individuals who used to wear nice clothes, like they do, but now wear rags would have evoked fear.[5] Parkin traces this fear back to Aristotle, who defined pity as the pain incurred by the sight of

---

[2] Similarly, Cam Grey, *Constructing Communities in the Late Roman Countryside* (Cambridge and New York: Cambridge University Press, 2011), 11–13, writes that the bulk of the church's resources and attention were devoted to aiding individuals who had fallen from a position of relative comfort into misfortune.

[3] Braudel, *Mediterranean and the Mediterranean World*, 892–900; Michel Mollat, *The Poor in the Middle Ages: An Essay in Social History* (trans. A. Goldhammer; New Haven, Conn., and London: Yale University Press, 1986), 26. For recent applications of the structural-conjunctural distinction, see Cohen, *Poverty and Charity*, 33–71; Morley, "The Poor," 28–29; Robin Osborne, "Introduction: Roman Poverty in Context," in *Poverty in the Roman World* (ed. M. Atkins and R. Osborne; Cambridge and New York: Cambridge University Press, 2006), 1, 5; Parkin, "An Exploration," 62–80; Whittaker, "Poor," 1–25.

[4] Gardner, "Who is Rich."

[5] Brown, *Poverty and Leadership*, 14–15.

misfortunes happening to people who do not deserve them.[6] Seneca writes that wealthy men are frequently reduced to beggary overnight and that people are often oblivious to the fragile nature of their fortunes.[7] "Am I to become a beggar?" was a typical question asked of the Oracle of Astrampsychus.[8] M. I. Rostovtzeff, in his classic work on the social and economic history of the Roman Empire, writes, "It was an everyday occurrence... for a man to become a beggar."[9]

Conjunctural poverty was likewise a preoccupation in biblical, Second Temple-era, and early rabbinic texts. Sudden impoverishment is addressed in Lev 25:35: "If any of your kin fall into difficulty and become dependent on you, you shall support them; they shall live with you as though resident aliens." Ben Sira was likewise concerned: "Assist your neighbor to the best of your ability, but be careful not to fall yourself" (Sir 29:20). Sudden impoverishment and its complement, sudden riches, are addressed in a number of early rabbinic texts that discuss reversals of fortune where individuals "become poor" or "become rich."[10] Emblematic is *m. Ketubbot* 6:6: "sometimes a man is poor and becomes rich, or he is rich and becomes poor."

Such reversals of fortune, particularly an unexpected plunge into poverty, could result from a number of factors. Roman Palestine during the era in which the Tannaim lived and worked saw a number of crises or conjunctures, including civil unrest, wars, natural disasters (e.g., droughts, earthquakes), as well as unanticipated taxes and dispossession of land by the Roman authorities.[11] Significant and sustained economic difficulties would descend upon Palestine in the middle of the third century, though the redaction of Tannaitic compilations was complete before the rabbis felt the impact and internalized the so-called third-century crisis.[12] Sudden poverty need not be the product of widespread disturbances or global events. Impoverishment is just as likely

---

[6] Aristotle, *Rhetorica* 2.8; Parkin, "An Exploration," 64.
[7] Seneca, *Ad Marciam de Consolatione* 9.1; as cited in Parkin, "An Exploration," 64.
[8] M. Rostovtzeff, *The Social and Economic History of the Roman Empire, Second Edition* (Oxford: Clarendon Press, 1957), 479.
[9] Rostovtzeff, *Social and Economic*, 480.
[10] E.g., *m. Pe'ah* 8:9; *t. Pe'ah* 4:14; *m. Nedarim* 9:4; *m. Sheqalim* 3:2. Conjunctural poverty is also addressed in Amoraic texts. See, for example, *Lev. Rab.* 34:13, which offers two interpretations of the "wretched poor" in Isa 58:7 as "those poor from their youth" and "those from good families who have fallen from their wealth." On the poor in *Leviticus Rabbah*, see Visotzky, *Golden Bells*, 121–34.
[11] Hamel, *Poverty and Charity in Roman Palestine*, 44–54; Millar, *Roman Near East*, 368; Pastor, *Land and Economy*; Russell, "Earthquake Chronology of Palestine," 37–59; Smallwood, *Jews Under Roman Rule*, 340–41, 477, 495.
[12] See Gray, "Formerly Wealthy Poor," 117–19, and my discussion in Chapter 2.

to result from individual action and misfortune, such as illness, profligate spending, and poor decision making.

The rabbis understood unexpected poverty or wealth to be mandated by God. We see this, for example, in *Mekilta, Amalek* 4:

> He [i.e., God] who had made one poor will in the end make him rich, and He who had made the other rich will in the end make him poor.[13]

For the Tannaim, conjunctural poverty was a function of one's behavior with respect to Torah:

> R. Jonathan said: He who fulfils the Law in poverty shall in the end fulfill it in wealth; and he that neglects the Law in wealth shall in the end neglect it in poverty. (*m. Avot* 4:9)

One earns merit by following the Torah and performing God's commandments, which in turn determines one's wealth or poverty. Likewise, merit is a more important determinant of wealth and poverty than one's profession:

> There is no trade in which both poor and wealthy men are not [employed]. Rather, all is according to the merit of [each] man. (*m. Qiddushin* 4:14)

Right living earns rewards, while the opposite leads to sudden and unexpected impoverishment – conjunctural poverty.[14]

THE *QUPPA* AS A CIVIC INSTITUTION

It can be particularly challenging to support and restore the conjunctural poor to their previous place in life. In Chapter 5, I discussed how this could entail an expensive outlay – providing even a horse and a slave. The rabbis also understood that restoring the conjunctural poor would require a collective effort. We see this, for example, in *Sifra*:

> *If any of your kin fall into difficulty and become dependent on you, [you shall support them]* (Lev 25:35)[15] Do not let him fall! To what then does this [case] compare? To the load on an ass's back: as long as [the ass] remains in place,

---

[13] Translation based on Jacob Z. Lauterbach, *Mekhilta de-Rabbi Ishmael: A Critical Edition, Based on the Manuscripts and Early Editions* (Philadelphia: Jewish Publication Society, 2004), 288, with my modifications.

[14] On the doctrine of merits, see A. Marmorstein, *The Doctrine of Merits in Old Rabbinical Literature* (London: Jews' College, 1920); E. P. Sanders, *Paul and Palestinian Judaism: A Comparison of Patterns of Religion* (London: SCM Press, 1977), 33–205; Jonathan Wyn Schofer, *The Making of a Sage: A Study in Rabbinic Ethics* (Madison: University of Wisconsin Press, 2004), 128–33.

[15] Translation according to NRSV.

one person may hold it and keep it standing; but when it falls, even five people cannot stand it up, [so that it is easier to support one's kinsman prior to his complete collapse]. And from what scriptural passage does one learn: Even if you have supported him four or five times, [you must] renew your support? Scripture specifies: *you shall support them*. (*Sifra, Behar, Parashah* 5)[16]

In this text, only one person is needed to keep the donkey and his load standing, but more than five people are needed to pick him up if he has fallen to the ground. Thus, the rabbis demonstrate an understanding that elevating the impoverished is a collective effort. This would be embodied by the *quppa*, which they model along the lines of a civic institution. Moreover, because poverty was a problem that adversely affected the lives of the poor and non-poor alike, finding remedies for poverty would elevate the well-being of the community as a whole.

I begin my examination of the communal, civic nature of the *quppa* by returning to the seminal texts on organized charity from Mishnah and Tosefta *Pe'ah*, which introduce the *quppa* by comparing it to the *tamhui*:[17]

> They do not give to a poor person, who travels from place to place, less than a loaf of bread worth a *pondion*, [made from grain valued at] one *sela* for four *seahs*.
> [If] he lodges, [then] they give him provisions for lodging.
> [If he lodges] over the Sabbath, [then] they give him food for three meals.
> One who has food for two meals may not take from the *tamhui*.
> One who has food for fourteen meals may not take from the *quppa*.
> And the *quppa* is collected by two people and distributed by three people.
> (*m. Pe'ah* 8:7)

And the parallel passage from Tosefta *Pe'ah*:

> A. They do not [give] to a poor person, who travels from place to place, less than a loaf of bread worth a *pondion*, [made from grain valued at] four *seahs* per *sela*.
> B. [If] he lodges overnight, [then] they give him provisions for lodging, oil, and beans.
> C. [If he lodges over] the Sabbath, [then] they give him food for three meals, oil and beans, fish and a vegetable.
> D. Under what circumstances does this apply?

---

[16] Based on the Hebrew text of Weiss, *Sifra*, 109a; translation based on Apothaker, *Sifra, Dibbura deSinai*, 137, with my emendations.

[17] On these texts, see also my discussions in Chapter 3.

E. In instances in which they do not know him.
F. But in instances in which they do know him, then they also clothe him.
G. [If a poor man] went from door to door [begging, then] they are not obligated to him in any way. (*t. Pe'ah* 4:8, A – G)

I have examined aspects of these important passages throughout this book. Here, I will focus on the importance of the role of geography and the poor man's place of origin in these pericopae. Both passages begin with the poor man who travels from place to place (lemma A in both texts). In the lines that follow, the Mishnah and Tosefta address different aspects of the vagrant's condition. The Mishnah picks up on the fact that he is both poor and away from his home. It follows that he would have insufficient provisions in hand, which becomes the focus of the Mishnah's instructions that one with fewer than two meals is eligible for the *tamhui*, while one with fewer than fourteen meals is eligible for the *quppa* (*m. Pe'ah* 8:7, D–E).

By contrast, the redactors of the Tosefta emphasize the poor man's place of origin. They elaborate upon his status as a transient – that is, the fact that he originates from a place different from the one in which he is presently located, different from the location in which he requests alms. This is seen in lines D–G, where the Tosefta distinguishes between those who are "recognized" or "known" and those who are "unknown."

An individual who is not recognized is eligible to receive food and shelter from the *tamhui*. A recognized individual is eligible for these plus clothing, which is provided exclusively through the *quppa*. What does it mean to be "recognized" or "known"? There are two probable explanations. The first, as Saul Lieberman suggests, is whether the individual is "known" to be poor. Is he genuinely in need? Has he already received alms from others? Or is he pretending to be poor, deliberately misrepresenting himself?[18] In late antiquity, it was common to be suspicious of those who claimed to be poor. This suspicion is likewise reflected in early rabbinic texts, as I will discuss in further detail in Chapter 7. Such behavior is dishonest, deviates from the proper observance of the Law, embraces dependency (which is otherwise to be avoided), and misallocates communal resources that were intended to support those who are truly poor. Assessing the needs of the poor would be the task of the charity supervisor.[19] Discovery of deception, moreover, discourages future giving by potential benefactors. A second interpretation, by Roger Brooks, is that a poor person is "known" or "recognized" if he

---

[18] Lieberman, *The Tosefta*, 1:57; Lieberman, *Tosefta Ki-Fshutah*, 1:183–84.
[19] See my discussion of the charity supervisor in Chapter 7.

resides in the town (*'ir*) in which the *quppa* in question is located.[20] I propose that Brooks's and Lieberman's interpretations should be reconciled, as one's present and past economic situation is more likely to be known if he is a resident and known to the locals as well as the charity supervisor.

The Tosefta goes on to flesh out the importance of one's geographic location and civic identity for the *quppa*:

C. The *tamhui* is for everyone.
D. The *quppa* is for poor people of the same town (*'ir*). (*t. Pe'ah* 4:9, C–D)

While the *tamhui* is for everyone, the *quppa* is only for the poor of the town in which the *quppa* is located. What, then, does it mean to be a poor person of a particular town? How would the *quppa*'s supervisors distinguish a local poor man from an itinerant poor man who stays a day, a night, a weekend, or longer? At what point does a visitor become a local and qualify for the elaborate alms that the *quppa* provides? The Tosefta takes up this very issue:

E. If he stays for thirty days, then he is like a resident of the town with regard to the *quppa*.[21]
F. And for clothing – six months.
G. For the town's taxes[22] – twelve months. (*t. Pe'ah* 4:9, E–G)

It is notable that the language of *t. Pe'ah* 4:9E–G is ambiguous, as scholars have understood it as addressing either the status of contributors or the recipients.[23] I suggest that the redactors' intention here is to address both. The point is that the *quppa* is closely linked to residence in the particular town in which it is located. That is, after a certain period of residence, all individuals become integrated into the community's system of organized charity – they become subject to its obligations or entitled to its benefits.

There is a tiered or graduated system of duties and entitlements, based on one's length of residence. One who resides in the town for thirty days is regarded "as if" he is a resident with respect to the *quppa*. If a poor man lacks a week's worth of provisions and resides in a town for thirty days, then he is entitled to food and money from the *quppa*. Likewise, after thirty days of residence, a non-poor individual is obligated to contribute, presumably

---

[20] Brooks, *Support for the Poor*, 147–48.
[21] See the explanation in Brooks, *Support for the Poor*, 148–49.
[22] On this reading and its textual difficulties, see Brooks, *Support for the Poor*, 148; Lieberman, *The Tosefta*, 1:57; Lohse and Mayer, *Die Tosefta*, 150.
[23] E.g., Frisch, *Historical Survey*, 102; Moore, *Judaism in the First Centuries*, 178, reads *t. Pe'ah* 4:9 as defining the contributors, while Brooks, *Support for the Poor*, 148, reads it as identifying the poor recipients.

money or food, to the *quppa*. After six months, the poor man would be entitled to the next level of provisions – clothing. Likewise, the non-poor must contribute clothing. If any individual resides in the town for a year, then he is subject to municipal taxes. Until twelve months have passed, he is considered "as if" he is a resident of the town for the purposes of the *quppa* alone. However, at twelve months, he is a full-fledged resident of the town, subject to taxes like everyone else.[24]

Two important points emerge from this passage. First, the Tosefta reflects an empathy for the poor, as one may receive alms from the town's *quppa* at one month, well before other civic obligations (i.e., municipal taxes) begin. Second, and more broadly, is that rabbis understand the *quppa* within the framework of one's civic standing and the obligations that go with it. The *quppa* is strongly associated with life in the ancient city and it is envisioned as a civic institution. Each *quppa*, moreover, has a special obligation toward the residents of the town in which it is located.[25] We see this, for example, in the Tosefta's instructions on how the charity supervisors should allocate the *quppa's* funds:

> An individual who in his town pledged to give to charity gives it for the poor of his town. [If he pledged to give] in another town, he gives it to the poor of that other town. The charity supervisors (*parnasim*) who in their town agreed to give charity must give it to the poor of their town. [If they promised it] in another town, they give it to the poor of that other town. One who pledges charity before the supervisors (*parnasim*) have taken possession of it is allowed to change it for another purpose. Once the supervisors (*parnasim*) have taken possession of it, he is not allowed to change it for another purpose, except with their knowledge (and consent). (*t. Megillah* 2:15)[26]

The *quppa* is a local institution, associated not only with civic life, but also with the life of the specific town in which it is located. Funded by local residents, the *quppa* funnels assets from benefactors to poor beneficiaries. It embodies the notion of collective responsibility that extends primarily toward assisting one's fellow residents.

---

[24] Whether or not the Romans taxed the poor lies beyond the scope of this study. For our purposes, the point is that the rabbis perceived that the poor would qualify as residents after one year and be liable to taxation. At twelve months, residents are also required to contribute toward the town's infrastructure (*m. Bava Batra* 1:5). As Cohen, *Justice in the City*, 98–100, observes, for the rabbis, twelve months of residency is the point in which one joins a town's "community of obligations."

[25] See *t. Bava Batra* 9:9 and the texts cited in the following.

[26] Translation is based on Fraade, "Local Jewish Leadership," 160, and Neusner, *The Tosefta*, with my emendations.

Responsibility toward the poor of one's own town even crosses the boundaries of identity and religion:[27]

> A town in which Israelites and gentiles dwell, the supervisors (*parnasim*) collect from the Israelites and the gentiles, for the sake of peace. They provide for the poor of the gentiles and the poor of Israel alike, for the sake of peace. (*t. Gittin* 3:13)[28]

In these as well as other texts, we find the notion that the poor of one's own town have a distinct social identity and that the *quppa* had a unique responsibility to them.[29]

The *quppa* is envisioned by the rabbis as an institution with civic standing and a part of everyday life among the town's residents. They place it alongside marketplaces, bathhouses, theaters, and other institutions that are typical of cities in Roman Palestine.[30] This supports Susan Holman's suggestion that the rabbis understood the contribution to and supervision of the *quppa* as a kind of *leitourgia*, the Greek word denoting a "liturgy" or "work for the people."[31] It encompasses a benefit or service that one provides to others, particularly one's fellow citizens.[32] Indeed, the *quppa* provides a number of benefits to the local community. Foremost, it benefits poor individuals. But poverty is not the poor's problem alone. Rather, the consequences of poverty extend to the community as a whole. The *quppa* benefits the non-poor by providing a systematic and reliable way to discharge their obligation to give *tsedaqah*. This was especially important in light of the imperfect nature of *tsedaqah*: How can one be sure that he has fulfilled the commandment of *tsedaqah* if the obligation itself is defined incompletely? The *quppa*, in a sense, is a means to perfect an obligation that is by nature imperfectly defined.[33]

The *quppa* also benefits the community as a whole as a form of social control, as it sought to eradicate the most visible form of poverty – begging.

---

[27] Cf. *Mekilta*, *Kaspa* 1 (to Exod 22:25), Lauterbach, *Mekhilta de-Rabbi Ishmael*, 458; Horovitz and Rabin, *Mechilta d'Rabbi Ismael*, 315, which prioritizes the Jewish poor of another town over the Gentile poor of one's own town. This text, however, addresses *lending* to the poor – it does not address support through the *quppa*.

[28] Translation based on Fraade, "Local Jewish Leadership," 160.

[29] *t. Megillah* 2:15; *t. Pe'ah* 4:9; *t. Bava Qamma* 11:3; *t. Bava Batra* 9:9.

[30] On Greek cities and their institutions, see A. H. M. Jones, *The Greek City from Alexander to Justinian* (Oxford: The Clarendon Press, 1940). On cities in Roman Palestine, see Sperber, *City in Roman Palestine*; Zangenberg and van de Zande, "Urbanization," 169–72.

[31] On liturgies, see Holman, *Hungry are Dying*, 21–25, 31–63, and the overview in Hornblower and Spawforth, *OCD*, 875–76.

[32] Holman, *Hungry are Dying*, 42–48.

[33] Here I apply Buchanan's work on perfecting otherwise imperfect obligations; see Buchanan, "Charity, Justice," 98–116.

Solicitations from beggars, in public spaces as well as at private doorways, were surely viewed as a nuisance by many. The sight of beggars produces negative emotions such as fear and pity that would not have been invoked otherwise. The frequency and magnitude of these negative emotions was doubtlessly amplified by the sight of beggars who everyone knew used to be well-off. "Beggars were horrifying physically and metaphysically," Parkin writes of the poor in the Roman world; "they evoked fear for what the future might hold."[34] More broadly, Sen writes that there is little doubt that the sight of the poor surely affects the well-being of the non-poor.[35] Begging was recognized as a problem for the community as a whole and there was a strong incentive to control and reduce it.[36] As an alternative to begging and giving to beggars, the *quppa* benefited poor and non-poor alike.

The *quppa* also served the community's interests by aiming to restore the wellborn poor in particular. The rabbis shared a sentiment held elsewhere in the Greco-Roman world that every individual ought to retain his or her proper station in life. Those born into the upper echelons of society were understood to be essential components of urban culture and civic life. Some held that the body politic might collapse without its most noble citizens fulfilling their expected roles.[37] Urban life during the age was unthinkable without the wellborn. The rabbis' interest in restoring the wellborn poor promoted stability, again benefiting the community as a whole.[38]

My findings here contribute to the body of scholarship that relates charity to civic life. Addressing mostly Greek, Roman, and Christian sources, Peter Brown, Arthur Hands, Paul Veyne, and others have noted that the main difference between Greco-Roman forms of giving (such as *euergetism*) and those of late antiquity (particularly Christian sources beginning in the fourth century) was the role of city life and urban culture. In Greek and Roman forms of giving, Brown writes:

> the community these public benefactors, the *euergetai*, addressed and helped define through their generosity was, first and foremost, thought of as a "civic community." It was always the city that was, in the first instance, the recipient

---

[34] Parkin, "An Exploration," 69.
[35] Sen, *Poverty and Famines*, 9.
[36] Likewise, see the effort to curtail begging in the *Codex Theodosianus* 14.18.1, which I discuss in Chapter 7.
[37] See especially the comments by the second-century B.C.E. Stoic writer Antipater of Tarsus, *SVF* 3.254.23–257.10 (Stobaeus 4.507.6–512) and the discussions in Deming, *Paul on Marriage and Celibacy*, 226–27; Satlow, *Jewish Marriage*, 13–14. A similar sentiment is expressed by Seneca, *Vita Beata* 24.1; see Saller, "Poverty, Honor," 15.
[38] Kate Cooper, *The Fall of the Roman Household* (Cambridge: Cambridge University Press, 2007), 96; Satlow, *Jewish Marriage*, 13.

of gifts, or, if not the city, the civic community. The *démos* or the *populous*, of the city. It was never the poor. What one can call a "civic" model of society prevailed. The rich thought of themselves as "fellow citizens" of a distinctive community – *their* city. It was their city they were expected to love. A rich man was praised for being a *philopatris*, a "lover of his home-city," never for being a *philoptôchos*, a "lover of the poor."... If some of them were occasionally spoken of as "poor," it was because they were citizens perceived to be in danger of impoverishment, of coming down in the world, not because they already lay at the very bottom of society. There was little room in such a model for the true urban "poor," many of whom would, in fact, have been impoverished immigrants, noncitizens, living on the margins of the community.[39]

While the Greeks and Romans spoke of citizens and noncitizens, from the fourth century onward Christian texts speak earnestly of "the poor" as a distinct social class. It was an economic, rather than political, understanding of society. Giving by Christian bishops, for example, was aimed at "the poor," a social category determined by one's economic position above all.

I find that intermediary stages of this shift can be detected in early rabbinic texts.[40] The *tamhui*, on the one hand, gives alms to all, regardless of one's civic standing or place of origin. It is based on a truly economic or material understanding of "the poor," as one is eligible to receive alms from the *tamhui* if he has fewer than two meals per day. The *quppa*, however, is more complex, as eligibility is based on both material holdings (fewer than fourteen meals per week) and residence. Therefore, it retains the vestiges of civic-minded Greco-Roman giving and foreshadows the economic approach predominant in later Judaism and Christianity. A poor man's eligibility for alms from the *quppa* is based on his material resources (less than fourteen meals per week) as well as his place of residence, as he must live in the city for thirty days to be eligible for the *quppa* and six months to receive clothing from it.

It is important to note that the *quppa* does not require "citizenship" per se. The Hebrew term for "citizen," *ezrah*, is not used in the texts at hand.[41] Rather, the Tosefta stipulates that eligibility is based upon the amount of time that one "stays" or "dwells" (*sheheh*) in a town. That is, one's affiliation with a

---

[39] Brown, *Poverty and Leadership*, 4–5. See also Peter Brown, "The Study of Elites in Late Antiquity," *Arethusa* 33 (2000): 338–39; Brown, *Through the Eye*, 53–90.

[40] I do not argue, however, that early rabbinic texts exercised direct influence on late-antique Christian writers.

[41] On *ezrah* in the Hebrew Bible and rabbinic literature, see the sources cited in Jastrow, *Dictionary*, 38; Ludwig Köhler et al., *The Hebrew and Aramaic Lexicon of the Old Testament* (Leiden and New York: E.J. Brill, 1994), s.v. ezrah.

town and its *quppa* is a matter of mere residence, without the political weight of citizenship. The Tosefta's emphasis on residence may be part of widespread social and political developments in the Roman world, especially those from the early third century onwards. The universalization of Roman citizenship in 212 C.E., shortly before the redaction of the Tosefta, diminished the value and meaning of citizenship. This combined with demographic changes to shift focus toward residential – and away from political – status.[42] The Tosefta is shaped in a way that is sensitive to and participated in the evolution of Greco-Roman urban culture. It engages in the Greco-Roman ideals of giving to one's fellow citizens, yet alters some of their attributes, and adds elements of the economic understanding of poverty that would later become dominant.

Peter Brown writes that the church in late antiquity had to satisfy the preferences and consciences of those givers who still adhered to the civic ideal.[43] Likewise, the rabbis had a distinct understanding of "the poor," but also preferred giving to the poor of one's own town. Similar to other civic *leitourgia*, contributing to and supervising the *quppa* benefited the town's poor, the non-poor, and thus the community as a whole.

Association with a town is a significant component of the rabbinic vision of the *quppa*. Seth Schwartz has written that discussions of organized charity played important roles in the development of the "town" or local community as a meaningful religious entity in rabbinic thought.[44] The idea of a local community constitutes a marked difference from the Hebrew Bible, which was focused on individuals and the nation of Israel as a whole. Towns and local communities would later become an important aspect of rabbinic Judaism and the *quppa* played a significant role.[45] We see this, for example, in the Babylonian Talmud:

> it has been taught: A scholar should not reside in a town where the following ten things are not found: A court of justice that imposes flagellation and decrees penalties; a *quppa* collected by two and distributed by three; a synagogue; public baths; a lavatory; a circumciser; a surgeon, a notary; a slaughterer, and a school-master. (*b. Sanhedrin* 17b)[46]

---

[42] See the summary in A. R. Birley, "Constitutio Antoniniana," in *Brill's New Pauly: Encyclopaedia of the Ancient World* (ed. H. Cancik et al.; Leiden and Boston: Brill, 2002), s.v.; Osborne, "Introduction: Roman Poverty in Context," 9–10.

[43] Brown, Poverty and Leadership, 32–34.

[44] Schwartz, *Imperialism and Jewish Society*, 228–30.

[45] Schwartz, *Imperialism and Jewish Society*, 228.

[46] Translation based on Isadore Epstein, ed., *The Babylonian Talmud: Translated into English with Notes, Glossary and Indices* (London: Soncino Press, 1935–1952), with my modifications. The importance of the *quppa* to civic life would be echoed by Maimonides in the twelfth century, whom I quote in Chapter 1.

ANONYMOUS GIVING

Having examined *what* (in Chapter 5) and *to whom* (this chapter, earlier) the *quppa* gives, I now turn to *how* it gives. Here, too, I find that the Tannaim are interested in protecting the dignity of the poor as they envision the *quppa* as a mechanism for giving and receiving charity anonymously. Giving alms in a way in which the benefactor does not know the beneficiary, and vice versa, is characteristic of Judeo-Christian approaches to charity.[47] The classic statement is from the Sermon on the Mount in Matt 6:1–4, where Jesus warns:

> (6:1) Beware of practicing your piety before others in order to be seen by them; for then you have no reward from your Father in heaven. (6:2) So whenever you give alms, do not sound a trumpet before you, as the hypocrites do in the synagogues and in the streets, so that they may be praised by others. Truly I tell you, they have received their reward. (6:3) But when you give alms, do not let your left hand know what your right hand is doing, (6:4) so that your alms may be done in secret; and your Father who sees in secret will reward you. (Matt 6:1–4)

To be sure, there is a wealth of scholarship on these verses and it would be impractical to review it here.[48] For our purposes, I will highlight a few aspects of this section of the Sermon on the Mount. Matthew warns against giving in public, especially in the synagogue. The object of Jesus's ire in Matt 6:1–2 was likely Greek and Roman forms of giving that emphasize visibility and conspicuity, such as *euergetism*. For Matthew, a benefactor who gives in secret will be rewarded by God, who sees all secrets. Note also that Jesus does not promote giving out of pure altruism, but rather out of the motivation that one should receive a reward – it is intangible and otherworldly, but it is nonetheless a reward for giving charity. The Tannaim express nearly identical sentiments in their discussions of charity, such as in *t. Pe'ah* 4:18, where a certain King Munbaz who gives away his fortunes in exchange for immaterial treasures in heaven or the world to come. Above all, Matt 6:3–4 uses vivid imagery to provide us with the paradigmatic statement of anonymous almsgiving: "do not let your left hand know what your right hand is doing, so that your alms may be done in secret" (6:3–4). The reference to hands in these verses plays

---

[47] The importance of anonymous giving was recognized and codified by Maimonides as the second-highest form of giving in his classic eight levels of charity, *Mishneh Torah, Hilkhot mattenot 'aniyyim* (Laws on Gifts to the Poor) 10.8–10.
[48] E.g., Hans Dieter Betz and Adela Yarbro Collins, *The Sermon on the Mount: A Commentary on the Sermon on the Mount, Including the Sermon on the Plain (Matthew 5:3–7:27 and Luke 6:20–49)* (Minneapolis, Minn.: Fortress Press, 1995).

on the image of a beggar's hand that is employed throughout biblical, Second Temple-era, and early rabbinic texts on poverty.[49]

How, exactly, does one give alms anonymously? While Matthew lays out the principle of anonymous giving, the Gospel does not provide the mechanics.[50] By contrast, the details are addressed by the Tannaim, where the *quppa* is constructed as a mechanism for anonymous charity. We read in Mishnah *Sheqalim*:

> There were two chambers in the Temple: One was the chamber of secrets and the other was the chamber of utensils.[51] The chamber of secrets: Those who feared sin put their contribution into it and the wellborn poor were maintained from it in secret. (*m. Sheqalim* 5:6)[52]

This Mishnah is paralleled in the Tosefta, which adds the following:

> Just as there was a chamber of secrets in the Temple, so too there was such a chamber in every town, so that wellborn poor could be maintained from it in secret. (*t. Sheqalim* 2:16, D–E)

In light of the references to "every town" and the "wellborn poor," it is clear that the Tosefta's redactors have the *quppa* in mind, as it was envisioned as a civic institution that aimed to support the conjunctural poor, devoting special attention to the wellborn poor.

While these passages cannot tell us much about the chamber of secrets in the pre-70 C.E. era, as I discussed in Chapter 1, they can tell us something about the ideas of the Tannaim who authored and redacted them in the late second and early third century. First, the passages indicate that the rabbis understood that conjunctural poverty had a particularly acute association with shame. If the extent of an individual's economic decline were directly proportional to his shame, then the wellborn poor, who suffered the greatest fall, would also suffer the greatest amount of shame. Second, the rabbis understand that the dignity and honor of these individuals can be protected by giving alms "in secret," whereby the benefactor and beneficiary do not

---

[49] E.g., Deut 15:11; Prov 31:20; Sir 7:32; Rev 13:16.

[50] See also *T. Job.* 9.8–10.4, where Job leaves the four doors of his house open so that the poor can enter his home to take alms without being seen; see the discussion in Becknell, "Almsgiving," 304–05. This could, at least theoretically, model how an individual could carry out anonymous charity. This, however, should not be mistaken for the kind of systemic approach to anonymous charity that the Tannaim propose in their discussions of the *quppa*.

[51] The "chamber of utensils" was understood as a place to contribute items that could be used or sold for the Temple's upkeep; see *m. Tamid* 3:4.

[52] On this text, see Neusner, *History of the Mishnaic Law – Sheqalim, Yoma, Sukkah*, 40; Safrai and Safrai, *Mishnat Eretz Israel: Tractate Skalim*, 189–92; see also the parallel in *SifreDeut* 117.

meet – that is, anonymous giving. The wellborn poor can be elevated with alms that restore them to their previous positions in society. By likening the *quppa* to something called a "chamber of secrets," the rabbis imply that the *quppa* too should operate in secrecy.

Anonymous giving protects the poor from the humiliation of begging. The importance of anonymous charity cannot be overstated, as it would become a hallmark of all subsequent approaches to charity in Judaism. In later texts, such as *Eccl. Rab.* 9:25 and *b. Hagigah* 5a, we read that it is better to give nothing than to give publicly and put the poor to shame. Bavli *Bava Batra* 9b claims that one who gives alms in secret is greater than Moses. Bavli *Ketubbot* 67b instructs that it is better for a man to throw himself into a fiery furnace than to publicly shame his neighbor. This text emphasizes the importance of the *quppa* for anonymous giving; suggesting that even the charity supervisor ought to avoid face-to-face interaction with the poor while distributing alms. Bavli *Ketubbot* 67b illustrates this point with the example of Rabbi Abba, who plays the role of charity supervisor. Abba distributes alms by wrapping money in his clothing, which he trails over his shoulder when he visits the poor so that they could help themselves secretly. He does peep sideways, however, so that he could keep an eye on those who claim to be poor, but are not. That is, Abba does his best to fulfill the supervisor's responsibility to give only to the deserving poor, while still allowing the poor to collect alms in relative privacy and anonymity.

EMPATHY FOR THE CONJUNCTURAL POOR'S DIGNITY

The attributes of the *quppa* discussed in this chapter and Chapter 5 all exhibit the Tannaim's interest in protecting the dignity of the conjunctural poor. Such empathy for the poor was rare in the Greco-Roman world. Whittaker, for example, writes that those who are not poor tend to view the structural poor as "a part... of the natural and ordained order of the world," while the conjunctural poor "are to blame for their own condition."[53] In most circumstances, this understanding of the causes of poverty promotes indifference and inactivity toward the poor, as it rationalizes one's inclination to keep his or her possessions instead of giving them to the poor. Moreover, because the conjunctural poor possessed adequate physical and mental capabilities, Whittaker writes, "conjunctural poverty... has always discouraged charity and welfare aid, since it is supposed to create lazy parasites and spongers."[54]

[53] Whittaker, "Poor," 1.
[54] Whittaker, "Poor," 2.

"I hate poor people," reads graffito in Pompeii, "If anyone wants something for nothing he is a fool. He should pay for it."[55]

Although the Tannaim similarly hold that one's poverty is determined by his or her merit in the eyes of God, they nevertheless promote empathy for the impoverished, encouraging readers to restore them to their former positions in life. The reason behind this empathy may be the Tannaim's own social location, as no Tanna was poor and it would be natural for them to fear impoverishment – just as other well-off ancient writers did.[56]

The shame of conjunctural poverty is further exacerbated by living in towns or other settings characterized by high population density. As I discussed in Chapter 2, urbanization reached its peak in Palestine during the era in which the Tannaim authored and redacted their texts. Just as Greco-Roman urban culture played an important role in shaping rabbinic discourses on interactions with Gentiles and idolatry, I find that urban living shaped rabbinic views on the poor and charity. Living in close quarters made the shame of poverty readily visible and the problem of poverty appear all the more urgent to the Tannaim, who largely resided in urban areas.

The rabbis' interest in and concern for the dignity and social well-being of the poor was unique in the Greco-Roman world in which they lived, where the poor were generally despised and derided.[57] "Put simply," Richard Saller writes, "if wealth was essential to civic honor, poverty entailed dishonor for the Romans."[58] Ramsay MacMullen writes that some Romans felt that the poor deserved to be held in contempt.[59] In Cicero's mind, P. A. Brunt

---

[55] *CIL* IV 9839 b; see Whittaker, "Poor," 3.
[56] Lest we think that the Tannaim were solely focused on the formerly wealthy poor, *m. Bava Qamma* 8:6 instructs that all poor individuals should be treated as if they were formerly wealthy poor.
[57] Whittaker, "Poor," 3. For a similar disrespectful treatment of the poor, see also Sir 13:23: "The rich person speaks and all are silent; they extol to the clouds what he says. The poor person speaks and they say, 'Who is this fellow?' And should he stumble, they even push him down." On Ben Sira and poverty, see Samuel L. Adams, "Poverty and Otherness in Second Temple Instructions," in *The "Other" in Second Temple Judaism: Essays in Honor of John J. Collins* (ed. D. C. Harlow et al.; Grand Rapids, Mich.: W.B. Eerdmans, 2011), 189–203; Benjamin G. Wright III, "The Discourse of Riches and Poverty in the Book of Ben Sira," *SBLSP* 37 (1998): 559–78. Likewise, see Eccl 9:16: "So I said, 'Wisdom is better than might; yet the poor man's wisdom is despised, and his words are not heeded'"; and 4QInstruction (fragment 4Q417 2 i 10; second–first century B.C.E.): "For what is more trivial than a poor man?" On contempt for the poor and beggars in late-antique Christian sources, see Finn, "Portraying the Poor," 134–39; Finn, *Almsgiving*, 188–89.
[58] Saller, "Poverty, Honor," 16.
[59] Ramsay MacMullen, *Roman Social Relations, 50 B.C. to A.D. 284* (New Haven, Conn.: Yale University Press, 1974), 97.

writes, the needy were virtually criminals.[60] Poverty was understood to be a cause of civil unrest and disorder.[61] Seneca writes that "poverty is taken as a disgrace," while Cicero and Martial intimate that poverty compels bad behavior. Likewise, Juvenal deems worthless an oath made by a poor man and Cicero discredits the poor's testimony in court. Poverty was associated with immorality and Sallust writes that it was a "disgrace."[62] The poor were the object of ridicule and scorn by the Greeks and Romans, particularly the wellborn poor. Tacitus writes that the Emperor Nero would publicly shame aristocrats who became poor.[63]

The lack of empathy for the poor helps explain the absence of charitable institutions in the Roman world. "In the absence of institutional relief for the poor," Saller observes, "the way to survive or get ahead in Rome was to cultivate the favor of those richer and more powerful. This was thought to be dishonoring, requiring public displays of deference or loss of independence."[64] It follows that institutional relief would provide a means for the poor to survive or advance without humiliating them. As such, rabbinic ideas on the *quppa* were unique. Whereas the Greeks and Romans expressed little interest in recognizing the poor's dignity, let alone restoring it, the rabbis instruct the supervisors of the *quppa* to restore the conjunctural poor to their previous places in society.

CONCLUSION

The recipients of the *quppa* are envisioned as conjuncturally poor, those who used to be non-poor but have since fallen into poverty. Conjunctural poverty and the shame that it carried were especially visible in the urban settings of Roman Palestine, where the Tannaim lived and worked. The *quppa* is modeled as a civic institution whose primary objective is to care for the conjunctural poor who are residents of the town in which it is located. In doing so, the *quppa* also benefited the non-poor and, in turn, the community as a whole. Identifying the *quppa* as a civic institution fills the gap between the

---

[60] P. A. Brunt, *Social Conflicts in the Roman Republic* (London: Chatto and Windus, 1971), 128; see also Saller, "Poverty, Honor," 16.
[61] Grey and Parkin, "Controlling the Urban Mob," 284–99; Saller, "Poverty, Honor," 17.
[62] On the sentiments of Cicero, Martial, Juvenal, and Sallust toward the poor, see Saller, "Poverty, Honor," 12, 17–19. Similarly, Philo (*Embassy* 123) notes the particular shame associated with going from a state of abundance to indigence. Indeed, impoverished members of the upper classes would later be dubbed the "shame-face poor"; see Brown, *Poverty and Leadership*, 60.
[63] Tacitus, *Annals* 1.74.
[64] Saller, "Poverty, Honor," 19.

urban-oriented giving of the Greeks and Romans, and later Christianity's focus on the poor. The *quppa* also played an important role in the emergence of the local community in rabbinic thought. Finally, the *quppa* serves as a mechanism for carrying out anonymous charity, whereby the benefactors and beneficiaries never meet. This process is facilitated by the charity supervisor, whom I will examine in the next chapter.

A common thread running throughout these features of the *quppa*, as well as those discussed in Chapter 5, is an interest in protecting the dignity of the poor. There are a number of possible reasons for this. The first is that the rabbis, like other well-off intellectual elites in the ancient world, feared the prospects of sudden, conjunctural poverty. The second is that the Tannaim empathized with those who originated from the same, well-off social circles that they did. The Tannaim likely knew some wellborn poor individuals, or their families, who were their economic and social peers. It may have been these individuals who the Tannaim had in mind when they conceived of the *quppa* as an alternative to begging for the conjunctural poor. If a Tanna had fallen into conjunctural poverty, he surely would have hoped that the *quppa* would restore him and protect him from the indignity of begging.

7

The Charity Supervisor

INTRODUCTION

The purpose of organized charity is to bring an end to begging by assisting the poor in a way that is communal, indirect, and anonymous. The charity supervisor plays a key role in this process. The supervisor was conceived by the Tannaim as an unpaid, voluntary public official who oversaw the operation of the *quppa*.[1] He is the intermediary between benefactors and beneficiaries, as he collects contributions from the town's residents for the *quppa* and distributes them to the poor. Ideally, the town's residents would give generously to the *quppa* and the supervisor, in turn, would assess the needs of each poor man and give him precisely what he used to have before falling into poverty. The poor man would willingly accept these alms, restoring him to his former place in society. By giving assets to the living poor in accordance with their needs, the supervisor would have completed his duties and all those who contributed to the *quppa* would have fulfilled the commandment of giving *tsedaqah*.

The rabbis, however, foresaw a number of possible problems that could disrupt this process and prevent the supervisor from fulfilling his duties. The first, which relates to the supervisor's charge to collect contributions, is that the official may lack legitimacy in the eyes of the public. He may lack the mandate or authority to demand contributions, or he may simply be perceived as not trustworthy enough to hold and manage the community's funds. The second set of problems is related to distribution. Some poor individuals might refuse to accept alms out of pride or fear of being labeled a "charity case." The supervisors would also face difficulties in accurately assessing those who claim to be poor as well as determining their precise needs. Are these individuals

---

[1] In later Amoraic texts, which I discuss in Chapter 8, the charity supervisor also oversees the *tamhui*.

genuinely in need or are they imposters? If they are in need, what assets would bring them up to their former standard of living? Another problem is that the poor could become dependent upon the supervisor – or even perceive the supervisor himself as their benefactor. If this were the case, then the poor would develop vertical, hierarchical relationships of dependency with the supervisor, engendering social inequalities, as the process would fall into the same pitfalls as giving to beggars.[2] The rabbis' objectives for organized charity, to provide an alternative to begging and giving to beggars, would thus fail.

To solve these problems or to forestall them altogether, the Tannaim provide instructions for how the supervisor should perform his duties.[3] In this chapter, I will first address the general nature of the charity supervisor, which includes looking at the two titles used for this position: *gabbai tsedaqah* and *parnas*. I will then examine the Tannaim's instructions on how he should go about the two fundamental tasks of his office – the collection and distribution of charity. I find that the rabbis model the charity supervisor as a synthesis of two officials – tax collectors and judges. By likening the supervisor to these communal officials, the Tannaim elevate the status of the supervisor and imply that he is an essential cog in the proper functioning of an ideal community. He is a perfect fit for the *quppa*, which is envisioned as a civic and communal institution, as he plays a decisive role in the Tannaim's vision of organized charity as an alternative to begging.

CHARITY SUPERVISOR

Tannaitic sources refer to the charity supervisor in two ways, as the *gabbai tsedaqah* or "charity collector" and *parnas* (plural: *parnasim*) or "provider." I will examine each in turn. While literally a "charity collector," the *gabbai*

---

[2] The rabbis perceived the construction of vertical relationships between humans to be problematic to their egalitarian ideals; see my discussion in Chapter 4 and Schwartz, *Were the Jews*.

[3] The earliest rabbinic discussions of institutional charity, t. Pe'ah 4:8–15, can be read as addressed to the charity supervisors. The subject of the text is the third person plural, which often indicates the impersonal. Thus, these passages may be understood as addressed to "one" – *one* does not give to a poor person less than a loaf of bread, *one* gives him new garments, *one* is persistent with him and maintains him [by] giving him [aid] as a loan, and so on. However, the third person plural may also indicate just that – the third person plural or "they." The passages would be read and understood as *they* do not give to a poor person less than a loaf of bread, *they* give him new garments but he returns old garments to *them*, *they* are persistent with him and maintain him [by] giving him [aid] as a loan, and so on. Given that the supervisors are to work in teams of two and three, it is possible – if not likely – that the redactors present their discourse in t. Pe'ah 4:8–15 as instructions to the charity supervisors.

tsedaqah in early rabbinic texts is depicted as one who oversees all aspects of the *quppa*, including the collection and distribution of alms. The latter also entails assessing the true needs of the poor individuals who request alms from the *quppa*. Because there are no extrarabbinic sources on this figure, the rabbinic discussions should be understood as the Tannaim's prescriptions and instructions for how they believed the *gabbai tsedaqah* ought to carry out his duties.[4] They are normative, as opposed to positive statements. The title *gabbai tsedaqah* is an adaptation of *gabbai*, which, when used on its own, refers to a tax collector.[5] In many ways, which I will explore shortly, the *gabbai tsedaqah* is modeled after the tax collector.

In early rabbinic texts, the *parnas* also supervised charity.[6] Who was the *parnas*? While we know nothing about the *gabbai tsedaqah* outside of rabbinic texts, there are a great deal of extrarabbinic sources on the *parnas* that can help us understand who this official was and shed light on who the rabbis wanted him to be. The Hebrew word *parnas* means "provider." It is a loan word from Greek, most likely related to *pronoetes* (plural: *pronoetai*), meaning "supervisor," "executor," or "administrator."[7] The *pronoetes* served important functions in the Greco-Roman world, many of which are attested by inscriptions from nearby Roman Syria. These inscriptions indicate that the *pronoetai* had a broad array of civil and administrative responsibilities. Often working in teams of twos and threes, they functioned as agents on behalf of individuals, families, and polities.[8] They supervised private estates and served as their executors. They oversaw public building projects and were generally associated with supervising a village or town's finances.

A similar image of *parnas/pronoetes* emerges from Hebrew and Aramaic extrarabbinic sources from Roman Palestine. Of particular interest are inscriptions and documents found in the Judean desert that date to the second century C.E., finds that are geographically and chronologically proximate

---

[4] On a possible, but unlikely, extrarabbinic source on organized charity and the charity collector, see my discussion in Chapter 1 of the "charity token" published in Kindler, "Bar Kokhba Coin," 73–75, plate 16.

[5] *m. Hagigah* 3:6; *t. Bava Metzi'a* 8:26; *t. Demai* 3:4.

[6] For rabbinic sources on the *parnas*, see those cited in Meir, "*Parnas*," and the earlier studies by Büchler, *Political and the Social Leaders*, 13–17; Yaacov Nacht, "Ha-parnas be-yisrael [Hebrew]," *Sinai* 12 (1942): 263–85. The studies by Büchler and Nacht are useful for their collections of sources and references, though their analyses and conclusions are largely untenable in light of modern academic critical approaches to rabbinic literature. As Levine, *Rabbinic Class*, 162, rightly notes, the precise definition of this office continues to elude scholars.

[7] See Fraade, "Local Jewish Leadership," 158–59, and his references to lexical works. See also Hezser, *Social Structure*, 272; Nacht, "Ha-parnas," 131n. 1. On the Greek, see Liddell et al., *Greek-English Lexicon*, 1490.

[8] Fraade, "Local Jewish Leadership," 159n. 6.

to the Tannaitic corpus.[9] Inscribed onto a lead weight found in the Judean foothills in Alim (near Beth Guvrin), *parnas* refers to an administrator for Bar Kochva, leader of the second revolt against Rome (132–135 C.E.). This *parnas* was responsible for administering commercial and financial matters. Three legal papyri from Nahal Hever also attest to *parnasim* working on behalf of Bar Kochva, where they deal with land-lease transactions.[10] A *parnas* is also mentioned as a local official in a document from Wadi Murabba'at, where he confirms ownership of an animal in advance of its sale.[11]

The functions of the *parnas/pronoetes* witnessed in extrarabbinic sources are also reflected in Tannaitic texts. As in the epigraphic and documentary sources from Roman Syria and Palestine, Tannaitic texts portray the *parnas* as a communal official whose responsibilities include supervising public properties and administering private estates.[12] Just as inscriptions show that they oversaw public finances and building projects, so too in rabbinic texts they have the final word on these matters. We see this, for example, in a text that discusses buying and selling synagogues and streets:

> R. Menahem b. R. Yose says, "[If they sold] a synagogue, they should not buy a street."
> Said R. Judah, "In what circumstances does this apply?"
> [It applies] when the *parnasim* of that town did not make a stipulation with them [that they may make use of the surplus for some other purpose].
> But if the *parnasim* of that town did make such a stipulation, they may make use of the funds for any other purpose which they choose. (*t. Megillah* 2:12)[13]

Contrary to current scholarly opinion, this passage does not address charity in the way that the Tannaim understood it, as giving to the poor.[14] Rather, in

---

[9] Fraade, "Local Jewish Leadership," 169–73; Amos Kloner, "Lead Weights of Bar Kokhba's Administration," *IEJ* 40 (1990): 58–67.

[10] Fraade, "Local Jewish Leadership," 172; Yadin et al., *Documents from the Bar Kokhba Period*, 42–64, 142–49.

[11] Pierre Benoit et al., *Les grottes de Murabba'ât* (Oxford: Clarendon Press, 1961), 155–59. Note that *parnas/pronoetes* would appear again, centuries later, inscribed in mosaic stones on the floors of the ancient synagogues in Na'aran (in Aramaic) and Hammat Tiberias (two references, in Greek). These may be local notables recognized for their contributions, titles indicative of a function specific to synagogue status or leadership, or oversight of local building activity; see Fraade, "Local Jewish Leadership," 172–73; Meir, "Parnas," 1–4.

[12] Fraade, "Local Jewish Leadership," 157–75.

[13] Translation based on Neusner, *The Tosefta*, with my emendations.

[14] See, for example, the translation of *parnasim* in this pericope as "charity-collectors" Neusner, *The Tosefta*. The Tannaim understood charity/*tsedaqah* in a very narrow sense as giving material provisions to the living poor. Giving to religious or other public causes, while

this passage the *parnas* serves as a public official, a representative of the community charged with managing communal properties (here, a synagogue) – precisely what we find in extrarabbinic sources.[15] Likewise, the role of the *parnas/pronoetes* as an administrator of a private estate and a third-party mediator in extrarabbinic sources is reflected in Tannaitic texts. We see this, for example, in a discussion of the grounds for annulling a marriage:

> [If] one places his wife under a vow not to derive benefit from him for up to thirty days, [then] he must appoint a *parnas* [to maintain her]. [If] for a longer period, [then] he divorces her and pays her marriage settlement. (*m. Ketubbot* 7:1)

In both Tannaitic and extrarabbinic sources, we also find the *parnas/pronoetes* working in teams of twos and threes.[16] For the most part, then, the image of the *parnas* reflected in early rabbinic texts is very similar to that attested in epigraphic, documentary, and other extrarabbinic sources: he was an official who performed a wide array of administrative and third-party services for public and private interests. There are, however, two functions of the *parnas* in early rabbinic texts that find no parallels in extrarabbinic sources: his depiction as a leader of the Jewish community, if not the nation as a whole, and his supervision of charity.

The image of the *parnas* as national leader has received a great deal of attention from scholars.[17] In particular, scholars have wanted to know the extent and reality of his authority, and whether or not the rabbis themselves served as *parnasim*. This issue lies at the heart of debates regarding the extent of rabbinic authority. Were the Tannaim leaders of the Jewish people, as later rabbinic texts and traditional interpreters make them out to be? Or were they a small group who exercised little real authority in Jewish society?[18]

That the *parnas* is connected with communal leadership is suggested by the locutions "*parnas* over Israel" and "*parnas* over the community" used in Tannaitic texts.[19] The identification of *parnasim* as national leaders is illustrated in texts that refer to biblical figures such as Moses, Aaron, Miriam, Joshua,

---

perhaps beneficent, was not understood as "charity" by the Tannaim; see *t. Pe'ah* 4:19 and my discussion in Chapter 1.

[15] It is notable that the parallel in *m. Megillah* 3:1 lacks any reference to the *parnas*.
[16] E.g., *m. Pe'ah* 8:7; G. M. Harper Jr., "Village Administration in the Roman Province of Syria," *Yale Classical Studies* 1 (1928): 126–27.
[17] See the discussions and references in Fraade, "Local Jewish Leadership," 165–69.
[18] On the Tannaim's lack of authority, see especially Goodman, *State and Society*; Schwartz, *Imperialism and Jewish Society*, 103–28.
[19] *Parnas* over Israel: *SifreNum* 141 (see also 105, 137, 138, 139); *parnas* over the community: *t. Rosh Hashanah* 1:18; *t. Avodah Zarah* 4:4; *SifreDeut* 157.

and David as *parnasim*.²⁰ Two Tannaitic passages seem to identify rabbis, such as Hillel the Elder, Yohanan ben Zakkai, and Akiva, as *parnasim*.²¹ As Fraade rightly notes, however, we cannot presume that these texts reflect a historical reality in which all (or any) *parnasim* were sages or the disciples of sages. Rather, these passages should be understood as reflecting and projecting rabbinic ideals, namely that rabbinic learning should be a preferred or even a necessary qualification for being appointed a *parnas* over a Jewish community.²² Later Amoraic texts claim that rabbis appointed *parnasim*, served as *parnasim*, or both.²³

While the sense of *parnas* as a communal leader is found only in rabbinic texts, the broader connection between the roles of a provider and political leader is likewise made by the Greeks and Romans. One way to acquire or maintain political authority in the Greco-Roman world was to provide a polity with the goods and services that it needs, such as means of defense, public games and spectacles, infrastructure, and food in times of famine. Indeed, the rabbis are cognizant of the similarities between a *parnas* and a Greco-Roman benefactor and they purposefully distinguish the two when discussing the *parnas*'s oversight of charity.²⁴

The *parnas/pronoetes*'s connection with charity is another important difference between his depictions in rabbinic texts and extrarabbinic sources. Some early rabbinic texts portray the *parnas* as a supervisor of charity, fulfilling the same functions as the *gabbai tsedaqah*. Yet the *parnas/pronoetes* is not associated with charity in any extrarabbinic sources. There are no inscriptions that suggest that the *parnas/pronoetes* was involved in giving alms to the poor. "We have no record," writes G. M. Harper Jr. in his seminal work on village administration in Roman Syria, "of a village expending any money for education, for public health, or for charity."²⁵

How can we explain this discrepancy between rabbinic and extrarabbinic sources? I suggest that the Tannaim prescriptively and wishfully added "charity supervisor" to the responsibilities of the *parnas*. In some ways, the *parnas* was a logical choice, as his other tasks included handling money and public finances.

---

[20] *t. Sotah* 11:8; *SifreDeut* 26; Fraade, "Local Jewish Leadership," 165.

[21] *SifreDeut* 306, 357. On these texts, see Fraade, "Local Jewish Leadership," 166–67; Goodman, *State and Society*, 121–22; Hezser, *Social Structure*, 270.

[22] Fraade, "Local Jewish Leadership," 163–64.

[23] *y. Pe'ah* 8:7, 21a, where Akiva is offered the position of *parnas* and R. Eleazar is a *parnas*. In *y. Pe'ah* 8:9, 21b and *y. Sheqalim* 5:6, 49a, R. Yaqob b. Idi and R. Yizkhaq b. Nachman are said to be *parnasim*. Cf. *Lev. Rab.* 25:1, where the *parnasim* are not sages, but rather the unlearned; see Hezser, *Social Structure*, 271–73, and my discussion in Chapter 8.

[24] See, e.g., the suggestive remarks about Elimelech in *t. Avodah Zarah* 4:4.

[25] Harper, "Village Administration," 153.

In a similar fashion, the *parnas* would be well suited to collect and manage the community's monetary and material contributions, and distribute them to the poor. It also aligns with the *parnas*'s role as a third party mediator, as the rabbinic vision of organized charity required a disinterested party to collect contributions from benefactors and distribute them to beneficiaries.

Adding oversight of the *quppa* to the *parnas*'s responsibilities infuses the charity supervisor with the authority of an existing and established public official. It places charity supervision – and organized charity with it – on the docket of political ventures that are essential to the proper functioning of a town. It also inextricably links charity with communal leadership. Organized charity could control a significant amount of funds and control the lives of the poor. Giving the *parnas* the powers of charity supervision also renders the *gabbai tsedaqah* – which was narrowly focused on charity – unnecessary.

All these aspects – the intersection of communal leadership and charity, as well as the diminution of the *gabbai tsedaqah* – become more pronounced in later, post-Tannaitic texts. We see this, for example, in Amoraic texts in which the rabbis appoint themselves as *parnasim*. The diminution of the narrowly focused *gabbai tsedaqah* in favor of *parnas* is especially apparent when comparing the Tannaitic and Amoraic discussions of organized charity. Whereas the key Tannaitic texts on charity use *gabbai tsedaqah*, this is replaced with *parnas* in Amoraic texts.[26] Thus, the connection between the *parnas*, charity, and leadership would become stronger in post-Tannaitic writings.

I will now examine the charity supervisor's duties in detail, first looking at the collection of alms, then their distribution. With regard to terminology, I will use "charity supervisor" or simply "supervisor" to denote the *gabbai tsedaqah* and *parnas* (i.e., in instances where the *parnas* is portrayed as overseeing charity).

COLLECTION

The rabbis instruct that all who have resided in a town for at least thirty days are obligated to contribute money to that town's *quppa*. Those who have resided in the town for six months or longer were also obligated to contribute clothing.[27] It important to note that the Tannaim do not specify precisely how much one should give. Charity, by nature, is an obligation that is imperfectly

---

[26] See, respectively, *t. Pe'ah* 4:8–21 and *y. Pe'ah* 8:7–9, 21a–b. While the root *prns* is used as a verb and to indicate "maintenance for lodging" throughout *t. Pe'ah* 4:8–21, the title *parnas* is not used to indicate the charity supervisor in this key discussion on organized charity.

[27] See *t. Pe'ah* 4:9 and my discussion in Chapter 6.

defined, allowing the giver to express his or her personal discretion. At the same time, it was necessary to fill the *quppa* with enough funds to provide for the poor in accordance with their needs, meeting their standards of living before they became poor. For some, such as the formerly wealthy poor, this could amount to astronomical sums.[28] It fell to the supervisor to raise enough money to fulfill the needs of the poor. It is possible that the supervisor himself would be responsible for any shortfalls.

The rabbis instruct the supervisor to raise funds in two ways: publicly and privately. Raising funds for the *quppa* in public entailed collecting contributions or pledges to contribute in public spaces, such as synagogues. The supervisor would then announce the contributions as a way to identify and honor the benefactor, elevate his social standing, as well as encourage others to give.[29] This approach resonates with a wider Greco-Roman ethos to honor individual benefactors in a public way, though because the *quppa* distributes to the poor anonymously, no particular beneficiary is subordinated to any particular benefactor.[30] Without specific instructions on how much one should give, the promise of public honor was a tool to motivate individuals to give as much as possible – and perhaps to reproach those who did not.

While powerful, broadcasting contributions also creates the potential for self-aggrandizing behavior. A sense of the distaste for such behavior is palpable in the previously discussed Sermon on the Mount, where Jesus instructs that one should refrain from boasting in public when giving alms.[31] It is notable that Matthew does not advocate giving without a return. Rather, the return for giving alms should be provided by God in secret – instead of in public by fellow humans. The rabbis recognize that such ostentatious behavior is inappropriate on festivals, which should be sacred and solemn.[32] For these days, they instruct the supervisor to promote modesty and decorum:

> Charity supervisors[33] do not collect on a festival and announce [the contributions] on a festival in the manner in which they collect and announce [the contributions] on a weekday. But without ostentation they collect [alms] in

---

[28] *t. Pe'ah* 4:10 and my discussion in Chapter 5.
[29] *t. Demai* 3:17; *t. Shabbat* 16:22.
[30] On Greco-Roman benefaction in Jewish society, see Chapter 1.
[31] Matt 6:1–2.
[32] Richard S. Sarason, *A History of the Mishnaic Law of Agriculture: Section Three, A Study of Tractate Demai* (Leiden: Brill, 1979), 119.
[33] The Hebrew reads *gabbai quppa* or "charity fund collector." This is the only instance of *gabbai quppa* that I know of in Tannaitic texts. The intention, however, is clearly to indicate the *parnas* or *gabbai tsedaqah* – the charity supervisor.

the folds of their garments. And they distribute [alms] in each neighborhood. (*t. Demai* 3:16)[34]

The emphasis here is on discretion and modesty during the festivals. Instead of collecting contributions and announcing them, the supervisor should simply collect them. And he holds the contributions in the folds of his clothing, a sign of discretion. The distribution to the poor is also discreet, as the supervisor delivers alms to the poor where they live, as opposed to distributing them in public.

Rabbinic authorities debate whether or not even a *pledge* of charity was acceptable in the synagogue on the Sabbath:

> And so Rabban Shimon ben Gamaliel said: "The House of Shammai said: 'They do not pledge charity to the poor on the Sabbath in the synagogue, even to marry off a male orphan and a female orphan; and they do not reconcile a man and his wife; and they do not pray for the sick on the Sabbath.' But the House of Hillel permits [these]." (*t. Shabbat* 16:22)

This passage is part of a larger debate between the Houses of Hillel and Shammai on various aspects of Sabbath observance. Shammai prohibits pledging charity on the Sabbath in the synagogue, even if the funds would finance an orphan's marriage. Not only do they shun the poor and the orphans, the Shammaites – frequently the foils in rabbinic legal discussions – also refuse to unite married couples or pray for the sick on the Sabbath in the synagogue. The House of Hillel takes a more lenient position, permitting these activities.

Using charity to distinguish between holy and profane days is characteristic of rabbinic discourse on almsgiving. As I discussed earlier, the rabbis prescribe that the alms given to the poor on the Sabbath and on Passover should differ from those given on weekdays, in order to fulfill the special material requirements of those days.[35] Likewise, the methods by which the supervisors collected charity had to be adapted to suit the character and requirements of festivals and the Sabbath.

In addition to collecting for the *quppa* in public, the rabbis also instruct the supervisors to raise money in a private way. They are to go door-to-door, asking people at their homes for contributions to the *quppa*.[36] The image of an individual going from doorway to doorway invokes begging. In *t. Pe'ah* 4:8, for example, a beggar is one who "goes around from door to door." Likewise, in *m. Shabbat* 1:1 a poor man comes to the door of a householder, soliciting

---

[34] Translation based on Sarason, *History of the Mishnaic Law – Demai*, 118, with my emendations.
[35] See my discussion in Chapter 4 and Gardner, "Let Them Eat Fish," 250–70.
[36] *t. Demai* 3:17.

alms by extending his hand from the public domain (outside the house) into the householder's private domain (inside the house).

Rabbinic attitudes toward door-to-door begging may also be a reaction to the realia of domestic living in Roman Palestine. Archaeological remains of dwellings suggest that people lived in close proximity, cheek-by-jowl, and their homes often opened into shared courtyards.[37] It is easy to imagine, therefore, a beggar going from one doorway to the next, asking for alms from everyone in a cluster of homes. The image of beggars at doorways is also found in extrarabbinic sources. Lucian, the second century C.E. Greek writer, called begging from door to door "shearing the sheep."[38] A beggar at the door is likewise depicted in a wall painting in Herculaneum.[39] Seneca tells of children being sent out on the streets to beg from door to door.[40]

The image of an individual going around from doorway to doorway is also reminiscent of the way that tax collectors are depicted in early rabbinic texts:

> the tax collectors go around continually every day and exact payment of men with their consent or without their consent. (*m. Avot* 3:16)[41]

Indeed, the rabbis consciously model the supervisor on the tax collector. This is immediately apparent in the title, as *gabbai tsedaqah* is a mere qualification of *gabbai*, which on its own indicates a tax collector. This nomenclature reflects the rabbis' vision that the supervisors would have the authority to demand payment to the *quppa* just as tax collectors can force payment. Tax collectors, for example, could enter the homes of those in arrears.[42] The rabbis hoped that the supervisors would have such authority to collect contributions for the *quppa*, which they viewed within the framework of civic obligations and as a kind of municipal tax.[43]

The rabbinic discourse on the supervisor's collection techniques consciously draws upon the images of beggars and tax collectors. Instead of the discomfort of being solicited by a beggar or the implied threat accompanied by a tax collector, the rabbis have replaced these with solicitations by the

---

[37] Baker, *Rebuilding the House of Israel*, 35–42; Galor, "Roman-Byzantine Dwelling," 109–24; Galor, "Domestic Architecture," 420–39.
[38] Lucian, *Fug.* 14.
[39] Charles Daremberg and Edm Saglio, eds., *Dictionnaire des antiquites* (5 vols.; Paris: Hachette, 1877), 3:2, p. 1713–14; Grey and Parkin, "Controlling the Urban Mob," 286.
[40] Seneca, *Contr.* 1.1.10. See also Philo, *Flaccus* 64.
[41] Translation according to Danby, with my modifications.
[42] *m. Hagigah* 3:6. To be sure, a tax collector's ability to enforce payment was not an entirely a positive characteristic; see the negative views toward tax collectors in *t. Bava Metzi'a* 8:26; *t. Demai* 3:4.
[43] *t. Pe'ah* 4:9 and my discussion in Chapter 6.

supervisor on behalf of the community as a whole. Supervisors do not collect for themselves (like beggars), nor for the government (like tax collectors), but rather to support the community's goals of fulfilling *tsedaqah* and ridding the town of begging. Having examined how the supervisors are to collect alms, I next turn to how they distribute them to the poor. Here, too, the Tannaim model the supervisor along the lines of a communal official.

DISTRIBUTION

The rabbis are particularly interested in working out how the supervisor would distribute alms from the *quppa* to the poor in a way that preserves their objectives for organized charity. Ideally, the supervisor would hand over money and clothing to the poor, giving them precisely what they need, and the poor would readily accept the alms. The rabbis, however, foresee a number of challenges that could complicate or disrupt this process. The first is that poor individuals may refuse these handouts out of pride. The second is the problem of the undeserving poor or imposters – deceptive individuals who solicit alms but are not truly in need. The rabbis provide instructions on how to deal with these two scenarios and enable the supervisor to fulfill his obligations.

The Poor Who Refuse Alms

The rabbis are apprehensive that some individuals who are truly in need would refuse to accept alms from the supervisor. Their concerns are legitimate. In the ancient Mediterranean, a man's ability to provide for himself and his household was highly valued. Economic independence was prized while dependency was shameful. These values were shared by the Tannaim.[44] It follows that some poor individuals would refuse to accept the supervisor's free gifts out of pride. The rabbis provide rather sophisticated and creative instructions on how to deal with individuals who are reluctant to accept alms, or refuse them altogether:

> [Regarding] one who says, "I shall not be maintained from the belongings of others." They[45] are persistent with him[46] and maintain him [by] giving

---

[44] See my discussion in Chapter 4 and Gardner, "Giving to the Poor," 116–19.
[45] The charity supervisors.
[46] Alternatively, "considerate" toward the poor man, see Brooks, *Support for the Poor*, 150; Lieberman, *The Tosefta*, 1:58–59; Jastrow, *Dictionary*, 1621. Cf. *T. Job* 11:1–10; Philo *Spec. Laws* 2.75.

him [aid] as a loan. But [when he cannot repay the loan],[47] they return[48] and give [it] to him as a gift – the words of Rabbi Meir. But the sages say, "They give [it] to him as a gift. [If he refuses][49] then they return and give [it] to him as a loan."[50] Rabbi Shimon says, "They say to him, 'Bring a pledge!' in order to persuade him." (*t. Pe'ah* 4:12)[51]

When one received a gift, it was common to give a gift in return, or a countergift. Here, however, the supervisor initially gives the gift as charity, that is, without the expectation of reciprocation or compensation. Anthropologists and social psychologists point out that giving a gift without the expectation of a return or compensation of any kind can demean a poor individual, labeling him as a "charity case."[52] If the poor felt demeaned by the supervisor's offer and refused it, then the sages instruct that the gift should be converted into a loan.[53] Rabbi Shimon adds that the supervisor should ask the poor to bring a pledge or collateral as security for the loan. This would convince him that the alms, in fact, are given as a loan instead of a gift. The poor man would then be more likely to accept the provisions.

Collateral is the key to understanding why the poor man would accept the alms, as it places him on level terms with the supervisor. Loans secured by pledges establish and maintain equity between the parties. Much like a contract, Pierre Bourdieu notes, a pledge ensures the "predictability and calculability" of the return of a loan. In such cases, the return is in a sense made – and the exchange complete – at the very moment that the loan is extended and the security is provided.[54] A loan secured by a pledge amounts to an immediate and equitable exchange, like a commercial transaction, and assumes equity between the two parties.[55] By contrast, "free" gifts, like loans

---

[47] Brooks, *Support for the Poor*, 150.
[48] Alternatively, they "retract" the terms of the transaction. On retracting or revoking transactions, see *m. Ma'aser Sheni* 1:6; *t. Bava Metzi'a* 1:17; Ze'ev W. Falk, *Introduction to Jewish Law of the Second Commonwealth* (2 vols.; Leiden: E. J. Brill, 1972–1978), 2:201.
[49] Lieberman, *The Tosefta*, 1:59; Lieberman, *Tosefta Ki-Fshutah*, 1:187.
[50] *milveh* in MS Vienna; *halva'ah* in MS Erfurt. Both are loans of money or some other fungible good; see Lapin, *Early Rabbinic Civil Law*, 186–93.
[51] Lieberman, *The Tosefta*, 1:59, explains that if he is allowed to retain his dignity, he will accept the aid.
[52] See Douglas, "No Free Gifts," vii–xviii; Schwartz, "Social Psychology," 1–11, and my discussion in Gardner, "Charity Wounds," 173–88.
[53] The Tosefta may be drawing upon and developing biblical and Second Temple-era traditions on supporting the poor through loans; see e.g., Deut 15:7–11, Sir 29, and the discussion in Anderson, *Charity*, 41–52.
[54] Bourdieu, *Logic of Practice*, 105.
[55] This is akin to Sahlins's concept of "balanced reciprocity," where reciprocation is the customary equivalent of the thing received without delay; see Sahlins, *Stone Age Economics*, 193–94.

that are unsecured or bear interest, subordinate the recipient into dependency and inferiority.[56]

Imposters

There was a perception, widespread throughout the ancient world, that many people who claimed to be poor were imposters. Many of the "beggars" on the streets, in marketplaces, near temples, and at one's own door were not truly in need. Rather, the thinking went, many of these individuals were only posing as destitute as a strategy to gain sympathy and handouts. What fueled the suspicion of imposters was the fact that it was so easy to pretend to be poor. As I discussed in Chapter 2, the ancients had a rather crude and superficial way of identifying poverty based on a simple semiotic code. If an individual wore rags, appeared to be disabled, or bore one of the other "signs of poverty," then he was perceived to be poor. To understand how simple it was to present oneself as lowly, Josephus recounts how King Herod the Great (first century B.C.E.) would disguise himself as a commoner and mingle among the people in order to identify and expose his opponents.[57] Whether this story is historical or apocryphal, it makes the point that one who dresses the part could easily appear worse off than he actually was. Because it was not difficult to present oneself as destitute in the ancient world, there was a deep suspicion of imposters.

It is important to bear in mind that the existence of imposters may have been more perceived than real, as begging and dependence were considered humiliating. But the possibility that a "beggar" was not actually poor could be used by the non-poor to rationalize one's choice to ignore the beggar or turn down his request. We know of episodes in the premodern world where imposture was believed to be so widespread that beggars who gathered in public areas were freely ignored.[58] Imposture, or, perhaps more accurately, the *suspicion* or *perception* of imposture, is a timeless issue that remains pertinent to this day.[59]

Deception was particularly problematic for the Tannaim. It could cripple the *quppa*. If potential contributors suspected that their funds were going to imposters, then they would surely stop giving. Moreover, because *tsedaqah* is

---

[56] This discussion summarizes and paraphrases my fuller treatment in Gardner, "Charity Wounds," 173–88.
[57] Josephus, *Ant.* 15.367.
[58] Alan J. Kidd, "Poor Relief," in *The Oxford Encyclopedia of Economic History* (ed. J. Mokyr; Oxford and New York: Oxford University Press, 2003), 4:220.
[59] See the modern studies of begging practices cited in Parkin, "An Exploration," 71n. 35.

defined as giving alms to the living *poor*, if these assets were given to someone who was not truly poor, then the religious obligation would not be fulfilled. Thus, the rabbis provide instructions for how the supervisor should handle potential imposters. They present two generic imposters. The first is one who claims to have insufficient means to support himself (*t. Pe'ah* 4:13), while the second pretends to be disabled (*t. Pe'ah* 4:14). I will examine each in turn.

> [Regarding] one who [has the ability to support himself, but[60]] says, "I shall not support myself." They are persistent with him and support him [by] giving him [aid] as a gift. [When he refuses], they return and give [it] to him as a loan. (*t. Pe'ah* 4:13)

This individual, at least as characterized by the rabbis, has the physical ability to work or financial capacity to support himself, but refuses to do so.[61] He is presented as a trickster and lazy, which was a common perception of the poor in the Greco-Roman world.[62] The Tosefta instructs the supervisor to offer aid initially as a gift and, if it is refused, to offer it as a loan. Thus far, these are the same instructions for dealing with one who is truly poor but refuses aid as a gift, as discussed earlier (*t. Pe'ah* 4:12). From this point forward, however, the two sets of instructions diverge. The truly poor man is encouraged to bring collateral, while no such instructions are given to the imposter. Providing collateral changes the terms of the loan and places the lender and recipient on equal footing. If the borrower fails to repay the loan, then the lender retains the collateral and the transaction amounts to an even exchange. By contrast, omitting collateral for the imposter leaves the recipient in a position of debt, in a position of social subordination, until he repays the loan. The rabbis draw upon the social ramifications of an unsecured loan to objectify and concretize the claimant's social subordination, and perhaps to deter further imposture by him or others.

The second type of imposter is one who pretends to be physically incapacitated and unable to work. Pretending to be an invalid was seen by many in the ancient world as a strategy for gaining sympathy and alms. The first century B.C.E. poet Horace, for example, mentions a beggar who feigns a broken leg, while Martial writes about shipwrecked sailors who lie in the

---

[60] See the explanations of this passage in Brooks, *Support for the Poor*, 152; Lieberman, *The Tosefta*, 1:59; Lieberman, *Tosefta Ki-Fshutah*, 1:188–89; Lohse and Mayer, *Die Tosefta*, 154.

[61] For a definition of poverty as a lack of financial means, see *m. Pe'ah* 8:8. That it might imply one's physical capacity to work is suggested by *t. Pe'ah* 4:14. See also *Codex Theodosianus* 14.18.1, where one's ability to support oneself is based on one's physical capacity.

[62] Grey and Parkin, "Controlling the Urban Mob," 284–99; Parkin, "An Exploration," 76.

streets faking injuries.[63] The first- and second-century C.E. Greek author Philostratus writes of an elderly beggar who closes his eyes in a way that makes him appear to be blind. This impostor would later be stoned to death.[64] Some perceived that the disabled were even used by other, more shadowy figures as "begging aids."[65] Faking injuries or wearing rags as a begging strategy is also noted by later writers, especially those from the fourth century, such as the bishops John Chrysostom and Ambrose.[66] Deception also underlies a Roman law that aims to control begging.[67]

The Tosefta provides the supervisor with instructions on how to deal with those who pretend to be physically incapacitated:

> One who blinds his eyes or distends his stomach or thickens his joints [to gain sympathy], he will not expire from this world until this actually is the case. (*t. Pe'ah* 4:14)

In contrast to *t. Pe'ah* 4:13, the rabbis do not offer gifts or loans to the imposter in *t. Pe'ah* 4:14. It stands to reason that it may have been difficult for supervisors to assess whether or not the individual was pretending. Should the supervisor guess wrong and accuse a genuinely disabled individual of pretending to be injured, it would be taken as an indignity. Preserving the dignity of the poor was a central objective of organized charity – all the more so for the poor who were disabled.

Instead, the rabbis instruct the supervisor to trust the claimant and provide him with alms. If he is not truly disabled, then his punishment will be meted out by God: at some point during his life, he will suffer from the very same disabilities that he pretends to have. The punishment will fit the crime, a clear manifestation of the rabbinic doctrine of "measure-for-measure."[68]

The use of the measure-for-measure principle to deter fraud is likewise reflected in other rabbinic texts. In the last line of the Mishnah's tractate

---

[63] Hor., *Epist.* 1.17.58–9; Martial 12.57.12; Hamel, *Poverty and Charity in Roman Palestine*, 217–18; Parkin, "An Exploration," 70–71, 76–77.
[64] *VA* 4.10; on these see Parkin, "An Exploration," 70.
[65] Seneca, *Contr.* 10.4; Grey and Parkin, "Controlling the Urban Mob," 289.
[66] John Chrysostom, *De Eleem.* 6 (*PG* 51.269); Ambrose, *Off.* 2.76.
[67] *Codex Theodosianus* 14.18.1, see Grey and Parkin, "Controlling the Urban Mob," 284–99.
[68] On measure-for-measure, see Lisa Grushcow, *Writing the Wayward Wife: Rabbinic Interpretations of Sotah* (Leiden and Boston: Brill, 2006), 166–69; Martha Himmelfarb, *Tours of Hell: An Apocalyptic Form in Jewish and Christian Literature* (Philadelphia: University of Pennsylvania Press, 1983), 104–5; Ishay Rosen-Zvi, "Measure for Measure as a Hermeneutic Tool in Early Rabbinic Literature," *JJS* 57 (2006): 269–86; Schofer, *Making of a Sage*, 260n. 76.

Pe'ah, following a discussion of who is eligible for *pe'ah*, gleanings, and other forms of agricultural support for the poor, the rabbis instruct:

> And he who does not need to take [*pe'ah*, gleanings, forgotten things, the poor tithe, etc.] but does take, will not die of old age[69] until he is in need of [support from other] men. (*m. Pe'ah* 8:9)[70]

Again, notice the principle of measure-for-measure at work here, as the individual who pretends to be poor will not die until he truly becomes poor.

Supervisors as Judges

A problem related to deception, and further complicating the supervisor's tasks, is how to assess the claimants and their true needs. The rabbis instruct that the *quppa* provide alms that are rather complex and highly individualized. The poor are to be given precisely what they used to have before they became poor – the exact income that they used to earn, clothing made of precisely the same fabric as the garments they used to own, and so forth. For these reasons, it was imperative for the supervisor to "know" the poor, to see past the superficial signs of poverty and evaluate their actual needs. This imperative is stressed in Tosefta *Pe'ah* 4:8, which distinguishes between the poor who are "known" and those who are "not known." The importance of knowing the poor is likewise apparent in other texts from late antiquity. In the *Didache* we read, "Let your charitable gift sweat in your hands until you know to whom you are giving."[71] And likewise Ambrose: "Many pretend that they have debts: let the truth be looked into. They bemoan that they have been deprived by robbers: give aid only if the misfortune is readily apparent, or the person is well known."[72]

What these authors, including the rabbis, have in mind is an assessment or judgment of those who claim to be poor. In many ways, the rabbis envision the supervisor as a judge who evaluates claimants to the *quppa* and their

---

[69] Printed editions read, "expire from the world"; see Albeck, *The Mishnah*, 1:65; N. Sacks, ed. *The Mishnah - Order Zeraim: With Variant Readings Collected from Manuscripts, Fragments of the "Genizah" and Early Printed Editions and Collated with Quotations from the Mishnah in Early Rabbinic Literature [Hebrew]*) (Jerusalem: Institute for the Complete Israeli Talmud, Yad Rav Herzog, 1972), 1:163.

[70] For later emendations to the text of *m. Pe'ah* 8:9, including the pericope's permutations in printed editions, see Walter Bauer, *Pea (Vom Ackerwinkel): Text, Übersetzung und Erklärung* (eds. G. Beer and O. Holtzmann; Giessen: A. Töpelmann, 1914), 71; Brooks, *Support for the Poor*, 151; Sacks, *The Mishnah*, 1:165–66.

[71] *Didache* 1.6; translation according to Aelred Cody, "*The Didache*: An English Translation," in *The Didache in Context: Essays on its Text, History, and Transmission* (ed. C. N. Jefford; Supplements to Novum Testamentum 77; Leiden and New York: E.J. Brill, 1995), 5.

[72] Ambrose, *Off.* 2.77, as cited in Grey and Parkin, "Controlling the Urban Mob," 291.

claims. The idea of judging the poor and evaluating their needs is likewise seen elsewhere. The *Didache* implores its readers to give to all who ask, yet also instructs that those who are not truly in need must be evaluated as if they are on trial:

> To all who ask you give, and do not ask back, for from their own gifts the father wishes to give to all. Blessed is the one who gives according to the mandate, for he is innocent. But the one not having need is given a hearing, into what he received and why. And in straits he shall be examined about that which he did, and he shall not go thence, until he has given back the last farthing. (*Didache* 1.5)[73]

Those who are genuinely in need are innocent, while imposters are guilty and must give back the alms. Steven Bridge writes that the moral responsibility of charitable activity falls squarely upon the beneficiary.[74] It seems to me, however, that the *Didache* relies less on the recipient's conscience and more on third party assessment and enforcement in the form of a hearing. Likewise, in the passage cited earlier, Ambrose calls for an investigation to look into the truth behind beggars' claims.

The idea that beggars and their claims must be evaluated as if on trial is also found in other texts, such as a Roman law from the fourth century. In 382, Severus, Prefect of the city of Rome, received an imperial rescript that aimed to control begging:

> If there should be any persons who adopt the profession of mendicancy and who are induced to seek their livelihood at public expense, each of them shall be examined. The soundness of body and the vigor of years of each one of them shall be investigated. In the case of those who are lazy and not to be pitied on account of any physical disability, the obligation shall be placed upon them that the zealous and diligent informer shall obtain ownership of those beggars who are held bound by their servile status, and as regards those who are attended only by the liberty of their birth, he shall be supported by a perpetual tenancy, provided that he shall betray and prove such sloth. The owners shall be entitled to an unimpaired right of action against those persons who happen to have offered either refuge to fugitives or the advice to adopt the profession of mendicancy. (*Codex Theodosianus* 14.18.1)[75]

---

[73] Translation according to Bridge, "To Give or Not to Give," 555.
[74] Bridge, "To Give or Not to Give," 555–56.
[75] Translation according to Grey and Parkin, "Controlling the Urban Mob," 284, which emends the translation of Clyde Pharr, *The Theodosian Code and Novels, and the Sirmondian Constitutions* (Princeton, N.J.: Princeton University Press, 1952).

This law attempts to control begging in ancient Rome. It assumes widespread suspicion of beggars' claims to poverty and outlines a system to judge or assess the true needs of those who claim to be poor. It is important to note a crucial difference between the Roman law and the rabbis' instructions. *Codex Theodosianus* attempts to control begging by making the poor man a tenant of one who is well-off. That is, this law seeks to prevent begging by intentionally fostering a hierarchical relationship of personal dependency between the two. This casts into high relief the rabbis' efforts to control begging in a way that purposefully obviates the formation of such vertical relationships.

The Tannaim participate fully in the ancient world's widespread suspicion of imposture and its conviction that these individuals ought to be examined or investigated, as if on trial. The supervisor, in his capacity as a distributor of alms, acts as a judge who assesses the veracity of the claimants and their claims. He then rules on who should receive what from the *quppa*. The idea that rabbis model the supervisor as a judge permeates their thinking. Mishnah *Pe'ah* 8:7 instructs that two supervisors are needed to oversee the *quppa's* collection, while three are needed for its distribution. In addition to recalling the two individuals needed to oversee public money and the three required to manage the Jerusalem Temple's finances, as well as the *pronoetai* who often worked in teams of twos and threes, these teams of two and three recall judicial themes.[76] Two witnesses are needed for a conviction and a three-judge panel is required to reach decisions on monetary rewards.[77] The term *tsedaqah* itself often carries connotations associated with judicial justice and courtroom proceedings in Tannaitic literature.[78]

In short, there was widespread suspicion in the ancient world that many individuals who claimed to be poor were nothing more than imposters. It follows that many, including the Tannaim, wanted to evaluate the claimants' and their claims. Such imposture was unsavory and would pose profound problems for the rabbis' vision of charity. Weeding them out, moreover, would benefit the community as a whole, as it ensures that charitable contributions go to those truly in need. As such, the Tannaim model the supervisor as a kind of judge to hear the claimant's claims, assess their veracity, and then

---

[76] *m. Sheqalim* 5:2; *m. Sanhedrin* 1:1, as noted by Brooks, *Support for the Poor*, 146–47. See also *t. Sheqalim* 2:15. To be sure, Goodman is correct to caution that these officials were not identical to those who served in the Temple Goodman, *State and Society*, 122.

[77] On two witnesses, see Deut 19:15; *m. Bava Qamma* 7:2; *m. Makkot* 1:7. On the three-judge panel, see *m. Sanhedrin* 1:1.

[78] E.g., *t. Sanhedrin* 1:3; see the discussion in Przybylski, *Righteousness in Matthew*, 71–72.

rule on the alms that they are to receive. The rabbis, therefore, model the charity supervisors as a synthesis of a judge and tax collector – two important communal officials.

SUPERVISORS AS COMMUNAL OFFICIALS

There are implications of modeling the charity supervisor after judges and tax collectors. Judges and their courts existed to punish crimes or offenses against the community, to provide remedies for wronged individuals, and to resolve disputes.[79] The Tannaim understand that courts were essential to the town and, indeed, constituted each town's central authority.[80] Taxes were levied by the Roman government upon all residents, who were obligated to pay the tax collector.[81] At least some of the tax revenue would be invested in public goods.[82] As such, the rabbis model the charity supervisor along the lines of two important communal officials, elevating the stature of the supervisor and organized charity. It is also important to recognize that the rabbis had no real authority over the actual judges and actual tax collectors in Roman Palestine.[83] The rabbis themselves were not appointed as tax collectors by the government.[84] Similarly, the rabbis were not judges.[85] At best, they were legal experts who might be approached as unofficial arbitrators on issues that were of no interest to the Roman authorities.[86] These included purity, dietary laws, tithes, and other aspects of Jewish law.[87]

---

[79] Jill Harries, "Courts and the Judicial System," in *The Oxford Handbook of Jewish Daily Life in Roman Palestine* (ed. C. Hezser; Oxford: Oxford University Press, 2010), 85–86.
[80] *SifreDeut* 144; see Goodman, *State and Society*, 122–23.
[81] Zangenberg and van de Zande, "Urbanization," 172–73.
[82] Sperber, *City in Roman Palestine*, 79.
[83] Goodman, *State and Society*, 101, 155–62; Harries, "Courts and the Judicial System," 88–95; Hezser, *Social Structure*, 475–80.
[84] The Tannaim expressed negative attitudes toward tax collectors, even implying that one could not be a tax collector and still remain within the rabbinic movement; see *m. Hagigah* 3:6; *t. Bava Metzi'a* 8:26; *t. Demai* 3:4.
[85] At most, the rabbis were legal experts who might be approached as unofficial arbitrators on issues that were of no interest to the Roman authorities; see Harries, "Courts and the Judicial System," 90–92; Hezser, *Social Structure*, 475–76. Moreover, Tannaitic attitudes toward judges were not wholly positive. See, for example, the antagonism expressed in *Mekilta, Kaspa* 3; Horovitz and Rabin, eds. *Mechilta d'Rabbi Ismael*, 172; Lauterbach, *Mekhilta de-Rabbi Ishmael*, 473; *SifreDeut* 14; 17; Goodman, *State and Society*, 158. See also G. Alon's "Those Appointed for Money," in Gedalyahu Alon, *Jews, Judaism, and the Classical World: Studies in Jewish History in the Times of the Second Temple and Talmud* (trans. I. Abrahams; Jerusalem: Magnes Press, 1977), 374–435.
[86] Harries, "Courts and the Judicial System," 90–92; Hezser, *Social Structure*, 475–76.
[87] Goodman, *State and Society*, 94–101.

The rabbis envision organized charity, with the supervisor playing a key role, as an essential component of the organization of Jewish communities. I showed in Chapter 6 how the *quppa* is conceived as a civic, communal institution, so too here the supervisor is modeled as an essential and authoritative communal official.[88] The Romans would have had little interest in organized charity and it is conceivable that the Tannaim saw this as an area in which they could assert influence over the local community; that being said, there is no evidence in Tannaitic compilations that the Tannaim formulated charity as a means to gain socioreligious authority. It would only be later that the Amoraim would attempt to use charity as a way to elevate their authority in a meaningful way.

INSTRUCTIONS FOR HANDLING FUNDS

The rabbis anticipate that certain problems might arise while the supervisor carries out his duties. In particular, their instructions address the possibility that the town's residents may not trust the supervisor. If the supervisor was believed to be biased, dishonest, or – above all – a thief who steals from the *quppa*, then no one would contribute and organized charity would collapse.[89] It was imperative that the supervisor be seen as honest and trustworthy – like a judge. Thus, the rabbis instruct the supervisor on how to conduct his duties and, in particular, how he should carefully distinguish between the funds that he holds for the *quppa* and those that belong to him personally. Optics are especially important, as the supervisor should not even be suspected of mixing his own assets with those belonging to the *quppa*. The Tannaim illustrate this principle by exploring the following scenario: what if the charity supervisor, while making his rounds collecting money for the *quppa*, happens to legitimately acquire money for himself? How should these coins be handled

---

[88] See also *m. Qiddushin* 4:5, where charity supervisors are paired with public officials.
[89] Given the Tannaim's concern with the dangers of relationships of personal dependency, it follows that they could be concerned that beggars become dependent upon private benefactors. They may even confuse the supervisor himself with a benefactor, misinterpreting his distribution of the *quppa* as donations from his own pocket. It may not have been readily apparent that the coins, clothing, and food that the supervisor hands out do not belong to him, but rather they come from the community as a whole. The title *parnas* – i.e., "provider" – might add to the confusion, suggesting that he *provides* alms out of his personal possessions. If the supervisor was mistaken for a private benefactor and his distribution was mistaken as direct almsgiving, it would undermine the central objective of organized charity to provide for the poor in a collective, anonymous, and indirect way. The transaction would incur the same undesirable effects as giving directly to beggars – creating relationships of dependency, shame, etc. – the very things that organized charity was designed to prevent.

so as not to arouse suspicion or create any wrong impressions? They instruct as follows:

> The charity collector is not permitted to separate this from that.[90] Even if his friend gave him silver coins (*me'ot*) that he owed him, even if he found silver coins (*me'ot*) in the road, he is not permitted to take them. As it is said: *you shall be clear before the Lord and before Israel* (Num 32:22). But he [may] separate this from that inside a courtyard or inside a store, and then collect [charity].[91] (*t. Pe'ah* 4:15)

The rabbis instruct that the supervisor may not in full public view sort out "this from that" – that is, sort his own, personal coins from those that belong to the *quppa*.[92] He should not do this even if the coins that he puts into his own pocket legitimately belong to him. Money that the supervisor receives as repayment of a loan clearly belongs to him. Scattered coins – and *me'ot* specifically[93] – are elsewhere used by the Tannaim as paradigmatic examples of objects that lack identifying marks and are acquired immediately by whoever finds them.[94] The supervisor would legitimately own these coins and would be "clean" or guiltless in the eyes of God, as the proof text from Num 32:22 indicates.[95] But the proof text also stipulates that he must be guiltless in the eyes of Israel – that is, his fellow Jews. If the supervisor is seen putting some *me'ot* into his pocket, some will surely suspect him of stealing from the *quppa*.

Moreover, a poor man who receives a *ma'ah* might understand this to come from the supervisor's own pocket, as opposed to from the *quppa*. To forestall the possibility of creating these misperceptions, the supervisor should sort out his personal funds in private, shielded from public view inside a store or within an enclosed courtyard. Once he has sorted out his personal coins from those of the *quppa*, he may continue his collection.

---

[90] They may not separate their own money from that which they collected for the *quppa*; see my following explanation.

[91] The charity supervisor is permitted to do this in private.

[92] They may not separate their own money from that which they collected for the *quppa*; see Brooks, *Support for the Poor*, 153. Cf. Lieberman, *Tosefta Ki-Fshutah*, 1:188. Lieberman reads "make change," in accordance with the printed edition over MS Vienna. This would also harmonize the reading with *t. Bava Metzi'a* 3:9. MS Vienna's "separate" is the more difficult language and therefore the preferred reading.

[93] The rabbinic redactors' choice of *me'ot* over other coins is significant, as these silver coins were mentioned earlier as items that the *quppa* would distribute to the poor; see *t. Pe'ah* 4:9.

[94] *m. Bava Metzi'a* 2:1; on this passage, see Lapin, *Early Rabbinic Civil Law*, 157–58.

[95] Num 32:22 is understood by the rabbis (in *m. Sheqalim* 3:2) as one's responsibility to satisfy both God and humans; see Jacob Milgrom, *The JPS Torah Commentary: Numbers* (Philadelphia: Jewish Publication Society, 1990), 272.

The supervisor must avoid, at all costs, the suspicion of mixing his personal funds with those of the *quppa*. He may not even use the *quppa*'s coins to make change for himself, as it may appear that he is pocketing the *quppa*'s money:

> Charity supervisors may make change for others. But they may not make change for themselves. (*t. Bava Metzi'a* 3:9, D)[96]

Likewise, the supervisor may not gain personal, earthly benefits from the *quppa*.[97] If he does, it would compromise the integrity of his work. Constructing a fence around this principle, the rabbis instruct the supervisor to avoid even the possibility that he could be perceived as reaping material or economic benefit. This is so even if the supervisor has completed his distribution and fulfilled his obligations, but has alms left over:[98]

> [If the] charity supervisors did not find poor men to distribute beans to, [then] they may sell them to others. But they may not sell them to themselves.[99] (*t. Bava Metzi'a* 3:9, A–C)

Even though he has provided for the poor in accordance with their needs and thereby fulfilled his duties, the supervisor may not sell the surplus beans to himself. This would raise suspicion that he sold the beans at a discount and pocketed the profits. He may, however, sell the beans to others and contribute the proceeds to the *quppa*.[100] Again, the rabbis' underlying principle is that the supervisor must avoid even the appearance that his personal interests intermingle with his responsibilities for public charity. In order to gain the public's trust and to ensure that organized charity meet its goals, the supervisor must be honest and impartial. Likewise, the Tannaim elsewhere discuss the importance of a judge being impartial and refusing personal gain.[101] To be sure, they should refuse earthly, material gain – as the rabbis promise that the supervisor who performs his duties properly will receive rewards in the world to come:

---

[96] Translation based Neusner, *The Tosefta*, with my modifications.
[97] To be sure, the Tannaim allow for the supervisor to reap the esteem and social capital that comes with the position, as well as otherworldly rewards; see my following discussion.
[98] See also *t. Sheqalim* 2:8, where the Tosefta instructs the supervisor on how to handle surplus money left over from the distribution to the poor. In particular, the money can be invested, albeit in a very conservative way so that the *quppa* would not incur losses; see the explanation in Meir, "*Parnas*," 16; Safrai, *Jewish Community*, 307.
[99] Translation based on Neusner, *The Tosefta*, with my emendations.
[100] This is indicated in *m. Sheqalim* 2:5, which instructs that surplus funds are to be given to the poor.
[101] E.g., *t. Sotah* 14:3–5; *Mekilta, Kaspa* 3.

On that basis, one who collects (*gby*) funds for charity and provides for the poor, one who performs deeds of kindness, how much the more so will he be given credit for his soul. (*Sifra, Vayyiqra Dibura Dehobah, Parashah* 12)[102]

The supervisors who perform these tasks will earn credit for their soul, a reward in accordance with the rabbinic doctrine of merits.[103]

CONCLUSION

The Tannaim saw organized charity as a means to end begging by giving alms to the poor in a way that was indirect, anonymous, and collective. The keystone was the charity supervisor, who would oversee the operation of the *quppa*. The rabbis instruct the supervisor on how he should perform his duties and handle the funds entrusted to him. The supervisor should make a visible distinction between his own possessions, on the one hand, and the interests and funds of the town's residents, on the other. This was done in order to avoid suspicion that he would steal from the *quppa* or compromise his objectivity by pursuing personal, material rewards for himself. Rather, the supervisor had to be an agent of the community as a whole and it must be readily apparent that he fulfills his duties with honesty, transparency, and fairness. The entire system of organized charity depended on it. He was to collect alms with the authority of a tax collector. Like a judge, the supervisor was to handle the funds in ways that avoided the misperception of personal gain and to properly assess the needs of the claimants. He would distribute alms with fairness and impartiality. If the supervisor fulfilled his obligations properly, rewards would await him in the world to come. The Tannaim envision the charity supervisor as a communal official who oversaw the *quppa* – itself envisioned as a communal institution. By properly carrying out his duties, the supervisor could provide a reliable alternative to giving to beggars and bring an end to begging, which would elevate the well-being of the community as a whole – poor and non-poor alike.

---

[102] Translation based on Jacob Neusner, *Sifra: An Analytical Translation* (3 vols.; Atlanta, Ga.: Scholars Press, 1988), with my emendations and based on the Hebrew of Weiss, *Sifra*, 27a.
[103] Similarly, see *t. Pe'ah* 4:18, where a benefactor forgoes earthly material rewards, but will be credited with immaterial rewards in the world to come.

8

Conclusion: After the Tannaim

ORGANIZED CHARITY IN PALESTINIAN AMORAIC TEXTS

The Amoraim of Roman Palestine (c. 250–500 C.E.), who succeeded the Tannaim (70–c. 250 C.E.), would significantly alter and develop rabbinic conceptualizations of organized charity. As I will show in this concluding chapter, the Amoraic discussions of organized charity differ from those of the Tannaim in four respects.[1] First, the Amoraim emphasize the role and scope of the *tamhui* whereas the Tannaim had focused more on the *quppa*. Second, the Amoraim had an acute sense of the urgency of poverty and that relief must be immediate. Third, whereas the Tannaim developed institutional charity as a means to address the dignity of the poor, the Amoraim understood that the *tamhui* and *quppa* could serve as vessels to convey and project social, religious, and political authority over Jewish society. Fourth, the Amoraim expand the

---

[1] This chapter illuminates the early reception and development of Tannaitic discussions of organized charity by exploring texts of the Palestinian Amoraim – the immediate successors to the Tannaim. As it would be unwieldy (and unnecessary) to review the entire reception history of Tannaitic literature, I have limited this chapter to Palestinian Amoraic texts because the subsequent works of rabbinic literature were redacted centuries later under very different social and political circumstances (e.g., the Bavli in seventh-century Sasanian Mesopotamia). Nevertheless, it is important to note that even though there is no tractate *Pe'ah* in the Babylonian Talmud (along with most of the Order of Seeds), the Babylonian Amoraim and Stammaim expressed interest in these issues, as discussions of sections of *m. Pe'ah* and *t. Pe'ah* are dispersed throughout the Bavli. See, for example, *b. Hagigah* 7a–b and *b. Shabbat* 127a–b (= *m. Pe'ah* 1:1); *b. Bava Qamma* 61a–b (= *m. Pe'ah* 2:1); *b. Mo'ed Qatan* 4b (= *m. Pe'ah* 7:5); *b. Sotah* 21b (= *m. Pe'ah* 8:5); *b. Bava Batra* 8b–11a (= *m. Pe'ah* 8:7; *t. Pe'ah* 4:8–21); *b. Ketubbot* 66b–68a (= *m. Pe'ah* 8:8; *t. Pe'ah* 4:8–15). Indeed, roughly half of the Order of Seeds is discussed in the Babylonian Talmud; see Yaacov Sussmann, "Babylonian Sugiyot to the Orders Zera'im and Tohorot [Hebrew]," (Ph.D. diss., Hebrew University of Jerusalem, 1969), 75–226, 245–90. Sussmann finds that topics from the Order of Seeds were discussed in Babylonian academies, but the Order of Seeds itself was not studied as an independent unit; see also Strack and Stemberger, *Introduction to the Talmud*, 191.

concept of charity beyond the Tannaitic definition of material support for the poor to include support for other ventures understood to be altruistic or beneficial to the community. This included raising funds for the rabbis themselves, the so-called collection of the sages, which was carried out by the rabbis and for the rabbis. These changes in attitudes among the Amoraim can be attributed to the lasting impact of the economic crisis of the mid- to late third century, which left an indelible mark on the rabbinic movement's collective consciousness and reshaped its socioeconomic structure. They can also be attributed to the influence of similar developments among Christians, where bishops employed charity as a means to organize the church and promote their own authority. The changes introduced by the Amoraim would become permanent features of Jewish approaches to charity. Exploring the Amoraic discussions will also highlight the uniqueness and idiosyncrasies of the original conceptualization of organized charity by the Tannaim.

THE *TAMHUI* AND *QUPPA* IN PALESTINIAN AMORAIC TEXTS

The most important texts on organized charity in Palestinian Amoraic compilations are found in Chapter 8 of Yerushalmi *Pe'ah*, which expands upon Tannaitic teachings, especially *m. Pe'ah* 8:7 and *t. Pe'ah* 4:8–15. It is illustrative to compare the Yerushalmi's introduction of the *tamhui* and *quppa* to that of the Tosefta:

t. Pe'ah 4:9

A. The *tamhui* [provides for] the entire day.
B. The *quppa* [provides] from Sabbath eve to Sabbath eve.
C. The *tamhui* [provides] for every man.
D. The *quppa* [provides] for poor individuals of the same town.

y. Pe'ah 8:7, 21a

A. The *tamhui* [provides] every day.
B. The *quppa* [provides] from Sabbath eve to Sabbath eve.
C. The *tamhui* [provides] for every man.
D. The *quppa* [provides] only for poor individuals of the same town.

The Yerushalmi largely matches the Tosefta, though there are two noticeable differences, which I have underlined. First, in lemma A of each text, the Tosefta instructs that the *tamhui* should provide support "for the entire day" (*kl hywm*) while the Yerushalmi instructs that the *tamhui* provide support "every day" (*bkl ywm*). Thus, whereas the Tosefta emphasizes the amount of food that the *tamhui* ought to provide, the Yerushalmi stresses the frequency. The *quppa*, by contrast, operates only once a week.² The second difference arises in the Yerushalmi's treatment of the *quppa* in lemma D. Both the Tosefta and the Yerushalmi define the *tamhui* as an institution for all men and the *quppa* for locals. The Yerushalmi, however, emphasizes the limited scope of the *quppa* by adding "only" – the *quppa* supports *only* the local poor. This casts into high relief the broad scope and application of the *tamhui*, as it addresses the needs of all men. With these two changes, the Amoraim instruct that the *tamhui* could have a greater and more frequent impact over society than the *quppa*.

In this vein, the Yerushalmi continues its discussion by fleshing out details of the *tamhui* that Tannaitic compilations did not address, such as its supervision:

> R. Huna said, "[The] *tamhui* [is distributed] by three people, because it is [allocated] on the spot." (*y. Pe'ah* 8:7, 21a)

Huna's instruction that the *tamhui* should be overseen by three individuals is repeated by R. Helbo in a text that I will cite and discuss further. By assigning three supervisors to the *tamhui*, the Amoraim place it on par with the *quppa*, which is collected by two and distributed by three (*m. Pe'ah* 8:7). Because charity supervisors, as I discuss in Chapter 7, embody control over the collection and distribution of economic assets, their presence here further concretizes the institutional character of the *tamhui*. Huna also instructs that the *tamhui* be distributed "on the spot," which can be taken in both temporal and geographical senses as "immediately" and wherever the supervisors and the poor happen to meet.³ By contrast, the *quppa* is fixed in both time and space, operating only in the synagogue on Sabbath eve. As such, the Yerushalmi conceptualizes the *tamhui* as an institution that is flexible, enabling it to achieve the broader aims of providing support for anyone in need at any time. In short, the Amoraim take more interest in the *tamhui* than the Tannaim, fleshing out its details and institutional structure and elevating its importance with respect to the *quppa*. As we will see, this interest in the *tamhui* complements the Amoraim's heightened sense of the

---

² Cf. MS Erfurt of the Tosefta, which reads like the Yerushalmi: "The *tamhui* [provides] every day." The reading in MS Vienna (Lieberman's edition), however, is preferred, as scholars have noted that MS Erfurt tends to reflect later (i.e., post-Tannaitic) emendations; see Eyal Ben-Eliyahu et al., *Handbook of Jewish Literature from Late Antiquity, 135–700 CE* (Oxford: Oxford University Press for the British Academy, 2012), 28; Schäfer, "Once Again," 92; Strack and Stemberger, *Introduction to the Talmud*, 158–59.

³ As noted in a comment in Jacob Neusner, *The Jerusalem Talmud: A Translation and Commentary* (Peabody, Mass.: Hendrickson, 2008), *ad loc.*

urgency of poverty, as the *tamhui* is designed to meet the poor's basic biological needs – that is, to keep them alive.

THE URGENCY OF POVERTY

More so than the Tannaim, the Amoraim perceived that poverty is a particularly urgent, immediate, and widespread problem. The Yerushalmi instructs that charity through the *tamhui* is not only a financial or civil matter – as it is in the Tannaim's vision of the *quppa* – but also a matter of life and death:

> R. Helbo, in the name of Abba bar Zavda, [said], "One does not appoint less than three *parnasim*."
> Come and look,[4] money matters are judged by three, matters of life and death not so much more?
> But then they should be twenty-three!
> Until one assembles them [the twenty-three], he [the poor man] is in danger.
> (*y. Pe'ah* 8:7, 21a)

Whereas the three supervisors assigned to the *quppa* are modeled in Tannaitic compilations on the three judges needed to oversee civil cases, the Amoraim reject this association for the *tamhui*. If anything, the Yerushalmi instructs, the number of supervisors for the *tamhui* ought to follow the twenty-three judges who oversee capital cases, demonstrating the understanding that the proper operation of the *tamhui* has life-or-death consequences for poor men in desperate need. However, the Yerushalmi recognizes that oversight by twenty-three individuals would be cumbersome and impede the speedy provision of alms. Rather, the *tamhui* must be a lithe and agile institution, where the supervisors can meet quickly to respond to a poor man's needs.

That the Amoraim perceive poverty as an immediate problem that requires an immediate solution is likewise seen later in the same text:

> R. Abba bar Zavda said, "Rav and R. Yohanan disagreed. One said, 'One investigates[5] before giving clothing, but one does not investigate for necessities of life.' The other said, 'Even before giving clothing one does not investigate, because of the covenant of the patriarch Abraham.[6]'"
> (*y. Pe'ah* 8:7, 21a)

This passage instructs that the necessities of life be given to the poor *before* the supervisor investigates or assesses their true needs. This contrasts with the

---

[4] I.e., take note.
[5] He assesses the needs of the poor.
[6] Because no Israelite should have to suffer the shame of being naked.

Tannaim's treatment of the *quppa*, which stresses the importance of determining the validity of the claimant and his claims before distributing alms. The Yerushalmi further instructs that if clothing is considered a necessity, then it too must be provided immediately. In Tannaitic sources, by contrast, clothing is provided by the *quppa* and is given for social and semiotic purposes.[7] In short, supervisors should give the poor man the necessities that he requests without stopping to assess the validity of his claims, which is seen here as a delay in the allocation of provisions.

The Amoraim's sense of the immediacy of biological poverty is likewise illustrated in narratives in which sages encounter poor men:

> R. Yohanan and R. Simeon b. Laqish went to bathe in the public baths of Tiberias. A poor man met them and said to them, "Acquire merit by me [i.e., give me charity]." They said to him, "When we return, when we return." When they returned, they found him dead....
> Nehemiah from Shihin[8] met a Jerusalemite who said to him, "Acquire merit [i.e., give me charity] by giving me that chicken." He said to him, "Here is its value, go buy red meat." He ate and died....[9]
> Nahum from Gamzo[10] was carrying a gift to the house of his father-in-law when he met a person afflicted with boils[11] who asked him, "Acquire merit [i.e., give me charity] from what you have on you." He said to him, "When I shall return." He [later] returned and found him dead." (*y. Pe'ah* 8:7–9, 21a – b)[12]

---

[7] See my treatment in Chapters 5 and 6.

[8] A town in the Lower Galilee, also known as Asochis; see Tsafrir et al., *Tabula Imperii Romani*, 70.

[9] Cf. Guggenheimer, *Jerusalem Talmud – Peah and Demay*, 341–42, who writes that he died because the poor are not accustomed to eating red meat. This narrative is substantially reshaped in *b. Ketubbot* 67b, where a poor man asks for fat meat and old wine, which are signs of extreme extravagance. R. Nehemiah, however, suggests that the poor man "live with me on lentils." That is, the poor man should live on humbler foods, just as Nehemiah does. The poor man ate the lentils and died. Nehemiah is initially blamed: "Alas for Nehemiah who killed this man!" But the Stammaim exonerate Nehemiah: "[The fact], however, [is that the man himself was to blame, for] he should not have cultivated his luxurious habits to such an extent." The Bavli has altered the details and the overall moral force of the narrative. The Yerushalmi's narrative exemplifies the principle that one should give the poor precisely what he requests *and* that one should do so immediately. This is in line with *y. Pe'ah*'s concern for the acute nature of poverty and the necessity to offer charity in accordance with the poor's needs as he himself defines them, and to do so immediately. By contrast, the Bavli's narrative is a warning against an extravagant lifestyle.

[10] A village near Lod; see Tsafrir et al., *Tabula Imperii Romani*, 128–29.

[11] Physical ailments are often understood as a sign of poverty; see my discussion in Chapter 7.

[12] Translation according to Guggenheimer, *Jerusalem Talmud – Peah and Demay*.

These narratives follow a similar pattern. A sage encounters a poor man, who requests alms or a certain kind of support, such as chicken. Any hesitation to give or deviation from the poor man's specific request results in his immediate death.[13] These narratives further illustrate the Yerushalmi's understanding of poverty as an urgent problem and one that requires immediate attention. Indeed, this is likewise reflected in other Amoraic texts.[14]

The Amoraim understood the urgency and immediacy of poverty, which complements their emphasis on the *tamhui*, whose main objective is to provide immediate relief to those who are biologically poor. By contrast, the Tannaim were more interested in discussing the *quppa*, which is primarily focused on semiotics and the social ramifications of poverty and charity.

ORGANIZED CHARITY AND AUTHORITY

Unlike the Tannaim, the Amoraim grasped that organized charity could be a means to claim or gain socioreligious authority. We see this in texts that portray the rabbis as controlling the appointments of supervisors or serving as supervisors themselves.[15] For example, in one passage, R. Yose implements R. Yohanan's instructions for appointing supervisors:

> R. Yose in the name of R. Yohanan [said], "One does not appoint two brothers as *parnasim*." R. Yose removed one of two brothers. He came and said before them, "There was not anything wrong with Mr. X [i.e., the removed brother], only one does not appoint two brothers as *parnasim*." (*y. Pe'ah* 8:7, 21a)[16]

The supervisors must be completely independent of one another, without familial relations that might influence their decision making. The overriding concern is to appoint supervisors to ensure a fair process or procedural justice.

---

[13] The connection between charity and death is also seen in Jewish interpretations of Prov 10:2: "Treasures gained by wickedness do not profit, but *tsedaqah* delivers from death," see also Prov 11:4. Postbiblical texts, from Tob 4:10 (second century B.C.E.) through the Babylonian Talmud (*b. Shabbat* 156a–b) interpret *tsedaqah* here as charity; see the discussions in Anderson, *Charity*, 54–66; Gardner, "Astrology in the Talmud: An Analysis of Bavli Shabbat 156," 314–38. It is notable, however, that these texts are concerned with delivering the life of the giver, as avoidance of death is couched as a reward and motivation for giving charity. By contrast, *y. Pe'ah* 8:7–9, 21a–b is concerned with saving the life of a recipient.

[14] E.g., *Lev. Rab.* 34:2; on this text, see Visotzky, *Golden Bells*, 132–33.

[15] See also *y. Berakhot* 2:8 (= 2:9 in Venice), 5d; cf. *t. Ta'anit* 1:7; and Fraade, "Local Jewish Leadership," 162n. 17; Hezser, *Social Structure*, 272–73; Levine, *Rabbinic Class*, 162–67; Schwartz, *Were the Jews*, 130–33.

[16] Translation according to Guggenheimer, *Jerusalem Talmud – Peah and Demay*, 326–27, with my emendations.

We also find rabbis offering honors or rewards to entice individuals to accept appointments as *parnasim*:[17]

> R. Yose went up to Kifra[18] and wanted to appoint *parnasim* there, but they [i.e., the appointees] did not accept [Yose's appointment]. He came and said before them, "Ben Bavai [an official in the Jerusalem Temple] is in charge of [maintaining] the wick [of the Temple's candelabrum]. If this one [i.e., Ben Bavai] had been appointed over the wicks and therefore merited to be counted with the leaders of his generation, you who are being appointed over the lives of the people, so much more." (*y. Pe'ah* 8:7, 21a)[19]

Notably, this text from the Yerushalmi elevates the supervision of care for the poor above a Temple ritual.[20] The portrayal of sages as controllers of organized charity is likewise seen in depictions of the rabbis themselves serving as *parnasim*.[21] We read in the Yerushalmi, "R. Jacob bar Idi and R. Isaac bar Nahman were *parnasim*" and "R. Henena bar Pappai used to distribute charity at night."[22] Rabbi Eliezer and Rabbi Akiva are both associated with service as a *parnas*:

> R. [E]liezer was a *parnas*. Once, he returned to his house and said to them [i.e., the members of his household], "What happened?" They said to him, "There came a group [of poor people], they ate and drank and prayed for you." He said to them, "That does not give much reward." Another time, he came to his house and said to them, "What happened?" They said to him, "There came another group, they ate and drank and cursed you," He said to them, "That gives much reward."[23] They wanted to appoint R. Akiva as *parnas*. He said that he had to take counsel with his house [i.e., wife]. They followed him and heard him say, "In order to be cursed, in order to be insulted?!" (*y. Pe'ah* 8:7, 21a)[24]

---

[17] Schwartz, *Were the Jews*, 130–33.
[18] Near Tiberias, see Tsafrir et al., *Tabula Imperii Romani*, 168.
[19] Translation based on Neusner, *Jerusalem Talmud: A Translation and Commentary*, with my modifications.
[20] This can be viewed as part of a more general rabbinic tendency, explored by Cohn, *Memory of the Temple*, to discuss Temple rituals in ways that highlight and elevate the rabbis' own interests.
[21] In addition to the sources cited here, see also *y. Berakhot* 2:8 (= 2:9 in Venice), 5d.
[22] *y. Pe'ah* 8:9, 21b.
[23] The narrative on Eliezer makes the point that we should admire those who serve as *parnas* without seeking gratitude or earthly honors in return; see the discussion in Schwartz, *Were the Jews*, 131–32.
[24] Translation based on Guggenheimer, *Jerusalem Talmud – Peah and Demay*, with my emendations and in light of the discussion in Schwartz, *Were the Jews*, 131–32.

An important theme of these passages is the reluctance to serve as a supervisor. We see this in Yose's appointments, which the appointees refuse. He entices them by elevating the prestige of a supervisor above that of a Temple official. Yose also tempts the potential appointees by touching upon the authority and importance of the office: "you... are being appointed over the lives of the people." The narratives on Eliezer and Akiva reflect the negative aspects of serving as a *parnas*. It could be a thankless task, as surely some poor claimants felt that they were short-changed and the non-poor could be irritated by the supervisors' solicitations to contribute.[25]

By empowering themselves to appoint *parnasim* or depicting themselves as *parnasim*, the Amoraim demonstrate how organized charity could be a means to gain social and political authority. This marks a significant development from Tannaitic compilations, where issues of power and authority may be implied or extrapolated, but rarely placed at the forefront of discussions as they are in the Yerushalmi.[26] The issues of charity, authority, and the role of the Palestinian Amoraim are explored in a short narrative in which a rabbi appoints a *parnas*:

> R. Haggai, when he inducted *parnasim*, let them carry the Torah, to indicate that every public office is given by the Torah: *Through me kings reign. Through me princes rule.* (Prov 8:15–16) (*y. Pe'ah* 8:7, 21a)

The *parnas*'s authority is expansive, encompassing social and political realms, as indicated by the choice of Prov 8:15–16 as the proof text. This authority, moreover, is based on the Torah, which is mediated by the rabbis – here, Rabbi Haggai.

The Amoraim's use of organized charity as a means to empower themselves reaches its apex in the so-called collection of the sages narratives, in which rabbis collect funds for other rabbis:

> *A man's gift eases his way and gives him access to the great* (Prov 18:16). Once R. Eliezer and R. Joshua and R. Akiva went to Holat Antiochia[27] to engage in the collection of the sages. There was there a certain Abba Yudan, who would do a *mitzvah* [i.e., give charity] generously and he became poor. When

---

[25] Likewise, see *b. Bava Batra* 8b, which further discusses the challenges of collecting for the *tamhui* and *quppa*.
[26] The lone exception, which I discuss in Chapter 4, is when the Tannaim instruct that the *tamhui* provide the poor with the materials needed to properly observe the Sabbath and Passover in the rabbinically prescribed ways. Even this, though, is a rather subtle attempt to assert socioreligious authority compared to what we see in Amoraic texts.
[27] A reference to the hot springs at Daphne, just outside of the city of Antioch on the Orontes in Syria; see Visotzky, *Golden Bells*, 124n. 17.

he saw the rabbis he went to his house and his face was downcast. His wife said to him, "What is with you, that you are downcast?" He told her the story: "The rabbis are here, and I do not know what I will do for them." His wife, who was a righteous woman [*tsadeket*], what did she say to him? "You still have a single field. Go, sell half of it and give it to them." He went and did it. When he gave it to them they said to him, "God will replace your loss." The rabbis left. He went to plow. When he had plowed half of his field, the Holy One, blessed be He, gave light to his eyes and the earth split before him and his cow fell in and [its leg] was broken. He descended to lift her up and found under her a treasure. He said, "For my good was the leg of my cow broken." When the rabbis returned they asked about this Abba Yudan, how he was doing. They said, "Who is able to see the face of Abba Yudan, Abba Yudan of the [many] goats, Abba Yudan of the [many] donkeys, Abba Yudan of the [many] camels." He [Abba Yudan] came to them [the rabbis] and said, "Your prayer for me made fruit and the fruit of fruit." They said to him, "Even though another man gave more than you, we will write you at the head of the scroll."[28] (*Leviticus Rabbah* 5:4)[29]

It is important to keep in mind the context of this passage. While it features Tannaim, this narrative and its parallels are found only in Amoraic compilations. Indeed, no such collection of the sages is mentioned in Tannaitic compilations. The narrative should not be read as a transparent history of the rabbinic movement in the second or early third centuries, but rather as an exhortation by rabbis in the fourth and fifth century to contribute to the rabbinic movement.[30]

The Amoraim frame the collection of the sages as an exercise in organized charity.[31] We see this in the Amoraic redactors' choice that *three* rabbis go around collecting contributions, recalling the *three* supervisors who oversee both the *tamhui* and *quppa*. Two of the three sages, Akiva and Eliezer, are associated with the office of the *parnas* in the text from *y. Pe'ah* 8:7, 21a discussed earlier. The passage uses *tsedaqah* and *mitzvah*, thereby invoking the language, as noted by Gary Anderson, that is common to rabbinic discussions of almsgiving for the poor.[32] The passage likewise invokes the concept of a

---

[28] That is, honor him by recording his name at the top of a list of donors; see Visotzky, *Golden Bells*, 125.
[29] Translation based on Satlow, "Fruit and the Fruit of Fruit," 246.
[30] As noted by Satlow, "Fruit and the Fruit of Fruit," 247.
[31] See also the collection of the sages in *y. Horayot* 3:6 (= 3:4 in Venice ed.), 48a.
[32] Likewise, note that *litra* is also used in the Tosefta's discussion of the *quppa* (*t. Pe'ah* 4:10). On *mitzvah* as charity, see the Amoraic passages cited earlier and Anderson, *Sin*, 174; Anderson, *Charity*, 16–17, 156–57; Lieberman, "Two Lexicographical Notes," 69–72; Tzvi Novick, "Blessings over *Misvot*: The Origins of a Category," *HUCA* 79 (2008): 84–86.

measure-for-measure reward – which is a common theme in texts on charity – when Yudan gives away his possessions but miraculously becomes wealthy again.[33] The redirection of funds from the needy to the rabbinic movement is presented in stark terms in a passage from the Yerushalmi:

> *And so with the surplus of the proceeds of any of these* (*m. Megillah* 3:1). That applies to what the charity supervisors (*gabbai tsedaqah*) collected and left over [those funds also may be used only for the purpose for which they were designated]. This accords with the following: R. Hiyya bar Ba came to Hamats,[34] and they gave him money to divide among orphans and widows. He went and handed them out to rabbis. (*y. Megillah* 3:1, 74a)[35]

Burton Visotzky is correct to observe that the collection of the sages does not constitute charity because it is not directed toward poor individuals per se, but rather toward the rabbinic movement. I submit, however, that this is an important point of the passage, as the Amoraim *present* the collection of the sages as an exercise in organized charity.

There are two important implications of the Amoraim's understanding and use of organized charity. The first is that they expand the concept of charity: beneficiaries are not limited to the poor, but rather can include other individuals as well as inanimate entities that do not directly address poverty, such as houses of study and the rabbinic movement. The Amoraic expansion of *tsedaqah*'s beneficiaries would become permanent. Earl Schwartz has rightly pointed out that the term *tsedaqah* has been hijacked for unintended purposes, as it is "frequently misapplied by Jews to describe any contribution to a not-for-profit organization ... regardless of how the contribution is actually used."[36] Schwartz illustrates his point with examples of how charity/*tsedaqah* is used to describe fundraising efforts for synagogues, swimming pools, and community centers. Of these contributions, Schwartz writes, "none qualify, in a historically authentic sense as *ts'adaqah*," which was intended for the poor.[37] Schwartz's observations are astute and significant, and they are paralleled by some medieval commentators, who likewise questioned whether contributions to Torah study, synagogues, or other Jewish communal entities

---

[33] Satlow, "Fruit and the Fruit of Fruit," 246–47. On the use of "measure for measure" in rabbinic discussions of charity, see *t. Pe'ah* 4:18 and more broadly my discussion in Gardner, "Giving to the Poor," 147–200.

[34] A city in Syria.

[35] Translation according to Neusner, *Jerusalem Talmud: A Translation and Commentary*, with my modifications.

[36] Earl Schwartz, "Land, Liens, and Ts'daqah," *Journal of Law and Religion* 14 (1999): 392.

[37] Schwartz, "Land, Liens, and Ts'daqah," 392.

not directly related to the poor could constitute *tsedaqah*.[38] I would clarify that contributions to such entities would not qualify under the Tannaim's conceptualization of *tsedaqah*, but they could be included in the *tsedaqah* of the Amoraim. The Amoraic conceptualization can be understood as more akin to philanthropy, which encompasses all kinds of efforts to promote the welfare of a wider swath of people than almsgiving, which is directed at the poor alone. Indeed, it is against this wider view of charity that we should view the substantial increase in donations to synagogues in the fourth and fifth centuries.[39] Another implication is the Amoraim's use of organized charity as a means to finance and strengthen their movement.[40] Such instrumental and political uses of charity are reminiscent of contemporaneous Christian sources, where organized charity is used to establish and maintain the authority of the bishops.[41]

A number of scholars have explored the ways that charity became a means of control over others in late antiquity. I stress, however, that charity can serve as a means of authority only if it can be controlled. Direct almsgiving, whose persistence is reflected throughout late-antique rabbinic texts, is an *ad hoc* and *ad loc.* practice. While it may result in an individual benefactor's control over an individual beneficiary, such discrete and disconnected economic processes cannot be harnessed to further the rabbinic movement's claims to authority over Jewish society. By contrast, institutionalization provides a means to control economic transactions, including charity. It controls the flow and transfer of assets, to and from certain people. The Tannaim put the institutional framework in place as a means to control charitable transactions to minimize the unsavory social costs that result from giving to beggars, namely the collateral damage caused to the recipient's dignity and honor. The Amoraim, however, understood that these institutions could also serve instrumental purposes. Controlling the flow and direction of charity could be employed to garner significant social, religious, and economic authority. The Christian church, indeed, took a similar tack.

Because charity was considered a communal obligation to which everyone was obligated to contribute, and because it amounted to significant

---

[38] Among others, the matter is discussed by the Rishonim and Maimonides; see the sources and discussion in Michael J. Broyde, "The Giving of Charity in Jewish Law: For What Purpose and Toward What Goal?," in *Toward a Renewed Ethic of Jewish Philanthropy* (ed. Y. Prager; New York: Yeshiva University Press, 2010), 241–74.

[39] As evidenced by dedicatory inscription inlaid into synagogues' mosaic floors; see Satlow, "Giving for a Return," 91–108.

[40] Levine also makes the point that Amoraic texts suggest that the rabbis tried to consolidate charitable giving into their own hands; see Levine, *Rabbinic Class*, 162–67.

[41] Brown, *Poverty and Leadership*.

control both over funds and people (e.g., the recipients), the administration of these funds would become an integral part of the general administration of the community. As such, the supervision of charity would become closely associated with authority over the local community.[42]

How can we explain the fundamental changes in organized charity made by the Amoraim?[43] One important factor was the third-century crisis (c. 235–284), which happened too late to be reflected in Tannaitic compilations, but is evident in Amoraic compilations. The third-century crisis introduced the possibility of widespread poverty. "Poverty is common," R. Ze'ora says in the Yerushalmi.[44] Because of the crisis, many rabbis surely became poor. Likewise, poverty and Torah study were no longer perceived as incompatible, raising the possibility that those born into poverty could become rabbis.[45] Whereas no rabbi is portrayed as poor in Tannaitic compilations, in Amoraic texts we begin to see impoverished rabbis.[46] Thus, unlike Tannaitic compilations, Amoraic teachings may include the perspective of rabbis who were not well-off. This sheds further light on the Amoraim's interest in the *tamhui* over the *quppa*. The *quppa*'s attention to the semiotic and social aspects of poverty is indicative of the way that the non-poor tend to construct charitable institutions. Institutions such as the *quppa* internalize the values of the well-off, where conspicuous consumption and decorum are prioritized over substance.[47] By contrast, if the poor were to design charitable institutions, they would surely formulate something closer to the *tamhui*, especially the Amoraic conceptualization of the *tamhui*. Here, the poor man's claims are readily believed and his exact requests are fulfilled.

A second factor influencing the Amoraic developments to organized charity was the influence of early Christianity. The church had become known for its charitable ventures and, as I discussed in Chapter 1, the bishops used their supervision over charitable institutions to influence the masses. The

---

[42] I have adapted the observations of Frisch, *Historical Survey*, 108, in light of modern methods and findings.
[43] The interest of Palestinian Amoraic texts in charity, more so than their Babylonian counterparts, is likewise reflected in their respective constructions of holy men; see Richard Lee Kalmin, "Holy Men, Rabbis and Demonic Sages in Late Antiquity," in *Jewish Culture and Society under the Christian Roman Empire* (ed. R. L. Kalmin and S. Schwartz; Interdisciplinary Studies in Ancient Culture and Religion 3; Leuven: Peeters, 2003), 213–49. I thank my student, Aoife O'Farrell, for pointing this out to me.
[44] *y. Nedarim* 9:4, 41c; on this text, see Gray, "Formerly Wealthy Poor," 118.
[45] Emblematic is the reconfiguration of the lives of Akiva and Eliezer as rags-to-riches stories; see Cohen, "Rabbi in Second-Century," 931–32; Azzan Yadin, "Rabbi Akiva's Youth," *JQR* 100 (2010): 573–97.
[46] See, for example, *y. Pe'ah* 8:9, 21b, where R. Hama receives a *dinar* from the *parnasim*.
[47] Ganley, "Poverty and Charity," 439; Veblen, *Theory of the Leisure Class*, 344.

Amoraim, it seems, envisioned a similar scenario in which charity could be used to assert their claims to authority.

CONCLUSION

In the first chapter, I discussed how modern understandings of charity are much broader than rabbinic Judaism's original conceptualization of charity. Some of these expansions can already be seen in Palestinian Amoraic texts, which enlarges the pool of legitimate beneficiaries beyond the poor alone to include schools and the rabbinic movement. The Palestinian Amoraim also understood, like the Christian bishops but unlike the Tannaim, that organized charity could be employed as a means to assert social and religious control. Thus, charity would play an important role in subsequent rabbinic claims to authority and influence over Jewish society.

Highlighting the changes to organized charity introduced by the Palestinian Amoraim casts into high relief the unique aspects of its original formulation by the Tannaim. This book has explored the earliest conceptualization of organized charity in rabbinic Judaism, demonstrating how the *tamhui* and *quppa* were transformed from vessels to institutions. The soup kitchen and charity fund, respectively, were seen by the Tannaim as remedies for the two ways that poverty was defined in Roman Palestine. The soup kitchen (*tamhui*) addressed the biological needs of all individuals while the charity fund (*quppa*) remedied the social effects of poverty, but only for the local conjunctural poor. The Tannaim developed the *tamhui* from Greco-Roman customs of hospitality and conceived of the *quppa* as a civic institution. Similarly, the Tannaim modeled the charity supervisor as a communal official akin to a tax collector who could compel people to contribute and exhibit the objectivity and fairness of a judge when distributing provisions to the poor. The *tamhui*, *quppa*, and charity supervisor served as intermediaries between benefactors and beneficiaries, thereby protecting the poor from the indignity of begging. Indeed, organized charity was conceptualized by the Tannaim as an alternative to begging and the problems that direct almsgiving caused.

Bibliography

Abegg Jr., Martin G. and Casey A. Toews. *Mishna: Based Upon the Kaufmann Manuscript.* Altamonte Springs, Fla.: Accordance 9.1 Bible Software, Oak Tree Software, Inc., 2010.

Academy of the Hebrew Language. *Ma'agarim: Historical Dictionary of the Academy of the Hebrew Language.* Jerusalem: Academy of the Hebrew Language, 1998.

Adams, Samuel L. "Poverty and Otherness in Second Temple Instructions," Pages 189–203 in *The "Other" in Second Temple Judaism: Essays in Honor of John J. Collins.* Edited by D. C. Harlow, K. M. Hogan, M. Goff, and J. S. Kaminsky. Grand Rapids, Mich.: W.B. Eerdmans, 2011.

Adan-Bayewitz, David. *Common Pottery in Roman Galilee: A Study of Local Trade.* Bar-Ilan Studies in Near Eastern Languages and Culture. Ramat-Gan, Israel: Bar-Ilan University Press, 1993.

Aharoni, Yohanan, Nahman Avigad, Joseph Aviram, Pessah Bar-Adon, Joseph Patrich, Ephraim Stern, and Yigael Yadin. "Judean Desert Caves: The Historical Periods," Pages 3:820–37 in *The New Encyclopedia of Archaeological Excavations in the Holy Land.* Edited by E. Stern. Jerusalem and New York: Israel Exploration Society, Carta and Simon & Schuster. 1993–2008.

Albeck, Hanoch. *Shishah Sidrei Mishnah = The Mishnah [Hebrew].* 6 vols. Jerusalem and Tel Aviv: Bialik Institute and Dvir Publishing House, 1952–1958 [repr. 1988].

Alcock, Susan E. "The Eastern Mediterranean," Pages 671–97 in *The Cambridge Economic History of the Greco-Roman World.* Edited by W. Scheidel, I. Morris, and R. P. Saller. Cambridge and New York: Cambridge University Press, 2007.

Alexander, Patrick H., John F. Kutsko, James D. Ernest, Shirley A. Decker-Lucke, and David L. Petersen, eds. *The SBL Handbook of Style: For Ancient Near Eastern, Biblical, and Early Christian Studies.* Peabody, Mass.: Hendrickson, 1999.

Allen, Joel. *Hostages and Hostage-taking in the Roman Empire.* Cambridge and New York: Cambridge University Press, 2006.

Alon, Gedalyahu. *Jews, Judaism, and the Classical World: Studies in Jewish History in the Times of the Second Temple and Talmud.* Translated by I. Abrahams. Jerusalem: Magnes Press, 1977.

Ameling, Walter. *Inscriptiones Judaicae Orientis: Kleinasien.* TSAJ 99. Tübingen: Mohr Siebeck, 2004.

Anderson, Gary A. *Charity: The Place of the Poor in the Biblical Tradition.* New Haven, Conn.: Yale University Press, 2013.

Anderson, Gary A. "Redeem Your Sins by the Giving of Alms: Sin, Debt, and the 'Treasury of Merit' in Early Jewish and Christian Tradition." *Letter & Spirit* 3 (2007): 37–67.

Anderson, Gary A. *Sin: A History*. New Haven, Conn.: Yale University Press, 2009.

Anderson, Gary A. "You Will Have Treasure in Heaven," Pages 107–32 in *New Approaches to the Study of Biblical Interpretation in Judaism of the Second Temple Period and in Early Christianity: Proceedings of the Eleventh International Symposium of the Orion Center for the Study of the Dead Sea Scrolls and Associated Literature, Jointly Sponsored by the Hebrew University Center for the Study of Christianity, 9–11 January, 2007*. Edited by G. A. Anderson, R. Clements, and D. Satran. Studies on the Texts of the Desert of Judah 106. Leiden and Boston: Brill, 2013.

Apothaker, Howard L. *Sifra, Dibbura deSinai: Rhetorical Formulae, Literary Structures, and Legal Traditions*. Monographs of the Hebrew Union College 28. Cincinnati, Ohio: Hebrew Union College Press, 2003.

Applebaum, S. "Economic Life in Palestine," Pages 631–700 in *The Jewish People in the First Century: Historical Geography, Political History, Social, Cultural and Religious Life and Institutions*. Edited by S. Safrai and M. Stern. *Compendia rerum Iudaicarum ad Novum Testamentum: Section 1*. Assen and Philadelphia: Van Gorcum and Fortress Press, 1974–1976.

Arterbury, Andrew E. "Abraham's Hospitality Among Jewish and Early Christian Writers: A Tradition History of Gen 18:1–16 and its Relevance for the Study of the New Testament." *Perspectives in Religious Studies* 30, no. 3 (2003): 359–376.

Arterbury, Andrew E. *Entertaining Angels: Early Christian Hospitality in its Mediterranean Setting*. New Testament Monographs 8. Sheffield: Sheffield Phoenix, 2005.

Avery-Peck, Alan J. "Charity in Judaism," Pages 1:335–47 in *The Encyclopaedia of Judaism*. Edited by J. Neusner, A. J. Avery-Peck, and W. S. Green. Leiden and Boston: Brill, 2005.

Avigad, Nahman. *Discovering Jerusalem*. Nashville, Tenn.: Thomas Nelson, 1983.

Avi-Yonah, Michael. *The Jews Under Roman and Byzantine Rule: A Political History of Palestine from the Bar Kokhba War to the Arab Conquest*. New York: Schocken Books, 1984.

Ayalon, Etan, Rafi Frankel, and Amos Kloner, eds. *Oil and Wine Presses in Israel from the Hellenistic, Roman and Byzantine Periods*. BAR International Series. Oxford: Archaeopress, 2009.

Baker, Cynthia M., *Rebuilding the House of Israel: Architectures of Gender in Jewish Antiquity*. Stanford, Calif.: Stanford University Press, 2002.

Bar, Doron. "The 3rd Century Crisis in the Roman Empire and its Relevance to Palestine During the Late Roman Period [Hebrew]." *Zion* 66, no. 2 (2001): 143–70.

Bar, Doron. "Was There a 3rd-c. Economic Crisis in Palestine?," Pages 43–54 in *The Roman and Byzantine Near East: Some Recent Archaeological Research*. Edited by J. H. Humphrey. Journal of Roman Archaeology Supplementary Series. Ann Arbor, Mich.: Journal of Roman Archaeology, 1995.

Bar Ilan University, *The Responsa Project: Version 20*. Ramat Gan, Israel: Bar-Ilan University, 1972–2012.

Bar-Adon, Pessah, *The Cave of the Treasure: The Finds from the Caves in Nahal Mishmar*. Judean Desert Studies. Jerusalem: Israel Exploration Society, 1980.

Barthes, Roland. "Toward a Psychosociology of Contemporary Food Consumption," Pages 166–73 in *Food and Drink in History: Selections from the Annales, économies,* sociétés, civilisations, volume 5. Edited by O. A. Ranum and R. Forster. Baltimore, Md.: Johns Hopkins University Press, 1979.

Bauer, Walter. *Pea (Vom Ackerwinkel): Text, Übersetzung und Erklärung.* Die Mischna: Text, Übersetzung und ausführliche Erklärung. Giessen: A. Töpelmann, 1914.

Baumgarten, Joseph M. "A Qumran Text with Agrarian Halakhah." *JQR* 86, no. 1/2 (1995): 1–8.

Becknell, Robert B. "Almsgiving, the Jewish Legacy of Justice and Mercy." Ph.D. diss., Miami University, 2000.

Beer, Georg, ed. *Faksimile-Ausgabe des Mischnacodex Kaufmann A 50*. The Hague, 1929 [repr. Jerusalem, 1968].

Beer, Michael. *Taste or Taboo: Dietary Choices in Antiquity.* Totnes, Devon: Prospect Books, 2010.

Beer, Moshe. "The Attitude of the Sages Toward Riding Horses [Hebrew]." *Cathedra* 60, no. 1 (1991): 17–35.

Ben Jehiel of Rome, Nathan Alexander Kohut, and Benjamin ben Immanuel Mussafia. *Aruch completum [Hebrew].* Vienna: Georg Brög, 1878.

Ben-David, Arye. *Talmudische Ökonomie: Die Wirtschaft des jüdischen Palästina zur Zeit der Mischna und des Talmud.* Hildesheim: Olms, 1974.

Ben-Eliyahu, Eyal, Yehudah Cohn, and Fergus Millar. *Handbook of Jewish Literature from Late Antiquity, 135–700 CE.* Oxford: Oxford University Press for the British Academy, 2012.

Benoit, Pierre, J.T. Milik, and R. de Vaux. *Les grottes de Murabba'ât.* Oxford: Clarendon Press, 1961.

Ben-Yehuda, Eliezer, Naphtali H. Tur-Sinai, and M. H. Segal. *A Complete Dictionary of Ancient and Modern Hebrew: Thesaurus totius Hebraitatis et veteris et recentioris [Hebrew].* 8 vols. New York and London: Thomas Yoseloff, 1960.

Bergmann, Judah. *Ha-Tsedakah be-Yisra'el [Hebrew].* Jerusalem: R. Mas, 1944; repr. 1974.

Betz, Hans Dieter and Adela Yarbro Collins. *The Sermon on the Mount: A Commentary on the Sermon on the Mount, Including the Sermon on the Plain (Matthew 5:3–7:27 and Luke 6:20–49).* Hermeneia: A Critical and Historical Commentary on the Bible. Minneapolis, Minn.: Fortress Press, 1995.

Birley, A. R. "Constitutio Antoniniana," in *Brill's New Pauly: Encyclopaedia of the Ancient World.* Edited by H. Cancik, H. Schneider, C. F. Salazar, D. E. Orton, and A. F. v. Pauly. Leiden and Boston: Brill, 2002.

Bokser, Baruch M. *The Origins of the Seder: The Passover Rite and Early Rabbinic Judaism.* Berkeley: University of California Press, 1984.

Bolchazy, Ladislaus J. "From Xenophobia to Altruism: Homeric and Roman Hospitality." *Ancient World* 1, no. 1 (1978): 45–64.

Bolchazy, Ladislaus J. *Hospitality in Early Rome: Livy's Concept of its Humanizing Force.* Chicago, Ill.: Ares Publishers, 1977.

Bolkestein, Hendrik. *Wohltätigkeit und armenpflege im vorchristlichen altertum; ein beitrag zum problem "moral und gesellschaft."* Utrecht: A. Oosthoek, 1939.

Bonz, Marianne Palmer. "The Jewish Donor Inscriptions from Aphrodisias: Are They Both Third-Century, and Who Are the Theosebeis?" *HSCP* 96 (1994): 281–99.

Bourdieu, Pierre, *The Logic of Practice.* Stanford, Calif.: Stanford University Press, 1990.

Boustan, Ra'anan S. "Jewish Veneration of the 'Special Dead' in Late Antiquity and Beyond," in *Saints and Sacred Matter: The Cult of Relics in Byzantium and Beyond.*

Edited by C. Hahn and H. Klein. Washington, D.C.: Dumbarton Oaks Papers, forthcoming.

Bowersock, G. W., Peter R. L. Brown, and Oleg Grabar, eds. *Late Antiquity: A Guide to the Postclassical World*. Harvard University Press Reference Library. Cambridge, Mass.: Belknap Press of Harvard University Press, 1999.

Bradley, K. R. *Slavery and Society at Rome*. Key Themes in Ancient History. Cambridge and New York: Cambridge University Press, 1994.

Brand, Yehoshua. *Ceramics in Talmudic Literature [Hebrew]*. Jerusalem: Mosad ha-Rav Kuk, 1953.

Braudel, Fernand. *The Mediterranean and the Mediterranean World in the Age of Philip II*. London: Collins, 1972.

Braund, Susanna Morton. *Juvenal and Persius*. Loeb Classical Library. Cambridge, Mass.: Harvard University Press, 2004.

Braund, Susanna Morton. *Juvenal: Satires: Book I*. Cambridge Greek and Latin Classics. Cambridge and New York: Cambridge University Press, 1996.

Bridge, Steven L. "To Give or Not to Give? Deciphering the Saying of Didache 1.6." *JECS* 5, no. 4 (1997): 555–568.

Bringmann, Klaus. "The King as Benefactor: Some Remarks on Ideal Kingship in the Age of Hellenism," Pages 7–24 in *Images and Ideologies: Self-Definition in the Hellenistic World*. Edited by A. Bulloch, E. S. Gruen, A. A. Long, and A. Stewart. Berkeley: University of California Press, 1993.

Brooks, Roger. *Support for the Poor in the Mishnaic Law of Agriculture: Tractate Peah*. BJS 43. Chico, Calif.: Scholars Press, 1983.

Broshi, Magen. *Bread, Wine, Walls and Scrolls*. London: Sheffield Academic Press, 2001.

Brown, Peter. *Poverty and Leadership in the Later Roman Empire*. The Menahem Stern Jerusalem Lectures. Hanover, N.H.: University Press of New England, 2002.

Brown, Peter. "Remembering the Poor and the Aesthetic of Society." *Journal of Interdisciplinary History* 35, no. 3 (2005): 513–22.

Brown, Peter. "The Study of Elites in Late Antiquity." *Arethusa* 33, no. 3 (2000): 321–46.

Brown, Peter. *Through the Eye of a Needle: Wealth, the Fall of Rome, and the Making of Christianity in the West, 350–550 AD*. Princeton, N.J.: Princeton University Press, 2012.

Broyde, Michael J. "The Giving of Charity in Jewish Law: For What Purpose and Toward What Goal?," Pages 241–74 in *Toward a Renewed Ethic of Jewish Philanthropy*. Edited by Y. Prager. New York: Yeshiva University Press, 2010.

Brunt, P. A. *Social Conflicts in the Roman Republic*. London: Chatto and Windus, 1971.

Buber, Salomon. *Midrasch Echa Rabbati: Sammlung aggadischer Auslegungen der Klagelieder [Hebrew]*. Hildsheim: Olms, 1899; repr. 1967.

Buchanan, Allen. "Charity, Justice, and the Idea of Moral Progress," Pages 98–116 in *Giving: Western Ideas of Philanthropy*. Edited by J. B. Schneewind. Bloomington, Ind.: Indiana University Press, 1996.

Büchler, Adolf. *The Political and the Social Leaders of the Jewish Community of Sepphoris in the Second and Third Centuries*. London: Jews' College, 1909.

Cancik, Hubert, Helmuth Schneider, Christine F. Salazar, David E. Orton, and August Friedrich von Pauly, eds. *Brill's New Pauly: Encyclopaedia of the Ancient World*. Leiden and Boston: Brill, 2002.

Caner, Daniel. *Wandering, Begging Monks: Spiritual Authority and the Promotion of Monasticism in Late Antiquity*. Transformation of the Classical Heritage. Berkeley: University of California Press, 2002.

Charlesworth, James H. "Community Organization in the Rule of the Community," in *Encyclopedia of the Dead Sea Scrolls*. Edited by L. H. Schiffman and J. C. VanderKam. New York: Oxford University Press, 2000.

Charlesworth, James H., ed. *The Old Testament Pseudepigrapha*. 2 vols. New York: Doubleday, 1983–1985.

Coase, R. H. *The Firm, The Market, and the Law*. Chicago, Ill.: University of Chicago Press, 1988.

Cody, Aelred. "The Didache: An English Translation," Pages 3–14 in *The Didache in Context: Essays on its Text, History, and Transmission*. Edited by C. N. Jefford. Supplements to Novum Testamentum 77. Leiden and New York: E.J. Brill, 1995.

Cohen, Aryeh. *Justice in the City: An Argument from the Sources of Rabbinic Judaism*. Boston: Academic Studies Press, 2011.

Cohen, Chaim E. "Masculine Nouns with Prefixed t- in Tannaitic Hebrew [Hebrew]," Pages 2:166–82 in *Sha'are lashon: Studies in Hebrew, Aramaic and Jewish Languages Presented to Moshe Bar-Asher [Hebrew]*. Edited by A. Maman, S. E. Fassberg, and Y. Breuer. Jerusalem: Bialik Institute, 2007.

Cohen, Mark R. *Poverty and Charity in the Jewish Community of Medieval Egypt*. Jews, Christians, and Muslims from the Ancient to the Modern World. Princeton, N.J.: Princeton University Press, 2005.

Cohen, Mark R. *The Voice of the Poor in the Middle Ages: An Anthology of Documents from the Cairo Geniza*. Princeton, N.J.: Princeton University Press, 2005.

Cohen, Shaye J. D. *The Beginnings of Jewishness: Boundaries, Varieties, Uncertainties*. Hellenistic Culture and Society 31. Berkeley: University of California Press, 1999.

Cohen, Shaye J. D. "Judaean Legal Tradition and the Halakha of the Mishnah," Pages 121–43 in *The Cambridge Companion to the Talmud and Rabbinic Literature*. Edited by C. E. Fonrobert and M. S. Jaffee. New York: Cambridge University Press, 2007.

Cohen, Shaye J. D. "The Place of the Rabbi in Jewish Society of the Second Century," Pages 157–71 in *The Galilee in Late Antiquity*. Edited by L. I. Levine. New York and Jerusalem: Jewish Theological Seminary of America, 1992.

Cohen, Shaye J. D. "The Rabbi in Second-Century Jewish Society," Pages 922–90 in *The Cambridge History of Judaism: Volume 3: The Early Roman Period*. Edited by W. Horbury, W. D. Davies, and J. Sturdy. Cambridge: Cambridge University Press, 1999.

Cohen, Shaye J. D., ed. *The Synoptic Problem in Rabbinic Literature*. BJS 326. Providence, R.I.: Brown Judaic Studies, 2000.

Cohn, Naftali S. *The Memory of the Temple and the Making of the Rabbis*. Divinations: Rereading Late Ancient Religion. Philadelphia: University of Pennsylvania Press, 2013.

Collins, Adela Yarbro. *Mark: A Commentary*. Hermeneia: A Critical and Historical Commentary on the Bible. Minneapolis, Minn.: Fortress Press, 2007.

Constantelos, Demetrios J. *Byzantine Philanthropy and Social Welfare*. New Rochelle, N.Y.: A.D. Caratzas, 1991.

Cooper, Kate. *The Fall of the Roman Household*. Cambridge: Cambridge University Press, 2007.

Corbier, Mireille. "The Broad Bean and the Moray: Social Hierarchies and Food in Rome," Pages 128–40 in *Food: A Culinary History from Antiquity to the Present*. Edited by J. L. Flandrin, M. Montanari, and A. Sonnenfeld. New York: Columbia University Press, 1999.

Corbier, Mireille. "Coinage, Society and Economy," Pages 393–439 in *Cambridge Ancient History, Volume 12*. Edited by A. K. Bowman, P. Garnsey, and A. Cameron. Cambridge: Cambridge University Press, 2005.

Cotton, Hannah and Hanan Eshel. "Hever, Nahal," Pages 1:357–61 in *Encyclopedia of the Dead Sea Scrolls*. Edited by L. H. Schiffman and J. C. VanderKam. New York: Oxford University Press. 2000.

Cotton, Hannah M., Leah Di Segni, Werner Eck, Benjamin Isaac, Alla Kushnir-Stein, Haggai Misgav, Jonathan Price, and Ada Yardeni, eds. *Corpus Inscriptionum Iudaeae/Palaestinae: Multi-lingual Corpus of the Inscriptions from Alexander to Muhammed*. Berlin and New York: De Gruyter, 2010.

Countryman, L. William. "How Many Baskets Full: Mark 8:14–21 and the Value of Miracles in Mark." *CBQ* 47, no. 4 (1985): 643–55.

Crook, Zeba A. "Fictive Giftship and Fictive Friendship in Greco-Roman Society," Pages 61–76 in *The Gift in Antiquity*. Edited by M. L. Satlow. Chichester, West Sussux, UK: Wiley-Blackwell, 2013.

Danby, Herbert. *The Mishnah: Translated from the Hebrew with Introduction and Brief Explanatory Notes*. London: Oxford University Press, 1933.

Danker, Frederick W., William Arndt, and Walter Bauer. *A Greek-English Lexicon of the New Testament and Other Early Christian Literature (= BDAG)*. Chicago, Ill.: University of Chicago Press, 2000.

Dar, Shimon. "Food and Archaeology in Romano-Byzantine Palestine," Pages 326–35 in *Food in Antiquity*. Edited by J. Wilkins. Exeter: University of Exeter Press, 1995.

Daremberg, Charles and Edm Saglio, eds. *Dictionnaire des antiquites*. 5 vols. Paris: Hachette, 1877.

Davies, W. D. and Dale C. Allison. *A Critical and Exegetical Commentary on the Gospel According to Saint Matthew*. The International Critical Commentary on the Holy Scriptures of the Old and New Testaments. Edinburgh: T. & T. Clark, 1988.

Deming, Will. *Paul on Marriage and Celibacy: The Hellenistic Background of 1 Corinthians 7*. SNTSMS 83. Cambridge and New York: Cambridge University Press, 1995.

Dothan, M., *Hammath Tiberias*. Ancient Synagogues Studies. Jerusalem: Israel Exploration Society, 1983.

Douglas, Mary. "Deciphering a Meal." *Daedalus* 101, no. 1 (1972): 61–81.

Douglas, Mary. "Foreword: *No Free Gifts*," Pages vii-xviii in *The Gift: The Form and Reason for Exchange in Archaic Societies*. By Marcel Mauss, trans. W. D. Halls. New York and London: W. W. Norton, 1990.

Downs, David J. *The Offering of the Gentiles: Paul's Collection for Jerusalem in its Chronological, Cultural, and Cultic Contexts*. WUNT 248. Tübingen: Mohr Siebeck, 2008.

Draper, Jonathan A. "Didache," Page 2:120 in *The New Interpreter's Dictionary of the Bible*. Edited by K. D. Sakenfeld. Nashville, Tenn.: Abingdon, 2006.

Drinkwater, John. "Maximus to Diocletian and the 'Crisis,'" Pages 28–66 in *Cambridge Ancient History, Volume 12*. Edited by A. K. Bowman, P. Garnsey, and A. Cameron. Cambridge: Cambridge University Press, 2005.

Duncan-Jones, Richard. *The Economy of the Roman Empire: Quantitative Studies*. Cambridge and New York: Cambridge University Press, 1982.

Eggertsson, Thráinn. *Economic Behavior and Institutions*. Cambridge and New York: Cambridge University Press, 1990.

Eisenstadt, S. N. "Institutionalization and Change." *American Sociological Review* 29, no. 2 (1964): 235–247.

Eisenstadt, S. N. "Social Institutions: The Concept," in *International Encyclopedia of the Social Sciences*. Edited by D. L. Sills. New York: Macmillan, 1968.

Eliav, Yaron Z. "Viewing the Sculptural Environment: Shaping the Second Commandment," Volume 3, pages 411–33 in *The Talmud Yerushalmi and Graeco-Roman Culture*. Edited by P. Schäfer. Tübingen: Mohr Siebeck, 1998–2002.

Ellis, Simon. *Roman Housing*. London: Duckworth, 2000.

Ellis, Simon. "Shedding Light on Late Roman Housing," Pages 283–302 in *Housing in Late Antiquity: From Palaces to Shops*. Edited by L. Lavan, L. Özgenel, and A. C. Sarantis. Late Antique Archaeology 3.2. Leiden and Boston: Brill, 2007.

Emerson, Ralph Waldo. "Gifts," Pages 533–38 in *Essays & Lectures*. Edited by R. W. Emerson and J. Porte. New York: Viking Press, 1844 [repr. 1983].

Epstein, Isadore, ed. *The Babylonian Talmud: Translated into English with Notes, Glossary and Indices*. London: Soncino Press, 1935–1952.

Even-Shoshan, Avraham and Moshe Azar. *Milon Even-Shoshan: meḥudash u-meʿudkan li-shenot ha-alpayim be-shishah kerakhim be-hishtatfut ḥever anshe madaʿ* [Hebrew]. Tel Aviv: ha-Milon he-ḥadash: Yorshe ha-meḥaber, 2003.

Falk, Ze'ev W. *Introduction to Jewish Law of the Second Commonwealth*. 2 vols. Leiden: E. J. Brill, 1972–1978.

Feliks, Jehuda and Shimon Gibson. "Agricultural Land-Management Methods and Implements in Ancient Erez Israel," Pages 1:471–86 in *Encyclopaedia Judaica*, 2nd ed. Edited by F. Skolnik and M. Berenbaum. Detroit, Mich.: Macmillan Reference and Keter Publishing House, 2007.

Feliks, Yehuda. *Agriculture in Erets-Israel in the Period of the Bible and Talmud* [Hebrew]. Jerusalem: Reuven Mas, 1990.

Feliks, Yehuda. *Plants and Animals of the Mishna* [Hebrew]. Jerusalem: Institute for Mishna Research, 1982.

Fine, Steven. *This Holy Place: On the Sanctity of the Synagogue during the Greco-Roman Period*. Notre Dame, Ind.: Notre Dame University Press, 1997.

Finkelstein, Aryay B. "Julian among Jews, Christians and 'Hellenes' in Antioch: Jewish Practice as a Guide to 'Hellenes' and a Goad to Christians." Ph.D. diss., Harvard University, 2011.

Finkelstein, Louis and Saul Horovitz, eds. *Sifre on Deuteronomy* [Hebrew]. 2nd. ed. New York: Jewish Theological Seminary of America, 1969; repr. 2001.

Finley, M. I. *The Ancient Economy*. Sather Classical Lectures 43. Berkeley: University of California Press, 1999.

Finley, M. I. *The World of Odysseus*. Pelican Books. Harmondsworth and New York: Penguin, 1979.

Finn, Richard. *Almsgiving in the Later Roman Empire: Christian Promotion and Practice (313–450)*. Oxford and New York: Oxford University Press, 2006.

Finn, Richard. "Portraying the Poor: Descriptions of Poverty in Christian Texts from the Late Roman Empire," Pages 130–44 in *Poverty in the Roman World*. Edited by M. Atkins and R. Osborne. Cambridge and New York: Cambridge University Press, 2006.

Flesher, Paul V. M. "Slaves, Israelites, and the System of the Mishnah," Pages 101–9 in *Literature of Early Rabbinic Judaism: Issues in Talmudic Redaction and Interpretation*. Edited by A. J. Avery-Peck. Lanham, Md.: University Press of America, 1989.

Flesher, Paul V. M. *Oxen, Women or Citizens? Slaves in the System of the Mishnah.* BJS 143. Atlanta, Ga.: Scholars Press, 1988.

Ford, J. N. "Another Look at the Mandaic Incantation Bowl BM 91715." *JANES* 29 (2002): 31–47.

Fraade, Steven D. *Legal Fictions: Studies of Law and Narrative in the Discursive Worlds of Ancient Jewish Sectarians and Sages.* Supplements to the Journal for the Study of Judaism 147. Leiden and Boston: Brill, 2011.

Fraade, Steven D. "Local Jewish Leadership in Roman Palestine: The Case of the *Parnas* in Early Rabbinic Sources in Light of Extra-Rabbinic Evidence," Pages 157–75 in *Halakhah in Light of Epigraphy.* Edited by A. I. Baumgarten, H. Eshel, R. Katzoff, and S. Tzoref. Journal of Ancient Judaism. Supplements 3. Göttingen: Vandenhoeck & Ruprecht, 2011.

Frankel, Rafael, Shmuel Avitsur, and Etan Ayalon. *History and Technology of Olive Oil in the Holy Land.* Arlington, Va., and Tel Aviv: Olearius Editions and Eretz Israel Museum, Tel Aviv, 1994.

Frankel, Rafi. *Wine and Oil Production in Antiquity in Israel and Other Mediterranean Countries.* JSOT/ASOR Monograph Series 10. Sheffield, England: Sheffield Academic Press, 1999.

Freidenreich, David M. *Foreigners and their Food: Constructing Otherness in Jewish, Christian, and Islamic Law.* Berkeley: University of California Press, 2011.

Frey, Jörg. "Essenes," Pages 599–602 in *The Eerdmans Dictionary of Early Judaism.* Edited by J. J. Collins and D. C. Harlow. Grand Rapids, Mich.: William B. Eerdmans, 2010.

Friedman, Shamma. *Pesah Rishon: Synoptic Parallels of Mishna and Tosefta [Hebrew].* Ramat Gan: Bar-Ilan University, 2002.

Friedman, Shamma. "The Primacy of Tosefta to Mishnah in Synoptic Parallels," Pages 99–121 in *Introducing Tosefta: Textual, Intratextual, and Intertextual Studies.* Edited by H. Fox, T. Meacham, and D. Kriger. Hoboken, N.J.: KTAV, 1999.

Frisch, Ephraim. *An Historical Survey of Jewish Philanthropy: From the Earliest Times to the Nineteenth Century.* New York: Macmillan, 1924.

Galor, Katharina. "Domestic Architecture," Pages 420–39 in *The Oxford Handbook of Jewish Daily Life in Roman Palestine.* Edited by C. Hezser. Oxford: Oxford University Press, 2010.

Galor, Katharina. "Domestic Architecture in Galilee and Golan During the Roman and Byzantine Periods: First Century B.C. to Seventh Century A.D." Ph.D. diss., Brown University, 1996.

Galor, Katharina. "Domestic Architecture in Roman and Byzantine Galilee and Golan." *NEA* 66, no. 1/2 (2003): 44–57.

Galor, Katharina. "Jewellery: The Archaeological Evidence," Pages 393–402 in *The Oxford Handbook of Jewish Daily Life in Roman Palestine.* Edited by C. Hezser. Oxford: Oxford University Press, 2010.

Galor, Katharina. "The Roman-Byzantine Dwelling in the Galilee and the Golan: 'House' or 'Apartment'?," Pages 109–24 in *Miscellanea Mediterranea.* Edited by R. R. Holloway. Providence, R.I.: Brown University, 2000.

Ganley, William T. "Poverty and Charity: Early Analytical Conflicts between Institutional Economics and Neoclassicism." *Journal of Economic Issues* 32, no. 2 (1998): 433–440.

Gardner, Gregg. "Astrology in the Talmud: An Analysis of Bavli Shabbat 156," Pages 314–38 in *Heresy and Identity in Late Antiquity*. Edited by E. Iricinschi and H. Zellentin. TSAJ 119. Tübingen: Mohr Siebeck, 2008.

Gardner, Gregg. "Jewish Leadership and Hellenistic Civic Benefaction in the Second Century B.C.E.." *JBL* 126, no. 2 (2007): 327–43.

Gardner, Gregg E. "Charity Wounds: Gifts to the Poor in Early Rabbinic Judaism," Pages 173–88 in *The Gift in Antiquity*. Edited by M. L. Satlow. Wiley-Blackwell, 2013.

Gardner, Gregg E. "Competitive Giving in the Third Century CE: Early Rabbinic Approaches to Greco-Roman Civic Benefaction," Pages 81–92 in *Religious Competition in the Third Century C.E.: Jews, Christians, and the Greco-Roman World*. Edited by N. DesRosiers, J. D. Rosenblum, and L. Vuong. Journal of Ancient Judaism: Supplements. Vandenhoeck & Ruprecht, 2014.

Gardner, Gregg E. "Cornering Poverty: Mishnah Pe'ah, Tosefta Pe'ah, and the Reimagination of Society in Late Antiquity," Pages 1:205–16 in *Envisioning Judaism: Studies in Honor of Peter Schäfer on the Occasion of his Seventieth Birthday* Edited by R. S. Boustan, K. Herrmann, R. Leicht, A. Y. Reed, and G. Veltri. Tübingen: Mohr Siebeck, 2013.

Gardner, Gregg E. "Giving to the Poor in Early Rabbinic Judaism." Ph.D. diss., Princeton University, 2009.

Gardner, Gregg E. "Let Them Eat Fish: Food for the Poor in Early Rabbinic Judaism." *JSJ* 45, no. 2 (2014): 250–70.

Gardner, Gregg E. "Who is Rich? The Poor in Early Rabbinic Judaism." *JQR* 104, no. 4 (in press): 515–36.

Gardner, Gregg and Kevin L. Osterloh, eds. *Antiquity in Antiquity: Jewish and Christian Pasts in the Greco-Roman World*. TSAJ 123. Tübingen: Mohr Siebeck, 2008.

Garnsey, Peter. *Food and Society in Classical Antiquity*. Key Themes in Ancient History. Cambridge and New York: Cambridge University Press, 1999.

Garnsey, Peter and Walter Scheidel. *Cities, Peasants, and Food in Classical Antiquity: Essays in Social and Economic History*. Cambridge and New York: Cambridge University Press, 1998.

Garnsey, Peter, Tom Gallant, and Dominic Rathbone. "Thessaly and the Grain Supply of Rome during the Second Century B.C." *JRS* 74 (1984): 30–44.

Gartner, Yaakov. "The Third Sabbath Meal: Halakhic and Historical Aspects [Hebrew]." *Sidra* 6 (1990): 5–24.

Gilat, Yitzhak D., *Studies in the Development of the Halakha [Hebrew]*. Ramat Gan, Israel: Bar-Ilan University Press, 1992.

Gnuse, Robert. "Debt, Debtor," Pages 2:76–77 in *The New Interpreter's Dictionary of the Bible*. Edited by K. D. Sakenfeld. 5 vols. Nashville, Tenn.: Abingdon Press. 2006–2009.

Goffman, Erving. *Relations in Public: Microstudies of the Public Order*. New York: Basic Books, 1971.

Goldenberg, Robert. "The Place of the Sabbath in Rabbinic Judaism," Pages 31–44 in *The Sabbath in Jewish and Christian Traditions*. Edited by T. C. Eskenazi, D. J. Harrington, and W. H. Shea. New York: Crossroad, 1991.

Goodblatt, David. "Towards the Rehabilitation of Talmudic History," Pages 31–44 in *History of Judaism: The Next Ten Years*. Edited by B. M. Bokser. Chico, Calif.: Scholars Press, 1980.

Goodman, Martin. "Kosher Olive Oil in Antiquity," Pages 227–45 in *Tribute to Geza Vermes: Essays on Jewish and Christian Literature and History*. Edited by P. R. Davies and R. T. White. Sheffield: Sheffield Academic Press, 1990.

Goodman, Martin. "The Pilgrimage Economy of Jerusalem in the Second Temple Era," Pages 69–76 in *Jerusalem: Its Sanctity and Centrality to Judaism, Christianity, and Islam*. Edited by L. I. Levine. New York: Continuum, 1999.

Goodman, Martin. *State and Society in Roman Galilee, A.D. 132–212*. London and Portland, Ore.: Vallentine Mitchell, 2000.

Goodman, Martin and Philip Alexander, eds. *Rabbinic Texts and the History of Late-Roman Palestine. Proceedings of the British Academy*. Oxford and New York: Oxford University Press for the British Academy, 2010.

Goody, Jack. *Cooking, Cuisine and Class: A Study in Comparative Sociology*. Cambridge: Cambridge University Press, 1982.

Gouldner, Alvin W. "The Norm of Reciprocity: A Preliminary Statement." *American Sociological Review* 25, no. 2 (1960): 161–78.

Gray, Alyssa. "Redemptive Almsgiving and the Rabbis of Late Antiquity." *JSQ* 18, no. 2 (2011): 144–84.

Gray, Alyssa M. "The Formerly Wealthy Poor: From Empathy to Ambivalence in Rabbinic Literature of Late Antiquity." *AJSR* 33, no. 1 (2009): 101–33.

Grey, Cam. *Constructing Communities in the Late Roman Countryside*. Cambridge and New York: Cambridge University Press, 2011.

Grey, Cam and Anneliese Parkin. "Controlling the Urban Mob: The *colonatus perpetuus* of *CTh* 14.18.1." *Phoenix* 57, no. 3/4 (2003): 284–99.

Grushcow, Lisa. *Writing the Wayward Wife: Rabbinic Interpretations of Sotah*. AGJU 62. Leiden and Boston: Brill, 2006.

Guggenheimer, Heinrich W. *The Jerusalem Talmud: First Order, Zeraim: Tractates Peah and Demay*. Studia Judaica 19. Berlin and New York: Walter de Gruyter, 2000.

Gutsfeld, Andreas. "Vegetables," in *Brill's New Pauly: Encyclopaedia of the Ancient World*. Edited by H. Cancik, H. Schneider, C. F. Salazar, D. E. Orton, and A. F. v. Pauly. Leiden and Boston: Brill, 2002.

Hamel, Gildas. "Poverty and Charity," Pages 308–24 in *The Oxford Handbook of Jewish Daily Life in Roman Palestine*. Edited by C. Hezser. Oxford: Oxford University Press, 2010.

Hamel, Gildas H. *Poverty and Charity in Roman Palestine, First Three Centuries C.E.* Near Eastern Studies 23. Berkeley: University of California Press, 1990.

Hamilton, David B. "Institutional Economics and Consumption," Pages 2:113–36 in *Evolutionary Economics*. Edited by M. R. Tool. Armonk, N.Y.: M.E. Sharpe, 1988.

Hammer, Reuven. *Sifre: A Tannaitic Commentary on the Book of Deuteronomy*. Yale Judaica Series 24. New Haven, Conn.: Yale University Press, 1986.

Hands, A. R. *Charities and Social Aid in Greece and Rome*. London: Thames & Hudson, 1968.

Harper, G. M. Jr. "Village Administration in the Roman Province of Syria." *Yale Classical Studies* 1 (1928): 102–68.

Harries, Jill. "Courts and the Judicial System," Pages 85–101 in *The Oxford Handbook of Jewish Daily Life in Roman Palestine*. Edited by C. Hezser. Oxford: Oxford University Press, 2010.

Harris, Jay M. "Midrash Halachah," Pages 336–68 in *The Cambridge History of Judaism: Volume Four: The Late Roman-Rabbinic Period*. Edited by S. T. Katz. Cambridge: Cambridge University Press, 2006.

Hasan-Rokem, Galit. "An Almost Invisible Presence: Multilingual Puns in Rabbinic Literature," Pages 222–42 in *The Cambridge Companion to the Talmud and Rabbinic Literature*. Edited by C. E. Fonrobert and M. S. Jaffee. New York: Cambridge University Press, 2007.

Hauptman, Judith. "How Old is the Haggadah?" *Judaism* 51, no. 1 (2002): 5–18.

Hauptman, Judith. *Rereading the Mishnah: A New Approach to Ancient Jewish Texts*. TSAJ 109. Tübingen: Mohr, 2005.

Hauptman, Judith. *Rereading the Rabbis: A Woman's Voice*. Boulder, Colo.: Westview Press, 1998.

Hauptman, Judith. "The Tosefta as a Commentary on an Early Mishnah." *Jewish Studies Internet Journal* 4 (2005): 109–32.

Hayes, Christine. "The 'Other' in Rabbinic Literature," Pages 243–70 in *The Cambridge Companion to the Talmud and Rabbinic Literature*. Edited by C. E. Fonrobert and M. S. Jaffee. New York: Cambridge University Press, 2007.

Hellinger, Michael. "Charity in Talmudic and Rabbinic Literature: A Legal, Literary, and Historical Analysis [Hebrew]." Ph.D. diss., Bar-Ilan University, 1999.

Hellinger, Michael. "Quppat ha-tzedakah ve-ha'aniyyim ha-machzarim al ha-petachim [Hebrew]." *Shema'tin* 174 (2009): 93–100.

Hempel, Charlotte. *The Laws of the Damascus Document: Sources, Tradition and Redaction*. STDJ 29. Leiden: Brill, 1988.

Hezser, Catherine. "Correlating Literary, Epigraphical, and Archaeological Sources," Pages 9–27 in *The Oxford Handbook of Jewish Daily Life in Roman Palestine*. Edited by C. Hezser. Oxford: Oxford University Press, 2010.

Hezser, Catherine. "The Impact of Household Slaves on the Jewish Family in Roman Palestine." *JSJ* 34, no. 4 (2003): 375–424.

Hezser, Catherine. *Jewish Slavery in Antiquity*. Oxford and New York: Oxford University Press, 2005.

Hezser, Catherine, ed. *The Oxford Handbook of Jewish Daily Life in Roman Palestine*. Oxford: Oxford University Press, 2010.

Hezser, Catherine. *The Social Structure of the Rabbinic Movement in Roman Palestine*. TSAJ 66. Tübingen: Mohr Siebeck, 1997.

Himmelfarb, Martha. *Tours of Hell: An Apocalyptic Form in Jewish and Christian Literature*. Philadelphia: University of Pennsylvania Press, 1983.

Hirschfeld, Yizhar. *The Palestinian Dwelling in the Roman-Byzantine Period*. Jerusalem: Franciscan Printing Press and Israel Exploration Society, 1995.

Ho, Ahuva. *Sedeq and Sedaqah in the Hebrew Bible*. American University Studies, Series VII, Theology and Religion 78. New York: P. Lang, 1991.

Holman, Susan R. *The Hungry are Dying: Beggars and Bishops in Roman Cappadocia*. Oxford Studies in Historical Theology. New York: Oxford University Press, 2001.

Hopkins, Keith. "Slavery in Classical Antiquity," Pages 166–91 in *Caste and Race: Comparative Approaches*. Edited by A. V. S. De Reuck and J. Knight. London: Churchill, 1968.

Horn, Robert C. "Use of the Greek New Testament." *Lutheran Quarterly* 1, no. 3 (1949): 294–305.

Hornblower, Simon and Antony Spawforth. *The Oxford Classical Dictionary*. Oxford and New York: Oxford University Press, 2003.

Horovitz, H. S. and I. A. Rabin, eds., *Mechilta d'Rabbi Ismael [Hebrew]*. 2nd. ed., 1931; repr. Jerusalem: Shalem Books, 1997.

Hort, F. "A Note by the Late Dr Hort on the Words." *JTS* 10, no. 40 (1909): 567–71.

Houtman, Alberdina. *Mishnah and Tosefta: A Synoptic Comparison of the Tractates Berakhot and Shebiit*. 2 vols., TSAJ 59. Tübingen: Mohr Siebeck, 1996.

Hurvitz, A. "The Biblical Roots of a Talmudic Term: The Early History of the Concept of tsedaqah [= charity, alms] [Hebrew]." *Language Studies* II-III (1987): 155–60.

Ilan, Z. and A. Izdarechet. "Arbel – An Ancient Town in the Eastern Lower Galilee [Hebrew]." *Qadmoniot* 22, no. 3–4 (1989): 111–17.

Ilan, Zvi. *Ancient Synagogues in Israel [Hebrew]*. Tel-Aviv: Ministry of Defence Israel, 1991.

Ilan, Zvi. "Meroth," Pages 3:1028–31 in *The New Encyclopedia of Archaeological Excavations in the Holy Land*. Edited by E. Stern. 5 vols. Jerusalem and New York: Israel Exploration Society, Carta and Simon & Schuster, 1993–2008.

Ilan, Zvi and Avraham Izdarechet. "Arbel." Pages 1:87–89 in *The New Encyclopedia of Archaeological Excavations in the Holy Land*. Edited by E. Stern. 5 vols. Jerusalem and New York: Israel Exploration Society, Carta and Simon & Schuster, 1993–2008.

Isaac, Benjamin, *The Limits of Empire: The Roman Army in the East (Revised Edition)*. Oxford: Clarendon Press, 1992.

Isaac, Benjamin. "Roman Administration and Urbanization," Pages 151–59 in *Greece and Rome in Eretz Israel: Collected Essays*. Edited by A. Kasher, U. Rappaport, and G. Fuks. Jerusalem: Yad Izhak Ben-Zvi, 1990.

Jaffee, Martin S. "Rabbinic Authorship as a Collective Enterprise," Pages 17–37 in *The Cambridge Companion to the Talmud and Rabbinic Literature*. Edited by C. E. Fonrobert and M. S. Jaffee. New York: Cambridge University Press, 2007.

Jaffee, Martin S. "A Rabbinic Ontology of the Written and Spoken Word: On Discipleship, Transformative Knowledge, and the Living Texts of Oral Torah." *JAAR* 65, no. 3 (1997): 525–49.

Jastrow, Marcus. *A Dictionary of the Targumim, the Talmud Babli and Yerushalmi, and the Midrashic Literature with an Index of Scriptural Quotations*. Reprint of Horev Press, Jerusalem. London and New York: Luzac & Co. and G. P. Putnams Sons, 1903.

Jensen, M. H. *Herod Antipas in Galilee: The Literary and Archaeological Sources on the Reign of Herod Antipas and Its Socio-Economic Impact on Galilee*. Tübingen: Mohr Siebeck, 2006.

Jeremias, Joachim. *Jerusalem in the Time of Jesus: An Investigation into Economic and Social Conditions During the New Testament Period*. Philadelphia: Fortress Press, 1969.

Jewish Publication Society. *Tanakh: The Holy Scriptures: The New JPS Translation According to the Traditional Hebrew Text*. Philadelphia: The Jewish Publication Society, 1985.

Jones, A. H. M. *The Greek City from Alexander to Justinian*. Oxford: The Clarendon Press, 1940.

Jones, A. H. M. "The Urbanization of Palestine." *JRS* 21 (1931): 78–85.

Jones, A. Heath. "Araunah," Page 1:230 in *The New Interpreter's Dictionary of the Bible*. Edited by K. D. Sakenfeld. Nashville, Tenn.: Abingdon, 2006.

Jongman, Willem M. "The Early Roman Empire: Consumption," Pages 592–617 in *The Cambridge Economic History of the Greco-Roman World.* Edited by W. Scheidel, I. Morris, and R. P. Saller. Cambridge and New York: Cambridge University Press, 2007.

Kahana, Menahem I., *Sifre on Numbers: An Annotated Edition [Hebrew].* 3 vols. Jerusalem: Hebrew University Magnes Press, 2011.

Kalmin, Richard. "The Formation and Character of the Babylonian Talmud," Pages 840–76 in *The Cambridge History of Judaism: Volume Four: The Late Roman-Rabbinic Period.* Edited by S. T. Katz. Cambridge: Cambridge University Press, 2006.

Kalmin, Richard. *Sages, Stories, Authors, and Editors in Rabbinic Babylonia.* BJS 300. Atlanta, Ga.: Scholars Press, 1994.

Kalmin, Richard L. *The Sage in Jewish Society in Late Antiquity.* London and New York: Routledge, 1999.

Kalmin, Richard Lee. "Holy Men, Rabbis and Demonic Sages in Late Antiquity," Pages 213–49 in *Jewish Culture and Society under the Christian Roman Empire.* Edited by R. L. Kalmin and S. Schwartz. Interdisciplinary Studies in Ancient Culture and Religion 3. Leuven: Peeters, 2003.

Kant, Immanuel. "Lectures on Ethics," in *The Cambridge Edition of the Works of Immanuel Kant.* Edited by P. L. Heath and J. B. Schneewind. Cambridge and New York: Cambridge University Press, 2001.

Katz, Jacob. *Tradition and Crisis: Jewish Society at the End of the Middle Ages.* New York: New York University Press, 1993.

Keane, Webb. "Semiotics and the Social Analysis of Material Things." *Language & Communication* 23 (2003): 409–25.

Kena'ani, Ya'akov. *Otsar ha-lashon ha-'Ivrit li-tekufoteha ha-shonot [Hebrew].* 18 vols. Jerusalem and Tel-Aviv: Masadah, 1960–1989.

Kerkeslager, Allen. "Jewish Pilgrimage and Jewish Identity in Hellenistic and Early Roman Egypt," Pages 99–225 in *Pilgrimage and Holy Space in Late Antique Egypt.* Edited by D. Frankfurter. Religions in the Graeco-Roman World 134. Leiden and Boston: Brill, 1998.

Kidd, Alan J. "Poor Relief," Page 4:220 in *The Oxford Encyclopedia of Economic History.* Edited by J. Mokyr. Oxford and New York: Oxford University Press, 2003.

Kindler, Arie. "A Bar Kokhba Coin used as a Charity Token." *Israel Numismatic Journal* 12 (1992–1993): 73–75, Plate 16.

Kindler, Arie. "Donations and Taxes in the Society of the Jewish Villages in Eretz Israel During the 3rd to 6th Centuries CE," Pages 55–59 in *Ancient Synagogues in Israel: Third-Seventh Century C.E.: Proceedings of Symposium, University of Hafia (i.e. Haifa), May 1987.* Edited by R. Hachlili. BAR International Series 499. Oxford: British Archaeological Reports, 1989.

Kloner, Amos. "Lead Weights of Bar Kokhba's Administration." *IEJ* 40, no. 1 (1990): 58–67.

Koenig, John. "Hospitality," Pages 3:299–301 in *The Anchor Bible Dictionary.* Edited by D. N. Freedman. New York: Doubleday. 1992.

Koenig, John. *New Testament Hospitality: Partnership with Strangers as Promise and Mission.* Overtures to Biblical Theology 17. Philadelphia: Fortress Press, 1985.

Kohl, Heinrich and Carl Watzinger. *Antike Synagogen in Galilaea.* Wissenschaftliche Veröffentlichung der Deutschen Orient-Gesellschaft 29. Osnabrück: O. Zeller, 1916 [repr. 1975].

Köhler, Ludwig, Walter Baumgartner, M. E. J. Richardson, and Johann Jakob Stamm. *The Hebrew and Aramaic Lexicon of the Old Testament*. Leiden and New York: E.J. Brill, 1994.

Komter, Aafke E., ed. *The Gift: An Interdisciplinary Perspective*. Amsterdam: Amsterdam University Press, 1996.

Komter, Aafke E. *Social Solidarity and the Gift*. Cambridge: Cambridge University Press, 2005.

Kovacs, David. *Euripidea*. Supplements to Mnemosyne. Leiden and New York: E.J. Brill, 1994.

Kraabel, A. Thomas. "The Diaspora Synagogue: Archaeological and Epigraphic Evidence Since Sukenik," Pages 1:95–126 in *Ancient Synagogues: Historical Analysis and Archaeological Discovery*. Edited by D. Urman and P. V. M. Flesher. StPB 47. Leiden and Boston: Brill, 1998.

Kraabel, A. Thomas, Eric M. Meyers, and James F. Strange, eds. *Ancient Synagogue Excavations at Khirbet Shema, Upper Galilee, Israel, 1970–1972*. The Annual of the American Schools of Oriental Research 42. Durham, N.C.: Published for the American Schools of Oriental Research by Duke University Press, 1976.

Kraemer, David. "Food," Pages 403–19 in *The Oxford Handbook of Jewish Daily Life in Roman Palestine*. Edited by C. Hezser. Oxford: Oxford University Press, 2010.

Kraft, Robert A. "Didache," Pages 2:197–98 in *The Anchor Bible Dictionary*. Edited by D. N. Freedman. New York: Doubleday, 1992.

Krauss, Samuel. *Griechische und lateinische Lehnwörter im Talmud, Midrasch und Targum*. 2 vols. Berlin: S. Calvary, 1898–1899.

Krauss, Samuel. *Kadmoniyot ha-Talmud 'al pi ha-ḥakirot yeha-tagliyot ha-ḥadashot [Hebrew]*. 2 vols. Odessa: Moriyah, 1914–1929 [repr. 1945].

Krauss, Samuel. *Talmudische Archäologie*. 3 vols. Leipzig: G. Fock, 1910–1912.

Kugler, Robert A. "Dead Sea Scrolls," Pages 520–24 in *The Eerdmans Dictionary of Early Judaism*. Edited by J. J. Collins and D. C. Harlow. Grand Rapids, Mich.: William B. Eerdmans, 2010.

Kulp, Joshua. "The Origins of the Seder and Haggadah." *Currents in Biblical Research* 4 (2005): 109–34.

Labendz, Jenny R. "The Book of Ben Sira in Rabbinic Literature." *AJSR* 30, no. 2 (2006): 347–92.

Lapin, Hayim. "The Construction of Households in the Mishnah," Pages 2:55–80 in *The Mishnah in Contemporary Perspective*. Edited by A. J. Avery-Peck and J. Neusner. Handbook of Oriental Studies 87. Leiden and Boston: Brill, 2006.

Lapin, Hayim. *Early Rabbinic Civil Law and the Social History of Roman Galilee: A Study of Mishnah Tractate Baba' Mesi'a'*. BJS 307. Atlanta, Ga.: Scholars Press, 1995.

Lapin, Hayim. *Economy, Geography, and Provincial History in Later Roman Palestine*. TSAJ 85. Tübingen: Mohr Siebeck, 2001.

Lapin, Hayim. "The Origins and Development of the Rabbinic Movement in the Land of Israel," Pages 206–29 in *The Cambridge History of Judaism: Volume Four: The Late Roman-Rabbinic Period*. Edited by S. T. Katz. Cambridge: Cambridge University Press, 2006.

Lapin, Hayim. "The Rabbinic Movement," Pages 58–84 in *The Cambridge Guide to Jewish History, Religion, and Culture*. Edited by J. R. Baskin and K. Seeskin. Cambridge and New York: Cambridge University Press, 2010.

Lapin, Hayim. "Rabbis and Cities in Later Roman Palestine: The Literary Evidence." *JJS* 1, no. 2 (1999): 187–207.

Lapin, Hayim. "Rabbis and Cities: Some Aspects of the Rabbinic Movement in its Graeco-Roman Environment," Pages 51–80 in *The Talmud Yerushalmi and Graeco-Roman Culture II*. Edited by P. Schäfer and C. Hezser. TSAJ 79. Tübingen: Mohr Siebeck, 2000.

Lauterbach, Jacob Z. *Mekhilta de-Rabbi Ishmael: A Critical Edition, Based on the Manuscripts and Early Editions*. Philadelphia: Jewish Publication Society, 2004.

Lawson, James. "The Roman Garden." *Greece & Rome* 19, no. 57 (1950): 97–105.

Lehmann, Joseph. "Assistance publique et privée d'après l'antique législation juive." *Revue des Études Juives* 35 (1897): i–xxxviii.

Leibner, Uzi. "Arts and Crafts, Manufacture and Production," Pages 264–96 in *The Oxford Handbook of Jewish Daily Life in Roman Palestine*. Edited by C. Hezser. Oxford: Oxford University Press, 2010.

Levi-Strauss, Claude. "The Culinary Triangle." *Partisan Review* 33, no. 4 (1966): 586–95.

Levi-Strauss, Claude. "The Principal of Reciprocity," Pages 84–94 in *Sociological Theory*. Edited by L. A. Coser and B. Rosenberg. New York: Macmillan, 1957.

Levine, Lee I. *The Ancient Synagogue: The First Thousand Years*. 2nd ed. New Haven, Conn., and London: Yale University Press, 2005.

Levine, Lee I. *The Rabbinic Class of Roman Palestine in Late Antiquity*. Jerusalem and New York: Yad Izhak Ben-Zvi and The Jewish Theological Seminary of America, 1989.

Lev-Tov, Justin. "'Upon What Meat doth this our Caesar feed...?' A Dietary Perspective on Hellenistic and Roman Influence in Palestine," Pages 420–46 in *Zeichen aus Text und Stein: Studien auf dem Weg zu einer Archäologie des Neuen Testaments*. Edited by S. Alkier, J. Zangenberg, K. Dronsch, and M. Schneider. Tübingen: Francke, 2003.

Lewis, Naphtali, Yigael Yadin, and Jonas C. Greenfield. *The Documents from the Bar Kokhba Period in the Cave of Letters*. Judean Desert Studies 2. Jerusalem: Israel Exploration Society, 1989.

Liddell, Henry George, Robert Scott, Henry Stuart Jones, and Roderick McKenzie. *A Greek-English Lexicon (Revised and Augmented Edition)*. Oxford and New York: Clarendon Press and Oxford University Press, 1996.

Lieberman, Saul. *The Tosefta: According to Codex Vienna, with Variants from Codex Erfurt, Genizah Mss. and Editio Princeps [Venice 1521] [Hebrew]*. 4 vols. New York: Jewish Theological Seminary of America, 1955–1988. [Reprint 1995–2002].

Lieberman, Saul. *Tosefta Ki-Fshutah: A Comprehensive Commentary on the Tosefta [Hebrew]*. 8 vols. New York: Jewish Theological Seminary of America, 1955–1988. [Reprint 1995–2002].

Lieberman, Saul. "Two Lexicographical Notes." *JBL* 65, no. 1 (1946): 67–72.

Lim, Timothy H., Philip S. Alexander, Emanuel Tov, and Noel B. Reynolds. *The Dead Sea Scrolls Electronic Reference Library*. Oxford, New York, and Leiden: Oxford University Press and Brill, 1997.

Ling, Timothy J. M. *The Judaean Poor and the Fourth Gospel*. SNTSMS 136. Cambridge and New York: Cambridge University Press, 2006.

Loewenberg, Frank M. *From Charity to Social Justice: The Emergence of Communal Institutions for the Support of the Poor in Ancient Judaism*. New Brunswick, N.J.: Transaction Publishers, 2001.

Loewenberg, Frank M. "On the Development of Philanthropic Institutions in Ancient Judaism: Provisions for Poor Travelers." *Nonprofit and Volunteer Sector Quarterly* 23, no. 3 (1994): 193–207.

Lohse, Eduard and Günter Mayer. *Die Tosefta, Seder I: Zeraim, 1.1: Berakot – Pea*. Rabbinische Texte. Stuttgart, Berlin, and Köln: Kohlhammer, 1999.

Longenecker, Bruce W. *Remember the Poor: Paul, Poverty, and the Greco-Roman World*. Grand Rapids, Mich.: Eerdmans, 2010.

Luz, Ulrich, James E. Crouch, and Helmut Koester. *Matthew 8–20: A Commentary*. Hermeneia. Minneapolis, Minn.: Fortress Press, 2001.

MacMullen, Ramsay. *Roman Social Relations, 50 B.C. to A.D. 284*. New Haven, Conn.: Yale University Press, 1974.

Magness, Jodi. "Heaven on Earth: Helios and the Zodiac Cycle in Ancient Palestinian Synagogues." *Dumbarton Oaks Papers* 59 (2005): 1–52.

Magness, Jodi. *Jerusalem Ceramic Chronology: Circa 200–800 CE*. JSOT/ASOR Monograph Series 9. Sheffield: JSOT Press, 1993.

Magness, Jodi. *Stone and Dung, Oil and Spit: Jewish Daily Life in the Time of Jesus*. Grand Rapids, Mich.: Eerdmans, 2011.

Mandel, Paul. "The Tosefta," Pages 316–35 in *The Cambridge History of Judaism: Volume Four: The Late Roman-Rabbinic Period*. Edited by S. T. Katz. Cambridge: Cambridge University Press, 2006.

Mantel, H. "The Date of the Usha Ordinances [Hebrew]." *Tarbiz* 34, no. 3 (1965): 281–283.

Marcus, Joel. *Mark: A New Translation with Introduction and Commentary*. Anchor Bible 27. New York: Doubleday, 2000.

Margulies, Mordecai. *Midrash Wayyikra Rabbah: A Critical Edition Based on Manuscripts and Genizah Fragments with Variants and Notes [Hebrew]*. New York and Jerusalem: Jewish Theological Seminary of America, 1953–1960 [repr. 1999].

Marmorstein, A. *The Doctrine of Merits in Old Rabbinical Literature*. London: Jews' College, 1920.

Marshall, Alfred. *Principles of Economics*. London: Macmillan, 1961.

Martin, Dale B. "Slavery and the Ancient Jewish Family," Pages 113–29 in *The Jewish Family in Antiquity*. Edited by S. J. D. Cohen. BJS 289. Atlanta, Ga.: Scholars Press, 1993.

Matthews, John. *The Journey of Theophanes: Travel, Business, and Daily Life in the Roman East*. New Haven, Conn., and London: Yale University Press, 2006.

Mauss, Marcel. *The Gift: The Form and Reason for Exchange in Archaic Societies*. Translated by W. D. Halls. New York: W.W. Norton, 1990.

Meir, Daniel. "The Parnas in Israel: Identity, Status, and Authority [Hebrew]." M.A. thesis, Hebrew University of Jerusalem, 2007.

Ménard, Claude and Mary M. Shirley, eds. *Handbook of New Institutional Economics*. Dordrecht: Springer, 2005.

Ménard, Claude and Mary M. Shirley. "Introduction," Pages 1–20 in *Handbook of New Institutional Economics*. Edited by C. Ménard and M. M. Shirley. Dordrecht: Springer, 2005.

Meszler, Joseph B. and Marc Lee Raphael. *Gifts for the Poor: Moses Maimonides' Treatise on Tzedakah*. Williamsburg, Va.: Department of Religion: The College of William and Mary, 2003.

Meyers, Eric M., A. Thomas Kraabel, and James F. Strange. *Ancient Synagogue Excavations at Khirbet Shema', Upper Galilee, Israel, 1970–1972*. The Annual of the American Schools of Oriental Research 42. Durham, N.C.: Published for the American Schools of Oriental Research by Duke University Press, 1976.

Meyers, Eric M., Ehud Netzer, and Carol L. Meyers. "Sepphoris: 'Ornament of All Galilee.'" *BA* 49, no. 1 (1986): 4–19.

Milgrom, Jacob. *The JPS Torah Commentary: Numbers*. Philadelphia: Jewish Publication Society, 1990.

Milgrom, Jacob. *Leviticus 17–22: A New Translation with Introduction and Commentary*. Anchor Bible 3A. New York: Doubleday, 2000.

Millar, Fergus. *The Roman Near East, 31 B.C. – A.D. 337*. Cambridge, Mass.: Harvard University Press, 1993.

Miller, Stuart S. *Sages and Commoners in Late Antique 'Erez Israel: A Philological Inquiry into Local Traditions in Talmud Yerushalmi*. TSAJ 111. Tübingen: Mohr Siebeck, 2006.

Miller, Stuart S. *Studies in the History and Traditions of Sepphoris*. SJLA 37. Leiden: E.J. Brill, 1984.

Mollat, Michel *The Poor in the Middle Ages: An Essay in Social History*. Translated by A. Goldhammer. New Haven, Conn., and London: Yale University Press, 1986.

Montefiore, C. G. and H. M. J. Loewe, eds. *A Rabbinic Anthology*. Cleveland, Ohio, and Philadelphia: Meridian Books and Jewish Publication Society of America, 1963.

Moore, George Foot. *Judaism in the First Centuries of the Christian Era*. Cambridge, Mass.: Harvard University Press, 1962.

Morley, Neville. "The Poor in the City of Rome," Pages 21–39 in *Poverty in the Roman World*. Edited by M. Atkins and R. Osborne. Cambridge and New York: Cambridge University Press, 2006.

Moscovitz, Leib. *Database of Sources and Parallels to the Yerushalmi [Hebrew]*. Available at http://www.biu.ac.il/js/tl/yerushalmi/. Bar-Ilan University, 2008.

Nacht, Yaacov. "Ha-parnas be-yisrael [Hebrew]." *Sinai* 12 (1942): 263–85.

Narkis, M. "The Snuff-Shovel as a Jewish Symbol." *JPOS* 15, no. 1–2 (1935): 14–28.

Nelson, Richard D. "Araunah (Person)," Page 1:353 in *The Anchor Bible Dictionary*. Edited by D. N. Freedman. New York: Doubleday, 1992.

Neusner, Jacob. *The Economics of the Mishnah*. Chicago, Ill.: Chicago University Press, 1990.

Neusner, Jacob. *A History of the Mishnaic Law of Appointed Times: Part One, Shabbat*. SJLA 34. Leiden: Brill, 1981.

Neusner, Jacob. *A History of the Mishnaic Law of Appointed Times: Part Three, Sheqalim, Yoma, Sukkah*. SJLA 34. Leiden: Brill, 1982.

Neusner, Jacob. *A History of the Mishnaic Law of Purities: Part Eleven, Tohorot*. SJLA 6. Leiden: Brill, 1976.

Neusner, Jacob. *A History of the Mishnaic Law of Women*. SJLA 33. Leiden: E. J. Brill, 1980.

Neusner, Jacob. *A History of the Mishnaic Law of Women, Part Three: Nedarim, Nazir*. SJLA 33. Leiden: E. J. Brill, 1980.

Neusner, Jacob. *The Jerusalem Talmud: A Translation and Commentary*. Peabody, Mass.: Hendrickson, 2008.

Neusner, Jacob, ed. *The Law of Agriculture in the Mishnah and the Tosefta: Translation, Commentary, Theology*. 3 vols. Handbook of Oriental Studies 79/1. Boston and Leiden: Brill, 2005.
Neusner, Jacob. *Method and Meaning in Ancient Judaism*. BJS 10. Missoula, Mont.: Scholars Press, 1979.
Neusner, Jacob. *Sifra: An Analytical Translation*. 3 vols. BJS 138, 139, 140. Atlanta, Ga.: Scholars Press, 1988.
Neusner, Jacob. *The Tosefta: Translated from the Hebrew with a New Introduction*. Reprint of *The Tosefta*, Hoboken, N.J.: KTAV, 1977–1986. Peabody, Mass.: Hendrickson, 2002.
Neusner, Jacob and William Scott Green, eds. *Dictionary of Judaism in the Biblical Period: 450 B.C.E. to 600 C.E.* Peabody, Mass.: Hendrickson, 1999.
North, Douglass C. *Institutions, Institutional Change and Economic Performance*. Cambridge and New York: Cambridge University Press, 1990.
North, Douglass C. *Structure and Change in Economic History*. New York: Norton, 1981.
Novick, Tzvi. "Blessings over Misvot: The Origins of a Category." *HUCA* 79 (2008): 69–86.
Novick, Tzvi. "Charity and Reciprocity: Structures of Benevolence in Rabbinic Literature." *HTR* 105, no. 1 (2012): 33–52.
Novick, Tzvi. "Crafting Legal Language: Four or Five in the Mishnah and the Tosefta." *JQR* 98, no. 3 (2008): 289–304.
Novick, Tzvi. *What is Good, and What God Demands: Normative Structures in Tannaitic Literature*. Supplements to the Journal for the Study of Judaism 144. Leiden and Boston: Brill, 2010.
Orshansky, Mollie. "How Poverty is Measured." *Monthly Labor Review* 92, no. 2 (1969): 37–41.
Osborne, Robin. "Introduction: Roman Poverty in Context," Pages 1–20 in *Poverty in the Roman World*. Edited by M. Atkins and R. Osborne. Cambridge and New York: Cambridge University Press, 2006.
Oxford University Press, *Oxford English Dictionary*. Oxford and New York: Oxford University Press, 2000.
Parkin, Anneliese. "An Exploration of Pagan Almsgiving," Pages 60–82 in *Poverty in the Roman World*. Edited by M. Atkins and R. Osborne. Cambridge and New York: Cambridge University Press, 2006.
Pastor, Jack. *Land and Economy in Ancient Palestine*. London and New York: Routledge, 1997.
Patrich, Joseph and Benny Arubas. "A Juglet Containing Balsam Oil (?) from a Cave Near Qumran." *IEJ* 39, no. 1/2 (1989): 43–59.
Peskowitz, Miriam. *Spinning Fantasies: Rabbis, Gender, and History*. Contraversions 9. Berkeley: University of California Press, 1997.
Pettit, Philip. "Institutions," Pages 2:858–63 in *Encyclopedia of Ethics*. Edited by L. C. Becker and C. B. Becker. 3 vols. New York and London: Routledge. 2001.
Pharr, Clyde. *The Theodosian Code and Novels, and the Sirmondian Constitutions*. The Corpus of Roman Law. Princeton, N.J.: Princeton University Press, 1952.
Pliny the Elder and H. Rackham. *Natural History*. The Loeb Classical Library. Cambridge, Mass.: Harvard University Press, 1938.
Przybylski, Benno. *Righteousness in Matthew and his World of Thought*. SNTSMS 41. Cambridge: Cambridge University Press, 1980.

Rajak, Tessa. "Benefactors in the Greco-Jewish Diaspora," Pages 305–19 in *Geschichte-Tradition-Reflexion: Fetschrift für Martin Hengel zum 70. Geburtstag*. Edited by H. Cancik, H. Lichtenberger, and P. Schäfer. Tübingen: J. C. B. Mohr, 1996.

Rathbone, Dominic. "Poverty and Population in Roman Egypt," Pages 100–14 in *Poverty in the Roman World*. Edited by M. Atkins and R. Osborne. Cambridge and New York: Cambridge University Press, 2006.

Rawls, John. *A Theory of Justice. Revised edition*. Cambridge, Mass.: Belknap Press of Harvard University Press, 1999.

Rawls, John and Erin Kelly. *Justice as Fairness: A Restatement*. Cambridge, Mass.: Belknap Press of Harvard University Press, 2001.

Reich, Ronny. "Stone Scale Weights of the Late Second Temple Period from the Jewish Quarter," Pages 329–88 in *Jewish Quarter Excavations in the Old City of Jerusalem: Conducted by Nahman Avigad, 1969–1982*. Edited by H. Geva. Jerusalem: Institute of Archaeology of the Hebrew University of Jerusalem and the Israel Exploration Society, 2000.

Reichman, Ronen. "The Tosefta and Its Value for Historical Research: Questioning the Historical Reliability of Case Stories," Pages 117–27 in *Rabbinic Texts and the History of Late-Roman Palestine*. Edited by M. Goodman and P. Alexander. Oxford and New York: Oxford University Press for the British Academy, 2010.

Renger, Johannes. "Wool," in *Brill's New Pauly: Encyclopaedia of the Ancient World*. Edited by H. Cancik, H. Schneider, C. F. Salazar, D. E. Orton, and A. F. v. Pauly. Leiden and Boston: Brill, 2002.

Reynolds, Joyce M. and Robert Tannenbaum. *Jews and God-Fearers at Aphrodisias: Greek Inscriptions with Commentary*. Cambridge: Cambridge Philological Society, 1987.

Richardson, Peter. "Towards a Typology of Levantine/Palestinian Houses." *JSNT* 27, no. 1 (2004): 47–68.

Ridder, A. De. "Parure de Jérusalem au Musée du Louvre." *Syria* 1, no. 2 (1920): 99–107.

Rosenblum, Jordan D. *Food and Identity in Early Rabbinic Judaism*. New York: Cambridge University Press, 2010.

Rosenblum, Jordan D. "Kosher Olive Oil in Antiquity Reconsidered." *JSJ* 40, no. 3 (2009): 356–65.

Rosenfeld, Ben-Zion. "Innkeeping in Jewish Society in Roman Palestine." *JESHO* 41, no. 2 (1998): 133–58.

Rosenfeld, Ben-Zion and Joseph Menirav. *Markets and Marketing in Roman Palestine*. Supplements to the Journal for the Study of Judaism 99. Leiden and Boston: Brill, 2005.

Rosenfeld, Ben Zion and Haim Perlmutter. "Foundations of Charitable Organizations in Judea at the End of the Second Temple Period According to Tannaitic Sources [Hebrew]." *Judea and Samaria Research Studies* 20 (2011): 49–62.

Rosenthal, Franz. "Sedaka, Charity." *HUCA* 23, no. 1 (1950/51): 411–30.

Rosen-Zvi, Ishay. "Measure for Measure as a Hermeneutic Tool in Early Rabbinic Literature." *JJS* 57 (2006): 269–86.

Rostovtzeff, M. *The Social and Economic History of the Roman Empire, Second Edition*. Oxford: Clarendon Press, 1957.

Rubenstein, Jeffrey L. *The Culture of the Babylonian Talmud*. Baltimore, Md.: Johns Hopkins University Press, 2003.

Rubenstein, Jeffrey L. *Talmudic Stories: Narrative Art, Composition, and Culture*. Baltimore, Md.: Johns Hopkins University Press, 1999.

Russell, Kenneth W. "The Earthquake Chronology of Palestine and Northwest Arabia from the 2nd Through the Mid-8th Century A. D." *BASOR*, no. 260 (1985): 37–59.

Sacks, N., ed. *The Mishnah – Order Zeraim: With Variant Readings Collected from Manuscripts, Fragments of the "Genizah" and Early Printed Editions and Collated with Quotations from the Mishnah in Early Rabbinic Literature [Hebrew]*). Jerusalem: Institute for the Complete Israeli Talmud, Yad Rav Herzog, 1972.

Safrai, S. "Home and Family," Pages 728–92 in *The Jewish People in the First Century: Historical Geography, Political History, Social, Cultural and Religious Life and Institutions*. Edited by S. Safrai and M. Stern. *Compendia rerum Iudaicarum ad Novum Testamentum Section 1*. Assen and Philadelphia: Van Gorcum and Fortress Press, 1974.

Safrai, Shemuel. *Pilgrimage at the Time of the Second Temple [Hebrew]*. Tel-Aviv: Am Hassefer, 1965.

Safrai, Shmuel and Zeev Safrai. *Mishnat Eretz Israel: Tractate Skalim [Hebrew]*. Jerusalem: Liphshitz Publishing House College, 2009.

Safrai, Zeev. "Agriculture and Farming," Pages 246–63 in *The Oxford Handbook of Jewish Daily Life in Roman Palestine*. Edited by C. Hezser. Oxford: Oxford University Press, 2010.

Safrai, Zeev, *The Economy of Roman Palestine*. London: Routledge, 1994.

Safrai, Zeev, *The Jewish Community in the Talmudic Period [Hebrew]*. Jerusalem: Zalman Shazar Center, 1995.

Safrai, Zeev. "The Roman Army in the Galilee," Pages 103–14 in *The Galilee in Late Antiquity*. Edited by L. I. Levine. New York and Jerusalem, 1992.

Sahlins, Marshall David. *Stone Age Economics*. London and New York: Routledge, 1972 [repr. 2004].

Sallares, Robert. "Ecology," Pages 15–37 in *The Cambridge Economic History of the Greco-Roman World*. Edited by W. Scheidel, I. Morris, and R. P. Saller. Cambridge and New York: Cambridge University Press, 2007.

Saller, Richard. "Poverty, Honor, and Obligation in Imperial Rome." *Criterion* 37, no. 2 (1998): 12–20.

Sanders, E. P. *Paul and Palestinian Judaism: A Comparison of Patterns of Religion*. London: SCM Press, 1977.

Sarason, Richard S. *A History of the Mishnaic Law of Agriculture: Section Three, A Study of Tractate Demai*. SJLA 27. Leiden: Brill, 1979.

Sarpaki, A. "The Palaeobotanical Approach: The Mediterranean Triad or is it a Quartet?," Pages 61–76 in *Agriculture in Ancient Greece: Proceedings of the Seventh International Symposium at the Swedish Institute at Athens, 16–17 May, 1990*. Edited by B. Wells. Stockholm: Svenska Institutet i Athen, 1992.

Satlow, Michael L. "'Fruit and the Fruit of Fruit': Charity and Piety in Late Antique Judaism." *JQR* 100, no. 2 (2010): 244–77.

Satlow, Michael L., ed. *The Gift in Antiquity. Ancient World: Comparative Histories*. Chichester, West Sussux, UK: Wiley-Blackwell, 2013.

Satlow, Michael L. "Giving for a Return: Jewish Votive Offerings in Late Antiquity," Pages 91–108 in *Religion and the Self in Antiquity*. Edited by D. Brakke, M. L. Satlow, and S. Weitzman. Bloomington: Indiana University Press, 2005.

Satlow, Michael L. "Jewish Constructions of Nakedness in Late Antiquity." *JBL* 116, no. 3 (1997): 429–54.
Satlow, Michael L. *Jewish Marriage in Antiquity*. Princeton, N.J., and Oxford: Princeton University Press, 2001.
Schäfer, Peter. "Die Flucht Johanan b. Zakkais aus Jerusalem und die Gründung des 'Lehrhauses' in Jabne," Pages 43–101 in *Aufstieg und Niedergang der Römischen Welt II.19.2*. Edited by H. Temporini and W. Haase. Berlin and New York: de Gruyter, 1979.
Schäfer, Peter. *Judeophobia: Attitudes toward the Jews in the Ancient World*. Cambridge, Mass.: Harvard University Press, 1997.
Schäfer, Peter. "Once Again the Status Quaestionis of Research in Rabbinic Literature: An Answer to Chaim Milikowsky." *JJS* 40, no. 1 (1989): 89–94.
Schäfer, Peter. "Rabbis and Priests, or: How to Do Away with the Glorious Past of the Sons of Aaron," Pages 155–72 in *Antiquity in Antiquity: Jewish and Christian Pasts in the Greco-Roman World*. Edited by G. Gardner and K. L. Osterloh. TSAJ 123. Tübingen: Mohr Siebeck, 2008.
Schäfer, Peter and Hans-Jürgen Becker, eds. *Synopse zum Talmud Yerushalmi*. TSAJ 31, 33, 35, 47, 67, 82–83. Tübingen: J.C.B. Mohr, 1991.
Scheidel, Walter. "Stratification, Deprivation and Quality of Life," Pages 40–59 in *Poverty in the Roman World*. Edited by M. Atkins and R. Osborne. Cambridge and New York: Cambridge University Press, 2006.
Scheidel, Walter, Ian Morris, and Richard P. Saller, eds. *The Cambridge Economic History of the Greco-Roman World*. Cambridge and New York: Cambridge University Press, 2007.
Schiffman, Lawrence H. "The Conversion of the Royal House of Adiabene in Josephus and Rabbinic Sources," Pages 293–312 in *Josephus, Judaism, and Christianity*. Edited by L. H. Feldman and G. Hata. Detroit, Mich.: Wayne State University Press, 1987.
Schlüter, Margarete and Peter Schäfer, eds. *Rabbinische Texte als Gegenstand der Auslegung: Gesammelte Studien II*. Edited by A. Goldberg. TSAJ 73. Tübingen: Mohr Siebeck, 1999.
Schneewind, J. B. "Philosophical Ideas of Charity: Some Historical Reflections," Pages 54–75 in *Giving: Western Ideas of Philanthropy*. Edited by J. B. Schneewind. Bloomington: Indiana University Press, 1996.
Schofer, Jonathan Wyn. *The Making of a Sage: A Study in Rabbinic Ethics*. Madison: University of Wisconsin Press, 2004.
Schürer, Emil, Geza Vermes, and Fergus Millar. *The History of the Jewish People in the Age of Jesus Christ (175 B.C. – A.D. 135)*. 3 vols. Edinburgh: Clark, 1973–1987.
Schwartz, Barry. "The Social Psychology of the Gift." *American Journal of Sociology* 73, no. 1 (1967): 1–11.
Schwartz, Earl. "Land, Liens, and Ts'daqah." *Journal of Law and Religion* 14, no. 2 (1999): 391–404.
Schwartz, Joshua. "A Holy People in the Winepress: Treading the Grapes and Holiness," Pages 39–53 in *A Holy People: Jewish and Christian Perspectives on Religious Communal Identity*. Edited by M. Poorthuis and J. Schwartz. *Jewish and Christian Perspectives* 12. Leiden and Boston: Brill, 2006.
Schwartz, Joshua. "Material Culture in the Land of Israel: Monks and Rabbis on Clothing and Dress in the Byzantine Period," Pages 121–37 in *Saints and Role Models in Judaism*

and *Christianity*. Edited by J. Schwartz and M. Poorthuis. *Jewish and Christian Perspectives Series 7*. Leiden and Boston: Brill, 2004.

Schwartz, Joshua. "Material Culture and Rabbinic Literature in the Land of Israel in Late Antiquity: Beds, Bedclothes, and Sleeping Habits [Hebrew]," Pages 197–208 in *Continuity and Renewal: Jews and Judaism in Byzantine-Christian Palestine [Hebrew]*. Edited by L. I. Levine. Jerusalem: Dinur Center for Jewish History, Yad Ben-Zvi Press, and the Jewish Theological Seminary of America, 2004.

Schwartz, Joshua. "'Reduce, Reuse and Recycle' Prolegomena On Breakage and Repair in Ancient Jewish Society: Broken Beds and Chairs in Mishnah Kelim." *Jewish Studies Internet Journal* 5 (2006): 147–80.

Schwartz, Joshua J. "The Material Realities of Jewish Life in the Land of Israel, c. 235–638," Pages 431–56 in *The Cambridge History of Judaism: Volume Four: The Late Roman-Rabbinic Period*. Edited by S. T. Katz. Cambridge: Cambridge University Press, 2006.

Schwartz, Seth. "Euergetism in Josephus and the Epigraphic Culture of First-Century Jerusalem," Pages 75–92 in *From Hellenism to Islam: Cultural and Linguistic Change in the Roman Near East*. Edited by H. M. Cotton. Cambridge: Cambridge University Press, 2009.

Schwartz, Seth. "Historiography on the Jews in the 'Talmudic Period' (70–640 CE)," Pages 79–114 in *The Oxford Handbook of Jewish Studies*. Edited by M. Goodman, J. Cohen, and D. J. Sorkin. Oxford and New York: Oxford University Press, 2002.

Schwartz, Seth. *Imperialism and Jewish Society, 200 B.C.E. to 640 C.E.* Jews, Christians, and Muslims from the Ancient to the Modern World. Princeton, N.J.: Princeton University Press, 2001.

Schwartz, Seth. "Political, Social, and Economic Life in the Land of Israel, 66–c.235," Pages 23–52 in *The Cambridge History of Judaism: Volume Four: The Late Roman-Rabbinic Period*. Edited by S. T. Katz. Cambridge: Cambridge University Press, 2006.

Schwartz, Seth. "Review of G. Hamel, Poverty and Charity in Roman Palestine, First Three Centuries C.E." *AJSR* 17, no. 2 (1992): 293–96.

Schwartz, Seth. *Were the Jews a Mediterranean Society? Reciprocity and Solidarity in Ancient Judaism*. Princeton, N.J., and Oxford: Princeton University Press, 2010.

Seccombe, David. "Was there Organized Charity in Jerusalem before the Christians?" *JTS* 29, no. 1 (1978): 140–43.

Segal, Arthur. *From Function to Monument: Urban Landscapes of Roman Palestine, Syria, and Provincia Arabia*. Oxbow Monograph 66. Oxford and Oakville, Conn.: Oxbow Books, 1997.

Segal, Eliezer. *Sanctified Seasons*. Calgary: Alberta Judaic Library, 2008.

Sen, Amartya. *Poverty and Famines: An Essay on Entitlement and Deprivation*. Oxford and New York: Clarendon Press and Oxford University Press, 1982.

Shemesh, Aharon. "The History of the Creation of Measurements: Between Qumran and the Mishnah," Pages 147–73 in *Rabbinic Perspectives: Rabbinic Literature and the Dead Sea Scrolls: Proceedings of the Eighth International Symposium of the Orion Center for the Study of the Dead Sea Scrolls and Associated Literature, 7–9 January, 2003*. Edited by S. D. Fraade, A. Shemesh, and R. Clements. *Studies on the Texts of the Desert of Judah* 62. Boston and Leiden: Brill, 2006.

Shemesh, Aharon. "Things That Have Required Quantities [Hebrew]." *Tarbiz* 73, no. 3 (2004): 387–405.

Shlezinger-Katsman, Dafna. "Clothing," Pages 362–81 in *The Oxford Handbook of Jewish Daily Life in Roman Palestine*. Edited by C. Hezser. Oxford: Oxford University Press, 2010.

Sigaud, Lygia. "The Vicissitudes of The Gift." *Social Anthropology* 10 (2002): 335–58.

Silber, Ilana F. "Echoes of Sacrifice? Repertoires of Giving in the Great Religions," Pages 291–312 in *Sacrifice in Religious Experience*. Edited by A. I. Baumgarten. Leiden and Boston: Brill, 2002.

Silber, Ilana F. "Neither Mauss Nor Veyne? Peter Brown's Interpretative Path to the Gift," Pages 202–20 in *The Gift in Antiquity*. Edited by M. L. Satlow. Chichester, West Sussux, UK: Wiley-Blackwell, 2013.

Simon-Shoshan, Moshe. *Stories of the Law: Narrative Discourse and the Construction of Authority in the Mishnah*. New York: Oxford University Press, 2012.

Smallwood, E. Mary. *The Jews Under Roman Rule: From Pompey to Diocletian: A Study in Political Relations*. SJLA 20. Leiden: Brill, 1981.

Smith, Adam. *An Inquiry into the Nature and Causes of the Wealth of Nations*. Chicago, Ill.: University of Chicago Press, 1776 [repr. 1976].

Sorek, Susan. *Remembered for Good: A Jewish Benefaction System in Ancient Palestine*. SWBA 5. Sheffield: Sheffield Phoenix Press, 2010.

Soskis, Benjamin. "The Problem of Charity in Industrial America, 1873–1915." Ph.D. diss., Columbia University, 2010.

Sperber, Daniel. *The City in Roman Palestine*. New York: Oxford University Press, 1998.

Sperber, Daniel. *Material Culture in Eretz Israel during the Talmudic Period [Hebrew]*. 2 vols. Ramat-Gan: Bar-Ilan University Press, 1993–2006.

Sperber, Daniel. *Roman Palestine, 200–400: Money and Prices*. Ramat-Gan: Bar-Ilan University Press, 1991.

Stahlin, Gustav. "Xenos," Pages 5:1–36 in *Theological Dictionary of the New Testament*. Edited by G. Kittel, G. W. Bromiley, and G. Friedrich. Grand Rapids, Mich.: Eerdmans, 1964–1976.

Stemberger, Günter. *Jews and Christians in the Holy Land: Palestine in the Fourth Century*. Edinburgh: T&T Clark, 2000.

Stern, David. *Parables in Midrash: Narrative and Exegesis in Rabbinic Literature*. Cambridge, Mass.: Harvard University Press, 1991.

Stern, Menahem. *Greek and Latin Authors on Jews and Judaism*. 3 vols. Jerusalem: Israel Academy of Sciences and Humanities, 1974–1984.

Strack, H. L. and Günter Stemberger. *Introduction to the Talmud and Midrash*. Translated by M. N. A. Bockmuehl. Minneapolis, Minn.: Fortress Press, 1996.

Strack, Hermann Leberecht and Paul Billerbeck, *Kommentar zum Neuen Testament aus Talmud und Midrasch*. 6 vols. München: Beck, 1922.

Sukenik, E. L. "Designs of the Lectern in Ancient Synagogues in Palestine." *JPOS* 13, no. 4 (1933): 221–25.

Sukenik, Eleazar Lipa. *The Ancient Synagogue of Beth Alpha: An Account of the Excavations Conducted on Behalf of the Hebrew University, Jerusalem*. Piscataway, N.J.: Gorgias Press, 1932 [repr. 2003].

Sussman, Varda. *Ornamented Jewish Oil-Lamps: From the Destruction of the Second Temple through the Bar-Kokhba Revolt*. Warminster and Jerusalem: Aris & Phillips and the Israel Exploration Society, 1982.

Sussmann, Yaacov. "Babylonian Sugiyot to the Orders Zera'im and Tohorot [Hebrew]." Ph.D. diss., Hebrew University of Jerusalem, 1969.
Tabory, Joseph. "Jewish Festivals in Late Antiquity," Pages 556–72 in *The Cambridge History of Judaism: Volume Four: The Late Roman-Rabbinic Period*. Edited by S. T. Katz. Cambridge: Cambridge University Press, 2006.
Tabory, Joseph. *Jewish Festivals in the Time of the Mishnah and Talmud [Hebrew]*. Jerusalem: Magness Press, 1995.
Tigay, Jeffrey H. *The JPS Torah Commentary: Deuteronomy*. Philadelphia: Jewish Publication Society, 1996.
Tsafrir, Yoram, L. Di Segni, Judith Green, Israel Roll, and Tsevikah Tsuk. *Tabula Imperii Romani. Iudaea-Palestina: Eretz Israel in the Hellenistic, Roman and Byzantine Periods: Maps and Gazetteer*. Publications of the Israel Academy of Sciences and Humanities. Jerusalem: Israel Academy of Sciences and Humanities, 1994.
Urbach, Ephraim. "Political and Social Tendencies in Talmudic Concepts of Charity [Hebrew]." *Zion* 16 (1951): 1–27. Reprinted with additions, pages 97–124 in *The World of the Sages: Collected Studies [Hebrew]*. Edited by Ephraim Urbach. Jerusalem: Magnes Press, 1988.
Uytterhoeven, Inge. "Housing in Late Antiquity: Thematic Perspectives," Pages 25–66 in *Housing in Late Antiquity: From Palaces to Shops*. Edited by L. Lavan, L. Özgenel, and A. C. Sarantis. Late Antique Archaeology 3.2. Leiden and Boston: Brill, 2007.
Veblen, Thorstein. *The Theory of the Leisure Class: An Economic Study of Institutions*. New York: Macmillan, 1912.
Veyne, Paul. *Bread and Circuses: Historical Sociology and Political Pluralism*. Translated by B. Pearce. London: Penguin, 1992.
Vidas, Moulie. "The Bavli's Discussion of Genealogy in Qiddushin IV," Pages 285–326 in *Antiquity in Antiquity: Jewish and Christian Pasts in the Greco-Roman World*. Edited by G. Gardner and K. L. Osterloh. TSAJ 123. Tübingen: Mohr Siebeck, 2008.
Visotzky, Burton L. *Golden Bells and Pomegranates: Studies in Midrash Leviticus Rabbah*. TSAJ 94. Tübingen: Mohr Siebeck, 2003.
Wagner-Hasel, Beate. "Egoistic Exchange and Altruistic Gift: On the Roots of Marcel Mauss' Theory of the Gift," Pages 141–71 in *Negotiating the Gift: Pre-modern Figurations of Exchange*. Edited by G. Algazi, V. Groebner, and B. Jussen. Veröffentlichungen des Max-Planck-Instituts für Geschichte 188. Gottingen: Vandenhoeck & Ruprecht, 2003.
Wagner-Hasel, Beate. "Hospitality: Greece and Rome," in *Brill's New Pauly: Encyclopaedia of the Ancient World*. Edited by H. Cancik, H. Schneider, C. F. Salazar, D. E. Orton, and A. F. v. Pauly. Leiden and Boston: Brill. 2002.
Wallace-Hadrill, Andrew, ed. *Patronage in Ancient Society*. Leicester-Nottingham Studies in Ancient Society 1. London and New York: Routledge, 1989.
Webber, Alan. "Building Regulation in the Land of Israel in the Talmudic Period." *JSJ* 27, no. 3 (1996): 263–88.
Webber, Alan. "A Consideration of the Dimensions of Walls Contained in Mishnah Bava Batra 1:1." *JSJ* 39, no. 1 (1998): 92–100.
Webster, Graham and John Updike. *The Roman Imperial Army of the First and Second Centuries A.D*. Norman: University of Oklahoma Press, 1998.
Wegner, Judith Romney. *Chattel or Person? The Status of Women in the Mishnah*. New York: Oxford University Press, 1988.

Weinfeld, Moshe. *Deuteronomy 1–11: A New Translation with Introduction and Commentary*. AB 5. New York: Doubleday, 1991.
Weiss, Isaac Hirsch. *Sifra de-ve Rav hu sefer Torat kohanim [Hebrew]*. New York: Om Publishing, 1862; repr. 1946.
Weiss, Moshe. "The Arrangement of the Mishna in Tractate Peah and its Relationship to the Tosefta [Hebrew]." Ph.D. diss., Barl-Ilan University, 1978.
Wewers, Gerd A. *Der Jerusalemer Talmud in deutscher Übersetzung: Pea, Ackerecke*. Tübingen: Mohr, 1986.
Whittaker, C. R. "The Poor in the City of Rome," Pages 1–25 in *Land, City, and Trade in the Roman Empire*. Edited by C. R. Whittaker. *Collected Studies Series*. Aldershot, Hampshire, and Brookfield, Vt.: Variorum, 1993.
Woolf, Greg. "Food, Poverty and Patronage: The Significance of the Epigraphy of the Roman Alimentary Schemes in Early Imperial Italy." *Papers of the British School at Rome* 58 (1990): 197–228.
Wright, Addison G. "The Widow's Mites: Praise or Lament – A Matter of Context." *CBQ* 44, no. 2 (1982): 256–65.
Wright, Benjamin G. III. "The Discourse of Riches and Poverty in the Book of Ben Sira." *SBLSP* 37, no. 2 (1998): 559–578.
Yadin, Azzan. "Rabbi Akiva's Youth." *JQR* 100, no. 4 (2010): 573–97.
Yadin, Yigael. *The Finds from the Bar Kokhba Period in the Cave of Letters*. Judean Desert Studies. Jerusalem: Israel Exploration Society, 1963.
Yadin, Yigael. "New Discoveries in the Judean Desert." *BA* 24, no. 2 (1961): 34–50.
Yadin, Yigael, Hannah Cotton, and Andrew Gross. *The Documents from the Bar Kokhba Period in the Cave of Letters: Hebrew, Aramaic and Nabatean-Aramaic Papyri*. Judean Desert Studies. Jerusalem: Israel Exploration Society, Hebrew University of Jerusalem, and Shrine of the Book, 2002.
Zahavy, Tzvee. *Studies in Jewish Prayer*. Studies in Judaism. Lanham, Md.: University Press of America, 1990.
Zangenberg, Jürgen K. and Dianne van de Zande. "Urbanization," Pages 165–88 in *The Oxford Handbook of Jewish Daily Life in Roman Palestine*. Edited by C. Hezser. Oxford: Oxford University Press, 2010.
Zeitlin, Solomon. "Slavery During the Second Commonwealth and the Tannaitic Period." *JQR* 53, no. 3 (1963): 185–218.
Zevulon, Uzah and Yael Olenik. *Function and Design in the Talmudic Period [Hebrew]*. Tel-Aviv: Haaretz Museum, 1978.
Zuckermandel, M. S. *Tosephta: Based on the Erfurt and Vienna Codices, with Parallels and Variants, with Supplement to the Tosefta by Saul Lieberman*. Jerusalem: Wahrman, 1970; repr. 2003.

Ancient Sources Index

Hebrew Bible
Genesis
2:3, 95n.59
2:18, 118, 118n.24
18:1–18, 102
18:19, 29n.105
19:1–3, 102n.100
19:4–11, 102n.100
24:10–61, 102n.100
45:5, 80n.89

Exodus
12:49, 101n.98
20:8–11, 95n.59
22:20–22, 101n.98
22:25, 147n.27
22:25–28, 127n.60
23:9, 101n.98
23:19–20, 127n.60

Leviticus
16:17, 120
19:9, 33n.119
19:9–10, 31
19:18, 101n.98
19:34, 101, 103n.110
23:10, 74n.69
23:22, 31
24:22, 101n.98
25:6, 103
25:35, 141, 142

Numbers
15:16, 101n.98
15:29, 101n.98
32:22, 177, 177n.95

Deuteronomy
5:12–14, 95n.59
10:17–19, 101
14:28–29, 31
15, 126, 127n.58
15:7, 28
15:7–8, 127
15:7–11, 168n.53
15:8, 118, 118n.24, 125–127, 132
15:11, 152n.49
17:15, 123
17:16, 123n.47
19:15, 174n.77
21:1–9, 12n.47
24:6, 127n.60
24:10–13, 127n.60
24:19–21, 31
26:12, 31
33:21, 28

Joshua
15:63, 130n.73

Judges
1:21, 130n.73
6:4, 80n.89
6:19, 73
17:10, 80n.89

2 Samuel
5:6, 130n.73

24:20–25, 130n.72
24:24, 130
24:25, 131n.77

1 Kings
1:5, 123n.47
10:28–29, 123n.47

2 Kings
4:1–7, 127n.60

Isaiah
58:7, 105n.122, 116n.16, 141n.10
58:13, 95n.59
59:17, 29n.105

Ezekiel
20:20, 95n.59
44:24, 95n.59

Psalms
23, 102n.99
37:21, 27n.94
104, 102n.99
112:4–5, 27n.94
146:9, 101n.98

Proverbs
8:15–16, 187
10:2, 29n.105, 185n.13
11:4, 29n.105, 185n.13
18:16, 187
22:9, 116
31:20, 152n.49

Job
31:32, 102n.100

Ecclesiastes
9:16, 154n.57

Esther
6:9, 123n.47
9:22, 3n.13

Daniel
4:24, 27n.94
12:3, 28

Nehemiah
5:1–13, 127n.60

1 Chronicles
11:4, 130n.73
21:15–28, 130n.72
21:25, 129n.69, 130
21:28, 131n.77

2 Chronicles
3:1, 130n.72
14:12, 80n.89

Apocrypha
Tobit
4, 19n.69
4:8, 129n.68
4:6–7, 6
4:10, 185n.13
12, 19n.69
14, 19n.69

Wisdom of Solomon
19:14–17, 101n.95

Sirach
7:32, 152n.49
13:23, 154n.57
26:3, 119
29, 168n.53
29:9, 6
29:20, 141
29:20–27, 101n.96
29:21, 56n.87
29:22, 109n.137
31:12–32:13, 101n.96
31:14, 69n.28
31:23, 101n.97
32:13, 102n.99
39:26, 95
40:28–30, 5n.21

Pseudepigrapha
1 En. 62:14, 102n.99
Ps. Phocylides 1.22–41, 106n.123
Sib. Or. 2.84, 105n.123
T. Ab. 1.1–2, 102n.101
T. Ab. 1.5, 102n.101

T. Job. 9.8–10.4, 152n.50
T. Job 10:1–3, 102n.100
T. Job 11:1–10, 167n.46

Dead Sea Scrolls
4Q270 3 ii 12–19, 33n.119
4Q417 2 i 10, 154n.57
4Q424, 27n.95
4QInstruction, 154n.57
4QWisd, 27n.95
CD 14, 21
CD 14:12–16, 19

Josephus
Against Apion
1.305, 5n.25

Jewish Antiquities
1.194, 102n.100
1.196–197, 102n.101
1.200–201, 102n.100
1.246–255, 101n.95
1.249–252, 102n.100
2.118, 43n.7
3.220–221, 69n.28
4:231–232, 33n.119
12.117, 69n.28
14.54, 43n.7
15.96, 43n.7
15.121, 46n.28
15.299–316, 13n.48
15.367, 169n.57
20.49–53, 13n.48

Jewish War
1.138, 43n.7
1.361, 43n.7
2.125, 20n.72
2.134, 19n.68
3.95, 73n.54
4.468, 43n.7
5.427, 50n.46

Philo
Abraham 107–18, 102n.101
Abraham 110, 102n.102
Embassy 123, 53n.70, 55n.83, 130n.71, 155n.62

Flaccus 64, 5n.22, 166n.40
Virtues, 90–94, 33n.119
Spec. Laws 2.75, 167n.46

New Testament
Matthew
5:42, 6, 77
6:1–2, 164n.31
6:1–4, 151–152
9:16, 113n.7
14:20, 71n.44, 73n.61
15:37, 73n.61
16:9, 73n.61
16:10, 73n.61
25:31–46, 101n.94
25:35–45, 105n.122
26:23, 69n.29, 69n.30

Mark
2:21, 113n.7
6:43, 71n.44, 73n.61
8:8, 73n.61
8:19, 71n.44, 73n.61
8:20, 73n.61
12:41–44, 17, 18
14:20, 69n.29, 69n.30

Luke
5:36, 113
6:30, 6n.27
9:17, 71n.44, 73n.61
14:1, 103n.111
21:1–4, 17, 18
24:13–35, 101n.94

John
6:13, 71n.44, 73n.61

Acts
3:1–5, 5n.25
3:2, 18n.63
9:25, 73n.61
10:23, 101n.94
11:27–30, 13n.48
28:7–8, 101n.94

Romans
12:13, 101n.94

1 Timothy
3:2, 101n.94
6:8, 56n.87

Hebrews
13:2, 101n.94

1 Peter
4:9, 101n.94

Revelation
3:20, 101n.94
13:16, 152n.49

Mishnah
m. Berakhot
2:7, 121n.40
6:8, 95n.57
7:1–2, 89n.22

m. Pe'ah
1:1, 86n.5, 135, 137n.105, 180n.1
2:1, 180n.1
2:4, 89n.24
3:1, 89n.25, 89n.26
5:4, 106, 106n.125
7:1, 89n.24, 89n.28
7:1–2, 89n.25, 89n.26
7:5, 180n.1
8:2–6, 31
8:5, 77n.82, 92n.43, 96n.70, 180n.1
8:7, 1n.2, 22n.77, 40n.128, 69n.31, 77n.82, 78, 81, 85n.1, 92n.43, 143–145, 161n.16, 174, 180n.1, 181, 182
8:8, 115n.14, 133n.86, 170n.61, 180n.1
8:9, 141n.10, 171–172, 172n.70

m. Demai
2:5, 74n.66
5:7, 74n.73, 94n.54

m. Kil'ayim
8:5, 89n.22
9:10, 70n.34, 75n.74

m. Shevi'it
8:4, 86n.6

8:6, 90n.31
8:7, 89n.29

m. Terumot
1:7, 70n.34, 74n.72, 75n.74
7:3, 89n.22

m. Ma'aserot
1:6, 88n.17
1:7, 68n.17
3:2, 70n.34, 74n.67, 75n.74

m. Ma'aser Sheni
1:6, 168n.48

m. Hallah
1:2, 89n.22

m. Shabbat
1:1, 62n.116, 124n.52, 165
2:2, 90n.38
3:5, 68n.17, 68n.23
4:2, 73n.62, 74n.74
8:2, 71n.40, 74n.74
10:2, 73n.63, 74, 74n.68, 74n.74
10:5, 89n.22
16:1–3, 92n.45
16:2, 77n.81, 93
17:1–18:1, 103n.112
18:1, 74n.65, 88
20:5, 98n.75
22:1, 92n.45
22:2, 94

m. Eruvin
8:2, 77n.82, 86n.6, 92n.43

m. Pesahim
3:2, 117n.20
7:2, 121n.40
10:1, 12n.47, 69n.25, 85n.1, 92, 96, 97
10:3, 94n.56

m. Sheqalim
2:5, 178n.100
3:2, 70n.38, 141n.10, 177n.95

3:3, 75n.74
5:2, 174n.76
5:6, 16, 152–153

m. Yoma
1:1, 120

m. Sukkah
2:1, 121n.40
2:6, 77n.82

m. Betzah
4:1, 70n.34, 72n.52, 73n.62, 74n.65, 75n.74
5:7, 103n.113

m. Megillah
3:1, 161n.15, 189
4:6, 113

m. Hagigah
3:6, 159n.5, 166n.42, 175n.84

m. Yevamot
16:7, 99n.81

m. Ketubbot
5:5, 122n.42
5:8, 88n.19, 89n.30, 98n.74, 116n.15
6:6, 141
7:1, 161
13:1–2, 12n.47, 30n.111

m. Nedarim
4:4, 68n.18, 68n.23, 69n.25
7:1, 88n.17
9:4, 141n.10

m. Nazir
1:5, 74n.67, 74n.68, 75n.74

m. Sotah
9:6, 103n.107

m. Gittin
8:9, 99n.81

m. Qiddushin
4:5, 176n.88
4:12, 99n.81
4:14, 142

m. Bava Qamma
7:2, 174n.77
8:6, 154n.56

m. Bava Metzi'a
2:1, 177n.94
2:8, 70n.34, 75n.74
7:1, 88n.18

m. Bava Batra
1:5, 146n.24
4:5, 90n.33

m. Sanhedrin
1:1, 174n.76
2:4, 123n.47
2:5, 123
8:2, 96

m. Makkot
1:7, 174n.77

m. Eduyyot
4:7, 99n.81

m. Avodah Zarah
2:3–7, 96n.66
2:6, 89n.29, 90n.34

m. Avot
1:5, 103n.110, 105
1:16, 86n.5
3:16, 166
4:9, 142

m. Zevahim
14:3, 131n.77

m. Menahot
8:3–4, 89n.26
8:3–5, 90n.32, 90n.37
8:6–7, 96n.66
10:1, 72n.51, 74n.69, 75n.74

10:3, 72n.51, 74n.69, 75n.74
10:3–4, 74n.70

m. Keritot
3:9, 68n.22

m. Me'ilah
6:1, 103

m. Tamid
3:4, 16n.58, 152n.51

m. Kelim
8:2, 75n.74
16:1, 68n.19, 68n.21, 68n.23
16:2–3, 70n.35
16:3, 74n.74
17:1, 74n.65, 74n.66
17:2, 68n.18, 68n.23
17:4, 75n.74
17:11, 77n.82, 86n.6, 92n.43, 95
27:4, 74n.74
28:6, 70n.34, 71n.41, 74n.74
28:8, 113
30:2, 68n.21, 68n.23

m. Ohalot
6:2, 70n.33, 74n.65, 75n.74

m. Parah
3:6, 89n.27

m. Teharot
9:1, 70n.39, 74n.67, 75n.74
9:4, 74n.67, 74n.71, 75n.74

m. Mikwa'ot
6:5, 70n.34, 71n.39, 75n.74
10:5, 71n.40, 74n.74

m. Makhshirin
2:8, 116
4:3–6, 70n.33
4:6, 74n.64, 74n.68
4:8, 70n.33

Tosefta
t. Berakhot
4:8, 94n.56, 96n.69, 102

4:15, 117n.21
6:2, 101n.97, 104

t. Pe'ah
1:1–2, 137n.105
1:1–4:7, 31n.113, 62n.115
2:13, 33n.120
2:18, 7n.30
4:1–7, 31
4:8, 7, 7n.30, 22n.77, 77, 78, 92, 143–145, 165, 172
4:8–9, 40n.128, 81
4:8–10, 85n.1, 133
4:8–15, 158n.3, 180n.1
4:8–21, 1n.2, 30, 163n.26, 180n.1
4:9, 69n.31, 78, 145n.23, 145–146, 147n.29, 163n.27, 166n.43, 177n.93, 181–183
4:9–10, 76n.77
4:10, 30n.112, 69n.31, 103n.106, 108n.129, 108n.130, 108–109, 112n.2, 120n.32, 111–128, 131n.77, 132n.81, 134, 134n.93, 164n.28, 188n.32
4:10–11, 131n.78
4:12, 127n.59, 167–169, 170
4:13, 170–171
4:14, 141n.10, 170n.61, 170–171
4:15, 177
4:16, 31
4:18, 13n.48, 28n.104, 130n.70, 137, 151, 179n.103, 189n.33
4:19, 27, 29, 30, 161n.14

t. Demai
3:4, 159n.5, 166n.42, 175n.84
3:12, 74n.66, 75n.74
3:16, 69n.31, 75n.75, 165
3:16–17, 1n.2
3:17, 164n.29, 165n.36

t. Shevi'it
4:16, 94n.54
4:19, 94n.54
5:21, 103n.108
6:27, 90n.31

t. Terumot
3:13, 74n.67
4:3, 89n.26

ANCIENT SOURCES INDEX

7:15, 96n.64
8:3, 88n.20

t. Ma'aserot
1:7, 68n.17
2:4, 95n.62
2:20, 105

t. Shabbat
2:3, 90, 91n.39
5:14, 71n.39
10:10, 71n.42, 75n.74
13:1–6, 92n.45
13:7–8, 92n.44
14:4, 74n.65, 75n.74
16:22, 164n.29, 165

t. Eruvin
6:9, 74n.67, 75n.74, 77n.82, 92n.43

t. Pesahim
2:15, 121n.40

t. Sheqalim
2:1, 70n.38
2:8, 114, 178n.98
2:15, 174n.76
2:16, 17, 152–153

t. Sukkah
3:15, 96n.65
4:11, 94

t. Betzah
3:10, 74n.65, 75n.74

t. Rosh Hashanah
1:18, 161n.19

t. Ta'anit
1:7, 185n.15

t. Megillah
2:12, 160
2:15, 146, 147n.29
2:18, 105n.121
3:27, 113n.5

t. Mo'ed Qatan
2:16, 121n.40

t. Hagigah
3:4, 68n.22

t. Yevamot
1:10, 99n.81

t. Ketubbot
5:8, 96, 98n.76
6:7–8, 30n.111
6:8, 98n.74, 99n.82

t. Nazir
1:3, 70n.33

t. Sotah
11:8, 162n.20
14:3–5, 178n.101
14:6, 75n.74

t. Gittin
3:13, 131n.76

t. Bava Qamma
2:6, 74n.65, 75n.74
11:3, 147n.29

t. Bava Metzi'a
1:17, 168n.48
3:9, 88, 177n.92, 178
7:9, 123n.47
8:26, 159n.5, 166n.42, 175n.84

t. Bava Batra
5:9, 134n.89
9:9, 146n.25, 147n.29

t. Sanhedrin
1:3, 174n.78
8:9, 103n.105

t. Avodah Zarah
1:21, 96n.66
3:11, 96n.66
3:16, 96n.66
4:1–2, 91, 96n.68
4:4, 161n.19, 162n.24
8:3, 90n.33

t. Menahot
9:5, 89n.26
9:5–8, 90n.32, 90n.37
10:23, 72n.51, 74n.69, 75n.74

t. Arakhin
4:27, 132–33

t. Kelim Bava Qamma
6:6, 70n.34, 70n.37, 74n.74

t. Kelim Bava Metzi'a
5:1, 71n.42
5:10, 68n.17
5:13, 70n.36

t. Kelim Bava Batra
3:1, 70n.35
6:2, 70n.34, 71n.41
6:6, 70n.34, 73n.62
7:10, 68n.17

t. Ohalot
4:2, 73n.55, 75n.74

t. Parah
8:4, 71n.41, 74n.74

t. Teharot
7:2, 71n.42, 74n.74
10:9, 74n.67, 75n.74
11:7, 95n.62
11:16, 90n.33

t. Mikwa'ot
6:15, 68n.17
6:16, 68n.17

Jerusalem Talmud

y. Berakhot
2:8, 5d, 185n.15, 186n.21

y. Pe'ah
1:1, 15b, 13n.48, 135, 136n.102
1:1, 15b–c, 1n.2
8:7, 21a, 77n.84, 162n.23, 181–184, 185–187, 188
8:7–9, 21a–b, 1n.2, 163n.26, 184–185, 185n.13
8:9, 21b, 162n.23, 186n.22, 191n.46

y. Demai
3:1, 23b, 1n.2

y. Sheqalim
5:6, 49a, 162n.23

y. Megillah
3:1, 74a, 189

y. Ketubbot
4:6, 28d, 135n.94, 136n.102

y. Nedarim
9:4, 41c, 48, 191n.44

y. Horayot
3:6, 48a, 9n.38, 188n.31

Babylonian Talmud

b. Shabbat
119a, 94n.53
127a, 102n.103
127a–b, 180n.1
156a–b, 1n.2, 185n.13
156b, 29n.105

b. Sukkah
49b, 1n.2, 29n.105

b. Mo'ed Qatan
4b, 180n.1

b. Hagigah
5a, 153
7a–b, 180n.1

b. Yevamot
61b–64a, 119n.29
79a, 29n.105

b. Ketubbot
49b–50a, 135n.94
50a, 136n.103
66b–68a, 1n.2, 180n.1
67b, 124n.51, 131n.78, 131n.80, 135n.94, 136, 153, 184n.9

b. Sotah
14a, 1n.2
21b, 180n.1

ANCIENT SOURCES INDEX

b. Gittin
7b, 109n.132
56, 130n.70

b. Bava Qamma
61a–b, 180n.1

b. Bava Batra
8a–11a, 1n.2
8b, 187n.25
8b–11a, 180n.1
9a, 77n.84
9b, 2n.3, 153
9b–10a, 29n.105
11a, 13n.48

b. Sanhedrin
17b, 150

b. Shevu'ot
35b, 102n.103

b. Arakhin
28a, 135n.94, 136n.103

Midrash

Mekilta of Rabbi Ishmael
Amalek 4, 142
Kaspa 1, 147n.27
Kaspa 3, 175n.85, 178n.101
Vayyisa 4, 92n.44

Sifra
Behar, Parashah 5, 142–143
Behar, Pereq 1, 88n.20, 103n.109, 103n.110
Emor, Parashah 13, 89n.26, 90n.32, 90n.37
Qedoshim, Parashah 2, Pereq 4, 71n.43, 73n.62, 75n.74
Qedoshim, Parashah 3, Pereq 7, 132n.81
Vayyiqra Dibura Dehobah, Parashah 12, 178–179

Sifre Numbers
6, 75n.74
141, 161n.19

Sifre Deuteronomy
14, 175n.85
17, 175n.85
26, 162n.20
47, 28
53, 103n.105, 104n.114
116, 103, 126n.57, 126–127, 131–132
117, 16n.59, 152n.52
144, 175n.80
157, 161n.19
232, 70n.34, 71n.43, 73n.62, 75n.74
306, 162n.21
320, 113n.5
343, 113
355, 28
357, 162n.21

Leviticus Rabbah
5:4, 1n.2, 9n.38, 9n.39, 137n.106, 187–188
25:1, 162n.23
34:1–6, 1n.2
34:2, 185n.14
34:13, 141n.10

Deuteronomy Rabbah
5:3, 1n.2

Ecclesiastes Rabbah
9:25, 153

Exodus Rabbah
31:4, 1n.2

Pesikta Rabbati
25:2, 135n.94

Early Christian Writings
1 Clement 10.7, 102n.101, 102n.102
1 Clement 11.1, 102n.100
Ambrose, Off. 2.76, 171n.66
Ambrose, Off. 2.77, 172n.72
Didache 1.5, 6, 173
Didache 1.6, 172n.71
John Chrysostom, De Eleem. 6 (PG 51.269), 171n.66
Shepherd of Hermas, Mandate 2.4–6, 6n.28
Sidonius Apollinaris, Epistulae, VII, 6, 80n.91

Greco-Roman Literature
Antipater of Tarsus, SVF 3.254.23–257.10, 120n.37, 148n.37

Apology of Aristedes 15, 106n.124
Artemidorus, *Interpretation of Dreams* 3.53, 5n.25
Cicero, *Off.* 1, 139, 101n.91
CIL IV 9839 b, 154n.55
Cleomedes, *On the Circular Motions of the Celestial Bodies*, 2.1:91, 5n.25
Codex Theodosianus 14.18.1, 148n.36, 170n.61, 171n.67, 173–174
Galen 6.529, 87n.10
Hor., *Sat.* 2, 3, 182, 88n.15
Hor., *Epist.* 1.17.58–9, 171n.63
Julian, *Ep.* 22, 7n.32
Juvenal, *Saturae* III, 10–18, 72n.53, 80n.91
Juvenal, *Saturae* III, 152, 114n.10
Juvenal, *Saturae* VI, 542–547, 72n.53, 80n.91
Lucian, *Fug.* 14, 166n.38
Macrobius. *Sat.* 1.12.33, 87n.10
Martial 12.57.12, 171n.63
Persius, *Saturae* 5.179–184, 93
Petronius, *Satyricon* 34, 69n.30
Philostratus, *VA* 4.10, 171n.64
Plautus, *Trinummus* 339, 7n.31
Pliny the Elder, *Natural History* 12.111–124, 43n.7
Pliny the Elder, *Natural History* 18.50, 87n.12, 88n.15
Pliny the Elder, *Natural History* 18.101, 87n.12, 88n.15
Pliny the Elder, *Natural History* 18.119, 87n.12, 88n.15
Pliny the Elder, *Natural History* 19.53–55, 51
Pliny the Elder, *Natural History* 22.154, 87n.12, 88n.15
Seneca, *Consolatio ad Helviam* 10.10, 128n.64
Seneca, *Contr.* 1.1.10, 166n.40
Seneca, *Contr.* 10.4, 171n.65
Seneca, *Vita Beata* 24.1, 148n.37
Stolebaeus, Flor. Xliv 41, 80n.91

Subject Index

Adiabene, 11, 13–15, 21
agoranomos, 60, 134
agriculture, 31
    crop yields, 45
    economic importance of, 43–47
Alexandria, 71, 90
alimenta, 10n.42
almsgiving. *See* charity
altruism, 3, 32, 101, 151
Amoraim, 31, 39, 41, 180
    approaches to charity, 9
    expanded charity, 189–190
    interest in *tamhui*, 181–183
Anderson, Gary, 5n.21, 15, 15n.54, 19n.69, 27n.94, 27n.95, 129n.68, 136n.98, 168n.53, 185n.13, 188, 188n.32
Aphrodisias, 23
Araunah. *See* Ornan, the Jebusite
Arbel, 66, 81
Avot d'Rabbi Natan, 40n.129

Babatha archive, 43, 65, 72
Babylonia, 13, 90
baraita, methodological issues, 41
barley, 36, 43, 49, 50, 51, 57
Barthes, Roland, 50, 58
balsam, 43n.7
beans, 76, 77, 78, 178
    See also legumes
beggars. *See* begging
begging, 5–7, 77, 152, 171
    alternatives to, 2, 35, 36, 39, 78, 79, 81–83, 84, 86, 139, 147–148, 153, 156, 158, 173, 174, 179
    at doorways, 7, 76, 77, 82, 144, 148, 165–167
    at sacred spaces, 5–6
    by wellborn poor, 140–141
    control of. *See* begging, alternatives to
    impact on non-poor, 35, 147–148
    in public, 6, 60, 169
    Jews as beggars, 5
    not giving to beggars, 7, 77–78, 169
    prevalence of, 2, 11
    problems with, 2, 4, 35, 158
    shame of, 5–7, 56, 62, 169
    See also dignity; shame
    visibility of, 34, 35, 38
Ben Sira. *See* Sirach
benefactor, 1, 4, 11, 14–15, 108, 152, 164
    See also charity; *euergetism*
beneficiary, 4, 33, 34, 36, 38, 151, 152, 164, 173, 190
    See also charity; *euergetism*; poor
Bergmann, Judah, 12n.47
Bet Alpha, 66, 67
Beth Shearim, 69
bishops, 8–9
Bokser, Baruch, 97n.71
Bolkestein, Hendrik, 10
Bonz, Marianne, 23
Bourdieu, Pierre, 168
Boustan, Ra'anan, 58

229

Brand, Yehoshua, 69
bread, 4, 56, 57, 75, 76, 77, 84, 88, 91, 107, 108
  and social status, 36, 49–50, 86, 116–117
  from *quppa*, 116–117, 126
  from *tamhui*, 86–87, 112
  of the poor, 116–117
  varieties, 49–50
  See also barley; wheat
Bridge, Steven, 173
Brooks, Roger, 144, 145
Brown, Peter, 8–9, 10, 15, 25n.90, 139, 148–149, 150
Büchler, Adolf, 25n.90, 125n.55

Cappadocia, 91
Cave of Letters, 52, 65
cereals. *See* barley; bread; wheat
chamber of secrets, 11, 16–19, 21, 152–153
charity
  amount to give, 38, 128–129, 134–137
  anonymous, 34, 38, 151–153
  as a means of control, 7, 9–10, 39, 81–83, 185–192
  as a religious obligation, 1, 9n.39, 35, 37
  as imitation of God, 1
  collection, 163–167
  defined, 32
  direct. *See* begging
  distribution, 167–172
  expansion of, 189–190
  Gentiles, 147
  indirect, 33, 34, 81, 82, 98, 105, 107, 109, 110, 124, 134n.93, 157, 176n.89, 179
  organized
    defined, 33–34
    question of pre-70 CE origins, 10–12
    question of reality, 22–26
  problem of, 1–5
  prodigious giving, 124, 134–137
  refusal of alms, 167–169
  replaces sacrifices, 1
  restorative, 111–134
  rewards for, 9n.39, 152
  Sabbath, 76–77
  Second Temple era, 10–21
  significance of, 1

  See also tsedaqah: as a religious obligation
charity supervisors, 34, 39, 49, 60, 67, 75, 80, 108, 112, 116, 124, 146, 153, 157–179, 183
  as judges, 174–175
  assessing the poor, 174–175
  collection by, 163–167
  distribution by, 167–172
  tax collectors, similarity to, 166–167
  See also gabbai tsedaqah; *parnas*
charity token, 22n.77, 159n.4
Christianity
  approaches to poverty and charity, 6, 9, 11, 37, 39, 107, 152, 191–192
citizenship, 10, 15
civic culture, 10–11, 32, 148–150
clothing, 30, 34, 36, 56, 108
  and shame, 113
  and social status, 36, 112–114
  archaeological finds, 49–53
  of the poor, 53, 113–114
Cohen, Aryeh, 146n.24
Cohen, Shaye, 125
collection of the sages, 9, 187–189
community, 35, 38, 39, 150
  hospitality, 104–105
conspicuous consumption, 127, 191
Cook, E., 20
cophinus. *See quppa*
Cyprus, 13

David, King, 130, 131
day of judgment, 1
Dead Sea Scrolls, 11, 19–21
deceptive poor. *See* poor, imposters
dependency, 4, 109, 120, 167–169, 174, 176n.89
  See also independence, economic
diet, 33, 49, 91
dietary laws, 90
difference principle, 91
dignity, 4–7, 34–35, 37, 38, 57, 125, 151, 171
  See also honor; shame
dinars, 115–116, 133
Douglas, Mary, 3, 4, 58
dress. *See* clothing

SUBJECT INDEX

droughts, 11, 13, 45, 46
　See also famines
dupondius. See pondion

economy
　of Roman Palestine, 43–48
　See also agriculture
Emerson, Ralph Waldo, 3, 4
Emmaus, 47
Essenes, 11, 19–21, 34
euergetism, 14–15, 16, 60, 148, 151
　different from charity, 33, 34

famines, 11, 13, 15, 60, 162
　See also droughts
favor, 16, 85, 100, 107, 155, 163
fish, 76, 77, 78, 87, 94, 107
Flavians, 59
food, 2, 5, 5n.25, 30, 34, 37, 51, 56n.87, 69n.24, 72n.53, 73n.61, 93n.47, 94n.55, 95, 95n.59, 101n.97, 116n.15, 144, 176n.89
　and social status, 4, 38, 49–51, 57–59, 96, 132
　for Passover, 96–97
　for Sabbath, 37, 70, 75–77, 92, 93, 143
　See also barley; bread; fish; grapes; legumes; olives; olive oil; wheat; wine
forgotten things, 31–33, 43, 106
forgotten sheaves. See forgotten things
formerly wealthy poor. See poor, wellborn
Fraade, Steven, 20, 162
Friedman, Shamma, 24
Frisch, Ephraim, 12n.47, 109

gabbai tsedaqah, 9n.39, 39, 158–159, 163, 189
　See also charity supervisors; *parnas*
Galilee, 59, 104
gemilut hasadim, 29, 30, 109
gifts, 14
　free gift, 3
　gift exchange, 3–5, 119–120
　refusal of, 167–169
　See also Mauss, Marcel

gleanings, 31–33, 43, 106
God
　as benefactor, 31
　as host, 101
　determines wealth and poverty, 142
　imitation of, 1, 101
Goldenberg, Robert, 94
Goodman, Martin, 48
Goody, Jack, 50
grapes, 31, 33, 43, 49, 50, 87, 87n.8, 96–97
　See also wine
Gray, Alyssa, 48, 122–125, 135
Grey, Cam, 140n.2
Greco-Roman approaches to charity and poverty. See poverty, Greco-Roman approaches to

Hadrian, Emperor, 59
Hamel, Gildas, 12n.47
Hamilton, David, 127
Hands, A. R., 10, 148
harvest, 32–33
　allocations for the poor, 31–32
　See also *pe'ah*; gleanings; forgotten things; poor tithe; agriculture
Hauptman, Judith, 24
Helena of Adiabene, 13
　See also Adiabene
Herculaneum, 166
Herod Antipas, 59
Herod the Great, 13n.48, 59, 169
Hezser, Catherine, 26, 121
Holman, Susan, 35, 147
honor, 14, 15, 16, 35, 122n.44, 123n.47, 127, 152, 154, 164, 186, 188n.28, 190
　See also dignity
horses
　and social status, 122–125
　given as charity, 118
hospitality, 16, 21, 37, 132
　and reciprocity, 105–109
　communal, 104–105
　different from charity, 105–109
　for the poor, 105–109
　relationship to *tamhui*, 99–110
　Second Temple era, 101

SUBJECT INDEX

householders, 7, 77, 103, 106, 120, 120n.34, 121, 122
   and status, 120–121
housing, 55, 57
   and social status, 36
   See also lodging; shelter

independence, economic, 4, 155, 167–169
   See also dependency
institutions in economic thought, 34, 81, 82
Izatus, 13
   See also Adiabene

Jerash, 69
Jeremias, Joachim, 12n.47
Jerusalem
   famines in, 11, 13, 130
Josephus, 11, 13, 19, 33, 43, 46, 50, 72, 101, 169
Judean desert, 42n.1, 52, 64, 64n.2, 65, 67, 71, 73, 98, 113, 134n.90, 159
judges, 19, 20, 39, 60, 158, 172–175, 183
Julian, Emperor, 7n.32

Kant, Immanuel, 2, 4, 35
kashrut. See dietary laws
Keane, Webb, 58
Khirbet Shema, 104
Kindler, Arie, 22n.77, 159n.4
Kohl, Heinrich, 66
kophinos. See quppa
Krauss, Samuel, 12n.47

Lapin, Hayim, 62
Legio X Fretensis, 47
legumes, 43, 49, 50, 58n.98, 73, 74, 84, 89, 91, 107, 116n.19
   See also beans
   and social status, 36, 51, 57, 58, 87–89, 110
leitourgia. See liturgy
lentils, 184n.9
leqet. See gleanings
Levine, Lee, 16n.55, 159n.6, 190n.40
Levi-Strauss, Claude, 58, 117, 119–120

Levites, 31
Lieberman, Saul, 144, 145
Ling, Timothy, 12n.47
liturgy, 147, 150
loans, 127, 167–169, 170
lodging, 15, 76, 77, 78, 84, 85, 98–99
   See also hospitality; housing; shelter
Loewenberg, Frank, 12n.47
Longenecker, Bruce, 108
Lysimachus, 5n.25

ma'ah, 114–116, 177
MacMullen, Ramsay, 154
Maimonides, 2, 2n.4, 32n.117, 109n.132, 135n.94, 150n.46, 151n.47
Marshall, Alfred, 61
Mauss, Marcel, 3, 119
me'ot. See ma'ah
meat, 50, 51, 58, 87, 184n.9
   and social status, 88, 103, 131–134
Mediterranean triad, 87
   See also barley, grapes; olive oil; olives; wheat, wine
Mekilta of Rabbi Shimon bar Yohai, 40n.129
merit, 142, 154, 184
Meroth, 67
mevaqqer, 19, 20
Midrash Tannaim, 40n.129
money, 2, 4, 23, 114–116
   from *quppa*, 114–116
   See also dinars; ma'ah; perutah; pondion
Monobazus, 13
   See also Adiabene; Munbaz
Moore, George Foote, 13n.47
Moses, 28
Munbaz, 137, 151
   See also Adiabene; Monobazus

Nahal Hever, 64, 72, 80, 160
Navtalah, House of, 129–131
Nazareth, 69
neoinstitutional economics. *See* institutions in economic thought
Nero, Emperor, 155
North, Douglass, 34
Novick, Tzvi, 38, 85, 109

SUBJECT INDEX

olive oil, 43–44, 77, 89–91, 107
   See also olives
olives, 31, 33, 43–44, 49, 50, 74, 89, 91
   See also olive oil
omer, 74
Ornan, the Jebusite, 129–131
orphans, 30, 31, 32, 99, 140, 165, 189
Orshansky, Mollie, 128
ossuaries, 65, 73

Parkin, Anneliese, 11, 108, 148
parnas, 39, 49, 134n.90, 159–163, 176n.89, 183
   See also charity supervisors; *gabbai tsedaqah*
Passover, 85, 96–97, 165
patella, 23
pe'ah, 31–33, 43, 89, 106
perutah, 108, 115
Philo, 5
Pliny the Elder, 43
Pompeii, 154
pondion, 22n.77, 75, 86, 115, 143
poor
   Amoraim who are, 191
   as givers of charity, 108–109
   as travellers, 106
   assessing their claims, 174–175
   clothing of, 113–114
   conjunctural, 38, 112–134, 139–142, 152–153
   disabled, 170–171
   empathy for, 146, 155
   Greco-Roman approaches to, 7, 153–155
   imposters, 82, 144, 169–175
   in Roman Palestine, 42–62
   obligation to reciprocate, 108–109
   relations with rich, 3, 4, 34, 61
   stealing from, 31
   Tannaim not poor, 125
   wellborn, 9n.39, 17, 38, 111–128, 132, 140–141, 148, 152–153
   who refuse alms, 167–169
   See also begging; poverty
poor tithe, 31–33, 43
poverty, 36
   and status, 128

biological approach, 36, 37, 56, 62, 85, 88, 91, 184
causes, 47, 191
   See also droughts; famines; Third-Century Crisis
conjunctural, 36, 38, 45, 139–142
   defined, 140–141
Greco-Roman approaches to, 10–11, 14–15
in Roman Palestine, 42–62
in the archaeological record, 42n.1
permanent, 45
structural, 45, 140
sudden impoverishment. See poverty, conjunctural
urgency of, 185
value-judgment approach, 36, 56, 57, 62, 89
visibility of, 6
priests, 68, 74
pronoetes. See *parnas*
Przybylski, Benno, 27, 29
ptochotropheia, 107

qe'arah, 68, 70, 79
Qumran, 20
quppa
   alternative to begging. See begging, alternatives to
   and restorative charity, 111–128
   and social status, 112–134
   archaeological finds, 67, 71–75
   as basket, 36, 63–64, 69–75, 80
   as charity fund, 2, 35, 36, 38, 75–79
   indirect charity, 34
   as civic institution, 150
   eligibility for alms, 145–146
   for conjunctural poor, 111–128
   for wellborn poor, 148
   in Greco-Roman sources, 75, 80
   institutionalization of, 79–83
   provides bread, 116–117
   provides clothing, 112–114
   provides money, 114–116

Rawls, John, 91

SUBJECT INDEX

reciprocity, 3, 4, 37, 81, 100–101, 103, 119–120
  absence of, 168
  and hospitality, 105–109
  and the poor, 108–109
  balanced reciprocity, 109
  generalized reciprocity, 107
  See also Sahlins, Marshall
residence, 34, 39, 77, 145–146
  and citizenship, 149–150
Reynolds, Joyce, 23
righteousness, 6, 26–29, 32, 137, 142, 188
  See also tsedaqah
Rosenblum, Jordan, 41n.131, 49n.44, 50n.51, 50n.53, 51n.57, 69n.26, 86n.3, 89n.29, 90n.36, 96n.66, 102n.104, 136n.100
Rosenfeld, Ben-Zion, 12n.47
Rostovtzeff, M. I., 141

Sabbath, 37, 70, 73, 76–77, 78, 85, 90, 91–95, 133, 165
  three meals on, 92–93
Sahlins, Marshall, 107, 109
  See also reciprocity
sal, 70, 73
Saller, Richard, 56, 154
saq, 70
Sasanians, 1, 23
Satlow, Michael, 24
Schwartz, Barry, 4
Schwartz, Earl, 189–190
Schwartz, Joshua, 55
Schwartz, Seth, 38, 62, 85, 109, 139, 150
Seccombe, David, 11
Segal, Eliezer, 118n.24
semiotics, 4, 38, 43, 50, 58, 64, 87, 111, 169, 184, 185, 191
  of bread, 116–117
  of clothing, 112–114
  of food, 57–59
Sen, Amartya, 35, 56, 89, 91, 128, 148
Sepphoris, 59, 131–134
servants. *See* slaves
Severans, 59
Severus, Prefect of the city of Rome, 173

shame, 4–7, 34, 35, 36, 38, 53, 56, 57, 62, 82, 113, 123, 152–153, 155
shelter, 30, 34, 36, 37, 77, 98, 105
  homelessness, 60
  of the poor, 53–56
  See also housing
Shemesh, Aharon, 20
shikhehah. *See* forgotten things
Sifre Zutta, 40n.129
Silber, Ilana, 18
Sirach, 5
slaves
  and social status, 122, 123–125
  as charity, 118, 121–125
  in Greco-Roman world, 121–122
Smith, Adam, 57
social exclusion, 3
solidarity, 3–4
Solomon, King, 130
sportula, 80–81
status, 14, 38, 50, 51, 58, 128
  and charity, 111–128
  and clothing, 112–114
Sukenik, Eleazar, 66
Sussmann, Yaacov, 180n.1
synagogues, 11, 15–16, 25, 30, 32, 66, 67, 78, 151, 160, 164
  as communal institutions, 104–105
  hospitality in, 104–105
  proper attire for, 113
  quppot in, 22, 23
  See also Theodotos inscription
Syria, 159, 160, 162

Tabi, 121
tamhui
  and archaeology, 69
  and hospitality, 105–109
  Aphrodisias, 23
  as alterative to begging. *See* begging, alternatives to
  as dish, 36, 64, 69, 80
  as soup kitchen, 2, 35, 36, 37, 75–79
  eligibility for alms, 145–146
  emphasis by Amoraim, 181–183
  institutionalization of, 79–83

provisions for Sabbath, 91–95
relationship to hospitality, 99–110
Tannenbaum, Robert, 23
tax collectors, 39, 166–167
taxation, 60
Temple
  begging near, 5
  contributions to, 17, 18
  See also chamber of secrets
Theodotos inscription, 11, 15–16, 21, 105
Thessaly, 73
Third-Century Crisis, 47–48, 191
Tiberias, 59, 104, 184
tithes, 74, 175
  See also poor tithe
towns, 17, 32, 76, 145
  See also city; urbanization
travellers, 16, 37, 75, 98, 104
  as poor, 106
tsedaqah, 1, 22n.77, 27n.96
  as a religious obligation, 37, 82, 108, 169
  as charity in the Babylonian Talmud, 185n.13
  as righteousness, 9n.39, 137, 188
  defined, 26–32
  on charity token, 159n.4
  See also charity; righteousness
Tyre, 114

Urbach, Ephraim, 8, 10, 12n.47
urbanization, 33, 59–62, 154
Usha ordinance, 129, 134–137

Veblen, Thorstein, 127
vegetables, 76, 77, 78, 91–95, 107, 132
Veyne, Paul, 8, 10, 15, 148
visiting the sick, 29, 32
Visotzky, Burton, 189

Watzinger, Carl, 66
wealth, 10, 18, 51, 54, 56, 58, 106, 118, 122, 124, 130, 132, 134, 141, 142, 154, 189
  of donor, 4
  Tannaim not poor, 125
  See also poor, wellborn
Wegner, Judith, 119
Weiss, Moshe, 106n.125
wheat, 36, 43, 45, 46, 46n.31, 49, 50, 50n.52, 61, 72, 72n.50, 73, 75n.76, 76, 153
  See also bread, wheat
Whittaker, C. R., 15, 61
widows, 30, 31, 140, 189
wife
  as charity, 118–121
wine, 51, 72n.52, 73, 85, 92, 93, 95n.61, 96n.65, 96n.66, 97, 97n.71, 97n.72, 104, 107, 184n.9
  for the poor, 96–97
  See also grapes

xenodocheia, 107

Yadin, Yigael, 64, 65

zuz. See dinars